DATE DUE

JY 28 '94			
SE 22 '04			

DEMCO 38-296

INVENTING
JAPAN

The Making of a
Postwar Civilization

William Chapman

PRENTICE
HALL
PRESS

New York   London   Toronto   Sydney   Tokyo   Singapore

PRENTICE HALL PRESS
15 Columbus Circle
New York, New York, 10023

Copyright © 1991 by William Chapman

PRENTICE HALL PRESS and colophons are
registered trademarks of Simon & Schuster Inc.

Library of Congress Cataloging-in-Publication Data

Chapman, William, 1930–
    Inventing Japan : the making of a postwar civilization
/ by William Chapman.
        p.,   cm.
    Includes index.
    ISBN 0-13-942921-2
    1. Japan—Civilization—1945–   2. Japan—Civilization
—American influences.   I. Title.
DS822.5.C453   1991
952.04—dc20   · 91-2990
                                                    CIP

Designed by Richard Oriolo

Manufactured in the United States of America

10 9 8 7 6 5 4 3 2 1

First Edition

For Christine

Contents

Preface

●

This book is an attempt to portray the Japanese as they have lived the period since the end of World War II. I have described some of the changes that came upon Japan in the crucial first years after the defeat, and have tried to show how those events determined what was to follow as Japan recovered and became rich. The theme, roughly put, is that the Occupation period was a great divide for the Japanese people. Their country was fundamentally remolded in those early years, and what Japan is today is largely the result of what flowed from that exciting and remarkably creative period.

This would seem an obvious conclusion except for the fact that so many observers—Japanese and foreigners, scholars and ordinary people—enjoy depicting today's Japan as an extension of her more distant past. During my fourteen years in Tokyo I have sometimes suspected that some conspiracy exists to interpret almost anything that happens as having been foreshadowed by traditions and habits that existed before the militarists took power in the 1930s and led Japan into war. When I arrived as a newspaper correspondent in 1977, the world was still fascinated by the Japanese way of manufacturing goods, and I set about reporting the obligatory story "explaining" the Japanese worker. Why, I asked a businessman, were the people in his factories so productive and adaptable? Simple, said the businessman. They were like the samurai of old who spent their days honing swords and polishing military skills. I asked a Nissan executive to explain the extraordinary loyalty to company. It was a transference of the old emperor-worship mentality, he replied. When, after the war, the emperor had been changed from god to mortal, the Japanese had needed some new focus for their devotion. The company replaced the emperor system.

Foreigners seem to delight in this imagery of a revived Japan owing all to her past customs and traditions. If an American magazine wishes to depict American business acumen, for example, it will present a cover photo of some dynamic-looking executive, his strong jaw jutting purposefully. But if it is Japan's economic power that is the focus, the photo will be one of an obese sumo wrestler, his arms holding aloft a globe of the world. In recent years, Chinese and Southeast Asians have become alarmed at Japan's growing military power. Invariably, their cartoonists resort to sketches of the World War II Japanese invader wearing a toothy grin beneath his spectacles and soldier's cap.

This view of Japan being what it is because of what it was would matter little if confined to such harmless bits of pop-mythology. But it is shared on a sophisticated level by learned people who have explored the country deeply. There exists, for example, a vein of scholarship that holds that Japan was little changed by the Occupation-era reforms. What Japan became in the postwar period was a continuation of trends that were visible in the prewar time (by "prewar," they refer not to the militarist 1930s but to the more "normal" times before). A good example is the late Edwin O. Reischauer, the Harvard scholar and ambassador who for a time was the foremost American authority on Japan. He believed that the Occupation reforms would have occurred without the Occupation, that they were largely prefigured by prior events. So what Japan became in the postwar era was due more to certain Japanese characteristics than to American intervention. The American Occupation did prevent certain extremes from happening, such as a Sovietization of Japan or a violent collision between left and right, Reischauer wrote. But:

. . . I contend that much if not most of what has developed within Japan during the past three decades would have come into being in broad outline even without the interference or guidance of the Occupation. The Occupation obviously speeded up many of these developments and gave them a certain coloration, but the results on the whole have probably been shaped more by Japanese characteristics, skills and past experiences and by general world conditions than by American design.[1]

The advantage of such a theory is that it can never be tested, but I find it as hard to accept as the absurd notion that modern Japanese workers are uniquely shaped by the samurai model. Who knows what might have happened had Japan been left to restructure herself? Just two of the Occupation changes—land and labor reform—fundamentally altered the circumstances under which a majority of ordinary Japanese people earned their living. There is little evidence in prewar history that Japanese authorities alone would have dared to go so far. Those two basic changes empowered classes of people who had been powerless. Would the Japanese have remained pacifists until today had not the "MacArthur Constitution" decreed that that was to be their destiny? I doubt it.

It is just as fanciful to suppose that Japan was reshaped by Occupation policy alone, a product solely of General Douglas MacArthur's Olympian pronouncements. In the first place, there were two distinct Occupations, not just one. The first was very liberal and sought to remake Japan into a clone of the United States. The second was conservative and reversed much of the original. The Japanese themselves were far from being passive objects of either of these. They altered and deflected many of the changes emanating from MacArthur's headquarters. The remolding of Japan was not an orderly, linear process. It was more like a series of shoving matches and tugs of war—the Occupation pulling first one way, then another, and the Japanese, themselves divided, pushing back and falling forward. It was all a very disorderly business in which happenstance and the sudden swervings of history were often more important than either MacArthur's edicts or the "Japanese character."

A realistic view of the times is offered in a small but incisive volume, *Japan's American Interlude*, written by a Japanese-American who actually witnessed them. Kazuo Kawai was educated in the United

States but was stranded in Japan when war broke out. During the Occupation period he was an editor of an English-language newspaper. He watched the Occupation unfold, observed what people actually did and thought, and was struck by the way in which circumstances of the time created their own changes. There was something ad hoc about the whole process. It fit, Kawai thought, with the way Japanese behaved in other periods. What propelled them sometimes toward, sometimes away from democratization were not institutions or traditions but the "imponderable demands of the moment." He wrote:

> There does not seem to be any such entity as the "Japanese soul" or the "Japanese temperament" which innately predestines the Japanese to any particular pattern of behavior. Of course, habit and tradition exert strong influences, but these relatively constant factors have been less decisive than the more variable factors of circumstances. History can be cited to argue that they are a revolutionary people as well as to argue that they are a conservative people. The determinant is to be found in the prevailing mood of a particular time as shaped by the circumstances of the moment.[2]

Out of these "circumstances," I think, emerged the shape of Japan as we know it. The new forms of economic life, the dominance of bureaucrats, the debasement of politics, pacifism, the dependence on and deference to the United States—all grew out of that period of compromise and accommodation. Much of this book's later parts are designed to show what flowed from those arrangements. The beliefs and institutions that were formed in those first years have persisted to this day and still determine, for example, Japan's predominant business culture, her attitude of aloofness from the world, and her inclination to follow the lead of the United States (except, of course, in military matters). For example, Japan is still bound by her early commitment to the expansion of her companies, so much so that she has largely ignored the comforts and amenities of her citizens. She still lives under the shadows of those first crucial years.

This is a journalist's book, which means that it is full of borrowed knowledge and the writer's prejudices about what is and is not important. It is based on a dozen years of interviewing Japanese as a newspaper correspondent and writer and on a great variety of written sources. I have relied on the memoirs of politicians, novels, government documents, formal histories, and many economic surveys in an attempt to piece together what could not be obtained through interviews. I found Japanese public-opinion polls to be of great assistance in determining what attracted and repelled the Japanese at important moments. To the greatest extent possible, I have used the words and actions of people who actually lived through the times described. Because I neither read nor speak Japanese, my research has required a great deal of translation, both for interviews and for written material. There is a great deal that I have missed.

I am much in debt to those scholars and journalists, both Japanese and foreign, who have been over the trail before me. Among the many people who have helped me, I wish to thank most of all Fukuo Izawa, a friend and guide who has shown me much about how Japan actually works and who has patiently translated great stacks of material that illuminated the Japanese experience. I was first introduced to Japan by Shigehiko Togo and Yasuko Maruta, both of the *Washington Post*'s Tokyo Bureau, and their patience in educating me about their country's ways was of immeasurable help. I also wish to commend Paul Aron, my editor at Prentice Hall, whose initial advice set me to work on the book and whose editing has improved it immensely. Finally, I thank my wife, Christine, whose own insights, criticisms, and editing talents got me through a great many rough patches.

WILLIAM CHAPMAN
Tokyo, January 1991

1
●

Surviving

At their headquarters base on the campus of Keio University in Tokyo, the group of young Japanese naval officers listened quietly as Emperor Hirohito, in his high-pitched voice and archaic court language, informed the nation in a radio broadcast that the war was over. For Lieutenant Senior Grade Kiyohisa Mikanagi and his comrades, the news was not unexpected. They were intelligence officers of the Imperial Navy and, unlike their ordinary countrymen, had guessed during the preceding weeks that surrender was inevitable. Their postwar duties were spelled out for them. First, they were instructed to burn all of the intelligence unit's important papers, which they promptly did. A few days later a number of them were assigned the unpleasant duty of meeting arriving ships of the U.S. Navy and guiding them to harbor at the port in Yokosuka, south of Tokyo. Mikanagi was instructed to proceed first to Yokosuka, where a small boat would take him to the contact point off the coast.

On the train down from Tokyo's Shinagawa station Mikanagi observed scenes he would long remember. His car was almost empty, but
the trains coming north from Yokosuka were crowded with civilian
passengers fleeing the port. The news had leaked out that Japanese
military forces had been ordered to vacate the coastal area and withdraw
to positions north of the Tama River, leaving Yokosuka an open city.
Thousands of civilians, children on their laps and belongings packed in
sacks and boxes, were moving north for protection behind Imperial
Army lines. Their faces were grim and taut and clearly they were frightened, but there was no evidence of panic. Mikanagi thought their flight
a natural reaction. "They had been taught for years to expect the worst,"
he recalled years later in an interview. Military leaders had drilled into
them the lesson that if the enemy landed there would be rape and killing
and looting. The *tonari-gumi*, or neighborhood associations, had been
told to prepare for hand-to-hand fighting, and women were handed
sharpened bamboo stalks to use as spears. "So after the emperor had
spoken," Mikanagi continued, "I thought it was natural that they should
run away when they heard the Americans were coming. They expected
to be treated very badly."[1]

The flight from Yokosuka that day meant more than military defeat
and the end of the war. It symbolized the end of Japan's grand vision of
herself, that of a proud and independent nation secure behind her
coastal borders. That vision had been supported by a national ideology
that had formed and hardened over a history of 150 years, and the core
of that ideology was fear of foreign control. Its origin lay in the early
nineteenth century, when foreign ships began probing Japan's shore-
lines and when the nation, like the rest of Asia, was threatened with
invasion and colonization. Fear, distrust, envy, and finally hatred of the
foreigner lay behind almost everything the country had accomplished,
everything that had propelled her to spectacular heights of achievement
and then to a terrible defeat. In 1945 the great vision and the ideology
that supported it were crushed. A few days after Lieutenant Mikanagi
took his train to Yokosuka, troops of a foreign power walked Japan's
streets and white men moved about like gods, regulating daily life,
restructuring the state, feeding its people amid the ruins. There was
nothing to do but, as Emperor Hirohito had admonished them, to
"endure the unendurable."

But mixed with the fear and shame was another emotion—relief. Fukuo Izawa remembers an end to the war that was the opposite of terror. Throughout that dreary summer of 1945, ever since the Imperial Army had drafted him in June, his mind had been filled with a single thought: "I am going to die." The anticipation of death had been pervasive, kindled by the stories of brave kamikaze pilots expressing their final thoughts before takeoff, by the scene of Tokyo in ruins, by the newspaper pictures of people, even women, preparing for the last defense of the homeland. One day shortly before the surrender, Izawa had seen a train from Hiroshima filled with refugees, their sunken eyes peering out from faces grotesquely disfigured. On August 15, 1945, his platoon had been instructed to assemble in the railroad station at Sekigahara to hear the emperor's address on the radio. The emperor speaking to his subjects on the radio? It was unimaginable. And it could mean only one thing: "I am going to die."

A Yokohama boy who had graduated from college in the spring, Izawa had been sent to a seaside base for training. In late July his platoon was ordered to fetch an artillery piece from Osaka Castle, the famous medieval bastion that had been transformed into an armory during the war. On August 10 they had hoisted the cannon onto a freight car, but because of the daily American bombing raids, it had taken them five days merely to reach the station at Sekigahara. Assembled there for the imperial address, the platoon sat quietly. None, of course, had ever heard the emperor's voice. Before the broadcast began, Izawa heard only one sound, that of cicadas whirring in the trees outside.

It was almost impossible to understand the emperor's words. The recording was scratchy and the radio reception poor. The emperor spoke in a squeaky voice, using old-fashioned court language unfamiliar to commoners. Gradually, Izawa grasped the message, and it was not what he had expected to hear—an imperial command for all Japanese subjects to fight to the death. Instead, the war was over. Japan was surrendering. He glanced around to see if his comrades had understood, but none displayed any emotion. He felt a great joy well up inside him: "I am not going to die, after all." Then he thought he was being selfish and unpatriotic, and, so that his happiness would not be detected, he fixed his face in a rigid frown. "I was overcome with joy and relief," he recalled years later, "but it was unthinkable that we could just stand up and shout *banzai* (long live the Emperor)." For several days afterward, he wondered if he had been the only one who had felt that surge of joy.

He questioned his friends quietly, one by one, about their feelings at the moment when the emperor spoke. All had felt as he had.[2]

Izawa's reaction, more common than he had first thought, explains much about those early days of defeat and occupation. Americans were puzzled at the undemonstrativeness of the conquered people and thought them strangely sullen. In fact, the Japanese were caught in that most primitive and stunning emotion: an overwhelming relief at having been spared. Almost all had expected to perish. For months they had lived in apprehension of death and national doom, brought on either by the Americans' ceaseless air raids or by national suicide on the beaches of Kyushu and Honshu. Deliverance had been simply stupefying. A Japanese-American citizen, an editor who had been trapped in Japan when the war broke out, witnessed the paralysis of the Japanese and later wrote: "The surrender came to them as a heaven-sent relief; the Occupation became a welcome symbol of deliverance from annihilation."[3] Sokichi Tsuda, a historian, had listened to the emperor's broadcast and could think of nothing to do but stare blankly at a wall. "When the realization of defeat first struck me, I felt a sense of relief," he remembered. "It is better this way, I thought, for Japan has at least escaped total destruction."[4] Shohei Imamura, who would become one of Japan's most creative postwar film directors, was eighteen years old when the emperor spoke. He had been expecting to die on the beaches of Chiba Prefecture when the Americans landed, and he felt a glorious sense of relief. "It gave me unlimited freedom," he remembered.[5]

Many, too, remember that as American troops began appearing on the streets, an unnatural calm prevailed, the sort that comes after a powerful typhoon has passed. True, many had sobbed at the Imperial Palace grounds, and some soldiers toyed briefly with the idea of resistance. But most simply did nothing, because they did not know what to do. They were prepared, as the emperor had said they must be, to bear the unbearable. But how? There were no rules to follow, no proper reaction to have, and they were a people accustomed to following directions from above. No one could imagine a part to be played out under an army of foreigners. Shigemi Hayashida, a former diplomat who had returned to his wasted homeland from China, traced the eerie calmness of those first weeks to the people's inability to decide on a proper role: "We had never experienced defeat before. We had never been occupied before. No one knew exactly how to behave." Japanese were prepared to cooperate, he thought, but did not know how and waited apprehensively for signs of what the occupiers would require of them. Hayashida recognized in their passivity the truth of an old Japanese proverb having to do with resignation to one's fate: *Manaita-no ue-no koi,* or "the carp is always calm as it lies on the carving board."[6]

It is not so strange, then, that the first encouraging moment that many remember was the arrival of General Douglas MacArthur. Newspaper photographs showed him at Atsugi Air Base unarmed and lightly guarded, a figure of studied casualness with his corncob pipe clamped in his teeth. No one could explain precisely why his appearance should be so reassuring, but it was. Perhaps it was because the arrival of any authority figure was somehow welcome. Better that than chaos. The mood changed perceptively. Little acts of voluntary cooperation were noted, even gestures of welcome. When a detachment of American troops camped on the outskirts of a village just outside Tokyo, leaders of the town put their heads together to consider a response that would be properly received and, they hoped, would ward off conflict. Their decision was pragmatic. Into an old charcoal-burning truck they bundled the town's prostitutes and drove to the encampment, where they explained that the girls would spend the night as a token of village friendliness. The GIs gave the women candy and waved them back into the truck.

Getting along with the foreigner was far from the major concern of the moment, however. Survival—the elemental task of finding food and shelter—was what mattered. The winter of 1945–46 was an excruciating, soul-searing experience, and even today Japanese accompany their accounts of it with shudders and grimaces of remembered pain. The terrifying incendiary raids of the previous spring had left Tokyo a level expanse of rubble surrounding the Imperial Palace, although the palace grounds were mostly unscathed. Beyond the placid moats, the emperor's subjects struggled to accumulate bits and pieces for shelter. They propped up sheets of fire-blackened tin, piled rocks and bottles for walls, and quarreled over bits of broken bricks. It was not only in Tokyo that the homeless slept in parks. Hiroshima and Nagasaki had simply vanished, and other major cities—Osaka, Nagoya, Kobe—were in ruins. Someone came up with the statistic that precisely 8,045,094 people were homeless. Ninety cities and towns, in all, were listed as essentially destroyed. Nearly one-third of what had been urban Japan was simply no longer there in any organized sense.

In those wastelands that remained, the most ordinary habits of daily life became absurdly burdensome. There were no matches, so men carried shards of optical glass in their pockets with which to light their cigarettes by magnifying rays from the sun. Those fortunate ones with jobs shuffled around their offices in long winter coats because there was no fuel for heat, not even in the new Central Liaison Office, which was staffed with English-speaking diplomats who dealt with the Occupation authorities. At night they slept wrapped in the same coats, many of them in railway stations, on and under benches. The struggle for food and shelter was so intense, so desperate, that families fell back on old country habits and hustled their daughters into prostitution, and so GIs strolling through the Ginza in that December were approached by young girls in kimonos who uttered, "Merry Christmas, Joe. Very good, Joe. Very cheap."

Hunger transformed Japan into a nation of barterers and grovelers. The wartime food allotment system were still in place that winter, and families were issued coupons that in theory could be exchanged for commodities at city shops. But most of the rice, fish, and vegetables had been diverted into the black market where prices were impossibly high. An official survey found that in October 1945, before the shortages were most severe, black-market prices for commodities averaged 132 times the official prices. There were weeks when even the black market was empty. Newspapers printed photographs and drawings of common weeds with instructions on which were edible, and children searched for them in the suburbs of Tokyo, where vegetation still grew. Later studies determined that the adult Japanese lived for nearly a year on rations averaging 1,050 calories a day, about one-third the amount required for physical well-being, and that during the first postwar years teenagers lost an entire year of physical development. The hunger lasted through the winter, and by the springtime mobs were in the streets with placards reading simply, "Give Us Rice."

There were moments when it seemed that the fear of starvation might tip Japan into revolutionary chaos. The supply of rice coming into Tokyo from the farming regions was only half the amount needed for a subsistence diet. By April the stock was down to less than a two-day supply. Rumors that authorities were hoarding rice for their own families (or for sale on the black market) swirled through the city, and "rice mobs" began collecting near official buildings. In January 1946 3,000 people smashed their way into the Itabashi Army Supply Depot and made off with bags of rice, charcoal, and soybeans. Communist leaders, jailed by the Japanese government during the war but freed under one of MacArthur's first reform edicts, sensed in the hungry mobs a vehicle for their party's renascence. They drew 2 million supporters to their first May Day rallies in eleven years, in part through slogans and placards that accused bureaucrats of concealing rice stocks. The Tokyo rally alone attracted 500,000 citizens. They were urged by Kyuichi Tokuda, the recently released Communist chief, to take the matter of obtaining food into their own hands. "Find the hidden foods," he shouted. "Destroy the bureaucrats and the imperial monarchy and establish a people's government." Building on that theme, the Communists and leftist labor unions organized a second set of rallies, called a "Food May Day," and marched to the edge of the Imperial Palace. It was an ominous and shocking challenge to the imperial institution itself and perhaps more than any other event of the period revealed the degree of desperation to which hunger had brought the people of Japan. One red-lettered placard waving outside the palace moat declared: "The Emperor Eats His Belly Full While His Subjects Die from Hunger."

There had been food shortages during the war, but this was something far worse because it affected the mind as well as the stomach. It changed the way people felt about everything: about themselves, their neighbors, and even their country. Wartime had created an equality of sacrifice and suffering when everyone ate less in order to support the troops and the imperial crusade in Asia. Hunger had been patriotic. But in 1946 people scrounged shamelessly and endured countless indignities, trading family heirlooms and other small treasures for their dinners. Those who did not were the rare exceptions. One of them was Yoshitada Yamaguchi, a judge of the Tokyo District Court, whose sad story was the talk of Tokyo for months. On a salary of 3,000 yen (about seven dollars) a month, Judge Yamaguchi could not hope to feed his family. But because of his position and his own sense of duty, he barred his wife from dealing on the black market. "How can the judge of the court break the law, even if it is a bad law?" he was reported to have asked his wife. He grew weak from hunger but insisted that his family live on government allocations. His wife begged him for permission to sell off family valuables. He refused. Judge Yamaguchi died of starvation.

Most, however, set aside their ethical doubts to satisfy their hungry stomachs. To feed their children more than a thin rice gruel, proper young matrons marched off to the black market in Shinjuku to sell their kimonos for cash or trade them in on old Army rations that had been stolen from military warehouses. The practice of *kaidashi*, or going out to the countryside to buy food, became a routine followed by housewives of all classes. Teruno Akabori remembers the train trips from her home in Saginomiya, on the outskirts of Tokyo. The trains left for the fields of Tokorozawa every thirty minutes, and all of them were packed with people seeking food. From the Tokorozawa station they would walk four or five kilometers in search of farmers willing to sell sweet potatoes, at the time a delicacy that also filled the stomach and stopped children from whining. Many of her friends brought kimonos and traded them on the spot. "There was no bargaining—we were grateful to get them at any price," she recalls. Mrs. Akabori, today a proud suburban housewife, remembers it as a time when the buyers, not the seller, bowed low and said, "Thank you." The trip back home could also be humiliating. If a policeman boarded the train, the foragers hung their bags of sweet potatoes outside the open windows or stuffed them under seat cushions. Walking home from the train station, Mrs. Akabori cautiously skirted all of the *koban*, or police boxes, for police often demanded that passersby open their bags for inspection and confiscated food that was in excess of legal rations. The least fortunate, those who had been bombed out, stole shamelessly from luckier neighbors. A cooking pot set out for airing would disappear in minutes. Wet laundry vanished from clotheslines. No one left laundry hanging out after sundown, Mrs. Akabori recalls.

As the dreadful winter wore on, the ranks of the unemployed swelled with the return of soldiers from former colonies, thin and wasted men who walked the streets in faded uniforms. By December an official count found that 13 million Japanese were jobless and looking for work. Those who did work were still impoverished—a factory worker earned only 882 yen a month. Women workers earned half that. Inflation shriveled even those meager wages, and in desperation, the government froze bank accounts, permitting the head of a family to withdraw only 300 yen a month. It did not work and prices continued to soar. A public-opinion poll found, not surprisingly, that four out of every five Japanese thought food and inflation were the most serious problems facing them. More than a year after the Occupation began, families were still selling off their possessions to make ends meet. An Asahi newspaper survey discovered in November 1946 that only 51 percent of the people survived on their wages alone. The rest relied on a combination of salaries and what they called "red ink income," a euphemism for the sale of family possessions.

Tokyo endured that winter on the workings of an illegal economy. The black market encompassed thousands of sellers and millions of buyers dealing in every commodity of daily life. It was also a vast jungle of lawlessness that began with thefts and led to gang killings, turf wars, and casual murders, becoming at last a criminal demimonde of immense proportions. It embraced all classes and kinds of people. When the war ended, sake, bread, clothing, shoes, sugar, and blankets had disappeared from military depots all over the country, pilfered wholesale by officers and enlisted men alike. Small thefts were the routine of daily existence. A bicycle snatched at Ueno's railway station turned up repainted and for sale two hours later at the station in Shimbashi. Koreans and Chinese, forced-labor immigrants during the war, prospered with goods smuggled from Hong Kong and Taiwan, and by the Occupation's ruling, they could not be arrested by Japanese police.

It was the beginning for many mobster organizations, some of whose descendants still operate today. In Tokyo there were eight major syndicates, each with its own piece of turf around the major train stations. There was the *Shibata-gumi*, operating out of Asakusa, and the *Sekiguchi-gumi*, in control of the streets around Ikebukuro station. Most notorious was the *Matsuda-gumi*, which organized the commuter hub around Shimbashi station. They fought among themselves and against other gangs, the Japanese mobs battling constantly for territory against the Koreans and the Chinese. Guns were plentiful, another result of looted army depots. Unable or unwilling to intervene, police let the gangs have at one another, and the shootouts continued for several years into the Occupation. One day in April 1948, two gangs—one Japanese, one Korean—fought it out with pistols in the Hamamatsu district. The next day, about one hundred Japanese returned to the attack on the Koreans' black market there and killed or wounded more than 15 men.

The murder rate soared all over the country. In 1947 it was nearly five times what it had been in 1940, the last year before total war began overseas. Gangland shootouts accounted for many of the killings, and the general populace was little troubled by them. But there were also bizarre and tragic murders over trifling matters, which deeply shocked people because they reflected so keenly the moral decline of the times. Nizaemon Kataoka, the famous Kabuki actor, his wife, their son, and two maids were slain on the night of March 15, 1946. Police said an apprentice in the theater world had killed them during what had begun as a squabble over food. A man killed his own brother, who had stolen his potato, and a youth murdered his father, who had taken some of his food. For a time, in 1946, the pervasive sense of decay and moral collapse was captured in newspaper stories about the case of a man who had been a successful company executive before the war. He had found postwar employment as a teacher, but the 700-yen monthly wage could not feed his family of eight. Old and desperate, he sneaked onto a farm and was making off with six kilograms of sweet potatoes when he was caught by a guard. He killed the guard with an iron bar.

Isamu Togawa, a journalist, later wrote a book about these postwar experiences in which he attempted to explain the descent into lawlessness and degradation. It was not difficult to understand most of the killings, he thought, because they had been committed by men who had been trained to kill during wartime. Hardened on the battlefield, they killed casually at home for money or food. It was the black-market trade that Togawa remembered as most aptly symbolizing the times. In the ashes of Shimbashi station, one would be approached by a repatriated army veteran clad in khaki and aviator's boots, who wanted to buy the suit off one's back, then another, who tried to sell a cheap watch smuggled from Hong Kong. The scenes reminded Togawa of the thieves' markets in Shanghai and Dairen when those cities were under Japanese occupation and their citizens were demoralized. According to Togawa, Japanese acted as they did, immorally and often cruelly, because there seemed to be no one—not even the police or the Occupation—to tell them that they were doing wrong. There was no longer authority in Japan, no government to respect, no rules to abide by. People lived, for the first time, by their own consciences, without a morality imposed from above. They did what they had to do to survive.[7]

●

At least one Japanese knew with absolute certainty what was right, both for himself and his country. On October 10, 1945, Kyuichi Tokuda, a prewar founder of the Japan Communist party, stepped from the gates of Fuchu Prison and was warmly greeted by a small band of followers. A solidly built, balding Okinawan, Tokuda had spent the last eighteen years in confinement thinking of the experience of Lenin and planning the party's revival. He was a man of extraordinary energy. (His nickname, formed from the first syllables of his family and given names, was *Tokyu*, which meant "special express train.") Nine days after his release, Tokuda was on the stump at a rally describing in quick, angry bursts what the party would stand for in the days of its liberation. The imperial system had brought on the war and must be destroyed. Big business must be crushed and the militarists exposed. The party could be rebuilt on the aspirations of the Japanese people, and its first step would be to hound the hoarders of food and feed the hungry. It was a rousing welcome for his old comrades, a speech full of both bitterness and hope, and Tokuda exuded self-confidence. His time had come.

Japanese communism had endured a pitiful history before the war. It had blossomed in the 1920s during those brief years when radicalism had enjoyed a certain respectability and the study of Marxism had been fashionable. A chosen few slipped off to Moscow, where they were embraced by the Comintern, and returned to Japan with money and literature to launch the party and organize the proletariat. From the start, it was weighed down with one enormous burden. Unlike other incipient Asian Communist movements, it was denied the role of representing nationalist aspirations. Nationalism in Japan was the property of conservatives and emperor worshipers. Communists were agents of a foreign power, and they never escaped that fatal label. The party was founded in 1922 with Tokuda, fresh from an international congress in Moscow, in a leadership post, but was almost destroyed a year later in a police dragnet. Reestablished in 1925 with him as chairman, it was demolished again in a new wave of arrests in 1928. Tokuda went to jail and was not to emerge until the war was over and Japan's new ruler, General MacArthur, ordered all political prisoners freed.

If the postwar scene was a dark abyss for most Japanese, it was a paradise for revitalized Marxists. Hunger and joblessness made people receptive to extremist appeals, and large crowds would gather around the hawkers of socialism who appeared on the streets and in the factories. Radicalism fit the times. Moreover, for the first time in Japan's history, radicals themselves were free to act. MacArthur had decreed that all speech was free. (So long, of course, as it did not exalt the old imperial system or malign the Occupation. Press censorship banned both.) Wherever people gathered in the ruins of Tokyo, Osaka, and other urban centers, they encountered red flags and speakers in headbands lettered with slogans extolling proletarian unity. In those early days, Marxism was especially appealing for one important reason: It filled an ideological vacuum created by the imperialists' defeat. Nationalism was in disgrace. That entire ideological structure which, with the imperial family at the top, had guided the thoughts of ordinary Japanese for nearly a century, had tumbled to the ground. Intellectuals in the media, universities, and even the bureaucracies turned to Marxism as a comforting set of beliefs that could both explain the terrible past and chart the course of the future.

And in a curious twist of history, Tokuda and his Communist followers found in the Occupation authorities—agents of the world's leading capitalist nation—allies who could advance their cause. This had nothing to do with the ideological bent of the Occupation's administrators but everything to do with the Communists' revolutionary schedule. It had been determined in Moscow that Japan was not ready for a proletarian revolt. The country must first pass through a preliminary, "bourgeois-democratic" stage, during which a capitalist economy and liberal state would gradually become ripe for revolution. Strikes and subversion would eventually bring it down. So Tokuda decided on a course of cooperation with the Occupation because he saw in its liberal, New Dealish ways the mechanism for advancing this intermediate stage. Civil rights, labor's freedom to organize, the purging of militarists, the destruction of the great corporations were, to Tokuda, all measures leading to some distant revolution. He began to court the Occupation by promising support for its goals and very quickly obtained easy access to its officers. It was in his movement's immediate interest to portray the Occupation and the Japan Communist party working hand in glove.

Tokuda was thus embarked on a delicate balancing act that tested all his talents as actor and manipulator. He displayed a different face in different scenes. On the streets of Tokyo he was the revolutionary-sounding orator promising a new dawn for the downtrodden with the birth of a worker's state. He did not call for armed revolution—that would have violated instructions from Moscow. What he wanted were massive protests that could create sufficient havoc to bring down the government, force new elections, and give his forces a role in the government that followed. In dealing with sympathetic unions he was more cautious. He sought to control them by outmaneuvering conservative factions in elections from the shop floors to national committees. To the officials in MacArthur's headquarters he presented himself as the model labor statesman, earnest, sincere, and pleased to work within the framework of laws that the Occupation had established.

A revealing display of Tokuda's cunning occurred one day in January 1946, when he led a delegation of locomotive drivers into the Occupation's Labor Division offices in the Daiichi Building, across the moat from the Imperial palace. To the officer in charge, Captain Anthony Constantino, he defiantly announced that the drivers had voted a national railway strike for better wages. Constantino coolly replied that a national rail strike would not be permitted because it would set back Japan's reconstruction. Further, he lectured Tokuda's group on the grief such a strike would bring to ordinary Japanese. Their winter supplies of rice and charcoal would be interrupted, adding to their already dangerous malnutrition. Tokuda listened as the rebuff was translated into Japanese, then turned to his followers, who had been unable to understand the translator. Almost word for word, he redelivered Constantino's speech as if it were his own. How, he asked, could the locomotive drivers risk such terrible hardships for the starving public? Then he turned to Constantino and declared that his drivers had nobly decided to cancel the strike because of the higher public interest. Having explained the sacrifice, he marched his men out.[8]

It was the era of "peaceful revolution," as Tokuda called it, when the Japan Communist party officially adopted the improbable slogan of "lovable" to characterize itself. The strategy worked brilliantly. From his headquarters in the Yoyogi section of Tokyo, Tokuda relentlessly drove his organizers to take advantage of the opportunities offered in free trade unionism. He maneuvered them into control of several new unions, which made exorbitant demands on impoverished companies. He championed the "production control" strikes in which workers displaced managers and ran the companies themselves. A celebrated strike at the Yomiuri newspaper came under Communist direction, and the party's Youth Corps, or *Seinen-tai*, captured control of the moderate Seamen's Union. A federation of Communist-dominated unions, called *Sanbetsu*, was formed in 1946 and grew quickly to a membership of more than 1.5 million workers. *Sanbetsu*, although smaller than the more conservative socialist-controlled federation, *Sodomei*, embraced unions in strategically vital sectors such as government and civil service workers and the communications and transportation industries. As its influence spread, the party's own membership increased dramatically. Before the war, the number of actual party members had never exceeded 1,000. Two years after Tokuda's release from Fuchu Prison, the total was estimated at 70,000.[9] For the first time, leftists were in a position to propel Japan in a radical direction and shape the nation's destiny.

Pumped up with confidence in his successes, sincerely believing that a revolutionary tide was rising, Tokuda hit upon a tactic that would prove pivotal not only for his party but for the entire postwar labor movement. A "general strike" involving millions of workers and leading toward chaos was a dream he had borrowed from European radicals. Out of a nationwide shutdown would somehow grow a People's Democracy ruled by militant unionists and guided by him from the Yoyogi headquarters. He saw his chance, in the winter of 1946, in a strike called by government workers who had been denied a wage increase. Tokuda's men won control of their strike committee. Twenty-five other unions joined in sympathy, and soon Tokuda dominated the "All-Joint-Struggle Committee." Under his direction, its demands escalated quickly to include both economic and political concessions, including the resignation of Prime Minister Yoshida. Management and the government dug in for a siege, and the workers' committee defiantly set February 1, 1947, as the date for Tokuda's general strike. As Tokuda had planned, Japan was indeed lurching toward chaos. The "Two-One Strike" (named for the date—second month, first day) would involve as many as 6 million workers throughout Japan, and it would shut down telephone service, railways, subways, schools, government offices, and hundreds of factories. Japan would be immobilized. It was an enormous gamble for the ambitious Communist leader not yet two years out of prison garb. Victory would crown him king of Japanese labor.

In fact, there was never any chance that the general strike would come off, for the simple reason that General McArthur would not permit it. But for reasons that were never clear, the general held his tongue until the last minute. His underlings in the Occupation's Economic Section and Labor Division were instructed to inform the workers' committee that they must cancel the strike. Tokuda ignored them. Unless MacArthur himself spoke, he decided, the "Two-One" could proceed, and his lieutenants agreed, after polling union leaders, that it would be successful. Through January, with workers massing daily in the Imperial Palace Plaza, the confrontation came closer and closer. In the Daiichi Building, the Occupation's frightened administrators shuttled to and fro, one moment warning Struggle Committee leaders to call off the strike, the next urging MacArthur to ban it in his own words. One wonders still why he held back, for his no-general-strike policy had been clear from the start. Perhaps he relished the high-noon melodrama. Perhaps he did not wish to put his own name to a command that would be viewed as antilabor. Literally at the eleventh hour, he issued a statement declaring the strike illegal because it would interfere with the Occupation's duties. Tokuda took one last poll of his unions. Would they strike in defiance of MacArthur? Back came the answer: They would not. Tokuda sent his militant lieutenant, Yashiro Ii, to the final meeting to break the news. Ii did so, tears in his eyes as he spoke.[10]

Precisely why radical labor retreated so submissively at the critical moment is still unclear. One obvious reason was the fear of armed retaliation from MacArthur's troops. Tokuda probably reasoned that it was preferable to fight again another day, although that day never came. Another explanation lay in the realization that broad public support for a chaotic general strike was lacking. Public-opinion polls taken immediately after the strike was canceled revealed that a large majority of Japanese sided with MacArthur and against the unions. People had peered into the abyss and had come away frightened. For all of the ferment in the streets preceding the "Two-One," there were limits to how fast Japanese could be led, and Tokuda undoubtedly sensed this. In any event, the aborted strike was a disastrous loss for him and his movement. In the next few months the labor movement as a whole took a step back. Many Communist leaders were removed from union offices. Newspaper editorials turned against them, too. Most important,

Tokuda had lost the cover he had fashioned as the Occupation's friend.

During the next few years the men in the Daiichi Building grew hostile to radicals. In 1950 they implicitly sanctioned the Japanese government's sweeping "red purge." Thousands of Communists and a large number of innocent non-Communists were ousted from unions, factories, and offices. That was the ultimate crushing moment for militant labor in Japan. But the failed Two-One affair had paved the way for the purge and had changed the course of Japanese history.

●

In the textbook version of the occupation of Japan, the citizens of that defeated country obediently accepted all that was thrust upon them in a spirit of willing cooperation. This was the version created by General MacArthur's media machine. He wanted it known that his reign was an unqualified success not merely because of his own great wisdom but also because the Japanese themselves saw that what was done to them was for their own good. A second version that emerged much later held that the democratization of Japan was a failure because the Japanese resisted at every turn and slyly evaded the Occupation's draconian edicts. In the end, Japan was little changed. The truth lies somewhere in between, for there were great differences among the Japanese themselves in their attitudes toward the Occupation. It appealed to many, infuriated others. Landlords and the conservative political establishment, for example, despised the American land-reform plan. Tenant farmers were ecstatic. Some cooperated totally, others tried by obfuscation and deceit to thwart the Americans.

But from the records of the times and recollections that came later, one pattern emerges clearly. All Japanese whose roles brought them into contact with the Occupation tried to bend its policies to their own interests. One is struck by how much bargaining went on between occupiers and the occupied. Prime Minister Yoshida had said that Japanese must play the role of "good losers," but he used all his talents to temper the Occupation's remodeling of Japan. So did labor leaders, unrepentant nationalists, landlords, village chiefs, Communists, *zaibatsu* (large corporation) families, and schoolteachers. Japanese of all opinions, once assured that they were not to be raped, looted, and murdered en masse, seemed to conclude that in the new order of things all was negotiable. There was in this collective response both an admirable spunkiness and an astounding audacity. Theodore Cohen, a shrewd chronicler of this interplay, has left us a revealing example of this attitude. Two days after the emperor announced surrender, the Japanese Foreign Office sent a remarkable message to Washington advising officials there on precisely how the Occupation could best be carried out. It declared that Japan's army should disarm itself, that no foreign troops should be stationed in Tokyo or other cities, that food and medicine should be supplied forthwith, and that prompt repatriation of Japanese troops overseas was imperative. MacArthur, of course, immediately rejected the advice, but the message itself had exposed the peculiar cast of mind prevalent in Tokyo. Defeat did not necessarily mean capitulation. Argument and compromise were still in order. As Cohen noted, in its first formal postdefeat reaction Japan had behaved "as though it were negotiating, not surrendering."[11]

Much of the give-and-take that did ensue was the inevitable result of a crucial decision made in Washington before MacArthur set foot in his new domain. Japan was not to be ruled, as Germany was, by a large military government. The civilian bureaucracy would be left largely intact, and MacArthur would govern through it. His administration in Tokyo, the Supreme Command of the Allied Powers (SCAP), was to issue commands, and a relatively small force of American soldiers was to see that they were complied with. MacArthur, moreover, soon pared his forces from 600,000 to 200,000 men, who were charged with supervising a nation of 70 million people. Most of them, after the first year, were raw recruits, young and inexperienced, so that in the most important years Japan's conversion was to be overseen by men in their teens and early twenties. These arrangements naturally created much leeway for evasion of Occupation directives, especially in the countryside, where only small units supervised entire prefectures. There was considerable opportunity to dilute the effect of SCAP's directives, and Japanese set about doing so with diligence.

There was also a disposition at MacArthur's headquarters not to be any more intrusive than was absolutely necessary. The Diet, purged of its militarists, continued to meet and actually to pass laws, subject to SCAP vetoes, of course. The emperor made his time-honored journey to the Grand Shrine at Ise to report to past gods. When the land-reform laws were forced through a recalcitrant Diet, they permitted committees of local farmers latitude in carrying them out. Thousands of politicians were purged from office, only to reappear promptly in new roles, wielding their same old power. None of these events could be charged to MacArthur's oversight. They were the natural result of deliberate policy. The Supreme Commander really did want the Japanese to democratize Japan.

For all of these reasons, a gap emerged between what SCAP thought it was accomplishing and what actually was happening among the Japanese. It is most vividly described in the pages of *Japan Diary*, an absorbing account of the Occupation's early years by an energetic American newspaper correspondent, Mark Gayn. Over the course of two-and-a-half years, until May 1948, Gayn compiled a half-million-word diary of his experiences. In it appear brothel-keepers, farmers, landlords, American generals, enlisted men, and many others. It is perhaps the finest single description available of how the Occupation was seen from both sides at the working level, and Gayn's interviews form a priceless record of how ordinary Japanese coped with their conquerors. Gayn was no unbiased observer, however. He had reported from China during the war and had observed the effects of Japan's cruel conquests there. In Japan he was predisposed to see the Occupation as a venture of dubious value. He believed that the Japanese were cleverly deflecting it at almost every turn, and he concluded that there was a vast "conspiracy" among them to block the SCAP directives. It was an error, he wrote, to attempt to remake Japan through the Japanese.

During Christmas season of 1945, Gayn rode rickety trains through northern Honshu, Japan's main island, to look closely at the Occupation's initial impact on rural Japan. What he saw in Sendai, Sakata, Akita City, and several villages convinced him that the impact was slight. American generals in Sendai told him that local Japanese sabotaged every directive as soon as it arrived from Tokyo. Men who had been purged from the old thought-control police were reemployed en bloc as municipal policemen. A dance hall ordered closed because of prostitution reopened quickly at another site. In Sakata, Gayn was told that all of the teachers in local schools had been hired during wartime on orders from the military, presumably for their extreme nationalist views. None was to be fired. An American officer told him that Japanese city officials submitted faked and inflated bills for housing GIs. They did so because they had been advised that the quartering costs would eventually be deducted from the nation's forced reparations payments. The American-Japanese Liaison Office in Sakata was staffed mostly with former thought-control policemen—even, Gayn discovered, the Japanese man who advised the American sentry as to which local Japanese should be allowed to enter the SCAP headquarters. He learned that a militant ultranationalist former general was secretly recruiting a new network of imperial-system loyalists in the countryside. He was doing so under the cover of giving lectures to farmers about the proper uses of yeast.

It was clear to Gayn from such stories that the Japanese had learned how to handle the Occupation. The occupiers scarcely knew what was happening around them, so thick was the wall of deception and obfuscation. Suspicions of illegal deeds were met with bland expressions, polite denials, and gracious displays of hospitality. Nowhere was this pattern clearer than in the Occupation's attempts to uncover evidence that Japanese schools were still teaching imperialist lessons and war preparations. Schools, Gayn wrote, had been the "breeding grounds of rabid nationalism" during the war and probably had not changed a bit. Proving this was another matter, although a wave of school inspections had been ordered to gather evidence. When visited, the classrooms were invariably cleansed of banned materials, and inspectors were greeted with elaborate courtesy, rice crackers, and tea.

In Akita Prefecture, deep in Christmas-season snow, Gayn and a Lieutenant Hartley hit upon a solution. Together they would make surprise raids at village schools to catch teachers in their treachery and confiscate textbooks containing subversive right-wing materials. Their first target was the snowbound village of Otuki, and they telephoned ahead for reservations at a local inn. It was a mistake. Arriving in Otuki, they were met by six neatly dressed gentlemen, including the mayor and deputy mayor. The next day, school officials greeted them warmly and implored them to visit their schools. Gloomily, the Americans inspected spotless classrooms. Their big find was a picture book depicting Japanese kamikaze planes sinking American ships. The principal explained that he intended to ink out these objectionable drawings but had not yet found the time.

Dejected, Gayn and Hartley planned a stealthier school raid. The local train from Otuki passed through four small towns on its way to the city. They would board it without telling anyone their destination, then hop off at the village of Mitumine and arrive unannounced at the local school. There would be no advance warning. Nothing could be concealed. At Mitumine, they bounded onto the platform to find a greeting party which included the mayor elegantly clad in a formal cutaway suit. Welcome to Mitumine, the mayor said. How would they like to visit the schools? Defeated once again, the two Americans glanced over more shiny classrooms and ate more tea and rice crackers. Later they discovered why their surprise raid was not a surprise. Police had alerted mayors and school principals at each of the train's four village stops. All down the line receptions had been prepared by smiling men in formal clothes and teachers with hot tea. Gayn and Hartley gave up.[12]

Gayn's eye for detail was magnificent, but it missed the larger picture. The Occupation did succeed in changing Japan fundamentally. It did not merely wipe away the militarism that had taken root in the decade before the war. It erased much of the social landscape that had existed since the Meiji Restoration of 1868. What the Occupation actually achieved is the subject of chapter 2, and what came of it all is for the remainder of this book to explain. The Occupation lasted for six years, seven months, and twenty-eight days. It was not a neatly ordered process of orders dispatched and automatically obeyed. It was a mixing-bowl process in which plans, pressures, counter-pressures, and sheer happenstance were swirled together. The Occupation ordered; the Japanese maneuvered to temper the orders; bargains were struck, original intentions changed, and more bargains struck. But when it finally ended, the old Japan was hardly recognizable.

2

●

Starting Over

General Douglas MacArthur never seems to have thought any small thoughts. He did not deign to accomplish missions. He engaged in grand crusades. If the task before him could not be pictured, at least in his own mind, as a matter involving mankind's destiny, it seemed to interest him little. This was true of both his greatest moments, as when he commanded vast American armies in the Pacific, and his minor ones, as when in the 1930s he commanded only the tiny army of the Philippines. And so he came to Japan in that autumn of 1945 not to disarm a defeated rival but to create a new country. It was to be a crusade worthy of his own view of his Olympian capacities. MacArthur, in a message to the War Department in 1947, described what he foresaw for a Japan placed under his control: "a complete reformation of the Japanese people—reformation from human slavery to human freedom, from immaturity that comes of mythical teachings and legendary ritualism to the maturity of enlightened knowledge and truth, from the blind fatalism of war to the considered realism of peace."[1] Only a MacArthur could have considered leading an entire people "to the maturity of enlightened knowledge and truth," but the phrase was no mere afterthought of an aging soldier. The general indeed regarded the Japanese as an immature people—he once referred to them as a nation of twelve-year-olds. (Momentarily embarrassed when that comment was printed, he explained that he had meant that in the stages of history leading to democracy they were only at age twelve.) He really did regard Japan as an unformed child who, with his enlightened guidance, could be brought to responsible maturity.

The postwar occupation of Japan is often regarded—especially by Japanese—as entirely the work of MacArthur. In fact, much of it had been planned in Washington before the surrender. Major strategic decisions, such as retaining the emperor as symbolic head of state and using Japanese bureaucrats to run the country, were part of that planning. So too were many of the specific elements, such as disarmament, reparations to formerly conquered countries, labor and land reform, and the purging of militarists. After some early bureaucratic skirmishes, during which the State Department's "old Japan hands," who favored a modest restructuring, were brushed aside, there was considerable unity in Washington. By the time MacArthur was given his orders, there was widespread agreement on a thoroughgoing democratization of the defeated nation. These instructions suited MacArthur's own view of the crusade that lay ahead. For the first two years of the Occupation there was little friction between him and Washington. Both the letters of instruction and a personal letter from President Truman had assured him that the manner of carrying the instructions out would be left solely to him as Supreme Commander of the Allied Forces. This meant that whatever its substance, the style of the Occupation would be MacArthur's. And the style was to become of much importance.

His list was a long one. Out went the Meiji Constitution and in came the MacArthur Constitution, binding Japanese to the renunciation of war forever. The emperor was demoted from god to mortal, and Shinto was disestablished as a state religion. Peasants would be freed from serfdom and given land. Workers would be permitted to organize unions and strike against their bosses. The *zaibatsu*, those huge commercial and industrial conglomerates, would be dissolved and replaced by an economic system that rewarded smaller enterprises. Japanese women would be elevated to sexual equality with men and released from ancient vows of servitude. Even the *ie*, or "family system"—a relic of the prewar civil code that made minimonarchs of fathers and husbands—would be erased. Nothing was to be left untouched. Makers of war would be purged, schools cleansed of rote learning and emperor worship, politics opened to the little man. And through it all the minds of Japanese would be scrubbed clean of that debilitating respect for authority and hierarchy, that ingrained obeisance to superiors, which had held back the march of democracy for centuries.

The immense scope of this reformation can be traced to two convictions that MacArthur held, one of them historical, the other personal. The first blamed Japan's history for the war in Asia. Her mad dash into the Pacific War had been the natural result of state repression at home, which in turn had flowed from centuries of feudalism. The term *feudal* turned up in hundreds of Occupation documents to describe the source of evils to be rooted out. It was used to explain the system of land tenantry, the impotence of workers, the attitudes of high school students. Militarism had been bred in the *bushido* ("way of the warrior") mentality of the shogun's samurai and when coupled with Shinto and the emperor system, led inevitably to Asian imperialism—and to Pearl Harbor. All of it had conspired in the subjection of the common man, who was reduced to an instrument of state power. Unbind him, give him rights and freedoms and a job, and the democratization of Japan would take care of itself. And so MacArthur set out to eradicate not merely a military class but centuries of Japanese history and culture.

The second conviction that guided MacArthur had to do with his personal view of American democracy. Despite his magisterial mien and exaggerated sense of destiny, there was in MacArthur a virile streak of old-fashioned American populism. The Occupation of Japan is often treated in history books as a transplantation of Roosevelt's New Deal. It is true that many civilian reformers sent out from Washington were dedicated New Dealers, and Japan's new labor laws would mirror reforms adopted in America in the 1930s. But MacArthur's own instincts—and they were what mattered in Japan at first—harked back to an earlier era and a simpler concept of reform. The changes he planned for Japan bore a strong resemblance to the ideals of populism. Break up the trusts. Protect the small farmer from exploitation. Create an economic environment hospitable to the independent businessman. Unfetter the talents of sturdy, hard-working men. Do all of these things and Japan would become, well, a sort of Asian Nebraska. Since his boyhood, MacArthur had lived most of his life overseas. What he knew of America in the thirties and forties was largely secondhand and had mostly to do with preparing for and fighting foreign wars. What he remembered of America was what he had learned long ago, and it was this older version, in all its simplicity, that he hoped to transfer to Japan.

The irony of MacArthur's role in remaking Japan was that he sought to implant a populist reformation by authoritarian methods. In theory, all of the reforms were to be freely enacted by popularly elected governments. In practice, SCAP, at nearly every stage had to compel those governments to act. The new constitution, for example, was written by MacArthur and his advisors and adopted by the cabinets and parliament only after rather crude threats. It was even poorly translated into Japanese, and a number of foreign-sounding phrases survived, enough of them to engender a measure of public cynicism. One popular joke was: "Have you read the new constitution yet?" "Oh, has it been translated into Japanese already?" The new charter unequivocally guaranteed freedom of the press. But on many occasions, MacArthur's watchful censors ordered news stories and editorials withdrawn before publication. The Occupation's own propaganda line dutifully portrayed the Japanese as cooperating splendidly in the process of democratic transformation. In fact, the occupiers suspected trickery and deceit on every hand. They even banned for a time productions of *Chushingura*, the old and beloved story of forty-seven samurai who avenged their master's death by murdering a shogunal aide. The Americans apparently feared that the story's popularity might encourage an assassination plot by supporters of executed war criminals.

Many of their suspicions were in fact correct, because postwar governments repeatedly attempted to dilute and obstruct Occupation-sponsored reforms. These governments included many liberal reformers, but their leadership for the most part objected to much of the program dished out from MacArthur's headquarters. There was more involved in these disputes than minor changes in approach. These leaders, especially Prime Minister Shigeru Yoshida, rejected in their hearts the historical premise of the Occupation, which viewed Japan's militarist period as a natural outgrowth of feudalism and Meiji-era nationalism. They deeply revered the old Meiji system as embodying the best of Japan and believed its nationalism a blessing that had been perverted by the militarists in the thirties. In their view, the Pacific War was not an inevitable consequence of feudal history, as MacArthur contended. It was an aberration. They held to the "stumble theory," which asserted that the dark age from 1931 to 1945 was a terrible mistake brought on by army fanatics. Furthermore, they could fairly point out, many in their own ranks were men who had opposed militarism and had been swept aside in its surge to power. There was, then, no cause for radical change in Japanese institutions, no sound reason for erasing a system that had once served Japan well and that had, before the generals came to power, sought a peaceful coexistence with the West.

These men shaped Japan's official response to the Occupation's demands, and the history of that period is largely one of tension between them and the occupiers. For it very quickly became apparent that, weak as she was, Japan would not accept the MacArthur reforms without at least haggling over them. Parrying here, delaying there, obfuscating, seeking endless "explanations," making singular interpretations of their own, the Japanese were, in fact, able to temper and even reverse some of the sweeping changes. Yoshida would later boast in his memoirs of having deflected some of them by demanding written instructions or by insisting that they did not suit, in his favorite phrase, "the actual conditions existing in Japan." He had learned very early how to play on the Occupation's aspirations and fears, especially its concern that the new spirit of radicalism evident in the street protests might sweep Japan toward communism. In 1946, with hungry people wandering in those streets, Yoshida deliberately delayed forming his first cabinet, signaling MacArthur's headquarters that he would not act until SCAP agreed to provide food for the starving. Yoshida is said to have remarked to his friends, "The Americans will certainly bring food to Japan once they see people waving red flags throughout the country for a whole month."[2] Later, at the height of his power, Yoshida skillfully exploited differences of opinion, not only those within SCAP (which had its own liberal and conservative factions) but also those within the community of foreign nations SCAP represented. He found ways to turn those divisions to Japan's benefit. A knowledgeable chronicler of those times, Masataka Kosaka, believed this was the prime minister's guiding principle: ". . . it was his opinion that if a defeated nation made clever use of the constantly shifting relations between the world powers, that nation could minimize the damage it suffered as a result of defeat. Japan, in other words, could by means of diplomacy transform defeat into victory. The thought was fundamental to his post-war policies."[3]

●

This conflict between conservative governments and MacArthur's command was played out in hundreds of skirmishes, of which the following were important examples:

1. *Labor.* SCAP was bent on establishing a strong and legally protected labor movement under laws similar to the Wagner Act in

the United States. Yoshida opposed all three of those laws, one of which, the Labor Standards Law, he said was being used by left-wingers as a vehicle of protest that intensified social unrest. His government tried, in vain at first, to hamper the law's administration and repeatedly urged SCAP to crack down on strikes and the political activity of union members.

2. *Land reform.* Occupation plans to disassemble the old farming structure and create a new class of free farmers was pushed through over Yoshida's objections. The minister he appointed to carry out the reform was hostile to it and tried to obstruct the vital land registration surveys on grounds that they were too costly. SCAP persisted, however, ending up with a successful program that made land owners out of 75 percent of the former tenant farmers.

3. *The* zaibatsu. SCAP's reformers insisted on breaking up the huge industrial and financial combines that had dominated Japan's prewar economy. Yoshida defended the *zaibatsu* at every turn as economically necessary to Japan's reconstruction and later regarded as a significant victory his campaign to let such former giants as Mitsubishi, Sumitomo, and Mitsui retain their corporate names. In the end, many corporations were rescued from dissolution and permitted to regroup.

4. *The purges.* Determined to erase all vestiges of militarism, SCAP purged tens of thousands of wartime government officials, business executives, politicians, and members of the news media. Yoshida protested indignantly that not all former officials had been militarists, that many had simply been forced to go along with the army clique and that, anyway, as he later wrote, the Occupation edicts prescribed "arbitrary standards based upon a misreading of history."[4] Most of these men were ultimately depurged, and many quickly regained influential positions in the government and political parties.

5. *Education.* Believing that the old Meiji education system produced not freethinking students but tools of the state, SCAP ordered changes from top to bottom. It banned instruction in ethics, abolished state control of textbooks, and shifted power from the Education Ministry to local school boards. Yoshida governments opposed several of these changes on grounds that they were too costly and deplored the trend toward encouraging students to act as

independent thinkers. The prime minister saw much of Mac-
Arthur's program leading to a lack of discipline and to classroom
chaos.

●

These conflicts were perhaps inevitable because of the decision to run
the Occupation through Japanese officials. This fit tidily with Mac-
Arthur's conviction that given a proper lead, Japanese themselves would
choose the right path to democracy. He encouraged cabinet leaders and
the bureaucracy to examine and approve his instructions before they
became final. Naturally, those governments attempted to reshape his
commands into forms more to their liking. As the Occupation wore on,
they became bolder and more forceful in making their own interpretations, and gradually a consistent pattern of resistance developed. Many
Americans became exasperated by the trend. In 1948 the U.S. Central
Intelligence Agency was moved to complain: "The leadership of the
Democratic Liberal Party is ideologically opposed to many Occupation-
initiated reforms, and there are indications that during the tenure of the
Liberal-led Yoshida cabinet the government sought to minimize the
effects, if not the implementation, of these reforms."[5]

Japanese resistance tempered the MacArthur reforms, but it was a
gradual change of heart by the Americans that did most to limit them.
By 1947 the United States was plunging into the cold war, and in both
Europe and Asia all acts were judged by their contributions to the
anti-Communist cause. What was wanted in Japan was not a democ-
ratized former foe but a sturdy partner in defense of that cause. In
Washington, MacArthur's reforms came gradually to be seen as destabilizing, even dangerous. They were creating not unity but turmoil and
were alienating those very pro-Western conservatives in Japan whom
Washington had come to trust and admire. The orders streamed into
Tokyo calling for restraint. By 1948 this policy of a "reverse course" was
official, and many of the reforms were stalled or softened. It was greeted
with enthusiasm by Japan's government, which hastened to put it into
practice. Limits were placed on union strikes, and in one massive stroke
more than 22,000 alleged Communists were purged. The zeal for trust-
busting evaporated, and in its place was a new tolerance for rebuilt
industrial and financial conglomerates. In the most astonishing turnabout of the entire postwar era, Washington began urging Japan to
disregard her own MacArthur Constitution and start forming a new
army.

●

Despite all of the tempering and backsliding, however, much of the MacArthur reformation endured, and Japan emerged from the Occupation in 1952 a changed nation. A great deal of the prewar Meiji system had been done away with and could never be revived. How much change really occurred is a fascinating puzzle that has kept armies of scholars busy for four decades. Some Westerners look at post-Occupation Japanese society and, because it does not function in a thoroughly Western way, see only superficial differences from the past. In fact, almost all of the country's political and economic relationships were changed and even some of the social habits and customs as well. There arose from the war and Occupation new relationships and new institutions that in some ways were as different from those of prewar days as the Meiji era's had been from those of feudalism's.

Labor, for example, found itself in a new position of power in postwar Japan and, despite the restraints imposed after 1947, emerged strong enough to challenge management in the most important considerations affecting workers' livelihood. Small farmers were in fact freed from tenantry and emerged a prosperous and politically powerful bloc capable of protecting themselves. The dissolution of the great *zaibatsu* was eventually abandoned, but the new corporate giants that replaced them were far different from the old family-owned, autocratic, union-busting ones of the prewar days. Political arrangements were sharply altered from the era when parties were weak and controlled. A solid opposition party did emerge and survive. The old imperial system was crushed, and Japanese showed little inclination to accept the rule of a small clique operating through the emperor. The new Japan did not, of course, much resemble the populist arcadia that MacArthur seemed to envision in the first days after the war, but neither did it resemble in its important institutions and working arrangements the society of prewar years.

The reason that so many of the Occupation's changes survived and flourished was that most of them were popular. Despite the conservative government's hostility and obstructionism, the reforms that most affected people's daily lives were accepted and approved, often overwhelmingly. Farmers did rush to claim their land from dispossessed owners, and the concept of land reform was endorsed in every public-opinion poll of that era. Workers did pour into the new legal unions, and the great majority remained even after the American-sanctioned retrenchment. Virtually every organized reading of the public mind in the postwar years registered approval. Eighty-five percent endorsed the emperor's new symbolic status as defined by MacArthur's constitution. Seventy-two percent agreed with the renunciation of war. Two out of every three approved the new legal equality of the sexes. Four out of ten even favored abolition of the *ie* system, which had regulated family life. In the closing months of the Occupation, several newspaper polls inquired whether Japanese, on balance, felt they had benefited from its experimentation. Nine out of ten said yes.

In a curious but very important way, the MacArthur reformation was self-fulfilling. The very reforms it instituted prompted a commitment to retain them. It created new constituencies with vested interests in these changes, especially among working people, farmers, and the civilian bureaucracy, and even among businessmen. All of them gained new power and rights in the postwar era. Labor bargained equally with bosses. Small farmers owned their own land. Economic bureaucrats began to guide the country, and a new class of businessmen soon took over the reins of corporations. They were not inclined, it turned out, to exercise their new powers in the same ways foreigners might have expected, but neither were they inclined to let them slip away. The radicalism of the first postwar years, when half of all Japanese had favored either the Socialist or Communist parties, rather quickly evaporated. But the reforms that had to do with how people earned a living and with what they could expect to achieve endured.

What survived from MacArthur's tenure in Tokyo was what the Japanese found acceptable, and in this respect the postwar reformation was somewhat similar to the Meiji Restoration. The Japanese had filtered out what they did not want of the Westernization process of the late nineteenth century, and they performed another filtering process during and after the Occupation. But there was a major difference. In the forties and fifties, it was a much-changed social system that did the filtering. What was to endure had to be acceptable to people who had been largely shut out of the system that existed before the war. The Occupation performed one act that ranked above all of the others. It elevated new kinds of people to positions of responsibility and power, assuring in the process a degree of social mobility unthinkable before the war. These people took control. Japan was placed in their hands, just as post-Meiji Japan had been placed in the hands of men who earlier would have been considered upstarts. And the changes they were to bring about were in many cases just as great as those of their Meiji predecessors.

How these changes unfolded is best told in the story of the postwar labor movement, and I have chosen to tell that story by describing what happened in a single union formed by steelworkers in the Yawata works. It is a fair microcosm, I think, of what was happening all over Japan. The saga shows how labor formed and defended a system vastly different from that which prevailed before the war. It reveals the upward thrust of a class that before had counted for little and the arrival of new men of power in the industrial system. And it shows how the Occupation actually acted on these events—first releasing radicalizing energies and then containing them. Out of all this pushing and shoving emerged the basic elements of Japan's system for organizing labor and management, for the ultimate compromise reached at Yawata was to be widely copied. I think the story suggests that there was little that was inevitable in the labor experience of those days. Things happened because certain men made them happen or because certain outside events shaped the way in which they were allowed to happen. Chance and happenstance played a big part. One cannot help thinking that the final result might have been very different.

●

In its forty-four years of operation, the Yawata Iron and Steel Works had become the glowing symbol of Japan's industrial modernization, a working monument to the Meiji-era's crusade to match the West in every way. People in the mill town and the nearby coal fields liked to call it the place where Japanese capitalism began. The blast furnaces, first fired in 1901, had been designed by German engineers imported for the task and were in large part financed by indemnities from China after Japan's first foreign military conquest, the Sino-Japanese War of 1894–95. A nationalized industry at birth, the Yawata works had been merged with five private companies in the depression year of 1934 to become part of the Nippon Steel Co. From her furnaces and rolling mill poured forth steel for the guns and ships used by the imperial forces as they swept through Asia in the Pacific War. Working three shifts a day, her work force never stopped so long as there was iron ore to turn into steel, and the small city in northern Kyushu became a national legend in the patriotic struggle to arm the emperor's troops.

But on August 15, 1945, the plant was almost silent. Part of a single furnace remained lit, but that was all, and the rolling mill was immobile. Yawata had been blasted repeatedly by America fire bombs, and vast sections of the works were simply rubble and twisted beams.

Bodies of workers killed in the most recent raids still lay in a room at one end of the mill. Young workers had been drafted very early into the armed forces, and those who remained to the end were older men bowed with fatigue from working double shifts. The streets were quiet as they listened to the emperor's voice that day, and when the speech was over the workers wandered about singly, lost in their own thoughts of what it would mean. Some would remember long afterward that from the mighty Yawata works all that emerged that day was a thin line of smoke climbing into the still summer sky.

In that remote corner of Japan, there had never been any talk of defeat and surrender; news bulletins had talked only of glorious victories. So the emperor's startling announcement was received more in puzzlement than in anger or remorse. They accepted it, because he was the emperor after all, but the times would be hard, they knew. An old saying was recalled to express their concern for the future: "It is easy to die in glory, but it is difficult to live in shame." The terms of the surrender, of course, were not known in Yawata, but the workers could guess that they would be severe. This much was realized, or guessed at: All that imperial Japan had won since the Sino-Japanese War a half-century in the past would now be gone. News reports told of a meeting the previous month, in some place called Potsdam, of the leaders of enemy nations who had decided what was to become of Japan. There had been a "Potsdam Declaration," the newspapers said. But where was Potsdam? What had Potsdam to do with Yawata?

The first to sense an answer to that question was Fujisaburo Oka. A middle-aged plant worker, Oka was a spirited man who had been active in what passed as a steelworkers' union before the military had absorbed all unions into the war machine in the 1930s. Four days after the emperor's address, he was at home reading a newspaper article that spelled out a few details from the terms of the Potsdam Declaration. Democracy was to be imported in Japan, the article said, and freedom of speech and the right to form political parties would be guaranteed. One paragraph stated: "The Japanese government shall remove all obstacles to the revival and strengthening of democratic tendencies among the Japanese people. Freedom of speech, of religion, and of thought, as well as respect for the fundamental human rights, shall be established." Oka instantly thought, "The time has come." Yawata would have a labor union, because democracy must include the right of workers to organize for their own welfare. Oka spent two days thinking through his idea, wondering how to start a union, worrying over whether others would see the opportunity he had glimpsed in the Potsdam Declaration.

On August 21, in a fortuitous meeting in the street, he encountered an old friend, Minobu Nose, and they began chatting. Nose had had the same idea—a union of steelworkers in Yawata. They talked eagerly there in the street and came to a conclusion: They must act fast or soon there might be others with the same ideas. Several unions could sprout at once, and the workers' power would be diluted from the start. In the following days, they gathered nine other friends and met in the evenings after work, first in a company office and then in an abandoned employees' recreation center owned by another factory in Yawata. Nose remembered they worked ten-hour shifts in the mill, for a thin stream of raw steel still was being produced there. Then they hurried to the recreation center where, weary but excited, they cooked their own meals, which consisted of the leaves and stems of potatoes and pumpkins, soybean paste, and occasionally some soup with a ball of flour floating in it. Each of the eleven men would report on the progress of his day organizing in the mill. On into September the meetings continued every night until, at last, they were ready to tell the factory manager what they had created: The Yawata Steel Works Labor Union.

●

If Oka, Nose, and Japan's other new labor organizers had looked back on the history of their country's union experience, they would have found few sources of inspiration. There was no grand tradition to revive. Prewar unionism had been characterized by periods of both suppression and growth, but on the whole it was far from militant and in general unsuccessful. In the early exuberance of the Meiji era, small associations of workingmen had been formed, and in the 1880s groups of printers and *rikisha* drivers had even managed brief strikes. Several of the first union advocates were graduates of American divinity schools and had imbibed both elements of the social gospel and the conservatism of the American Federation of Labor. They were a timid lot on the whole. Their first national federation was masked under the inoffensive title of *Yuaikai,* or the "Friendly Love Association." Serious unionists had to confront government suppression, management hostility, and a chaotic labor market in which workers were periodically hired off the streets and quickly discharged at the slightest signs of militance. By 1920 the organized labor movement consisted of only about one hundred thousand members.

The period around World War I was a more hopeful one. Companies enriched by wartime trade began hiring full-time workers to form a stable, experienced work force, and some exhibited a new tolerance for unions. It was a time of democratization and new freedoms for Japanese in many walks of life and also one of renewed copying of Western institutions. Unions were free to organize with little government interference. Still, the results were marginal. Many of the new unions were mere extensions of management, their leaders given to making secret deals with company officials and using their jobs as representatives of working men as ladders for their own promotions. A new crop of leftist agitators entered the field to preach the theories of class struggle and revolution. Most of them spent more time analyzing Marx and Lenin than in organizing the rank and file. The movement peaked in 1931 with only 8 percent of the industrial work force in unions, and one-third of them were members in a single union of seamen. The energies of labor were gradually absorbed into the enormous patriotic surge engineered by the military. Marxists were jailed and strikes suppressed. Finally, all independent unions were banned by law, and workers were free to join only a government-sponsored federation known as *Sampo*, an abbreviation for *Sangyo Hokokukai*, or the "Patriotic Industrial Association."

Defeat in the Pacific War introduced a radically new chapter. Of all the postwar reforms introduced into Japan, none was more solidly supported by the occupying powers than the movement of organized labor. Even the Far Eastern Commission, a generally important body that embraced all the allied powers, including the Soviet Union, agreed with the goal of free and democratic trade unions. SCAP, the real ruler of Japan then, was united in its commitment. New Dealers, generals, and diplomats all envisioned a strong labor organization modeled on American lines—in part because of their own liberal views and in part because labor was seen politically as a check on the revival of giant corporations that had abetted Japan's militarism. In their general instructions to MacArthur, the U.S. Joint Chiefs of Staff had called for "the development of organizations in labor . . . on a democratic basis." On October 11, 1945, MacArthur used a social visit by the new prime minister, Kijuro Shidehara, to introduce a list of five reforms that the new government was to enact "as readily as they can be assimilated." Second on the list was this requirement: "the encouragement of the unionization of labor so that it may be clothed with such dignity as will permit it an influential voice for safeguarding the working man from exploitation and abuse and raising his standards of living to a higher level." That same month, MacArthur instructed his officers and civilian planners that their mission was to remove all barriers to union organizations. Moreover, he said in one of his more fateful commands, Japanese workers were to be free to strike when they pleased. Only if a strike appeared to threaten interference with actual "military operations" was it to be thwarted. There were to be no restrictions on the type of unions, on their size, or on their political coloration. If anything, leftists seemed to be favored in the initial application of MacArthur's edicts. Shortly after the general met with Shidehara, SCAP ordered the release from prison of all Communists jailed before and during the war. Among them was the prewar firebrand, Kyuichi Tokuda, who was soon to make life miserable in SCAP's Labor Division.

SCAP's role would be not simply to tolerate Japan's unions but to assist in organizing them. Its Labor Division, located four floors beneath MacArthur's own offices in the Daiichi Building, became a sort of union-boosting service center where the new labor leaders came to seek advice. It was staffed largely by American labor union organizers and U.S. Department of Labor veterans, almost all of them New Dealers, all of them dedicated to a Japanese labor movement as militant as the one back home. They wrote the movement's magna carta, the Trade Union Law, modeling it on the New Deal's Wagner Act. They passed out literature explaining how union meetings were held, what shop stewards did, how strikes were organized. Through their offices passed almost all of the new Japanese union chiefs, tough revolutionaries quoting Marx and conservatives preaching prewar passivism. All of them came seeking advice, but many also came to enlist the prestige of SCAP behind their own campaigns for union power. Even Communist delegations were led in by their chief, Tokuda, who was eager to demonstrate that he enjoyed SCAP support. A quick meeting with a Labor Division clerk could be transformed into a gesture of support, and that gesture itself could be transformed further into evidence of SCAP's support. Every conceivable type of union trooped in for these interviews. Heads turned quickly one day when a trio of geisha, dressed in kimonos and *getas* (wooden shoes), their hair trimmed with bells and trinkets, marched in to announce the formation of their own new union.

In charge of the Labor Division was one of the more remarkable of the men dispatched by Washington to guide Japan into the new world of labor-management relations. Theodore Cohen was a feisty New Yorker who, like many of his generation, had been attracted to radical ideas during the depression years. The son of Russian Jewish immigrants, he had gone to college in New York and at Columbia University had written a master's-degree thesis on the labor history of Japan. When he arrived in Tokyo in 1946, he was familiar with the records of most prewar labor leaders because their names were preserved on the file cards used for his thesis. He was a witty, scrappy young man with a sharp tongue that provoked many confrontations with his seniors in SCAP, including some of MacArthur's close military aides. At times he was attacked for being too soft on Japanese radicals, at times for bowing too quickly to SCAP's latter-day conservatism. He served for a year-and-a-half as chief of the Labor Division before being kicked upstairs as an advisor to the leader of the economics branch. After the Occupation ended, he remained in Japan as a private businessman for three decades.

Cohen was the most energetic of all the "Occupationaires" (as they called themselves) and was passionately devoted to the cause of unionism. He hustled around the country spreading the new organizing sermon, dropping down into coal mines and talking to women workers in textile mills. He was tireless in his rounds, telling workers of their new rights and managers of their new responsibilities. With the latter, he was often brash and insulting. Once the president of the Nippon Iron and Steel Corporation, Shigeo Nagano, asked Cohen to explain what the phrase "labor problems" meant because, he said piously, there had never been any labor problems in Japan before. Cohen tartly told him that if there had been no labor problems there had certainly been "management problems." On another occasion, a group of coal operators came seeking exemption from a new law prohibiting women from working in the mines. They claimed, in apparent seriousness, that some of their coal seams were too narrow for men to enter; only slender young women could do the job. The issue was settled when Cohen crisply asked the operators if they would be willing to send their own wives into the mine shafts.[6]

Cohen was the brightest beacon of hope among the new generation of Japanese labor organizers who emerged in the early months of the Occupation. His devotion to free unions and his power to help them succeed seemed limitless. One of those awed by his commitment was Eiichi Ochiai, who had formed a new electrical workers' union at a Toshiba plant in Kawasaki. Ochiai was himself an unusual young man, and the story of his involvement in the trade union movement provides a revealing glimpse of the topsy-turvy character of the times and the sometimes peculiar origins of postwar unionism. He was a college graduate with a degree in engineering, and when the war ended, he had been the boss of some three hundred workers at Toshiba. As the era of war contracts was closed out, the company seemed to flounder. Managers seemed unsure of what they should do now that peace was staring them in the face. They made no effort to revive a line of products that would be serviceable. Production lines were producing nothing, and workers stood around helplessly, fearing their jobs would soon be abolished. Ochiai became outraged at management's seeming paralysis and drew up a plan to begin manufacturing lines of radios and telephones, both in short supply. Managers turned him down. He turned next to the workers, urging them to form a union and force the company to act. And so the first postwar union in Toshiba's Kawasaki plant was organized in an attempt to get management to manage something.

By October 1946 Ochiai had called a strike in the American style. The employees spent each day squatting on the plant floor. Suddenly, one day, a young American army lieutenant appeared and ordered them out of the building, informing them that he had been instructed to halt the strike. "I started yelling at him," Ochiai remembered in an interview years later. " 'Strikes are legal—why are you trying to get us out?' " The lieutenant left but returned later with a written order. Ochiai agreed to vacate the plant but then rushed down to Cohen's office. "I told Mr. Cohen about it and said something was wrong. He picked up the phone and called the provost marshal's office in Yokohama. I never knew what he said, but two days later the commanding officer came to me with an apology. The young lieutenant had been transferred. Our strike went on. Cohen was so powerful."[7]

Given prodding and protection by SCAP, Japanese workers responded with a remarkable burst of organizing. New unions popped up by the hundreds in the first year of the Occupation. Some were Communist, some were Socialist, and some were conservative unions of the old stripe. New labor federations—*Sanbetsu* for the leftist unions, *Sodomei* for the more conservative—sprang into existence and competed vigorously for local affiliates. Hardly a day passed in Tokyo without a parade of workers wearing cloth headbands called *hachi-maki* and marching to proclaim the birth of some new union. Between October 1945, when MacArthur had first laid down the law to Prime Minister Shidehara, and the summer of 1946, union membership increased on an average of a half-million people a month. By the end of 1946 organized labor in Japan counted 4.5 million members, nearly ten times the number on union rolls at the prewar peak.

For company owners and managers, those first months of the Occupation were the worst of times. First of all, they themselves were under the Occupation gun, threatened with the forced dissolution of their companies and, in many cases, with jail terms for having supported the military during the war. Second, they faced an indigenous labor movement that was not at all the sort with which they had been comfortable before the war. This was a militant, often radical, crusade backed up by the highest power in the land, General MacArthur. It was as if the emperor of old, suddenly smitten with affection for the proletariat, had commanded managers to heed the workers and run factories for their benefit. As the wave of unionism mounted, as striking workers actually began locking up bosses in their own offices, as protesters in white *hachi-makis* and red armbands surged through the streets chanting about revolution, the managerial class, or what was left of it, shuddered in fear. In their fright and confusion, they ceded many of the early demands without a struggle. One observer wrote: "Employers were stunned by the defeat, disorganized and uncertain, fearful of antagonizing the Occupation forces, and in some cases, no doubt, apprehensive of revolutionary developments."[8]

There were, in fact, several memorably radical strikes that carried portents of social revolution. One of them was at the *Yomiuri Shimbun*, an important newspaper, where employees, urged on by a Communist leadership, took control of the editorial departments and proclaimed a people's press. Another was an industry-wide strike of electrical-power workers in the fall of 1946—a well-prepared action in which workers backed their demands by shutting off power to selected industries. But more often than not, the confrontations that year were harmless affairs marked by ingenious arrangements rather than damaging assaults. A peculiarly Japanese form of cautious militance emerged, dramatically radical in appearance but modest in its ultimate goals. In some plants, workers locked up their managers and continued to work, promising to release them when wages went up.

The most distinctively Japanese actions were "production control strikes" in which workers occupied plants, continued to work without bosses, and then prudently placed the business receipts in company bank accounts. At the Keisei Electric Railway Co., workers ousted management, continued to run the trains, collected fares, paid themselves slightly higher wages, and banked the profits in the company's name. Throughout the "October Offensive" of 1946, when it sometimes seemed that all Japan was on strike, only 1.21 percent of the total man-days were actually lost. There were many examples of middle-level managers actually joining the strikers, and it was not uncommon for them to be elected to union offices. So closely did workers and managers seem to work together in many companies that SCAP agents frequently urged the unionists to be more independent. One incident in particular seemed to suggest that, for all the revolutionary sloganeering and confrontational tactics, the soul of Japanese labor was not really engaged in the new radicalism. In the autumn of 1945 the telephone workers in Sendai, consumed with the exuberance of the moment, went on strike. They remained at their switchboards, however, and answered customers with the following greeting: "*Moshi, Moshi* (Hello, Hello). We are on strike. Long live Democracy. Number please?"[9]

●

The important truth to be found in all this was that the Japanese labor movement was anything but monolithic. It embraced militants, moderates, Marxist radicals, mild-mannered Socialists, old-fashioned conservatives, and a great many workers indifferent to any ideology. Its drift certainly was in the direction of an independence and activism that had been unknown before the war. The influence of radicals—in these early days before a great reaction set in—were enormous, and had they not been curbed by outside forces they might have transformed the movement into something truly revolutionary. Indeed, one is struck by how unpredictable it all really was in the early stages, and how, given but a minor shift in circumstances, it all might have turned out differently.

●

While all these events were unfolding that winter and spring, the steel workers in Yawata were playing out their own union strategy in the shadows of the famous old mill. Before any talks began with management, a group of their elders spent a great deal of time thinking about the history of unionism in Japan, especially about the record of unions at their own plant. They found little encouragement there. The first Yawata union, founded in 1917, had been bursting with energy and in the new freedom of that time, had displayed an uncommon militance. A bitter ten-day strike in 1920 over working hours and wages had marked a new stage in the national development of independent unions in Japan. Their rallying cry had been incredibly radical: "Turn off the furnaces." Closing down blast furnaces would have been a drastic step, possibly ruining the plant and at least delaying production for a long period. The threat was long remembered in labor lore as unionists' bravest hour, although it was never carried out. One hundred and forty-one strikers were fired, but the union won a nine-hour day and a small wage increase. Management, frightened by the new attitude in the mill, became more cooperative. But time and the appearance of managerial indulgence dulled the union's militance, and Yawata became a company union town. So indifferent did the rank and file become that union leaders were forced to hold "*udon* meetings" to attract them, serving hot meals of noodles (*udon*) as inducements for attendance. The rising nationalism also curbed labor's fighting spirit. As early as 1933, a national steel-union manifesto listed its priorities first as expansion of the industry's production for national defense and only second as the betterment of workers' welfare. By 1938 the Yawata union was absorbed without a fuss into *Sampo*, the military regime's tame labor federation.

Memories of that prewar decline hung like a cloud over Yawata in the fall of 1945 as Oka, Nose, and their friends sought to sign up new members. Soon they would make their statement to the company's managers, and solidarity among the workers, they knew, was essential if they were to get a serious hearing. But as they combed through their recruiting lists, they found many workers rejecting their appeals for one reason in particular. They remembered prewar union leaders as opportunists who used their roles in the labor movement for their own selfish purposes. They had taken company payoffs and had manipulated union power to advance their own careers both within the company and in local political life. Oka and Nose found themselves suspected of similar motives. Discouraged, they met one night at Nose's house and admitted to each other that the union was dead unless the clouds were dispelled. In desperation, they drafted a formal pledge in which each member of the Preparation Committee agreed that he would not use union office for financial or political gain. The next day they circulated the paper throughout the plant and rolling mill. It worked. One by one, the reluctant steelworkers abandoned their suspicions and joined the union. Younger ones were particularly drawn to a small union faction called *Seinen-tai*, which was composed of impatient young activists speaking a strange language of class struggle.

Its ranks now filled and united, the union was ready to test the company. During meetings in September and October, four members of the Preparation Committee explained the new union to Takashi Miki, the assistant factory manager of the Yawata works. His response seemed cordial. Miki began by promising that in the new spirit of the times the company would not oppose the idea of having a union at Yawata. But then, in a discursive speech full of platitudes and vague statements about harmony, he set out the terms of management cooperation. During the war there had been a healthy spirit at the plant, he said, and it had been largely due to the efforts of *Sampo*, the military-imposed union federation. He would be sorry to see the *Sampo* spirit destroyed. Besides, he went on, it did not seem a good idea to leave something so important as the establishment of a new union to the laborers in the plant. "Is it really such a good thing to place this matter in the hands of a labor union which has come up from the bottom?" Miki asked. It would be better, he thought, to establish the company's own union, which all would be free to join. The union could be called *Shinwakai*, which translates roughly into English as "The Intimate Harmony Association." Into that organization would be poured the old *Sampo* spirit. There would be cooperation, not conflict, Miki concluded, and the glory and industrial might of the Yawata works would flourish anew.

It was a clever speech, full of appeals to sentiments close to the heart of all Japanese. It embraced patriotism, group harmony, and that strong inclination to welcome instructions from the top of a hierarchy. It placed Oka, Nose, and the other union founders in a difficult spot. The choice was clear. They could stick with their own independent union concept and risk company displeasure, which could mean firings and harassment. Or they could accept *Shinwakai*, which they knew the company would expect to dominate but which, in the prewar fashion, would probably assure workers' jobs. The choice was security or independence, the past or what promised to be the future. Oka, Nose, and the others chose the future. Politely, they explained to Miki that they would be careful and moderate in their actions, for they recognized that times were hard. Japan was a defeated country, and Yawata a stricken mill, barely able to meet a payroll. But these were new times, and the spirit of those times called for independent and democratic labor unions. The spirit of *Sampo* would not suffice. *Shinwakai* was rejected.

For months thereafter, the fateful decision brought nothing but good fortune to the Yawata Steel Labor Union. The timing was spectacular, because just as its choice of independence was being announced, the news from Tokyo brought waves of encouragement. General MacArthur served notice that companies could no longer control labor unions. *Sampo*, the wartime federation, was officially disbanded. Workers were to be liberated, the bulletins said, and actively encouraged to form their own unions. Collective bargaining and the right to strike without reprisal were specifically guaranteed. A branch of the Occupation headquarters had recently been established in nearby Fukuoka, and its officers had sternly informed the managers at Yawata that the new orders were to be strictly obeyed. Until then, the Yawata union leaders had relied chiefly on the vague words of a declaration written in some place called Potsdam. Now the highest authority in the land had backed them up. In the same month of October that had seen company unionism rejected in Yawata, the new labor law was proposed in Tokyo, and the government was compelled to enact its every feature.

Faced with a united union and instructions from SCAP, the Yawata company backed down as gracefully as it could. To trim payrolls, it fired hundreds of white-collar clerks, but not a single blue-collar worker lost his job. To maintain harmony and satisfy the first sizable wage demands, the company sold off several properties for cash. Oka's union prospered, enlisting new members every day, and moved with a full-time staff of thirty into an office in an old warehouse. The union's first newspaper appeared, its editorials insisting on independence and self-discipline. Its headline slogans called for a soldier's commitment: "Sacrifice and Cooperate." It rejected outside influence of any kind. By the end of 1945, less than five months after the article on Potsdam had stirred Oka to act, the essential form of Japan's postwar trade unions was taking shape in the steelmaking town. The union was strong, but it also sought amicable relations with management and cooperated to save jobs for its members. Its horizons were limited to the boundaries of Yawata steel, and little thought was given to joining with industrial unions around the country to form a national political force. But within those bounds it was something completely new—a union of workers that bargained from strength with the managers.

The arrangement had its detractors, however, and they were to put Yawata through the same bitter crisis that was being played out across Japan in 1946 and 1947. The Yawata union had been shaped by middle-aged and older workers who, although determined on independence, often displayed an old-fashioned concern for the company's welfare. Job preservation was their primary goal, and they were often willing to concede other issues to attain it. Within the union a small group of younger members found the pattern of conciliation unsatisfactory. It smacked to them of the outdated spirit of *nemawashi*, of "consensus-seeking," in which union leaders sought favors through private collusion with the company. Several of them, too, were newly minted Marxists who saw unionism as the preparation for class struggle. Protest, not agreement, they declared, was the union's rightful role. A small cell of Communists began to form and grow, centering its attention on a band of disaffected younger workers grouped in *Seinen-tai*, or Youth Corps.

Yawata thus became an example of a struggle that was common all over Japan. The future of Japanese labor was largely determined in those months of late 1946 and early 1947. The forces pushing and pulling the movement all had seemed to gather strength in that second winter of the

Occupation. In the center was the new breed of union activists, men like Oka and Nose who had quite early grasped the opportunity to found unions that were both democratically ruled and independent of management. They were, in general, men of moderation whose attentions, once their union was born, were riveted on a single labor issue: preserving the jobs of their members. What the rank and file wanted most was job security. Even wage increases were secondary. To achieve that security, they were prepared to cooperate with management in a rather old-fashioned way, promising to help keep production lines rolling at a steady pace. They would sacrifice much—although not the independence of their union—to keep their men at work. With millions of Japanese still unemployed and hunger still a genuine threat, theirs was by no means an irrational choice. They pragmatically opted for bread on the table.

Pulling against these centrists, in Yawata and elsewhere, were unionists of a different stripe. Younger than the leadership and more adventurous, they were easily attracted to a more militant view of a union's purposes. Many of them were army veterans who were embittered by the experiences of war and defeat and easily susceptible to arguments that they had been forced to fight a capitalists' war. Very few were committed Communists or Socialists, but the organized left had an advantage in the struggle to win their minds. They had suffered and their comrades had died while plant managers and company owners had survived comfortably and even prospered, at least until the final year of the war. For the disaffected young searching for meaning in the postwar chaos, the left also offered one idea that had broad appeal: "worker control." The laboring man, through militant unions, should take control of industry and run it for the benefit of workers. Top Communist leaders hoped that this concept would eventually be extended to workers' control of the Japanese state, but at the grass-roots level, where union power was being fought over, the idea of controlling production was uppermost in the minds of young militants. They objected strongly to the moderates' willingness to settle for job security. That was a limited tactic, they claimed, which guaranteed that the essential control of production would remain with management. Communists seized on this difference in plant after plant across Japan, using it in attempts to dislodge the union leadership. Their appeal was great to young men like Yoshiji Miyata.

Miyata had been a teenaged apprentice in Yawata before the war but had managed to attend a high school before being drafted and sent to Korea in 1943. A diligent and ambitious student, he also had somehow attained certification as an engineer-technician. When the war was over, he expected to return to Yawata and cash in on those attainments. He felt certain that he was destined for the company's elite track as an engineer. Instead he was assigned to the unskilled blue-collar work force. The rebuff was humiliating. For months he stewed and grumbled at his work bench. Miyata's political conversion began in the course of a single conversation. Near him worked a covert Communist, Hisashi Tanaka, who one day began discussing conditions in the plant, the idea of worker control of production, social democracy, and revolution. He and Miyata agreed that the union's leaders were too passive, too addicted to *nemawashi*. Tanaka described the works of Lenin, which designated labor as the driving force in the class struggle. Its duty was not compromise but protest—constant, unyielding protest. Miyata began to read the works of Marx and an assortment of pamphlets passed on to him by Tanaka. Given his own grievance against the steel company, he found himself excitedly agreeing with all that Tanaka urged. Finally, Tanaka put the question to him: Would he join the Communist party? "Let's do it,' Miyata replied instantly. Years later, remembering that moment, Miyata agreed that he had been motivated primarily by his personal sense of humiliation by the company. "It was a very simple motivation," he said.

Together Miyata and Tanaka used the youth group, *Seinen-tai*, like a hammer to pound the union leadership. They accused it publicly of playing secret games with the bosses, of selling out. Yawata was at last beginning to make both steel and profits, and the younger workers demanded a bigger share. They were a tiny minority. Only fifty young workers showed up for *Seinen-tai*'s first meeting. When May Day, 1946, rolled around, it was clear that militants were in no position to challenge the leadership for control. Only about three thousand of Yawata's twenty thousand workers marched through the rain that day. The union's officials were not pleased with the appearance of Marxists in their ranks and were determined to bar all outside influences, Communist or otherwise. They were firmly opposed to holding production-control strikes, as some of the big-city unions were doing. Still, the dissidence of Miyata and others alarmed them. Something should be done to keep the young workers loyal, they felt. They finally agreed to incorporate them into the union's directorship as a new *Seinen-bu*, or Youth Section. By the end of 1946 the Communists had moved inside the union's power structure. Miyata was named to its executive committee.

Strike fever came to Yawata in January 1947, as it did to the rest of

Japanese unionism, and it was partly due to a Communist minority. The campaign began with a demand for elimination of a complex, company-designed class system that divided and then subdivided all employees into job classifications with distinct, and discriminatory, wage scales. Blue-collar workers were lumped into the lowest class and paid by the hour instead of by the month. If a blue-collar worker was absent for sickness, his pay was docked; a white-collar clerk was paid even while ill. The issues were ideal for a class protest, and *Seinen-bu* agitated with all its might for a strike. The time was right. All over Japan, suddenly radicalized unions were preparing to hit the streets in the "Two-One," the general strike scheduled for February 1. The more conservative leadership at Yawata was reluctantly swept along in the tide. It did take the precaution of advising MacArthur's headquarters that its strike would be separate from the large general strike. To stress that it should not be considered part of the Tokyo radicalism, the Yawata union scheduled its strike for February 7.

SCAP, it turned out, was rethinking its policy on all strikes, not merely the "Two-One." It was drifting from that original policy of encouraging militance and tolerating strikes to the new conviction that Japan's economy must be stabilized. All strikes could be destabilizing, especially a national steel strike. In Tokyo, where industry-wide steel negotiations were taking place, MacArthur's men quietly let union bargainers know that a steel strike would be a violation of Occupation policy. Back in Yawata, the local's executive committee ran for cover at the news, voting nineteen to fifteen to suspend the strike indefinitely. But the rank and file, still imbued with the new radical spirit and emboldened by the plentiful Communist rhetoric, thought otherwise and, ignorant of SCAP's private warning, voted to hold the strike by a margin of 69 to 31 percent. *Seinen-bu*, with Miyata taking the lead, pushed relentlessly for a walkout. In Tokyo SCAP got tougher, ordering the broadcast of a national radio message calling for the strike. The national union agreed but submitted a script for the broadcast blaming the cancellation on "pressure from GHQ." MacArthur's representatives did not want to take the blame for strike-blocking and insisted that the message be rewritten. The union bowed again and prepared a new script saying that the strike was canceled "because of new developments."

Back in Yawata the local union, fired up again by Miyata and the *Seinen-bu*, still refused to call off the strike. They had carefully explained to the local representatives of SCAP that theirs had nothing to do with the general strike in Tokyo, that their grievances were local, and that, anyway, GHQ had always told them strikes were a right of all workers. A mere broadcast from Tokyo would not deter them. On February 6, the eve of the chosen day, the local membership again vowed to strike and set the time for 10:00 A.M. the next morning. It was the crucial moment toward which all their energies had been directed for many weeks, a moment that would determine just what sort of union theirs would be. They had, it is true, been maneuvered to this crossroads by radicals, but the strike votes showed a preference for militance that went beyond the Communists' influence. The company had not budged far on the vital issue—equality of pay for blue-collar workers—and the time of testing had come. Miyata was delighted.

Again SCAP intervened, this time directly, and the moment was lost for all time in Yawata. Union leaders were summoned that evening to the nearby community of Kokura to meet with a representative of the U.S. military government. He had warned them before, but this was to be different. He read them a message from General MacArthur himself. The strike must be canceled. It would be a violation of Occupation policy. There could be no doubt this time, and the union leaders were hustled in a military jeep back to Yawata to announce the news. There, the strike committee argued on until midnight, while an angry crowd milled about outside. However, the outcome was inevitable. The strike was off.

The next morning a heavy snow was falling as some 12,000 workers gathered to hear the final decision. There was no real argument in favor of defying MacArthur. The union elders, flourishing the latest command from SCAP, announced that they would not risk disobedience to armed authority and called for a no-strike vote. The rank and file, which through several prior votes had wavered between militancy and accommodation, agreed and walked away from the strike. The power of MacArthur had been demonstrated again.

Seinen-bu was furious and tried to keep the crowd boiling. Many wept openly and others began making up brief, sorrowful songs of defeat and betrayal. Speaker after speaker had his turn, and each said the same thing: MacArthur could not be defied. Finally the youngest militants were invited to say their piece and up stood Miyata, representing *Seinen-bu*. It was his first speech to so large an audience, and he fashioned it into a mixture of rage and sadness. Their strike was right, SCAP was wrong. It was all a great betrayal. It had been the Americans who preached a union's rights and duties, the Americans who had talked of the right to strike. SCAP itself was destroying union democracy in Yawata. Miyata finished, and the meeting began breaking up, the workers drifting away. The strike was abandoned.

It was the end of a brief era, in Yawata and the rest of Japan. The young radicals tried repeatedly to keep the strike issue alive, but they were rejected and discovered that much of the rank and file had turned against them. They were blamed for the failed strike, accused of fomenting a crisis for their own political interests and of placing politics above the workers' need for jobs. But as the leftists' dreams evaporated, so too did the company's hopes of reviving the old prewar style of company unionism. For a time, it tried to keep its last vestige of that era, *Shinwakai*, as its official union, but the workers would have none of it. The decisive event occurred in a bargaining session at which the union asked for emergency rations of rice at company expense. The company, sensing it had the upper hand for a change, said it would make its reply through the *Shinwakai*. The real union refused to accept that. Finally, *Shinwakai* was dissolved as a labor union and transformed into a company-sponsored sports and recreation club. There followed a period of down-to-earth, undramatic collective bargaining that ushered in the new age of labor relations that was to become familiar across the country. The union promised to help the company increase production; the company said no one would be fired, not even when times were bad. By 1950 the Yawata union membership had grown to 47,000 employees, the largest in Japan.

Miyata, the youthful firebrand, drifted on the leftist fringe of labor politics, but he finally became dissatisfied with its politics and quit the Communist party in 1948. Over the years he became highly successful in moderate union organizing, rising to several high positions in the house of labor. Forty years after the failed strike he was a respected elder statesman of the Japanese labor movement. He looked back on his Communist days as a time of youthful foolishness. Time had cooled his anger at the Americans' intervention and, in an interview in 1989, he agreed that MacArthur had done the right thing. "It was quite natural that the Americans called off the strike," he said. "Our purpose [in 1947] was revolutionary. We weren't interested in wage increases or other issues. We thought we were going to bring the government down. We just wanted to create a disturbance there in Yawata. It was inevitable, what the Americans did."[10]

3
●

Trials of the
Spirit

A kitsugu Yamazaki wanted to be rich. By the standards of the day, he was already on the customary path to success. A veteran of the war, he was a third-year student in the elite Tokyo University School of Law, which even in those difficult times was the proper place to launch a successful career in government or business. But in January 1948 the twenty-seven-year-old Yamazaki thought that was not enough, and he designed for himself a fast track to wealth. All around him were Japanese desperate for cash. They needed money to pay bills, enjoy a night in a bar, support a mistress, finance a son through prep school. Money was tight, prices were high, and the nation was showing few signs of rising from the ashes of defeat. Yamazaki and a medical-school friend scraped together 6 million yen in borrowed funds and set about lending it at exorbitant rates, sometimes as high as 10 percent for ten days. The venture, which Yamazaki named the "Hikari Club," was instantly suc-

46

cessful. Profits rolled in, he borrowed more capital to make even greater profits, and throughout one of Japan's most miserable years, he amassed spectacular riches. He was seen constantly in expensive restaurants in the company of pretty young women. Yamazaki was as coolly calculating in romance as he was in business. Instead of promising marriage, he negotiated "free-will contracts" guaranteeing love for money with a series of girl friends.

The law caught up with Yamazaki in July 1950, when he was arrested and charged with loan-sharking under the Price Control Act. Shocked creditors descended on his offices, demanding repayment of debts, and the "Hikari Club" plunged into bankruptcy. At first he seemed to have taken the honorable way out—he committed suicide. But he left behind a diary and some personal letters that contained no hints of remorse. Later collected and published as *Memoirs of a Loan Shark*, the thin volume was a publishing sensation. It described in intimate detail his sexual relations, but it was most remembered for the cold-blooded self-justification of his exploitation of friends. Japanese tradition called in such circumstances for apology and pleas for forgiveness, but Yamazaki posthumously broke even that rule. "To do business by making cunning use of others is a clear principle of economics," his memoirs declared. His transition from Tokyo University student to loan-sharking predator was amusing, he thought—"like a clam being turned into a sparrow." And in a climactic burst of egoism, he wrote: "Life is a drama. I write the scenario, produce and direct the play, and act the hero. I bet my life and I do not take death seriously."[1]

●

The "Hikari Club Affair" became one of those rare events that symbolizes an entire era. Those who lived through it remember the decade of 1945–55 as much for its atmosphere of moral decadence as for its deprivation and poverty. Yamazaki's exploitation of friends, his crass relations with women, and his celebration of pure avarice served as a metaphor of the times. Three novels were written about the affair, including one—*Ao No Jidai*, or *The Blue Age*—by Yukio Mishima, who was to become one of Japan's most celebrated postwar novelists. Loan-sharking, of course, had been a common practice for many decades, a slightly dishonorable yet generally accepted trade. But Yamazaki had been no low-life trickster. He was of good family, and as a student at Tokyo University had been prepared for a career of almost certain success and respectability. In the "Hikari Club" he created a model of greed and unrepentance that has stood time's test as the symbol of a mean and shoddy decade.

In literature and in people's memories, the mores of that time are often contrasted with those of prewar Japan. Japanese remembered the Meiji and Taishō eras as pinnacles of good taste and lofty principles. Under the harsh postwar circumstances, this exaggerated nostalgia was perhaps natural. The sense of lost values was acute. Prewar Japan seemed a kind of golden age of civility in which neighbor trusted neighbor and exploiters were cast into shame. In those comfortable times, the head of the house could live on credit with obliging tradesmen, paying grocers, druggists, and clothiers once a month. Postwar relations were reduced to cash on a vicious black market. If there was one virtue that the old Japan had exalted above all others it was that of *giri*, one's sense of duty and obligation toward others. Postwar Japanese believed that *giri* was tarnished beyond recovery. When they were asked in a 1952 public-opinion survey whether they believed the loss of *giri* was "a disaster," nearly three out of four said that they did.[2]

This feeling of lost personal values translated, too, into a perception that the social cohesion so remarkable in the old Japan had withered. In the late nineteenth century, as he attempted to instill a sense of nationalism, Emperor Meiji had admonished his subjects to "let all Japanese hearts beat as one," and that injunction had been learned by every schoolchild. It had guided the generations that pulled Japan into the modern world. The wartime suffering reinforced it, because the burdens were shared by all in equal measure. Pride in common sacrifice had sustained the people through terrible times. Now "nationalism" had become a dirty word, soiled by the perverse purposes to which the military had put it. The postwar world reflected, in almost every aspect, a decline of selflessness. The simplest daily exchange of money for food had a beggar-thy-neighbor quality about it, and that great national consensus that had taken a century to build seemed to have disappeared.

There was confirmation of this in the frightening increase of serious crimes. While prewar Japan had not been the age of innocence that many thought they remembered, it had been generally peaceful. The postwar crime rate soared. There were four times as many murders in 1947 as in 1940, the last year before war with the United States broke out. Many were gangland killings in the black-market districts. But especially chilling were the bizarre and calculated murders of innocent people. One that seemed to mark a new low in decadence was unraveled in January 1948, after a man was discovered pushing a cart bearing the corpses of four infants. He was traced to a nursery, the Jusan-in, in Yanagi-cho, owned by one Mrs. Miyuki Ishikawa and her husband. The nursery had run a brisk business in caring for unwanted babies, charging fees ranging from 5,000 to 8,000 yen a month. After collecting their payments, however, the Ishikawas neglected to feed the babies. Eighty-five of them, it was discovered, had died of starvation, their bodies later being hauled on carts to isolated burial sites.

It was in that same month that Japan's most spectacular postwar crime occurred. At 3:30 P.M. on January 26, a man appeared at the rear door of the Teikoku Bank in Shiinamachi. He identified himself as a "Dr. Matsui" of the Tokyo Metropolitan Government's Quarantine Service and solemnly reported to the bank manager that an epidemic of dysentery had broken out, requiring the entire population of Tokyo to drink a certain immunizing potion that he was charged with distributing. The man coolly asked for drinking cups and served all sixteen employees with a cloudy mixture from his bottles. They promptly began keeling over. By the time the police arrived, twelve of them were dead and the "doctor" had escaped with 164,000 yen in cash. After an exhaustive investigation, police eventually traced the mass murders to one Sadamichi Hirasawa, a Japanese-style painter. Hirasawa was sentenced to death, but the order was never carried out, in part because of lingering suspicions that the police had seized the wrong man. Hirasawa died in prison in May 1987 at the age of ninety-five, still contending that he was innocent.

Such terrifying events as the Jusan-in and Teikoku Bank murders might have been dismissed as the work of sick and deluded minds, perhaps to be expected in the aftermath of war. But another series of investigations disclosed a pattern of lawlessness in the corporate world and government that was in some ways more shocking because it involved studied corruption by Japan's elite. Three months after the two spectacular mass murders—1948 seems to have been a banner year for criminal behavior of all types—the Showa Denko scandal began unfolding. Showa Denko was the country's major producer of fertilizers, the leader of a vital industry nurtured by the government in its eagerness to increase agricultural output for a hungry nation. The company had received a large loan from the Reconstruction Finance Bank, a government institution modeled on the lines of an American depression-era credit program. Investigators delving into anonymous reports found a trail of bribery and graft that would have made Boss Tweed envious. Financial documents confiscated at the company's headquarters revealed proof of widespread bribe-taking by government and political leaders and of lavish entertainment of both by Showa Denko executives. The trail of tainted money led on to such eminent public figures as Prime Minister Hitoshi Ashida, the minister of finance, the vice-minister of agriculture, the chief secretary of the Liberal party, and a high-ranking Ministry of Finance official named Takeo Fukuda. In November 1948 the Ashida Cabinet was forced to resign and, as the probing continued through the years, a total of sixty-four men were indicted.

The Showa Denko scandal confirmed for many Japanese the notion that in their new era of demoralization no one and no institution was to be trusted. Men at the pinnacle of Japan's elite, men entrusted with the duty of reviving a stricken nation, had been caught in a callous betrayal of the public. Corruption in the political world was not particularly surprising; politicians had not been highly regarded even in the old days. But Japan's bureaucracy had, since the Meiji period, enjoyed a reputation for probity and selflessness. The Showa Denko revelations found some of them, too, to be untrustworthy. Moreover, as the months and years wore on, it became apparent that few would be punished, that the political-bureaucratic world could protect its own. Only two of those indicted in the Showa Denko case were convicted of crimes. (Takeo Fukuda went on to become, three decades later, a prime minister of Japan.)

In that first postwar decade, the war itself seemed to recede from the public consciousness. It is rarely discussed explicitly in the literature, film, and memoirs of the time. Crime, corruption, and daily indignities were what troubled Japanese, and these bred a cynicism about state and society that was completely new. Since Meiji, Japanese had been filled with a sense of their country's purity, of its essential goodness, and had reveled in its ascent to a position of power and respect in the world at large. There was now an overwhelming sense of shame, not so much about what her armies had done in Asia but about the catastrophe that had followed defeat. Japan was back at the bottom—poor, forced to beg from the West, an object of either scorn or hatred. She was dunned abroad for war reparations and for repayment of postwar loans. In China and Southeast Asia she was reviled for her troops' inhuman behavior. Not many Japanese traveled abroad in those days, but those who did felt the sting of shame most acutely. Manila was then the crossroads of Asia for trans-Pacific air flights. When the first Japanese businessmen ventured to fly overseas, they were advised not to leave the plane during refueling stops in Manila because of fear that Filipinos would assault them.

In Europe, Japan's emissaries encountered huge claims for indemnities due badly treated prisoners of war, and even America was beginning to insist that recovery loans be repaid. The embarrassment was great. In 1954 Prime Minister Yoshida ventured abroad on a trip to Europe and the United States to meet old friends. The hostility toward Japan shocked him. He later recalled, "I had been met everywhere by demands for the payment of money due—rather in the manner, I felt, of the president of a shady company."[3] Japanese shrank defensively from conversation with foreigners or seemed to spend encounters with them bowed to the floor in apologetics. The shame was so great, and so intensely personal, foreigners discovered, that ordinary conversations almost always included expressions of Japanese unworthiness. Edward Seidensticker, the Japanologist and translator, found such performances embarrassing. "Back in the years after the war," he later recalled, "the Japanese sense of inferiority was so painful that one wanted to tell them to be quiet about it, at least, if they could not overcome it."[4]

●

The sense that Japan's traditional cohesion had been fragmented was nowhere more sharply defined than in the perception of her modern youth, the *après-guerre* generation. The *après*, as they came to be called, were presumed to have lost all respect for authority—for their parents, teachers, government, and emperor—and to have determined to lead lives of degeneracy and extreme eogism. Much melodramatic prose was devoted to the notion that postwar youth rejected all of their elders' ethical codes. Imbued with the new democratic spirit brought to Japan by the Occupation soldiers, they were seen to be rebelling against all that had held the society together in the past. In his memoirs, Prime Minister Yoshida deplored the excesses of the young who, he complained, "regarded it as democratic to despise their teachers and make light of their elders generally."[5] Yoshida was preeminently a man of the Meiji generation, but his opinion was shared by younger and more liberal observers. Kazuo Kawai, a newspaper editor of modernist views, was equally appalled. "To the *après*," he wrote, "the concept of a social order of any kind seems to be incomprehensible, and they exhibit an attitude which might be characterized as a sort of passive nihilism."[6]

Postwar youth were indeed a restless bunch, undoubtedly affected by the new cynicism of their parents and inspired by Occupation dogma to celebrate the new emphasis on individual rights. Some of them did mock their elders, kiss on street corners, practice casual sex, criticize their teachers, and preach the right of alienated youth to challenge all that was old. And certainly the public saw in such attitudes an irrepressible tide of disobedience. A public-opinion survey in March–April 1952 asked adults if they thought that the number of children who paid no attention to parents had increased recently. Sixty-six percent said yes.[7]

But the *après* phenomenon appeared far more threatening than it really was. Surveys of attitudes among young people themselves revealed few signs of rebellion or radicalism, and in general they described a generation only modestly less conservative in social attitudes than its elders. A series of UNESCO public-opinion polls analyzed by Jean Stoetzel found that a majority of youth differed only slightly from their parents in the degree of respect for authority. More than half of them felt that American-style democracy would not suit Japan. They demonstrated strong affection for Japanese traditions, including the emperor system. Instead of wildly embracing democratic rights, they were only slightly more inclined than their parents to become active in politics. Stoetzel summarized their political leanings with this comment: "The anxiety of people in Japan and elsewhere who fear lest the youth of the country may plunge into an excessive form of liberalism appears . . . to be ill-founded."[8]

However much exaggerated, these fears of a new generation of savages continued throughout the decade and reached a zenith of sorts when a young writer named Shintaro Ishihara bounded onto Tokyo's literary scene. A graduate of Hitotsubashi University, Ishihara had been a brash and inventive student writer whose first novel, dealing with college life, had been published in a campus literary magazine. He startled the nation in 1955 when his second work, *Taiyo No Kisetsu*, or *Season of the Sun*, was published. It won the prestigious Akutagawa Award, sold 300,000 copies in the first year, and became the theme of three popular movies. The book was far more than a literary event. Japanese took it to represent the literal truth about a whole generation. For a time it was the most notorious piece of social commentary in Japan, regarded as a definitive description of alienated youth and postwar degeneracy. The *après* it portrayed were callous, amoral, defiant, egotistical, insensitive young hedonists concerned only with their own pleasures, and their exploits confirmed every fearful suspicion of the adult generation. The dismay was doubled when Ishihara, while promoting his best seller, declared that he was not condemning the young but merely depicting the reality of their lives.

Season of the Sun tells the story of Tatsuya, a handsome college boxer who enjoys inflicting physical pain on his sparring partners and emotional suffering on his girl friends. He moves with a crowd of young pleasure-seekers whose ties are primarily those of money:

> All the group were very good friends, but theirs were not the generous friendships each had had in high school days. There was no element of self-sacrifice in their relationships, but instead a carefully balanced system of debit and credit. If the debit column grew too long, the friendship would break up. Everything they did and said was calculated; they never risked a wild venture that might drastically upset their accounts.[9]

Money is valued over affection; *giri* is a subject of scorn. At one point Tatsuya discovers that his girl friend, Eiko, is also admired by his own younger brother. He resolves this dilemma by selling her to him for 5,000 yen. "And did you think I'd agree?" asks Eiko when she learns of the transaction. "It's nothing to do with you," Tatsuya replies. "It's my affair, not yours."[10] Sex is shockingly casual and frequently used for comic effect by the author. In one scene, Tatsuya, seeking more inventive ways of demonstrating his contempt for Eiko, rams his hardened penis through a *shoji* screen into a room where she is reading a book. Eiko responds by throwing her book at his penis.

Inevitably, Eiko becomes pregnant, an event that brings out her lover's most brutal instincts. At first, he instructs her to bear the child because he thinks it would be fun to show to his friends as a kind of prize he has won. This turns out to be a passing whim. "But he got a kind of pleasure from watching Eiko's reactions, like inspecting ties he had no intention of buying in order to irritate the salesgirl."[11] Too late, Tatsuya changes his mind and orders Eiko to have an abortion. She dies four days after the operation. Her funeral becomes the setting for the novel's baffling climactic scene. Angered by the smiling photograph of Eiko in the visitation room, Tatsuya smashes it to bits, shouting, "God-damn you." Then he turns on her family and, as if the tragedy had been all their fault, screams, "None of you understand."[12]

As a work purporting to represent an entire generation, *Season of the Sun* was a bit of a fraud, and one suspects in the end that Ishihara was merely pulling the leg of an adult society already predisposed to think the worst of the *après*. But it did capture part of the spirit of his times, specifically that descent into cynicism and materialism that characterized many Japanese of all ages. One can imagine that it caused many to wonder, "Is this where we are heading?" Ishihara was taken seriously by the critics as a knowing guide to the *après* world. Among the young he was a durable pop-hero, and the worshipful cult he spawned became known as the *taiyozoku,* or "sun tribe," their common bond being the distinctive "Shintaro" haircut, modeled after Ishihara's own. The worship was prolonged by the production of three extremely popular movies based on the novel. One of them starred Ishihara's younger brother, Yujiro, who was instantly established as "the James Dean of Japan," a living symbol of youth in revolt. Ironically, Shintaro Ishihara, after his fame diminished, was rather quickly enveloped by the conservatism of a later age, being elected to both houses of the Diet as a member of that most conservative of institutions, the Liberal Democratic party.

●

The *après* and the *taiyozoku* were important fads of that first postwar decade, but the cinematic and literary mainstream was far more serious. Japan's new movies probed deeply into the seaminess of the times, laying bare that streak of amorality and corruption that characterized the era. A new generation of directors emerged almost as soon as peace was announced, and they created a golden age of movies, producing works of power and artistry that have not been matched since. Their age was made to shine more brightly by comparison with what followed—an era of film renowned for transcendent silliness and adolescent mush, which continues to this day. Like so many Japanese institutions, the movie industry was born anew in 1945 and entered into a fresh landscape shaped by the aftermath of war and the foreign occupation.

In a curious way, it was the Occupation authorities who cleared the stage for the new cinema. Their plan to remake Japan included the censoring of all forms of public entertainment, and movies, which had been enormously popular before the war, were a major target. SCAP naturally banned any theme associated with militarism and extreme nationalism, but it went beyond this to forbid almost anything having to do with Japanese history. Period pieces were taboo, especially those that exalted nationalist feelings or portrayed feudalism in a favorable light. Bowing was erased from the silver screen. In their place, SCAP wanted films depicting a new Japan moving toward democracy and egalitarianism and enjoying her new freedoms. It also purged many of the old industry leaders deemed guilty of serving the military's propaganda interests during the war. The result was a grand opening for a new generation of directors and actors free to experiment with novel techniques and themes, so long as they did not cross swords with SCAP's censors.

Into this opening they poured a stream of films that deplored militarism and extolled democratic freedoms. The emancipation of women became a popular theme. So did labor's rights. Many of the new film industry leaders were disposed toward liberalism and left-wing causes, and a number of them were Communists inflamed by the proletarian sagas popular in the Soviet Union. Almost any institution was, with SCAP's blessings at first, fair game. Heartless corporations, indifferent bureaucrats, the corrupt press—all were frequent targets. So, too, were the black-market gangsters and the fast-buck hustlers who preyed on people struggling to survive. There arose a genre known as *shomin-geki*, the theater of common people, which took up the causes of ordinary folk striving to remain honest in a sea of corruption. It was an extraordinary time in Japan's history, when social and political protest were not only tolerated but encouraged by authorities in power. Not since the Meiji Restoration had institutions been subjected to such assaults. The only one exempt was SCAP itself. [13]

Many of the protest movies and the *shomin-geki* were high in political content but low in artistry. Some were merely left-wing diatribes full of exploited women (even the geisha system was exposed and deplored) and heroic strikers. Yamamura's *The Crab-Canning Ship* (1953), for example, was a proletarian tract about depression-era seamen turned revolutionists who are finally overwhelmed by the military. Yotoyoshi Oda's *Lady from Hell* (1949) portrayed a cornucopia of corruption and indicted every known example of postwar exploitation: black-marketeering, crooked politicians, blackmailing journalists, and a decaying aristocracy. There were films of evil *zaibatsu* bosses who murdered to protect profits and crushed strikes of honest working men. Thin as many of them were in artistic terms, they did expose and capture on film that sordidness, meanness of spirit, and sense of moral collapse that people recognized as part of their daily life, and collectively they left their mark on the times. As two foreign critics put it, "The postwar spirit was, with reason, so gloomy, so critical of crumbling institutions, so pessimistic in outlook, that one of the few signs of health in the industry was the very awareness of the wretchedness of life." [14]

But the times also produced film-makers who combined the common touch with great artistic talent and who moved Japanese cinema for a few years into the world's top ranks. The giant among them was Akira Kurosawa, who turned out a remarkable series of films in that decade and who is still Japan's foremost director (although now dependent on foreign support because his own nation's movie moguls will not finance his work). Kurosawa is best remembered in the West for such epic productions as *Rashomon* (1950), *The Seven Samurai* (1954), and much later, *Kagemusha* (1979). But in the early postwar years he set himself firmly in the line of protest and *shomin-geki*.

Kurosawa was born in Tokyo in 1910 and for a time struggled along as a painter. He drifted into film-making in 1936 simply by answering a newspaper advertisement placed by a studio that was seeking young assistant directors. He proved adept at directing, conceptualization, and scenario writing and was taken under the wing of one of the period's most successful directors, Kajiro Yamamoto. After working on many scripts for Yamamoto, Kurosawa made his debut in 1943 with *Sanshiro Sugata*, a period piece set in the Meiji era and acceptable to the wartime military propagandists because it celebrated proficiency in the martial art of judo.

Kurosawa moved easily into the postwar world when a new batch of censors reversed their previous demands and called for antimilitary plots. In 1946 his first such effort appeared. *No Regrets for Our Youth* was the tale of a young girl set alongside a case of military repression of the thirties: the dismissal of a university professor because of his left-wing beliefs. In the series of popular films that followed, Kurosawa discovered the mix that made him famous—a blending of underdog themes with characters of wonderful depth. In most of these films, rather ordinary people struggle against fate and the unfairness of life with great determination, and under Kurosawa's direction they become memorable and real. Always in the background are the seamy and corrupt sides of daily life. *Drunken Angel* (1950) is set in a world of gangsters and extortionists. In *Scandal* (1950), Kurosawa attacked one of his favorite targets, the press, which in those days was much given to blackmailing and extortion of public figures. One of Kurosawa's best is *Stray Dog* (1949), which is both a fascinating detective story and a penetrating social drama. A young detective searching for his stolen revolver takes the audience on a revealing journey through the low-life districts of Asakusa and Ueno. The line of social protest films continued until 1960, when Kurosawa made *The Bad Sleep Well*, a story full of anger at corruption, betrayal, and murder in the corporate world.

Kurosawa's marriage of film art and social protest reached a pinnacle in 1952 with the production of *Ikiru*, or *To Live*, which many critics regard as Japan's finest cinematic work. It is a gentle, moving, and sometimes maudlin tale of an elderly municipal bureaucrat, Kanji Watanabe, who discovers that he has stomach cancer and has but a few months to live. A lonely widower who has done little but stamp papers for thirty years, he wanders self-pityingly through boozy scenes until suddenly becoming convinced that he can still do something memorable with his life. A group of neighborhood women hoping that a fetid pond can be turned into a children's park provides his opportunity. With a strength and persistence that surprises everyone, himself included, Watanabe pushes his park plan through the bureaucracy. He dies after a memorable scene in which he rocks on the new park's swing, singing an old tune about living life to the full.

Ikiru is essentially a story of personal redemption, a modern existentialist drama of man working out his salvation through his acts. But it is also a social document mirroring the times. It is filled with glimpses into the demoralizing circumstances of postwar Japan, especially those that the average struggling Japanese might encounter in his or her daily life. Scenes of bureaucratic callousness are vivid. When the neighborhood women first come to the city offices on behalf of their park, they encounter icy, stone-faced officials at every turn. Thugs threaten Watanabe as he pursues his park (the gangsters apparently prefer a new red-light district to a children's park). Everywhere in his search the hero encounters obstacles and indifference among people of his own class, and he prevails by sheer obstinance. Along the way are glimpses of the materialism of a people without values, grasping for every spare yen. Watanabe's estranged son and scheming daughter-in-law are ignorant of his impending death and anxious only that their eventual inheritance not be dissipated. Watanabe's own funeral wake is transformed into a celebration of selfishness by his bureaucratic colleagues who are trying to claim credit for the park he created. A final scene finds a new man stamping away at papers at Watanabe's old desk. Nothing has changed.

●

In one corner of the sprawling Tokyo suburb of Mitaka stands the Zenrinji Temple and its adjacent small cemetery. Each June 19 since 1948 a crowd of people has gathered there around a small tomb to pay respects to the man whose ashes lie within. One by one they offer a brief Buddhist prayer and leave small gifts—a cigarette, a glass of sake, fruit, or a small can of beer. Young or middle-aged, they quietly honor the spirit of the novelist, Osamu Dazai, whose body was pulled from the nearby Tamagawa Reservoir on this date in 1948, and who became posthumously regarded as the writer who best captured the gloomy spirit of the postwar years. A worshipful cult has grown up around him since that summer night when he and a lover committed suicide in the water. In part it recognizes a fine writer who died young. It also pays tribute to one whose life and death reflected the streak of despair characteristic of Japan's most painful decade.

The mainstream postwar novel was, not surprisingly, one of gloom and anger. Many of the writers were leftists, some were Communists, and they produced a number of polemics attacking militarists and capitalist bosses. The best and most remembered, however, dwelt on the spiritual collapse of the time. The war and the Occupation formed the backdrop but were less important to the novelist than the pitiful, struggling condition of Japanese life in the postdefeat malaise. Characters moved about in a wasteland of deteriorating families and alienated individuals. Materialism and spiritual corruption were major themes, and the doings of the nouveau riche were pilloried. The sordidness was often contrasted with memories of prewar times, which were portrayed as an era of simple virtue and loyalty to one's family and friends. Many of the more appealing characters in these novels are older people left over from Meiji times and naturally bewildered by the callousness and amorality of modern Japan. The mainstream of this literature was known as the *burai-ha*, or "school of decadence," and Dazai is remembered as its finest talent.

It is somewhat ironic that Dazai is seen today as representing the social theme of postwar decay, because his own degeneracy predated the war and was essentially personal. The tenth child of a rich, proud family in remote northern Japan, he was anything but a child of his times. Raised largely by maids and aunts, he was estranged from his family at a young age and spent a lifetime either quarreling with its members or trying to reestablish the broken connections. He was a precocious and rather precious child who began writing stories in his teens and who acquired a modest reputation before the war. His personal life was always troubled. At college in Tokyo, he took up drinking and, after a stint in a mental hospital, drugs. These problems led to a series of disastrous emotional affairs with women and at least three suicide attempts, in one of which a woman companion drowned. Dazai drifted into left-wing politics, was briefly a member of a Communist cell, and recanted all of it when caught by police. For money, he turned repeatedly to an older brother or wrote self-pitying letters to friends, one of which he signed "Homeless Swallow." His great fortune was to be befriended by a major novelist, Masuji Ibuse, whose influence was responsible for the publication of Dazai's early works. His dissolute life and deep personal pessimism are captured in a photograph taken in 1947. Dazai appears as a pale weakling, a cup of sake at hand, his haggard face propped on a fist as if he is too fragile to sit erect.[15]

It was in that year, however, that Dazai completed *The Setting Sun*, the work that made him instantly famous and established his reputation as a novelist of despair. It is the story of a once-proud family fallen on hard times after the war, their land and most of their property gone. The family is modern Japan in miniature, its sun setting on a world of defeat and abandoned dreams, and Dazai seems to have modeled the work on Chekhov's *The Cherry Orchard*, which he admired. The son, Naoji, has returned from the war a wasted and indifferent young man periodically addicted to opium. He rejects his mother and sister, while sponging off both to support his habit, and enters a prolonged period of despair in which he frequently contemplates suicide. A relentless self-pitier, Naoji traces his weakness to a sheltered childhood of wealth that left him physically inferior to sturdier friends. His personal degeneration represents a decaying aristocracy that is too weak to survive in a hurly-burly era of the common man. "It is painful for the plant which is myself to live in the atmosphere and light of this world," Naoji explains. "Somewhere an element is lacking which would permit me to continue. I am wanting. It has been all I could do to stay alive up to now."[16]

●

Dazai's work was concerned as much with personal tragedy as with social malaise. Another writer, Jiro Osaragi, was a more accurate chronicler of the times, and his most famous novels, *Homecoming* and *The Journey*, stand out even today as excellent descriptions of Japan at its nadir. He was born into a comfortable middle-class business family in 1897 and after college took a position in the Foreign Ministry, largely because his father, who was engaged in foreign trade, wanted an inside source on international events. He began writing in his spare time, adopting the pen name of Osaragi to conceal his identity. Abandoning the bureaucratic world after three years, he began writing full time and produced in his life a large number of novels, plays, historical biographies, and children's books.

Osaragi's two postwar novels are rich in detail and nearly journalistic in their precision. The characters are stereotypes, but they are excellent stereotypes that reveal the dishonesty and cynicism of the era. Hustlers, nouveaux riches, intellectual frauds, and those who have abandoned all hope and pretension roam through his pages, and they leave a picture of a society spiritually spent and lacking in all conviction. The exceptions are older Meiji-era men and women who have retained some pride in the past and a bit of the old-fashioned confidence. Osaragi was bitter about the war; he blamed it totally on the military class that had taken power. The main character in *Homecoming*, Kyogo, confronts a former admiral whose own son died in the naval battle of Midway: "You've killed in this mad war, even your son you've killed, and you're still alive yourself," Kyogo explodes. "You and your kind have smashed Japan to pieces, have made people suffer agonies . . ."[17]

It is an age of great dishonesty that Osaragi illuminates, and no one is treated more disdainfully than the schemers of the intellectual world. A minor character in *Homecoming*, Professor Oki, is an opportunist who has prospered in both war and peace by carefully balancing his works to please whichever authority is in power. In wartime he had served the Japanese military in China as a cultural advisor. The postwar period finds him a newly minted liberal, albeit a cautious one. Oki's latest books include just enough nationalist sentiment to curry popular favor but not so much as to arouse the Occupation censors' attentions. He writes an essay glowing with praise for the happiness of the new Japanese home in which women are liberated and honored; then he berates his own wife as though she were a dumb dog. A pompous fence-straddler, he writes only what will enhance his reputation as a "man of character" (he hopes to run for the new parliament):

> Whatever the political climate, Professor Oki managed to seem temperate and fair, thus avoiding danger to himself and preserving the esteem of his respectable readers. . . . Professor Oki understood everything moderately. It wasn't likely that the high tide of cultural activity after the war would leave Professor Oki on the beach.[18]

Major characters in both novels are caught up in the new materialism. There are men who gamble recklessly and sell cars to rich Americans, bar hostesses who offer their bodies to any customer, and women whose charms are purchased by corporate schemers. One of the characters in *Homecoming* is Saeko, a willful, self-centered woman who seeks to control and exploit her friends, often through gifts of large diamonds. Her cunning young friend, Toshiki, is a hustler without conviction who publishes left-wing books not because he respects them but because they sell best. *The Journey* presents the character of Kaoruko, a voluptuous woman employed by a Japanese firm that caters to American clients. Poised and clever, she maintains a young Japanese lover whose haplessness lands him in debt. In a memorable scene, Kaoruko icily speaks for all of the postwar hucksters as she pressures her young lover to repay money she has loaned him. At first he attempts to seduce her to take her mind off money, but she is unrelenting. Finally, exasperated, he tries to minimize the importance of debt:

> "It's silly, isn't it, all this talk about money?"
>
> "Not in the slightest," retorted Kaoruko, and her tone was more glacial than ever. "So far as I'm concerned, money is strength. There's certainly nothing else I can depend on in this world. And you don't have any reason to consider it silly either. If there's one thing I can't stand, it's irresponsibility in money matters."[19]

The dominant character in *Homecoming* is Kyogo, a former expatriate who spent the wartime years abroad and who is therefore able to observe postwar Japan with some detachment. He is a man of the past filled with sorrow at the sight of his countrymen forced by poverty to think only of their daily bread and ignorant of what Japan had been before the war. The callousness and sheer mean-spiritedness of the *après* depress him most. Kyogo hears a street-corner speech by an angry young man complaining of low wages and is saddened by the brutishness of his tone:

> Kyogo couldn't forget the broadcast. It had showed him how much of the grace had gone out of Japanese life. Nowadays, poverty had only an evil effect, even on Japanese. It had made everyone terribly impatient. Post-war Japan was really a desert. The young were devoid of subtlety—as one might expect of a generation stripped of its past.[20]

The atmosphere of a spiritual wasteland is relieved only by the intrusions of elderly characters who exude an old-fashioned virtuousness and simplicity. Like the aging mother in Dazai's *The Setting Sun*, the character of Professor Segi in *The Journey* stands for the old values. He is a charming, often whimsical academic whose sentiments are painfully out of place in the postwar gracelessness. Tipsy with sake in one scene with a favorite student, Segi delivers a rambling sermon on love among young moderns. Love, he claims, has become so frivolous and superficial that it makes him physically ill. "I suppose I'm sort of a relic of the Meiji Period," he apologizes, reminiscing about the steady faithfulness that he believes characterized old-fashioned love and marriage:

"And such love doesn't seem to exist much any longer. This is a period of insincerity, and people think they can get by without being sincere. And I don't mean only in matters of love. It seems to apply to everything. Now if someone's really in love, I expect him to be prepared to sacrifice himself completely. But nowadays it's the exact opposite. The young men and women of today love each other with the intention of getting something out of it. The spirit of thieves or pickpockets seems to have spread in the world."[21]

Kyogo wanders like an alien through this world of lost values, weighed down with a nostalgia for the good old days. He looks anxiously for signs of regeneration and finds none. Everywhere are people blinded by materialism and ignorant of the gentler time before the war. Japan has been irrevocably severed from her history. "Perhaps, as some people said, the surrender had made everyone suddenly indifferent to the Japanese past," he muses:

> The young people, especially, had lost all faith in their country's history. . . . The young wanted only to push ahead, and the past of Japan could not hold them back. It hadn't been a bad country. But it was ended now. That made him sad. He felt sorry for the young savages who were growing up in these post-war days, ignorant even of what had been good in the past.[22]

Osaragi emerged as the most pessimistic of Japan's "wasteland" novelists. Even Dazai's *The Setting Sun* concluded with a fragile theme of regeneration. Osaragi saw no hope in a period that produced the *après*, corruption, and gross materialism. Japan was, quite simply, finished, Osaragi believed, her great adventure of a hundred years a terrible failure. Depression, war, control by foreigners, the new poverty—all of these traumas had rendered her lifeless. What made Osaragi special in an age of writers who all employed the theme of despair was his acute sense of history. The ugly new Japan always stands, in his work, in contrast to a noble and beautiful past. Near the end of *Homecoming*, he has Kyogo deliver a bleak sermonette that is intended to sum up the age. His friend Ushigi, the former admiral, quotes a Chinese poet: " 'The sun sets and the myriad aimless movements cease.' " Kyogo responds:

> "But Ushigi, . . . it's still aimless movement. The state is dead but the aimless movement hasn't ceased. Is there anyone

in Japan who lives in accordance with his own definite opinions? That's what I wonder about. . . . It's a narrow land. And the people—they're so poor, so terribly poor. There's no room to dream, no leeway. The Japanese can only work up enough courage to grab somebody's leg and beg for food. A pathetic people."[23]

4

●

The Price
of Independence

In the daily struggle to earn a living and feed their families, the
Japanese, as the Occupation lingered on, were not much inclined
to contemplate the world outside. When they did think about their
future as a nation, they had two concerns: They wanted to be independent and then to be left alone. They were weary of the Occupation and
wanted most of all to sort out for themselves what kind of country they
would be. They wanted no part of the cold war that had begun to divide
the postwar world. By 1949 their newspapers were speculating that
Japan would be forced to seek shelter from this new global storm in the
anti-Communist security structure being erected by the United States.
A public-opinion survey found that only one-fifth of Japanese were
willing to accept dependence on America. Distinguished figures from
the universities and public life formed the Peace Problem Council,
dedicated in part to hastening a peace treaty and in part to stating
explicitly what Japan wished from the world. Its prescription was a Japan

free of foreign soldiers, a country disarmed, neutral, and disengaged from outside conflicts. It was not a radical position. Indeed, it was very close to what the Americans had once told them they had to expect. It was, after all, General MacArthur who had vowed that Japan would become "the Switzerland of the Pacific," and that was good enough for most Japanese.

Japan formally reentered the society of nations in September 1951, when her prime minister signed a peace treaty in San Francisco with the United States and forty-seven other nations. But it was a peace far different from the sort that she, and even General MacArthur, had envisioned. She was not to become a nation of unarmed neutrality, one at peace with all the world. Under the "San Francisco System," as it came to be called, Japan was to embrace a number of propositions not included in the treaty itself. She was transformed into a fully pledged anti-Communist partner in the cold war. She became a vast staging ground for American troops, warships, and planes, an anchor of the forward U.S. defense strategy, which assumed that Asian communism would be fought on Asian soil. She was compelled to establish her own armed forces, despite an American-imposed constitution that banned war-making forever. She was denied a chance to make peace with old enemies that were by then in the Communist bloc and was pressured into abandoning hopes of a rapprochement with the Chinese on the mainland. All of these terms composed the price Japan paid for postwar independence.

Establishment of the "San Francisco System" was the most mo-mentous—indeed, the only meaningful—event in her postwar diplo-matic history. It shaped her relations with other countries for four de-cades and predetermined almost every move she would make on the world stage. It also became the only source of real division and discon-tent with Japan. Today there are those who accept the "San Francisco System" and those who resent it, but all recognize it as something that was forced on a reluctant country in 1951. It was in many ways like one of those Japanese arranged marriages in which a recalcitrant bride is hustled to the marriage chamber, bowing grimly to the inevitable.

In an arranged marriage the matchmaker is called the *nakodo*, and in Japan's "wedding" to the West that role was played by the most remarkable of her postwar leaders. Prime Minister Shigeru Yoshida dominated his time as none of his successors has even tried to do, a star performer in a system that distrusts standouts. Japanese prime ministers are as a rule cautious men who rule by nudging colleagues toward consensus, building slowly, a block at a time. Yoshida, as *nakodo*, had neither the time nor the disposition to move with patience. Instead, he moved by intrigue and secret dealings of his own design to seal the match with the United States. In his bargainings, Yoshida achieved much that he thought was right and accepted much that he thought wrong, but he was always certain that the "wedding" must go on. He was publicly contemptuous of Japanese who dissented, especially those who did not recognize the "bride's" limited choice in the matter. He was a singular figure on the postwar landscape, a leader who led by force of personality and individual talent. Japanese still refer to him as *"Mr. Wan Man"* ("Mr. One Man").

●

The 1870s had been a time when all things seemed possible in Japan. The bold, strong-willed men who had replaced the Tokugawa shogunate with Emperor Meiji were piecing together the new empire, and for the imaginative, adventurous, and determined the future seemed limitless. A new army, a modern government of able men, intriguing contacts with the West, intoxicating tastes of political freedom, openings for clever merchants and entrepreneurs—all of these were part of the so-called Meiji spring. There was a thrilling sense of rebirth and creativity in the air for the ambitious. By 1878 the Restoration was history, the Meiji era was ten years old, and the nation was theirs to build. Shigeru Yoshida was born in that year, and throughout his life he carried with him something of the exuberance and self-confidence of the men of Meiji.

He was the natural son of an ambitious former samurai who dabbled in politics and a woman whose identity remains uncertain but who probably was a geisha. By prearrangement, the father passed the infant on to an adoptive father, Kenzo Yoshida, one of those eager entrepreneurs who had taken advantage of the times to amass considerable wealth as a merchant and shipping agent. Kenzo Yoshida died while still a relatively young man, leaving the bulk of his wealth to the nine-year-old Shigeru. The boy grew up in comfort, tended by servants and a fond but not especially indulgent adoptive mother. His was the world of a young prince, one almost certain to produce a self-assured adult accustomed to having his way. It bred a haughtiness that characterized his relationships long into his old age. The *"Mr. Wan Man"* label, which stuck because of his autocratic ways, troubled him not at all. Yoshida himself traced this streak of arrogance to his childhood, recalling on several occasions his adoptive mother's judgment: "This child is a proud child."[1]

Although never strong academically, Yoshida managed to pass through Gakushuin and Tokyo Imperial University, elite institutions for sons of the titled and wealthy. Because of periodic interruptions, he was twenty-eight years old when he obtained his university degree. Disliking business, he chose diplomacy as a career and passed the competitive Foreign Ministry exams in 1906. But the most important event of young manhood was his marriage into the nobility. In 1909 his wedding was arranged with the daughter of a count, Nobuaki Makino, who was the son of one of the early-Meiji-era's prominent families. The arranged marriage brought the young diplomat within a circle of men who, largely through family and imperial connections, were to play important roles in diplomacy and politics for nearly three decades. Yoshida embarked on his career, then, with all of the enviable credentials: wealth, degrees from the approved schools, and acquired connections with Japan's powerful. All derived from the fortunes of birth, adoption, and marriage.

The Japanese state he served had already entered its heady imperialist phase, and Yoshida's career was to coincide with its rise and fall as an Asian power. Meiji's new army had been victorious in two wars, first against a pitifully weak China and then against a supposedly powerful Imperial Russia. Both wars fed the victor's ambition for expansion in Asia and implanted the conviction that Japan's destiny was to be the vanguard state of an entire continent. The militarists who were to carry out this notion were not yet in power, but in varying forms it appealed to all of the leaders and factions who mattered, including that patrician circle into which Yoshida had married. What all Japan wanted, even then, was what the Western nations already had: colonial power and influence over her Asian neighbors. And just as the West had done, she created a concept of benevolent imperialism to justify a course of conquest.

As a young diplomat, Yoshida enthusiastically shared this view of manifest destiny and never really surrendered it. He approved of the 1910 annexation of the Korean peninsula, and he supported aggressive enforcement of Japan's new treaty rights in Manchuria, to which he was posted on his first overseas assignment. He also subscribed to the majority view taking shape in Tokyo that somehow China was to be tamed and guided through diplomatic and political pressures to recognize Japan as an Asian mentor and to serve her economic interests. Expansion into China was the great challenge of the times, and Yoshida did not blink, then or later. When he was an old man, he wrote in a peculiar passage that Japan had been a superior power dragged down by lesser Asian countries whose duty, one infers, was to be led up the slopes to civilization by an enlightened Japan. Expansion into those countries was unavoidable, he felt: "The vitality of our people which had been responsible for our national development continued to seek some further outlet—and it was only natural that this should have been found in China, from Manchuria southwards, and in the Pacific area."[2]

In this matter of controlling China, Yoshida's quarrel with the military centered on the matter of tactics. It must be accomplished, he thought, without disrupting relations with those Western powers that already had carved out their shares of that unfortunate nation. Yoshida was a life-long Anglophile who regarded the Japan-Britain alliance as the cornerstone of Meiji-era foreign policy, and his approach was that of the aristocratic circle to which his career had been joined by marriage. Theirs was a vague and inevitably futile policy of trying to exploit China without alienating either England or the United States. Manchuria could be colonized and northern China brought into Japan's sphere of influence, they contended, without disturbing the West if only Japan moved cautiously through diplomatic and political means. That process was deemed too slow by the generals, who wrote Yoshida off as a conciliator of the "Anglo-American Clique" and hence untrustworthy. Yoshida opposed the military's "Twenty-One Demands" on China, which made extravagant claims of Japanese privilege, realizing they would anger the West and might conceivably lead to war.

The rift between the pro-Western circle and the military widened in the twenties and was sealed by a watershed event, the London Naval Conference of 1930, which limited Japanese fleet expansion. Yoshida's friends urged acquiescence in the agreement that left Japan's fleet inferior to that of the United States and Great Britain, a settlement that infuriated the Japanese Navy. By the mid-thirties Yoshida was entered in the military's book as a hopelessly Western-oriented diplomat. In 1936 he was briefly proposed as a candidate for foreign minister but was quickly vetoed by the Army and Navy. When war finally came, he was despondent, certain that Japan would lose, and he periodically worked with a small circle of friends, secretly pushing for negotiated settlement. In 1944–45 he helped Prince Konoe and others draft a memorandum to the emperor that pressed for negotiations by warning that Japan was threatened with both a crushing defeat from without and a Communist revolution within. In April 1945 Yoshida was arrested for his role in that scheme and was jailed by the military police for several weeks.

There was a reason deeper than national policy at the root of

Yoshida's conflict with the generals. The military as a new powerful class was a threat to the entire Meiji-style social and political structure in which he had grown up, undermining as it did that alliance of nobility, business barons, and bureaucratic elites that had governed Japan since his birth. Yoshida was a minor cog in that apparatus, but his relationship with such real powers as Prince Konoe and Count Makino, his father-in-law, was close enough to make him sense their declining influence and prestige. His ideological enmity was mixed with his sense of a loss of power for his class. The military cliques, he later wrote, had wanted "to gain power at the expense of those around the Throne and those in responsible positions within the civilian government who advocated a policy of friendship with Great Britain and the United States."[3] "Those around the Throne," were Yoshida's friends and mentors. His contempt for these interlopers, as he regarded them, was deep, and he was not cowardly in revealing it. At one conference of rightists he listened impatiently to generals and nationalist intellectuals denounce the United States and Great Britain. Then he sarcastically told the gathering that they reminded him of "books on American history in which the North American Indians discussed among themselves how they might best get rid of the white men."[4]

Yoshida therefore entered the Occupation period with several credentials that recommended him to American authorities. MacArthur's men seem to have been suspicious of him from the start and were never entirely comfortable with his holding power in postwar governments. But he had many influential supporters in Washington. Until the brink of war, he had been friendly with United States Ambassador Joseph Grew and Grew's influential assistant, Eugene Dooman. For them, Yoshida had represented the cause of peaceful association with English-speaking powers. There were those in the State Department who believed that there had been both "good" and "bad" Japanese and that Yoshida had been among the former because of his known differences with the military. Moreover, Yoshida was a demonstrated anti-Communist, a fact that was to become more and more important as the cold war unfolded. His hatred of the Japanese military and opposition to their wartime policies had been certified by his brief jail term.[5]

●

The cold war in Asia produced a line of national leaders distinguished by a common role, that of the American ally required to fit his country into the anti-Communist strategies designed in Washington. The list includes South Korea's Syngman Rhee and Park Chung Hee; the Philippines' Ramón Magsaysay and Ferdinand E. Marcos; and the Diems, Nguyen Van Thieu, and Nguyen Cao Ky of South Vietnam, to mention the most obvious. Most were anti-Communists themselves, willing in the main to move their nations along paths charted by the Americans, but each at times faced opposition at home because of unpopular decisions forged in the United States. Each maneuvered and struggled in his own way to balance American demands against a contrary national opinion. In Japan the burden of accommodation was carried through the crucial years by Shigeru Yoshida.

Yoshida was sixty-seven years old when the postwar era began, and he was to serve eighty-six months as prime minister and two terms as foreign minister. It was his lot to represent a defeated nation in dealing with the allied occupation of Japan and to negotiate the political rapids that led to the peace treaty of 1951. In doing so he was required to confront two of the most arrogant of American emissaries, General Douglas MacArthur and Secretary of State John Foster Dulles. The demands of these two men were extremely different. The first had initially wanted a demilitarized and neutral Japan; the second insisted upon a rearmed ally in the cold war. Through it all, Yoshida had to lead a crushed but proud people who wanted most to be left alone. When his tour was over in 1954 and Japan had again become a sovereign nation, a majority of his countrymen were disappointed. Many felt he had compromised too much, and the most hostile among them called him an American puppet. But history was kinder, and most Japanese look back on Yoshida today as a worthy national leader. He dominated his age as no other postwar prime minister dared and did so largely because of his personality.

Personal glimpses of Yoshida passing through his country's trials do not fit a portrait of what one would expect of the defeated national leader. He was still, in his sixties and seventies, a true son of Meiji, and groveling was not in his nature. To the foreigners who spoke with such great authority, he was tenacious, scrappy, bold, evasive, and defiant, depending on the pose required of the moment. Some of them called him, admiringly, "Japan's Churchill." Even when dealing with the imperious MacArthur, he was determined not to behave as an underling but as an equal partner. He told his colleagues that it was important, for Japan's sake, to confront the conquerors in a self-assured manner. One member of his cabinet secretariat from 1950 to 1952 was Kiyohisa Mikanagi, the former navy officer mentioned earlier who had witnessed the flight of Japanese civilians as the war ended. He remembers that

Yoshida constantly advised his staff to be correct but firm in dealing with the Americans and to avoid displays of obsequiousness. He said in an interview, "Yoshida was determined that, personally, he would deal on equal terms with MacArthur. He felt, he told us, that he had to show self-confidence during their talks and he really made himself act like that. He told all of his assistants to do the same, and he was always unhappy to see a Japanese official speaking to Americans as a subordinate."[6]

The same Yoshida, however, dominated his own aides as if they were a boatload of galley slaves. He insisted on hard work and long hours and rather frequently turned on them with imperious lectures that kept them in their place. "He was not an easygoing person," recalls Akira Matsui, who was the prime minister's personal secretary from 1950 to 1952. Matsui still remembers one evening when he was called upon to act as translator at a small dinner Yoshida was giving. Throughout the meal, Yoshida and his guests chattered on and on, with Matsui struggling to translate the flow of conversation. Plate after plate was placed in front of him, but he had no chance to sample any of them. When the dinner party was over, Matsui lightly remarked that it had seemed to be a delicious meal but that he had been unable to manage a single bite because of his duty as translator. Yoshida turned on him coldly: "Were you thinking of eating? That was wrong of you."[7]

Yoshida could be stubborn and evasive in his dealings with Americans. Sometimes he simply outtalked them. Returning from the San Francisco conference in 1951, he stopped over in Honolulu, where protocol required a social call on an American admiral. The visit worried him, he told a private secretary accompanying him, because the admiral often insisted on a discussion of the Japanese attack on Pearl Harbor. How could he avoid it? he wondered. Arriving at the officer's residence, he spotted the family's pet dog and instantly perceived the answer. The admiral loved dogs. When they met, the prime minister lavished praise on the dog and began to talk of his own pet, "Chipper." On and on he rambled, discussing the lineage of dogs, the habits of dogs, the comforts of owning dogs. He had two new puppies, he said, and intended to name them "Sanny" and "Franny" in honor of the peace conference he had just attended. If he got another, he would name it "Cisco." For two hours he and the admiral talked dogs. Pearl Harbor never came up.[8]

He told those around him that Japanese must always act with tact and good grace in their encounters with foreigners, and he often rebuked those who even inadvertently showed disrespect. Once he

abruptly canceled the overseas assignment of a young Japanese diplomat
who had caused offense by leaving a reception before the American
guest of honor. He thought Japan could best be represented by a leader
who accepted her defeat gracefully. Yoshida often repeated the advice
given him immediately after the war by Kantaro Suzuki, an old friend
and former prime minister. Suzuki had told him that preserving their
civility would be important in the days of occupation to come and that
Japanese should conduct themselves like "good losers." Yoshida was to
use that phrase frequently as a guide to his own conduct. "I must be the
good loser," he would tell his associates.

Often arrogant, just as often civil and charming, Yoshida cut an
odd figure in the new democratic times ushered in by the Occupation.
He was in many ways an anachronism. His manners were those of the
Meiji aristocrat, a role learned from his association with the likes of
Prince Konoe and Count Makino and enhanced by a lifetime of admiration for the British upper class. Even his appearance was tailored to
the style of an older generation of gentlemen. He peered out at the world
through a pince-nez and to the end favored stiff wing collars. His favorite drinks were Tio Pepe sherry and a particular French wine, tastes
acquired in English dining rooms during an assignment in London in
the late thirties. He wore only suits made in England by a Saville Row
clothier whom he equipped with a mannequin of his own torso for
proper fittings when he ordered from Tokyo. He had also acquired the
British habit of smoking after-dinner cigars and insisted on only the
finest Havanas. When a Filipino guest once offered him an inferior
Philippine brand, Yoshida stiffly told him that he never smoked cigars.

It was, then, a man temperamentally rooted in the past whom
history chose to lead a new Japan into the future, a man in wing collars
confronting the freewheeling ways of modern democracy. Conflict was
inevitable, because what the Occupation intended to change was not
merely the militaristic spirit of the past decade but patterns of life ex-
tending much further back, patterns that Yoshida revered. The Occupation's charter was reformation of politics, education, women's life,
labor relations, the industrial structure, the state religion (Shinto), and
the emperor system. It entailed the uprooting not just of General Tōjō's
militarist state but of older values, practices, and deeply held beliefs.
Yoshida adored the emperor, defiantly attended Shinto shrines, deplored democratic manners, regarded women as beings of little importance, and was most comfortable with an economic system run by
strong-willed patriarchs of good family. None of those beliefs had anything to do with militarism, which he regarded as a perversion of the

Japanese tradition. He was being called on to preside over the eradication of a way of life to which he was deeply attached.

It was in many ways an impossible mission, and we see this most clearly in Yoshida's role as politician. *Antipolitician* is perhaps the better word. He detested political parties and their incessant feuding in the Diet, even after he had been chosen in 1946 to lead the Liberal party in order to become prime minister. At first he had refused to join any party. "I had always thought the bickering and back-biting rampant between contending groups were the curse of the Japanese political world . . ."[9] he wrote in his memoirs. Privately, he referred to the Diet as a "zoo" and to its members as "monkeys." He often simply refused to attend Diet interpellations, forcing aides to scurry around with false excuses that he was ill or fatigued. When he did agree to attend, advisors prepared elaborate written answers with which to parry opposition questions. Invariably, he carried those rolled in his fist and never deigned to glance at them. It was his conviction that such grillings demeaned a prime minister. Once, in the 1960s, when he had already retired, he watched on television as Prime Minister Satō painstakingly and courteously replied to each question addressed to him in the Diet. Yoshida turned to a secretary and asked why Satō was so obliging, especially since the conservative party's majority was then so large. "Why does he talk so long?" he asked.[10]

Yoshida never cared to learn the art of *nemawashi*, which in its political sense means nurturing a consensus in order to achieve a success in parliament. He was the despair of assistants and party colleagues who attempted to build bridges that he saw no need to build. A classic example was Yoshida's response to a group of Manchurian army veterans who wanted their wartime bank accounts honored by the postwar government. The veterans asked for a meeting. Yoshida refused. Aides argued that the veterans' group was large and politically powerful. But the government had no money with which to honor their demands, Yoshida insisted. His friends implored him to employ the time-honored dodge of meeting with the veterans and agreeing to "study" their problem, a formula for saying no without giving offense. That would be dishonest, Yoshida countered. Finally, an aide and Yoshida's daughter prevailed on him to grant a brief interview. But he would only listen in silence, and he assigned to Eisaku Satō, then his chief cabinet secretary, the demeaning task of promising to "study" the veterans' request.[11] Such displays of contempt for ordinary politics were often misinterpreted as incompetence. In 1948 MacArthur called him "monumentally lazy and politically inept."[12] MacArthur had missed the point, for at the root of these performances was an aristocrat's distaste for wheeling and dealing in the modern style. As one Japanese scholar put it:

> Yoshida . . . was not by temperament suited to ruling in an age of freedom; he was neither a popular politician nor a party politician. What he liked and was eminently able to do was to manipulate people within an elite circle, a circle in which he himself had been active as a diplomat. But he refused to function in a wider sphere, to take into consideration the ambitions of other politicians, the opinions of opposition parties, or the sentiments of the people at large. He would neither seek to earn their support for his own point of view nor compromise in an attempt to bring his point of view nearer to theirs. He was in some ways an anachronism in the new age.[13]

It was precisely Yoshida's ability "to manipulate people within an elite circle" that made him so successful a postwar leader. Diet politicians were of far less importance in those days than General MacArthur and his officers. Occupation directives determined Japan's path, and it was the "elite circle" of the Occupation that Yoshida learned to manipulate skillfully. He did so with the fine hand of a Meiji noble or career bureaucrat, winning points here, losing others there, always pressing, chipping away for small victories when larger ones were impossible—in other words, exercising that pliancy, patience, and persistence that comprise the Japanese adversarial style. His memoirs, written long after the adversaries had departed, celebrate his team's diligence: "We Japanese, for our part, never lost an opportunity to demand the revision and readjustment of those Occupation policies which we judged to be impractical and not suited to the actual conditions existing in Japan."[14]

His goal was to defeat or dilute the sweeping social and economic reforms that MacArthur's crews intended to impose. In the first months, SCAP presented a monolithic front, insisting on the total transformation of Japanese society. The "MacArthur Constitution" was adopted, under extreme pressure, exactly as the general wanted it. Yoshida himself was present at the grim meeting in which General Courtney Whitney informed the Japanese government that unless it accepted the constitution completely, the document would be submitted directly to the people in a referendum. ("Mr. Yoshida's face was a black cloud," Whitney later recalled.)[15]

In time, Yoshida discovered the cracks in SCAP's front and set about exploiting them in the best divide-and-conquer tradition. He learned of two principal factions behind that front—the "idealists" and the "pragmatists," as he called them. The former, located in the Government Section, followed a literal interpretation of their chief's charter and pressed for thorough social and democratic change. The latter were based in General Charles Willoughby's G-2 Section, and they were fearful that radical changes might bend Japan toward communism. Playing one faction off against the other was the Yoshida team's standard tactic. He used Willoughby's preference for law and order to temper several reforms, including administration of the labor law and the Government Section's scheme to decentralize Japan's police force. As reform after reform poured forth, Yoshida pounced on each in turn, sometimes attacking their cost, sometimes questioning (in his favorite phrase) their applicability "to the actual conditions existing in Japan." He insisted that all purge orders from SCAP be in writing. When formal argument failed, he could always run to G-2 with warnings of a proposed reform's left-wing origin and radicalizing impact. Exploiting SCAP's liberal-conservative schism provided him with some of his proudest moments. His private secretary for four-and-a-half years, Takaaki Kagawa, watched with fascination Yoshida's twists and turns as he attempted to manipulate the factions in MacArthur's headquarters. Many years later, in an interview, he explained the prime minister's tactics:

> Yoshida knew how to use SCAP and how to use SCAP's rivalries for the benefit of Japan. He had private channels outside the Central Liaison Office (the formal structure for dealing with the Occupation) to both Willoughby in G-2 and to Government Section. He felt that there were many leftists in Government Section. So if Yoshida got a memo from SCAP to do something—if it were important and Yoshida thought it was due to leftist influences—we would go to G-2 and block it. Then G-2 and the Government Section would begin fighting internally, among themselves. Finally, if the result was still a bad order, Yoshida would go directly to MacArthur. Almost every time, we had success. Yoshida was very shrewd in that way.[16]

●

Among the many postwar encounters between conqueror and conquered, none is more revealing than the conference held on a day in

June 1950 at the residence of an American diplomat in Tokyo. On one side was John Foster Dulles, already, though only a State Department advisor, pressing with missionary zeal the plan to build a wall around communism. On the other was Shigeru Yoshida, suspicious as ever about new American schemes for his country. They were a good match. Each was stubborn, clever, and arrogant. The issue that day was military power and Japanese security, and the American drove straight to the point: How would Japan be protected against the Communist hordes? Yoshida was at his evasive best—bantering, casting out diversions, grinning his puckish grin. Security, Dulles said, was the overriding question. Yoshida retreated into parables. Defense, Dulles insisted. Security, Yoshida said at last, could be taken care of by the Americans. Then he enigmatically added: "But Japan's *amour propre* must be preserved in doing so." What did that mean? Japan had little interest in military security, he explained. She would be democratic, demilitarized, and peace-loving and rely on the world's good opinion for protection. Exasperated, Dulles broke off. Later he seemed baffled and depressed by the encounter. He had felt, he told a friend, "like Alice in Wonderland."[17] A fellow diplomat described Dulles as "completely frustrated and almost bitter."[18] The meeting with Yoshida, this diplomat recalled, had been a "dismal failure."[19]

Yet in the months ahead this odd couple effectively shaped Japan's position in the postwar world, and the bargain they struck has lasted four decades. The stakes were always the same. Yoshida wanted independence and a peace treaty to end the years of tiresome occupation. Dulles wanted a Japan tightly bound to the Western alliance. The pattern of their exchanges was always similar as well—Dulles pressing and demanding, Yoshida hedging, haggling, sometimes yielding. Dulles, first as advisor to Truman's State Department, then as secretary of state, was Washington's chief agent in the grand strategy for containing communism in Asia. He carried with him President Truman's special instruction "to secure the adherence of the Japanese nation to the free nations of the world, and to assure that it will play its full part in resisting the further expansion of communist imperialism."[20] But Japan was always a special worry for Dulles. He fretted constantly that she would bolt to the Communist camp. Sometimes he saw her intimidated by Soviet Russia, sometimes attracted by trade and historical associations to Communist China. Japan was fickle and potentially unfaithful, he believed, and would pursue her own interests unless locked legally into the West's alliance. Even after all of the papers were signed, he feared that if, for example, Southeast Asia went Red, Japan would sense the power balance shifting and move to the Communist bloc. "From there on out the Japs would be thinking on how to get on the other side," he once said.[21]

●

There were five distinct elements in the overall *Pax Americana* plan as it unfolded for Japan in the early fifties:

1. *Rearmament.* The United States wanted Japan to ignore the American-made constitution and launch a rearmament that would eventually grow to a force of 350,000 men.

2. *A separate peace.* Fearing Soviet interference and growing influence, Washington pressed for a treaty only with the West and its anti-Communist Asian allies.

3. *Non-neutrality.* No more "Switzerlands" here—the United States wanted a committed ally in Northeast Asia, not a neutral bystander.

4. *American military bases.* The United States insisted on basing air, naval, and ground-force facilities as part of its strategic forward-basing policy confronting the Soviet Union and China.

5. *Recognition of Taiwan.* Japan, Washington insisted, must abandon hopes of dealing with mainland China and embrace only the nationalist government.

With these five pillars in place, the United States planned to build Japan into a bastion of defense against international communism. In return, Japan would receive independence, more economic assistance, and gradual inclusion in the Western trade bloc then being pieced together.

What the Japanese wanted was something very different. They wanted most an end to the Occupation. They had accepted it in the depths of their war-weariness, and at no time had they attempted serious resistance. But as the years wore on and the interference in domestic life continued, the resentment grew. There was irritation with the rich style lived by Occupation families, especially those of military officers and their wives, which clashed so visibly with Japan's poverty. Moreover, the soldiers who had first occupied Japan were gradually replaced by less disciplined troops, and the number of nasty incidents involving civilians increased.[22] Both Yoshida and MacArthur recognized the dangers of prolonged occupation, and both wanted an early peace settlement. But both also knew that what the United States would ask in return would not be popular.

When the Japanese public glimpsed what the price might be, the passive mood began to change. What the early signals suggested was shocking: a rearmed Japan tied to the West and the continued presence of U.S. forces in their midst. The habit of resigned acceptance was first shaken by intellectuals and academics from the left, who formed the Peace Problem Council, its platform calling for neutrality, disarmament, withdrawal of U.S. forces, and a "comprehensive" peace treaty with all of Japan's old enemies, including Soviet Russia and the People's Republic of China. Japan's Communist party was active in this campaign but was not its main force. In April 1950 all of the non-Communist opposition parties formed a joint council urging a comprehensive peace treaty and neutrality. Much of the press agreed. The reasons varied—fear of being dragged into a new world war, doubts that the United States would really protect Japan in a crisis, concern that a revived military would repeat the repression of the thirties.

There was, overall, a disinclination to become engaged in any fashion in the cold war. All of the signs of the times—the press, public-opinion surveys, accounts of competent observers—registered a clear indifference to the new power alignments taking shape in the world. One of the most astute of foreign observers then was Baron E. J. Lewe Van Aduard, a Dutch diplomat who left behind a revealing memoir. He reported that the mainstream Japanese did not want their country anchored to either side. "It was now abundantly clear that the Japanese people were, in fact, sitting on the fence in the ideological battle between the Western democracies and the Soviet bloc," he wrote. When in the fall of 1949 the American insistence on a separate treaty with only the Western camp became public knowledge, Van Aduard observed that the sudden outspokenness of the Japanese astonished the Americans:

> Strangely enough, the United States had been wrongly informed as to the attitude of the Japanese. Undoubtedly, the United States had hoped that after all the benevolent assistance extended to the Japanese people under the Occupation, Japan would be only too glad to take the American side, to declare herself a faithful member of the community of free nations, opposed to any rapprochement with Russia or Red

China. The Japanese reactions in the autumn of 1949, however, showed that these expectations were erroneous.[23]

In June 1950 the Korean War erupted, bringing the reality of the cold war close to Japan's own shores. It was a shock that caused some Japanese to reassess their views and prompted Washington to press its own even more forcibly. It is sometimes assumed that the invasion of South Korea forced the Japanese people to scurry for shelter and embrace the American demands. But did it? There is abundant evidence that it did not. Japanese remained hostile to the five United States demands before, during, and after the Korean War. Public-opinion polls and the reports of observers on the scene show that the Japanese did sense that the fighting would reinforce American insistence, making it more difficult, if not impossible, to obtain independence without giving in to the demands. But the notion that the Korean War provoked a Japanese about-face and sent them rushing into American arms for protection, having suddenly seen the light of reality, is a dubious one.

In fact, the Japanese became, if anything, even more opposed to an alignment with the United States as the Korean War was being fought. Public-opinion polls of the time show a clear trend of increased sentiment for neutrality and opposition to a military alliance. For example, in September 1950, 55 percent of all Japanese had believed that in general, Japanese foreign policy should be pro-American; three years later, only 35 percent thought so. The proportion of people favoring outright neutrality increased from 22 to 38 percent in the same period, which coincided with the fiercest fighting of the Korean War.[24] The plan for a military security pact with the United States was always extremely unpopular. In November 1949 only 21 percent of all Japanese favored dependence on the United States for their security.[25] In September 1951, shortly after the security treaty was signed and with the Korean War blazing furiously, a Yomiuri newspaper poll determined that only 31 percent believed it would enhance Japan's own security.[26]

Japanese also wanted a comprehensive peace treaty that embraced both China and Soviet Russia. This was not because of any ideological sympathies with the cause of international communism. Masao Maruyama, Takeo Kuwabara, and other intellectuals wanted it not because they were pro-Communist—most were emphatically not—but because they felt true neutrality was impossible without it. Many observers noted that this was the mainstream Japanese opinion, not merely a preference of leftists. Van Aduard estimated that a majority opposed the U.S. plan for a separate peace. An experienced State Department official, Robert A. Fearey, reported a "strong preference for a treaty participated in by all the Allies."[27] The new Japanese elite overwhelmingly favored peace with the two Communist giants, despite the war raging across the Sea of Japan. A poll of Japanese businessmen, labor leaders, scholars, and government officials in 1954 underscored the broad conviction. Sixty-two percent of the businessmen polled in that survey wanted diplomatic relations with China, and 57 percent wanted the same with the USSR. That particular survey turned up convincing evidence that prominent Japanese did not share the American government's visceral fears of communism. Examining details of the poll, Lloyd Free, the American public-opinion analyst, found that a mere 3 percent of all those leaders expressed fear of communism or Communist aggression.[28]

Least popular of the American demands was that which called for the continued basing of foreign troops in Japan. Their presence prolonged the stigma of Occupation, even though their new mission ostensibly would be the protection of Japan. The extent of that presence was not fully realized until disclosure after the San Francisco treaty of a secretly negotiated "administrative agreement," the terms of which angered Japanese. It gave the U.S. military forces rights to as many as 1,400 installations—airfields, naval bases, private residences, barracks, and training areas—covering a total of 245,000 acres. Resentment of that immense militarization grew instead of waned as the Korean War wore on. A newspaper poll in August 1951—fourteen months after the fighting began—found that only 18 percent endorsed U.S. bases (although 34 percent acknowledged that U.S. pressure made them inevitable). Douglas H. Mendel, an American researcher, uncovered surveys showing that throughout the 1950s the bases were never approved by a majority of Japanese and that the initial modest support for them actually decreased. About 30 percent approved of the bases in 1950 (before the enormous scope of the administrative agreement was publicly known), and this number decreased over the years to a mere 8 percent in 1958. It was not simply that the troops symbolized Japan's defeat. Many Japanese felt their presence would be a "magnet" drawing Japan into a new war between the USSR and the United States. "Far from believing [the United States forces] to be 'vital' to their national security, a plurality of Japanese have felt such foreign troops actually endangered the peace of Japan," Mendel wrote.[29]

American insistence that Japan rearm also became less, not more, popular during the war in Korea. In 1953, with the war still raging, only

36 percent favored Japan's rearming, according to a Mainichi newspaper poll.[30] A clear majority in all surveys during that period believed that rearmament was being demanded for America's benefit, not Japan's. Only 10 percent of those questioned in a 1953 Asahi newspaper poll thought that rebuilding Japan's army helped their country in any way.[31] The notion that opposition to rearmament was an exclusively leftist position is belied in every poll taken during that period. Even in the higher ranks of the conservative government there was a strong sentiment against rearmament, which was seen as being forced on Japan by foreigners. Americans had at first forbidden Japan an army, then reversed the policy and insisted on rearming her. In August 1953 Akira Kodaki, parliamentary vice-minister for foreign affairs, told an interviewer:

> You Americans forced us to disarm not only physically and legally, but spiritually. Then Dulles reviled us for not rearming faster. The Occupation wanted to destroy Japanese militarism, but went so far as to undermine the patriotism on which any nation's self-defense must be built. Can you blame us for being confused and a bit angry when America has pushed us in such opposite directions over the past few years?[32]

The final cost of independence was to be American insistence on placing China off-limits for Japan, a price that aroused resentment in every quarter. It became clear, once the peace treaty was signed, that the U.S. Senate would refuse to ratify it unless Japan formally abandoned mainland China and embraced the Nationalist government on Taiwan. There could be no diplomatic relations and not even trade with the Beijing government. (The U.S. Battle Act barred trade with Communist China for those countries receiving American economic aid.) These facts embittered sentimentalists who longed for relations with China and diplomats who felt that Japan's postwar course lay in friendship with Asian countries. They also irritated Japanese businessmen, who were eager to restore trade with China's huge market and who cared not a whit that Red commissars would become their trading partners. The leadership survey in 1954 showed that 70 percent of Japan's elite believed that trade with China would contribute to Japan's well-being, and the proportion increased during the 1950s.[33] In June 1953 an Asahi poll revealed that only 10 percent approved the policy that meant the loss of China. Only 40 percent of the Yoshida government's own supporters endorsed it.[34]

•

It was Yoshida's fate to be the marriage broker between these two seem-
ingly irreconcilable partners. In the Japanese mate, he faced a public
restless for independence but increasingly opposed to the five American
demands. The American partner insisted on all five and left no doubt
that they were the price of Japan's sovereignty. In the end, Yoshida
risked his government by accepting all of the five demands, at least in
part, some of them in that spirit of resignation that Japanese express as
shikata ga nai—"It cannot be helped." At intervals he would tell members of his staff and political friends that it mattered little what Japan
hoped for. America would write the terms of peace and independence.
Things changed in time, he would say; no relationship was ever carved
in stone. By then in his seventies, as eager for independence as any
Japanese, he would become most irritable with those countrymen who
pretended that Japan had any course other than to submit. He scath-
ingly denounced leftist intellectuals who, in their ivory towers, grandly
insisted on Japan's own terms. He once called the president of Tokyo
University "a prostitute of learning." He was furious when his own
Foreign Ministry inexplicably published a document advocating a peace
treaty that included both Communist China and the Soviet Union.

Yoshida was resigned to the role of leading his country into the new
Pax Americana. But he never fully shared Washington's consuming fear
of communism. He did have a real dread of domestic radicalism and
was delighted when the Occupation cracked down on Communists in
the labor unions. But the international threat was not great, he felt, and
his relaxed view of it baffled Dulles in their encounters. To his aides,
and occasionally in public, Yoshida said that the American fear of
Communist aggression was an inflated one. "We do not have the slightest expectation that the Communist countries will invade Japan," he
told the Diet in January 1951.[35] He detested Communist Russia, but
China was a different matter entirely. China's Communist phase would
not last, he thought. "China has a self-rejecting mechanism which will
get rid of communism eventually," he told a secretary.[36] In 1949 he
acknowledged to an American journalist that he personally disliked
Communist authoritarianism. But he did not care "whether China is
red or green," because Japan needed her markets regardless of their
political coloration.[37] And he was convinced that the alliance between
the Soviet Union and China would not last; they were fundamentally
incompatible. Long before those giants parted ways, Yoshida predicted

to a private secretary, Takaaki Kagawa, that they would inevitably separate and that Japan could hasten that separation. Kagawa remembers that the prime minister was very sure of that judgment. In an interview, he said:

> Mr. Yoshida always said that Chinese communism was different from Russian communism. He said that although they were now united "like a rock," that they were very tight with each other for the moment, China and the Soviets were quite different from one another and someday would part. Japan's role in this, he would say, was to help drive a wedge between them, to try to accelerate this process of their coming apart. He felt that Japan should be a kind of "showroom" for China and show her how a capitalist democracy would work. He disagreed with the United States completely on the subject of China. [38]

What drove Yoshida toward compromise with the United States was not a fear of communism but a pragmatic conviction, rooted in history, that Japan's place in the world lay with the West, with Europe and America. This had been the essential guidepost of Meiji-era diplomacy when he was a young man. He would have preferred a policy centered on Great Britain, the sophisticated great power of his youth. But England was now second-rate. Power had flowed to America, and it was the United States to which, like it or not, Japan must cleave. Like any clever diplomat, Yoshida might describe this choice in terms of flowery sentiment and cast praise on America's civilizing mission in Asia, but the attachment was always grounded in economic pragmatism. Japan had to survive by becoming a maritime trading nation, and that meant alignment with the rich, powerful maritime nations of the West, among which America was now supreme. There was nothing to be gained by rejecting the West in favor of Asian countries. Time and again, his closest assistants urged him to concentrate on Asia, to rebuild relations with former enemies regardless of what the Westerners wanted. Yoshida repeatedly spurned their advice. Japan must side with the strong, he insisted. Kagawa, the private secretary, remembers Yoshida stressing the point of playing to strength in world affairs:

> Yoshida once said to me that in diplomacy there are always active and passive powers. Europe and the United States had always been active, capable of influencing other countries. He said we should always deal first with those strong, active pow-

ers. There were men around him always saying that Japan
should affiliate with the neutrals, the passive countries like
Thailand or India. He always rejected that. He would always
say that since the Meiji period Japan should have been with
the strong maritime countries and that our failure to do that
[during World War I] was our undoing.[39]

On the issue of rearmament, Yoshida was partially successful in
defending Japanese interests. He obeyed MacArthur's instructions to
establish a national police force of about 75,000 men. And he dutifully
argued before a skeptical Diet that its creation had not breached the
constitution. But he rejected Dulles's pleas to escalate that force into a
350,000-man modern army. Yoshida recognized the bitter opposition of
his people, and he also knew that Japan's sluggish economy could not
support a large military. There was something very personal in his
opposition as well. He had hated the old Japanese military, and he
deeply feared a revival of uncontrolled militarism. An American diplomat, John M. Allison, attempted several times to convince Yoshida that
a revived Japanese military would be subject to civilian control guaranteed by the constitution. There was nothing to fear, Allison told him,
because a new army would lack the means to subvert a civilian government. Allison later wrote, "Mr. Yoshida would look up at me with
twinkling eyes and an impish grin and say, 'Yes, but they have guns,
haven't they?' "[40]
    By the spring of 1950 Yoshida had reached the point of crisis.
There had been no real progress toward independence and a peace
treaty with the allied nations. The restiveness at home was growing into
public criticism. The year before, Americans had insisted on an extremely austere fiscal reform that had, as expected, thrown Japan into a
recession. Thousands of government employees had been laid off. In
acceding both to continued occupation and a harsh economic line,
Yoshida was more and more regarded as an American toady following
whatever new policy the Americans dreamed up. Public-opinion polls
that spring revealed that his government's approval rating had sunk to 32
percent.[41] An Upper House election was coming up, and it was not at
all certain that his Liberal party could win.
    Only a dramatic breakthrough, Yoshida realized, could save his
government and set his country on a peaceful course with the West. The
principle obstacle lay in Washington, where stalemate persisted over the
issue of basing U.S. forces in Japan after a peace treaty. The Pentagon

was insisting on a huge military presence and wanted Japan's acquiescence before she was cut free to become a sovereign nation. To break that stalemate, Yoshida determined on a daring plunge, the riskiest venture of his career, one that he prepared in total secrecy and launched with a flair for intrigue and backstage maneuvering that astonished even his closest friends. Using his finance minister, Hayato Ikeda, as emissary, he made an offer: Give us independence and Japan will not only accept but invite American troops to remain on her soil.

The gambit began with almost comic furtiveness. First, Yoshida deceived MacArthur, telling him that Ikeda was flying to Washington to consult on economic issues. Yoshida had guessed, probably correctly, that the egotistical supreme commander would have scrubbed a peace mission that was not originated by himself. Ikeda and a young aide, Kiichi Miyazawa, arranged two weeks of meetings in Washington, principally with Joseph Dodge, the banker who, as a special economic advisor, had imposed the austere budget plan a year earlier. Yoshida's penchant for secrecy was so great that not until the last minute did he inform even Ikeda of the real message he was to bear. In Washington, Ikeda met privately on a Sunday night with Dodge, both men agreeing that MacArthur must not know of their purpose.

The message Ikeda delivered for his chief was shrewdly calculated to stir almost every fear latent in official Washington. It said that anti-American feeling was rising in Japan because of the Occupation's meddling, the harsh new economic policy, and lack of progress toward independence. Yoshida's pro-American government might not survive the next election. Japan's opposition parties were united in favoring a peace treaty embracing China and the USSR. There was a strong chance that those Communist nations would offer their own separate treaty aligning Japan with them. Moreover, many Japanese felt that the United States would not, in fact, defend them if an invasion came, and the message cannily recalled that a high American official had hinted at precisely that in a statement a year earlier.

To move the pace forward, Yoshida—through Ikeda—said that Japan would take the risk of inviting American forces to stay. But Washington must deliver independence "at the earliest possible time." The message, with its dark warnings and hints of disaster, quickly circulated in Washington, and the stalemate was broken. It would take more than a year for Dulles to work out the details, but Yoshida's ploy was successful. Sovereignty came, on America's terms but at Japan's initiative, and relations between the two nations were fixed for decades to come.

The young aide, Miyazawa, later wrote a step-by-step account of the secret talks, correctly calling them "the basis of future military alliance between the two countries."[42]

Sixteen months later Yoshida went to San Francisco for the signing of documents. There in the Opera House Dulles adroitly fended off Soviet objections, and the peace treaty—without the USSR and the People's Republic of China—became history. Despite the price his countrymen had paid, Yoshida had achieved independence at last. He was in an exuberant mood, reading his speech from a long Japanese scroll that dangled from the dais. To the end, the rules were set by the Americans. The State Department found his original speech unsatisfactory and ordered it rewritten. There was one more act to be played out. As soon as the ceremony was over, Yoshida rushed from the hall, telling an aide, "We haven't got a minute to lose." After a quick lunch, he sped off to an isolated military installation out of the news media's view. There he signed the Japan–United States Security Treaty containing the terms of alliance that were the cost of independence.[43] The "San Francisco System" was in place.

There was a final indignity still to come, one that must have pained Yoshida deeply. Throughout the negotiations, he had managed to preserve some leeway in the matter of how Japan would deal with the competing Chinas, the Communists who held Beijing and the Nationalist government in Taipei. His sympathies clearly lay with the mainland government, which he most certainly intended to recognize at a later date. A month after San Francisco, no doubt thinking himself free to act as sovereign at last, he told the Diet that Japan would decide "from a position of realistic diplomacy" whether to recognize Communist China. It was a popular statement in Tokyo, but it ignited a firestorm in Washington. Fifty-six senators implied in a statement that they would reject the peace treaty and keep Japan occupied if Yoshida did not reverse himself. An angry Dulles, accompanied by two of the most prominent senators, scurried once again to Tokyo to bring Yoshida to heel. The result, known ever after as the "Yoshida Letter," promised that Japan had "no intention to conclude a bilateral treaty with the Communist regime of China." It was the most embarrassing public reversal of Yoshida's career. And it was especially humiliating because drafts of the "Yoshida Letter" were in fact written by Dulles.[44]

The joy of independence pushed Yoshida's popularity to an all-time high in the days after San Francisco, but the decline set in quickly. Approval of his cabinet slipped to 33 percent in a few months. One can speculate about the cause. The China letter was certainly one, reviving accusations that he catered too much to Washington whims. Also, the precise terms of the administrative agreement, spelling out terms of the enormous American military presence, became known, and people joked sourly that the Occupation had not, after all, gone away. Anti-American hostility erupted in a near riot on May Day 1952, and by September, a year after San Francisco, only 20 percent wanted Yoshida to continue as prime minister.[45] His government lingered on for two more years, but Japanese were clearly weary of him and wanted a true postwar, post-Occupation government. By the time he finally retired in December 1954, three out of every four citizens wanted him out.[46]

●

Yoshida is an honored man in Japan today, although his legacy is still subject to debate. Japan learned to live with the restrictions he accepted on her sovereignty, and she was to prosper enormously from the economic arrangements that went along with them. She benefited substantially from the aid and technology that flowed her way. Most of all, she benefited from her admission into the worldwide trading and currency systems with which the United States sought to unite the anti-Communist nations. In time, the bilateral relationship with America ripened into something approaching real friendship, despite the many irritations Japan felt with it. And in one sense, the "San Francisco System" did revive something important for Japan. It retrieved the old Meiji-style goal of alliance with the greatest power of the West (although it would be three decades before a Japanese prime minister felt sufficiently secure actually to use the word "alliance" because of its unpopular military connotations).

But in more fundamental ways, the pattern of foreign relations that the system established was something totally new and different from what had gone before. It was a product of the times and in retrospect stands in sharp contrast to what Japan had claimed in the past as her destiny. She had always feared most of all a dependence on a Western power. She had wanted an alliance with the West but one that left her free to play her own role in Asia, to have her own sphere of influence. The postwar treaty system did not confer that kind of role. Japan became in some respects a ward of the United States and accepted that country's guidance in most important matters of foreign policy. Many nations of Asia regarded her as diplomatically unimportant, and the Soviet Union treated her with disdain as a kind of American lackey. Yoshida's wise prediction that China would split with the Soviet Union proved to be accurate, but it was twenty years after San Francisco before Japan could deal with the mainland diplomatically. What she had was a conditional sovereignty. "It could not be said," wrote the historian John Dower, "that sovereignty brought with it the capability of pursuing an independent foreign policy."[47] The limitations rankled two generations of Japanese diplomats and intellectuals who felt that Japan should cast them off, if only to escape the psychological stigma that continued American influence inflicted. In the early 1970s, a Japanese editor wrote, "In a sense, Japan has yet to emerge from the Occupation. The Occupation itself may not have been despotic, but its aftermath is, for Japan continues to be limited in autonomy and freedom of choice."[48]

Yoshida, one suspects, would have dismissed such judgments as the brayings of leftist intellectuals who were removed from reality and totally lacking in that trait he most admired—"diplomatic sense." His memoirs show that he believed he had got the best bargains possible from Dulles and MacArthur. "He was proud that he had not made any real concessions on rearmament, for example," a former private secretary recalled. "He felt he had done his best to limit it. Yoshida was proud that he had taken much from Dulles."[49] Yet with outsiders, he was reluctant to talk of the security arrangements he had accepted and frequently withdrew into cautious evasions when asked about them. Once, long after his term in office had ended, an American affiliated with the Princeton University library arrived to tape-record an interview with him and asked many questions about his bargains with Dulles. Yoshida parried them all with non sequiturs and senseless comments, even insisting that he had no idea how many times he had met with Dulles. Finally, the interviewer said he supposed that Japan's rearmament must have been a big issue in those talks. Yoshida merely looked at him blankly and said, "Is that so?"[50]

If Yoshida ever felt that he had traded away too much for independence, the public record does not reveal it. Always self-assured, filled with certitude about the course he had followed, *Mr. Wan-Man* remained convinced that the bargain was a fair one. Yet he knew that many Japanese distrusted him, and he let his fears be known in a revealing moment as he returned from the San Francisco conference in 1951. A large crowd greeted his airplane, and flag-waving schoolchildren lined the streets as his limousine moved into Tokyo. His secretary, Akira Matsui, was traveling with him and was surprised at one point to see Yoshida's eyes fill with tears. Yoshida suddenly acknowledged that he had worried about the reception he would receive on this occasion. He recalled a time from his youth when a foreign minister,

Jutaro Komura, had returned from negotiations that had ended the war with Russia in 1905. Nationalists thought he had not extracted enough concessions from Japan's great victory, and Komura was jeered, his house stoned by mobs. Yoshida told Matsui that he had feared a similar fate after San Francisco. Then he turned back to the window and continued waving at the schoolchildren. "I am tired of looking at the back of my hand," he joked, and something in his voice caused Matsui to look closely. Tears were streaking down his cheeks.[51]

5
•

The Miracle
Machine

When Japanese businessmen reminisce about the economic miracle their nation achieved after the war, they are likely to begin with a familiar joke about the steel industry. The best thing that ever happened to it, they say, was its near destruction by American bombers in the closing months of the war. The industry had no choice but to rebuild from scratch, and it did so in the 1950s with American aid and technology. It emerged as the most modern steel industry in the world, capable within a short time of dominating international markets with the finest, cheapest steel to be found anywhere. Even a quarter of a century later, Japan's factories and furnaces were still more productive and cost-efficient than America's aging plants. The crucial event had been the war's destructiveness, which left Japan the single option of building anew.

There is a kernel of truth in this story, and it could serve as a metaphor for the entire postwar economic experience in Japan, that

Phoenixlike rebirth that was to astound and eventually frighten the West. That success was established on foundations that were almost all new after the war. Japan rebuilt on a blank landscape. This was true not only of factories and mechanical processes but of nearly all of the institutions and relationships among people that go into the shaping of a modern economic system. Some elements of these were, it is true, visible in the period just before the war, but the way in which all of the pieces were put together amounted to something new under the sun. In the ashes of defeat, Japan invented a way of organizing economic life.

The two aspects most obviously changed were management and labor. The Occupation at first dissolved the old family-controlled *zaibatsu*. Later, these regrouped but their manner of operation was very different from that of the prewar days. Most important, the *zaibatsu* bosses themselves were gone. MacArthur's team purged 2,210 officers from 632 *zaibatsu* companies and about 2,500 high-ranking officers and stockholders from other corporations. They became known as *shay-ozoku*, or "the tribe of the setting sun."[1] They were replaced by men from lower and middle management, clerks and technocrats suddenly elevated and handed powers that at first bewildered them. In addition, as we have seen, the labor movement was vastly transformed. The rejuvenated movement, under pressure from the Occupation's "reverse course," soon lost its radical spirit. But what survived was formidable. By June 1949 Japan had nearly 35,000 unions with 6.5 million workers. Despite their setbacks, they were strong enough to bargain with the new breed of managers who sat across the tables.

That portion of the government bureaucracy that was engaged in economic planning also reappeared in a new posture. In the final prewar years the economic bureaucracy had been of marginal importance in Japan. Meiji-era governments had played an important initial role in modernization and had done much to foster embryonic industries. They had built national railways and communications networks, arranged for investments through people's savings, subsidized fledgling manufactures, and created a marvelous new enterprise, the trading company. But the government's influence rather quickly receded as the new industrial giants emerged—the *zaibatsu* tended to run the governments rather than the other way around. Not until the late 1920s, when a worldwide depression threatened to ruin all that Meiji's men had built, did the economic bureaucracy assert itself, only to be absorbed in a few years into the generals' war machine. It reemerged intact after the defeat, sheltered from Occupation purges because MacArthur's economic team needed it to carry out the reconstruction of Japan. Leaving that

group of experienced bureaucrats in place was, in retrospect, perhaps
the most important decision the Americans made.

These, then, were the three pieces of the new Japan economic
structure: new and uncertain managers of dismembered companies,
militant unionists whose power was tamed, and a government bureaucracy intact but experienced primarily in authoritarian control of a
wartime economy. How would the pieces be fitted together? The answer
would come in the 1950s as the three elements struggled against one
another, then formed a tenuous bond and became Japan's new miracle
machine. Their performance would dazzle the world and make the
Japanese far richer and more secure than anyone in those early days
dared dream. But as the decade dawned, in poverty and an overriding
sense of helplessness, no one knew what would work. No one had a plan
for meshing these pieces into a working whole. There was no accepted
notion of what sort of economic structure should or could be put together. Japan survived in those days on American aid and the bounteous
fallout of the Korean War, which produced the *tokujyu*, the boom in
special procurements of war matériel ordered by the United States.
What pattern of economic life lay ahead was a great unknown. The only
certainty in economic behavior for Japan was that there were no cer-
tainties. Japan was free to choose. Like the wasted tracts of rubble where
steel mills once stood, the landscape was bare.

The rest of the world was engaged in its struggle between competing economic ideologies—socialism and capitalism. But Japan had
never really had, in modern times, an economic ideology, a system of
fixed beliefs to guide it in making choices among economic institutions.
In the Meiji period she had imported the basics of Western capitalism
because they seemed to work but had accompanied them with a strong
dose of national control and government sponsorship. That eclectic mix
was followed in the Taishō era (1912–26) by a period of freebooting
capitalism dominated by huge family enterprises that did not welcome
government interference. But that lasted hardly a quarter of a century
and all but disappeared under the system of state control imposed by the
militarists. In the first postwar years a romantic brand of revolutionary
socialism became fashionable. But that, too, waned quickly, especially
once the Occupation threw its weight against it. In all of its modern
history, Japan had only one genuine ideology, that of nationalism.
Choices were made according to what seemed best for national survival
and imperial power. Even the new capitalists of the late Meiji and
Taishō eras justified their deeds by resorting not to Adam Smith or other
capitalist gods but to the dogma of "national will." No capitalist ideol-

ogy as such ever took root. And in 1945 Japan's only real ideology, nationalism, was despised and bankrupt.

A great search has been underway, both in Japan and abroad, to trace the origins of her postwar economic success. Many analysts are irresistibly drawn to cultural explanations. Because Japan succeeded without a background in Western-style ideology, they believe, her secret must be rooted in her own cultural history. Japan's miracle is unique and so must be attributed to her cultural uniqueness. As they have looked more closely, they have found this system to be neither fish nor fowl, neither capitalist nor socialist, but some peculiar hybrid that had no known precursor abroad. This search seems to have begun sometime in the 1970s when it became apparent that Japan's achievement was no temporary phenomenon and that she was destined to become a permanent member of the advanced industrial club until then dominated by the United States and Europe. Essays and whole books poured forth with learned explanations tapping deep historical interpretations, and one began to hear Japanese businessmen, normally a no-nonsense crowd, describing the cultural origins of the miracle they had wrought.

It was noted, for example, that capital investment in Japan was fueled by an extraordinarily high rate of personal savings. This was due, it was solemnly asserted, to the traditional frugality of a people who saved every unused thread and uneaten morsel of food. Why had large Japanese companies and workers settled on a personnel system that presumed lifetime employment in a single firm? The answer lay in a Tokugawa aphorism about a peasant's loyalty to his lord: "A man should not serve two masters in his life." Protectionism in foreign trade, by which Japan blocked out foreign imports, was a relic of the xenophobic tradition found as far back as the seventeenth century. Foreign analysts, some of whom had spent very little time in Japan, uncovered wondrous cultural traits to explain each unusual feature of Japanese industry.

One of the most admiring of the foreigners was Peter F. Drucker, the eminent American analyst of business management. He discovered cultural inheritances in such practices as making decisions through group consensus and in the flexibility of Japan's labor force. The Japanese worker's supposed willingness to undergo repeated training throughout his work life, Drucker wrote in a famous article, could be linked with the samurai's practice of calligraphy and swordsmanship. Constant training and the ability to move from job to job were economic traits predating modern business, and they could not be emulated by the rest of the world's corporations. "It would be folly for managers in the West to imitate these policies," Drucker warned. "In fact it would be impossible. Each policy is deeply rooted in Japanese traditions and culture. Each applies to the problems of an industrial society and economy the values and the habits developed far earlier by the retainers of the Japanese clan, by the Zen priests in their monasteries, and by the calligraphers and painters of the 'great schools' of Japanese art."[2] Drucker was not alone. Indeed, the noble samurai was invoked in countless articles and cartoons as the source of modern skills and industrial invention. All of Japan's cultural nooks and crannies were ransacked for evidence of a special inheritance that somehow predestined her to economic success in the third quarter of the twentieth century. Another American observer, James Abegglen, found parallels between Japan's factory system in 1958 and the nation's clan or kinship organization. Business cartels, he wrote, were ". . . the furthest extension of kinship-type relations in the economic and industrial sector."[3]

●

These explanations were mainly nonsense. Virtually all of Japan's modern miracle can be explained by events that took place on that empty landscape left by war and occupation. The elements of success were formed by the special circumstances of the times, by decisions men made, by the interactions of people and social forces, and sometimes by the sheer luck of the draw. New institutions were developed and new relationships between them were constructed, not because of any cultural predisposition but because certain choices were made and certain understandings took root. A few features of this new economic system can be traced to the war years or the decade immediately preceding them, but the fact that they survived into the fifties and sixties was due to conscious choices made, not to some special cultural trait of the Japanese. Japan simply invented her economy anew.

The cooperative labor-management system that was one of those elements, for example, was almost entirely newborn. The prewar system was anything but cooperative; it was characterized by union-busting, repression, and an often harsh paternalism. The idea of workers and bosses discussing mutual problems and negotiating contracts was an alien one before the war. Similarly, there is little truth to the notion that some native instinct for frugality created the postwar penchant for personal savings and fueled the vast investment pool. Historically, the Japanese had been too poor to save. The samurai is the poorest of metaphorical figures to justify such a myth. Many of them in the late Tokugawa period were spendthrifts and deadbeats indebted to moneylenders. Savings as a national trait was first encouraged in the late nineteenth century by Meiji governments intent on raising cash for new industries. Economic historians have shown, moreover, that Japan's prewar savings rate was unremarkable and consistently lower than that in the United States.[4] The high postwar rate is the result of government decisions that encouraged savings (tax policy and the postal savings program) and of such realities as the low level of government welfare, which forced people to save for retirement.[5]

Perhaps the most distinctive feature of postwar economics was the activist role played by government bureaucrats and planners. Their prominence can be traced no further back in history than the 1930s, when depression and the coming of war required central planning. The notion that their dominance in the fifties and sixties is a legacy of wise Tokugawa-era officials is fanciful. Japan had never had an economic mandarinate. The postwar one was born in the desperate need to create purpose and direction out of chaos. The style of political economy that is established—oligopolies guided by government pressures—had no precedent, except perhaps in the few years when Meiji governments nurtured fledgling industries. The new mandarins, operating in uncharted waters, designed many of the distinctive features that produced Japan's miracle. They amassed the first batches of investment capital, fostered and sheltered new industries, planned the era of huge exports, limited imports, and controlled the currency. Each was a pragmatic reaction to events to the times. Armed with new powers, targeting new goals, creating new economic institutions where none had existed before, they built a new structure with little history or culture to guide them.

Many important early elements in Japan's recovery were not Japanese at all but were fashioned abroad. Some are obvious and well known, such as American financial aid and the special-procurements boom afforded by the war in Korea. The latter poured $3 billion into Japan's economy at a critical time, saved companies such as Toyota from collapse, earned the first substantial amounts of foreign currency, and overall had such enormous impact that a Bank of Japan official referred to it as "divine aid." It was also from foreign countries, primarily the United States, that Japanese first acquired the basics of the new industrial technology and learned the rudiments of quality control on assembly lines. Far more important was the absorption of Japan into the Western economic system, with all of its potential for sustained growth. By accepting American aid after the peace treaty was signed, Japan had to foreswear trade with China, but she was richly rewarded with an

opening to the West. It provided her with continued access to the best
technology and linked her permanently to the free-trade system that the
United States was guaranteeing. She won access to American and European markets while being allowed to close her own to foreign imports.
Many of the internal changes that advanced Japan's growth were in fact
responses to pressures and inducements from outside. It was in a sense
a replay of the Meiji experience. Naohiro Amaya, who was a Ministry
of International Trade and Industry official when all of this was unfolding, described the process in 1987:

> The main reason Japan was able to achieve miraculous eco-
> nomic development during the Meiji Era and after World
> War II lies in the fact that the system, ethics and life-style of
> Japanese society were changed substantially and appropriately
> at the time Western technology was introduced. . . . In re-
> viewing Japan's history over the last 130 years, changes in
> values, ethics and systems for the most part took place as a
> result of major external pressure. Cynically speaking, perhaps,
> today's Japan should be more concerned about the lack of
> external pressure . . . than the excess.[6]

Finally, if Japan's modern success story were dependent on some
unique cultural heritage, why have her Asian neighbors been able to
emulate it so successfully? A decade or so after her own economic
lift-off, South Korea, Taiwan, Hong Kong, and Singapore were in hot
pursuit, using many of Japan's techniques and strategies. What they
borrowed were not her cultural traits—they cared very little about samurai habits—but her organization, planning, and technology, all of
which were of postwar origin. One can argue that South Korea's surge
was far more remarkable than Japan's had been. Korea had never benefited from a Meiji-style modernization, had suffered through a cruel
Japanese occupation, was in ruins caused by another war eight years
after Japan's was over, and even today assumes a much heavier military
spending burden than Japan ever shouldered. Given all that, South
Korea's rise as a developed country seems a greater achievement than
Japan's. Does that mean, then, that the Korean cultural inheritance is
even more economically serviceable than Japan's?

The truth of Japan's dizzying climb out of poverty is that, unen-
cumbered by ideological baggage and having little regard for her own
economic history, Japan wrote her own success story. She filled the
blank landscape with new institutions and new relationships of her own
devising. Most were the products of pragmatic choices made under

pressure. Government, management, and labor lurched forward a step at a time. In the beginning, there were very few signs of that vaunted consensus some picture as the essential foundation of her success. Arguments and pitched battles raged both within and among the various economic institutions. Only years later, when they discovered that the creation worked rather well, did Japanese and foreigners begin to marvel at its cohesiveness and to invent a mythical past to explain it all.

●

As Japan groped for a footing in the world of defeat and hunger, one can imagine her constructing any of several economic systems. She might well have returned to the prewar stage in which huge *zaibatsu* and powerful cartels dominated commercial life with very little government interference. Many wanted it that way, including Prime Minister Yoshida and his conservative supporters. Or she might have veered leftward toward the Socialist model. A radical fever ran through Japan for two years after her defeat: in 1946, public-opinion polls showed, about half of all Japanese aligned themselves with either the Socialist or Communist parties. Then, too, she might have drifted into a system of small, competitive industries lightly regulated by the central government. That was the model first favored by the populist trust-busters in MacArthur's headquarters. Or why not the welfare-state system that had evolved out of depression and war in the West? The United States and Great Britain offered appealing examples of regulated laissez-faire arrangements that helped the poor.

Instead of any such obvious models, the economic system that evolved in the first postwar decade was something as distinctive and new to Japan as it was to most of the world. It was a curious mixture of systems, actually, a government-guided capitalism that fit none of the classical molds. Large corporations competed in commercial struggles for turf and profit. But they did so under the very heavy hand of government. At the center of it all was a supremely powerful bureaucracy which for the first fifteen years of the postwar era shaped economic life. It directed and managed and organized that life, bending private enterprise to its will. It supplied the capital and determined which corporations would get it. It identified the industrial sectors that were important to the nation and determined which companies would enter them. It selected the technology Japan would need and decided which enterprises could buy it. It chose the foreign markets that companies should enter and taught those companies how to succeed in them. It selected the competitors and set the rules of engagement. Indeed, the whole thing appeared to be a mammoth sumo contest in which the fiercest wrestlers survived but in which all the contestants were trained and managed by the government.

The process by which this new system was put in place was so full of twists and turns, so much the result of conflicting ideas and clashing needs, that it almost seems, in retrospect, to have been an accident of history. The most drastic twist was the American abandonment of the plan to leave Japan economically powerless. By 1947, as the cold war loomed, what the United States wanted was not an impotent former foe but an economically viable ally. Japan and Germany, said Dean Acheson, then a State Department official, should become "two of the greatest workshops of Europe and Asia."[7] The architect of the new containment strategy, George F. Kennan, grumbled that MacArthur's purges and industrial dismemberings were causing turmoil and embittering the upper classes most congenial to the United States.[8] Moreover, a weakened Japan might be forever an expensive American ward. All of these concerns came together in a new design requiring Japan to be built up, not torn down, economically. Business purges were abandoned, dissolution orders were shelved. Old *zaibatsu* were permitted to retain their treasured name and many of their old properties. Holding companies were still banned, but large industrial groupings reappeared, centered around large banks. The old vision of populist minimalism was erased. The new SCAP priorities were growth, efficiency, and contribution to cold-war needs.

Throughout all of this pushing and pulling, tearing down and building up, one permanent Japanese institution remained in place. This was the economic bureaucracy that SCAP had inherited from the wartime governments. Its members were a varied group of economists, planners, clerks, and career officials who had been thrust into command of Japan's economy as the country geared up for war in the 1930s. For more than a decade they had struggled to keep the military supplied with the instruments of war and to keep a resource-starved domestic economy producing enough for survival. The experience had transformed these rather ordinary men into a close-knit team that possessed one important collective talent: It was comfortable with bigness. It had dealt in budgets of billions of yen and planned expenditures of enormous size. It had meshed together huge corporations, amassed stockpiles of vast quantities of war goods, and delivered enough equipment and supplies to support an army spread throughout Asia. No other Japanese institution except for the military itself had ever managed an enterprise of such magnitude. No other group of Japanese had ever learned so well the art of managing bigness. The survival of this bureaucracy into the postwar years was the most vital fact of economic life. Among the several components that became the Japanese miracle machine, it was the most important. Had this mandarinate not endured the defeat intact, and had it not been kept intact for the job of economic recovery, the shape of Japan's future would have been far different.

When peace came, most of the experienced technocrats were quickly fitted into the fledgling SCAP-designed agencies that were to inaugurate the recovery, principally the reconstituted Ministry of Commerce and Industry and the Economic Stabilization Board. Given little independent authority, they were mainly clerks for SCAP. But in 1949 many were assigned to yet another new economic conglomeration that was given cabinet status and charged with revitalizing Japan for the cold war. The Ministry of International Trade and Industry, or MITI, did not at first seem a formidable instrument. Its powers were broad but vague, and it was, of course, subject to Occupation control. But in a very short time, MITI established itself as the real economic power in Japan. For the next fifteen years it was the strongest institution on the scene. Hundreds of books and memoirs, and at least three novels, have been written to describe its commanding presence in Japan's recovery. It became the model for state-developed capitalism that third-world countries turned to. In the West, MITI acquired a rather sinister reputation as the mysterious and secretive organization that plotted a global economic conquest and saw to it that it was carried out.

The connection between Japan's wartime planning and the postwar economic miracle has been expertly delineated by Professor Chalmers Johnson.[9] But perhaps the closest observer of the process is a mild-mannered bureaucrat-turned-scholar who has followed MITI's trail both inside and outside its headquarters in Tokyo. Yasuyuki Maeda was a fresh young college graduate looking for a lively spot in the government when, in 1953, he joined MITI's Business Research Division. For seven years he watched the ministry grow in power. He became fascinated by the people above him who guided Japan's recovery and even more fascinated by their past careers in wartime planning. Maeda resigned in 1960 to become a professor of economics at Hosei University, but he continued to watch MITI from a distance and eventually became involved in the writing of the ministry's official history. He has traced the path of those wartime economic czars who were transformed by SCAP into the master builders of the world's most successful economy.

In several lengthy interviews with me, Maeda described his conclusions about those formative years in MITI. Not surprisingly, he believes that the key to Japan's economic success lay not in the business world but in the bureaucratic world. It was the strong hand of government that propelled the stricken nation forward. The important mandarins were to be found in MITI and to a lesser extent in the Ministry of Finance. Their supremacy and the ways in which they exercised it had no precedent in prewar history. They were a product of the war and the years that followed it, the richest irony of all being that the men who planned the economic side of the war also planned the peacetime recovery. As Maeda remembers it:

> You have to think back to wartime. The military had the power then and resources were very scarce. To win the war the government had to have strict control over the economy. They did this through the ministry of Commerce and Industry and later the Ministry of Munitions. When we were defeated, the army was gone, but the economic bureaucrats remained, and they went on to become the founders of MITI. Their purpose was changed, of course, from winning the war to the recovery and rehabilitation of postwar Japan. But the people were the same. And their way of achieving the new goals was not changed.[10]

The principle of government control over the economy was carried over into peacetime. Even the methods of control remained the same:

> Even the things they had to work with, to concentrate their efforts on, were much the same as in the war. During the war they exercised their control mainly to produce coal, steel, light metals, and ships. In the years after the war the emphasis was only somewhat changed. They concentrated on steel and coal, just like in the war, and they added textiles and fertilizers, because we needed food and clothing to survive. The purpose was different, but the people and their method of organization and even some of the industries were the same. That is how we got this system of strong government control into the economy. It was just the same men doing the same things they had done during the war.[11]

Indeed, Maeda contends that it was in some ways easier for the bureaucrats to control the economy after the war then during it. During wartime, the bureaucrats had been frequently challenged and pulled between contending forces, mainly the business *zaibatsu* and the generals. Then came SCAP, which was by the nature of its task a totalitarian organization determined to manage everything without interference. It gave Japanese administrators more autonomous power than they had wielded in the old Ministry of Munitions. Maeda discovered that the Japanese were delighted with the centralized control apparatus handed to them by MacArthur's men:

> I can remember one of the highest officials of those early days [after the defeat] admitting to me that it was much easier to run things after the military was ousted. The big improvement was that the United States was in control instead of the old Japanese military, and the United States had more realistic ideas of how the economy should run. There were some conflicts among them, but it was much easier in the long run for the Japanese bureaucrats. The United States was more rational in its decisions, this official told me.[12]

The new mandarins spent little time philosophizing about their role or about the overall shape of Japan's new economic system. The rest of the world was absorbed in a bitter and fundamental conflict over economic philosophy. It was the time of the great ideological debate when economic systems were attacked and defended in sweeping moral terms. Communism versus capitalism. The free world versus authoritarian socialism. State control versus free-market economics. Even in much of the Third World, where poor countries were just emerging from colonialism, new leaders were choosing sides in the great debate. But not in Japan. Socialism remained the vague ideal of a leading opposition party, but its tenets were irrelevant to those actually running the state, those rising technocrats clustered in MITI after 1949. There were many in the conservative political world who grumbled about state control and warned of a drift toward socialism. But in the corridors of MITI, Maeda remembers, the only questions discussed were those of how to induce economic growth and escape from poverty:

> In reality, there was very little discussion of whether what they were doing was socialism or not. Some outsiders saw it as socialism, because of the control management by the bureaucrats. But what happened just grew piece by piece. It was all very nonideological. In the days before the war, our guiding philosophy had been to become the leader of Asia, the head of the Greater East Asia Co-Prosperity Sphere. But that was destroyed in the war. Our only principle after the war was the

rehabilitation of the economy and the expansion of it. That was our philosophy—not capitalism or socialism. We had abandoned political ideology entirely and took up the idea of economic expansion as our only philosophy. [13]

During the first years after the defeat, the bureaucrats and SCAP ran Japan with rigid controls, as if a wartime economy were still in place. The main agencies were the revived Ministry of Commerce and Industry (which became MITI in 1949) and the Economic Stabilization Board. Just as they had during the war, the peacetime czars settled on a "priority production system," which called for concentrating available resources in the most crucial industries. Coal and steel production were given the top priority, followed by fertilizers, electric power, shipping, and textiles. The government apparatus and SCAP controlled distribution of all commodities, doled out the limited supply of investment capital, fixed prices of essentials, and at one point, in a desperate attempt to stifle inflation, froze people's savings accounts. The program was almost pure socialism, although not called by that name, and resembled very closely the war-mobilization planning of the 1930s. It did not work very well. By 1950, despite all the spurring of essential industry, the index of manufacturing production was only one-third of the 1931 level, which itself had been a low one. Not until the Korean War broke out and Japanese firms benefited from the procurements boom it engendered did the Japanese economy begin to revive. In the spring of 1952, when the Occupation ended and Japan's bureaucrats were left to run things alone, there was not a great deal to be proud of, except that Japan had survived.

Maeda arrived in MITI as a fledgling bureaucrat in 1953, several months after the Occupation ended. He found the mood not terribly encouraging. He recalls:

They were neither very optimistic nor very pessimistic. On the one hand, there was a sense of ease, because we were preparing to do everything by ourselves at last, with the Americans gone. But the United States was still supporting Japan, and American taxpayers were objecting to the fact that so much money was going to an enemy country. We felt that eventually we could do it by ourselves, but there also was a lot of anxiety. [14]

Left at last to their own devices, the Japanese set about building their new economic system. It was not at all what the American populists had intended, and it was different from those that had developed in the capitalist and Communist worlds. MITI's essential strategy was the sponsoring of large corporations in each of the important industrial sectors and the shaping of those companies into government-guided cartels. The underlying premise was that these corporate giants would be encouraged—forced if necessary—to expand in ways that benefited Japan's national interest and that this national interest would be primarily defined by the men of MITI. It was a style recalled from the experiences of the war-mobilization years. The great *zaibatsu*, once tamed under government control, had proved to be extraordinarily productive in turning out ships, tanks, and planes for the war effort. Big companies, directed from above, had proved to be efficient users of capital and scarce resources. Their efforts properly concentrated, they had become adept at developing new technology—the Zero fighter plane and the great battleships were testimony to that talent. It was to those proven achievements that MITI turned in the 1950s. They simply revived what had worked before. Concentrating scarce capital and resources in large industrial concerns had worked during the war and could be made to work again. The wartime analogy was always on their minds. One of the MITI technocrats, Yoshihisa Ojima, would later describe it in an appropriate military metaphor. "According to Napoleon and Clausewitz, the secret of a successful strategy is the concentration of fighting power on the main battlegrounds," he said in 1970. "Owing to good luck and wisdom spawned of necessity, Japan has been able to concentrate its scant capital in strategic industries."[15]

The early planners faced one enormous obstacle left behind by the departing Occupation authorities: the Anti-Monopoly Law. A vital piece of SCAP's early populism, that law prohibited cartels, price-fixing, market-sharing arrangements, and any other collusive activities. It was therefore anathema to MITI's plan to erect a system of large corporations through which it could supervise entire industries. MITI was not hostile to competition per se. But it preferred the managed competition of the 1930s, when the older bureaucrats had created cartels of *zaibatsu* and guided the war effort. They did not understand the postwar Anti-Monopoly Law. It seemed contrary to everything they had learned about national economic management during the war. Big companies were efficient producers. The law's "antibigness" feature genuinely confused postwar planners, who at first assumed it was part of the Occupation's plan to gain revenge on Japan for having waged war. Maeda remembers hearing MITI's top planners discuss antitrust policy as if it were a severe penalty:

Most of them thought that enforcing the antimonopoly law was part of Japan's punishment. Getting even with Japan, somehow. For example, Mitsui Bussan had been divided up into ten or twenty separate companies. In the beginning, the SCAP concept of antitrust was very severe, and we thought it was a form of punishment. We didn't really understand the idea of free enterprise then.[16]

The bureaucracy's attempts to escape the Anti-Monopoly Law were unrelenting. A revealing episode in 1948–49 showed how determined the planners were to thwart SCAP policy at a time when they were supposed to be carrying it out as part of a conquered state. In 1948 SCAP had insisted on the passage of a law sharply reducing the role of industrial trade associations. Remnants of the wartime production system, these associations had been used by bureaucrats principally to allocate critical materials among member companies, and they were a vital part of the network by which private industry had been controlled. After the war, SCAP viewed them as integral parts of the old monopolistic structure, prone to price-fixing and market-sharing. It ordered the associations dissolved and refused the Japanese bureaucracy's pleas to relent. The Ministry of Commerce and Industry (MCI, the forerunner of MITI) regarded the associations as essential to its plans for continued control of the economy; it was far easier to transmit instructions through a few industrial associations than to deal directly with dozens or hundreds of separate companies. Maeda recalls that MCI resolved its dilemma with a clever end run around SCAP: It simply put the trade associations' managers on the payroll as government officials where, without SCAP's knowledge, they continued to follow the bureaucracy's instructions just as in the past. After the Occupation pulled out, one of the independent government's first deeds was to repeal the Trade Association Law and revive the associations in their old form as de facto instruments of the government.[17]

With the Occupation ended, MITI had no need for subterfuges and embarked on its campaign to "cartelize" almost all of Japanese industry. It was stymied at first by rulings of the Fair Trade Commission, which had been created under the Anti-Monopoly Law to oppose precisely the kind of collusive activities MITI favored. For more than a year a bitter struggle was fought between the Commission, a relic of Occupation populism, and MITI. Finally, MITI prevailed and in September 1953 the law was drastically weakened. There followed a long period in which industry after industry was "cartelized." Many in the Diet and in the business circles opposed the campaign, considering it a variant of socialism, but MITI almost always prevailed. Sometimes it argued that "excessive competition" in a particular industry threatened stability. At other times it would contend that cartels were needed to strengthen and protect an industry against foreign imports. By 1959 the contest was over, and cartels under MITI's supervision were dividing up markets and fixing prices in almost every important industry. By 1961 a total of 477 cartels were in place.[18]

MITI built this new industrial structure block by block in the years when its powers were sweeping. It selected the industries it considered important to Japan's national interest—steel, chemicals, shipbuilding, and heavy machinery—and poured the country's capital and resources into them. It chose the companies that would lead those industries and favored them with attention and assistance. It formed and shaped the cartels through which entire industries could be guided toward efficiency. Companies it approved of flourished. Those it counted too weak to contribute to national well-being did not. The weakest were frequently merged into other corporations and given their proper place within the overall structure.

The tools it used were ones of compulsion and inducement similar to those inherited from the war period and enhanced by the greater authority delegated by SCAP. The bureaucrats in MITI and the Ministry of Finance held life-or-death control over much of the nation's capital, and they saw to it that it was funneled into industries on the approved list. They controlled the flow of foreign currency, so that companies could buy abroad only those things that the planners deemed valuable. Subsidies, tax breaks, and research grants went to companies the bureaucrats endorsed. The ministries controlled bank loans, access to new foreign technology, and importation of natural resources. The revived *zaibatsu* often objected and criticized the controls, but they had little choice but to go along with them. Without the nod from MITI they were hardly able to function. But they were also rewarded. They were shielded from foreign competition by a web of rules MITI devised to keep Western products and companies out of Japan's marketplace. The power to control currency exchange meant that no Japanese firm could import foreign products without a special exception from the bureaucracy. MITI permitted joint ventures with foreign firms only when the benefits of new technology were substantial, and it placed limits on foreign ownership of Japanese companies. It was the policy, overall, of the carrot and the stick, but the bureaucracy wielded a very large stick.

In this design there was very little national ownership of industry, almost nothing that would merit the label of "socialism." Only the telephone and telegraph industries, part of the railway system, and the tobacco industry, were nationally owned, less even than in prewar days when steel had been a national property. Nor did this structure resemble the free-market capitalism of the West. It was something strangely different—government-guided oligopoly is perhaps the best definition. In each industry that MITI's Enterprises Bureau selected as vital, between three and ten companies were encouraged to compete. Compete they did, but in a fashion decreed by MITI. Price-fixing, production limitations, and other collusions were permitted, often even encouraged. If competition became "excessive"—a bugaboo word for more than a decade—MITI weeded out the least efficient through mergers and arranged bankruptcies. Throughout the 1950s, on the average, the top five companies in each industry accounted for two-thirds of that industry's output. The goal was always the same: large, strong companies protected from foreign competition until they were able to stand on their own feet in the international arena. Saburo Okita, a world-renowned economist with the Economic Planning Agency and later a foreign minister, explained it all very simply: "The policy was: carefully select industries, prevent ruinous competition at the infancy stage, nurse them up to a competitive stature, and then expose them to outside competition. This has more or less been the industrial policy of Japan."[19]

For years after the war, the bureaucracy shepherded Japanese industry toward the goal of international strength, until the day came when it needed little help at all. Gradually, the bureaucracy's direct controls were eased, and the stick of outright compulsion was put away. It was replaced by MITI's famous "administrative guidance," a process mysterious to foreigners and even to most Japanese. The shepherding continued, but it was accomplished by subtle warnings, inducements, and requests that corporations abide by the national interest. The companies grew larger and stronger and seemed to the outside world to be freewheeling giants operating on their own instincts. In fact, MITI's direction was always felt, prodding here, fixing there, bailing out failed firms, strengthening the weak, curbing the dissidents, appealing always to the businessman's sense of national duty. "Government by admonition," the noted economist, William W. Lockwood, called it, writing in the 1960s:

> The hand of government is everywhere in evidence, despite its limited statutory powers. The Ministries engage in an extraor-

dinary amount of consultation, advice, persuasion and threat. The industrial bureaus of MITI proliferate sectoral targets and plans; they confer, they tinker, they exhort. This is the "economics by admonition" to a degree inconceivable in Washington or London.[20]

In that famous essay, which is still the surest guide to Japan's early development years, Lockwood went on to say that "a new industrial order is taking shape" through a series of "groping experiments" by government, not by a single coherent blueprint.[21]

Indeed, it had all been pieced together out of the circumstances of the times. It grew from no ideological commitment whatsoever. Pragmatism was the method, expansionism the goal, and these were the only "isms" that really mattered. Success was woven of several threads—a few from the Meiji period, many from the experiences of war, bits and pieces from the Occupation era—all of them stitched together by the bureaucracy in the first fifteen years after the great defeat. What seemed serviceable was retained, what was not was discarded. Somehow, it all fitted, worked, blended into a whole.

It evolved into a period of extraordinary economic growth that made Japan rich and also made her famous as the model for a developing economy. Because it succeeded so well, some have concluded that it was meticulously planned from the start on the order of those multiyear plans common in socialist countries. No such grand design ever existed. Yasuyuki Maeda, looking back on those days, said he could not recall that any high-growth, long-term plan was ever conceived within the bureaucracy. A series of five-year plans existed on paper, but few paid much attention to them—they were more hopes than plans, really. MITI's own men were frequently astonished at their success, Maeda remembers, and over the years a popular saying emerged to explain it all: "We just came forward, walking up one step at a time, and when we looked up we were at the top of the stairs."[22]

●

The emergence of government-guided capitalism was one of the two major elements of the new economic order that transformed Japan after the war. The other was a novel style in relations between workers and management. Its essence was an uncommon harmony between them within the structure of the company. This ideal of harmony was based on the assumption that the workers and bosses had shared interests in the welfare of the corporation, that the well-being of the employee was inextricably bound up with the performance of the entire company, and that both would prosper so long as management and worker proceeded to work out their problems in a spirit of cooperation. This understanding differed considerably from the relationship that had grown up in Western capitalism. There, an enduring hostility was presumed to be the natural order. The Western worker rented out his labor for a price, and to drive that price up had to threaten to withhold his labor. Confrontation was both inevitable and normal. In the new Japanese model, which flowered in the 1960s, confrontation was discouraged except in extreme cases, because the company's stability and long-term growth were presumed to be more important than any immediate gains workers might achieve through a strike. This, at least, was the ideal preached by both unions and management. Although the ideal was often violated and was never really accepted in much of Japanese industry, it did prevail in the important, successful corporations. Looked at from Western shores, it was something as new and strange as the concept of government-guided capitalism.

There were three pillars underpinning this peculiar structure, and they are familiar to anyone who has read anything at all about Japanese society. The first was "lifetime employment." When joining a large company after graduating from high school or college, an employee made an unstated commitment to remain with that company throughout his working life. In turn, the company tacitly promised that the employee would not be discharged before retirement except for the most serious reasons. The second pillar was management's assurance that the employee's wages would be raised as he grew older and his years with the company increased. Pay-by-age, or *Nenko*, was a system that assured that a worker's benefits would rise as his needs in life increased. The third pillar was the company union. Workers were organized within each company and had only minor associations with workers in other corporations. The union's activities were concentrated almost exclusively on the betterment of life within the company; solidarity with other unions was celebrated in word but not in fact. These three elements came to be accepted as the set of understandings that made Japanese capitalism unique, and they were accorded an almost mystical significance in explanations of how it all worked. Even today, when much of their mystical aura has been dispelled, it is not uncommon to hear them referred to, sometimes seriously and sometimes in jest, as Japan's "three sacred treasures." (The real "three sacred treasures" are the sword, mirror, and jewel, which, according to legend, have belonged to the imperial dynasty for 2,600 years.)

Like the structure of guided capitalism that the bureaucrats built, this Japanese employment system is so distinctive that it is frequently depicted as the product of a peculiar culture. It is said to have evolved out of some unique Japanese penchant for harmony and conciliation that is different from, and superior to, the Western style, which stresses confrontation. In particular, lifetime employment is seen as an extension of the old principle of serving but one master during one's lifetime or of some possibly Confucian ideal having to do with respect for authority. The notion that Japan's modern employment arrangements were prefigured in a past society, and that they represent some special Japanese virtue, was so ardently embraced that as late as 1977 it was still the official explanation offered by the government. In that year the Ministry of Foreign Affairs published in English a guidebook attributing lifetime employment to Tokugawa-era practices. Its origins, the guidebook stated, lay in the feudal apprenticeship system in which a young man worked many years for a single master before leaving to launch his own enterprise. According to the guidebook, "this custom of long years of faithful service can be considered the forerunner of today's lifetime employment system."[23]

It is all a pretty legend, with as little substance as the parallel notion that Japan's brand of guided capitalism is an extension of traditional practices. For one thing, the apprenticeship system cited by the Foreign Ministry was not, in fact, unique to Japan. It existed in similar form in feudal Europe and was even used in the United States in the eighteenth century. Yet the official myth endures in the pop-sociology books and is accepted by some foreign authors. The lifetime employment legend seems to be an indestructible example of some insistent Japanese need to discover institutional roots in the past where none exist. It is a sample of what Professor Robert S. Ozaki of California State University (Hayward) has called the "circular reasoning" inherent in most attempts to interpret Japan through the cultural model approach. "Whenever an aspect of Japanese behavior cannot otherwise be explained, it is attributed to Japanese culture," Ozaki has written. "To say 'the Japanese behave like Japanese because they are Japanese' is not particularly revealing."[24]

In truth there are only the faintest traces of lifetime employment in prewar Japanese industry. It was not the common practice in the Meiji era (1868–1912), when Japan's first industrial structure was being shaped, nor in the Taishō era (1912–25) that followed. Throughout those eras, the employment system in industry was a chaotic affair, characterized by indifference to labor as a significant part of the economic picture. The usual practice followed in new, burgeoning companies was for blue-collar workers to be employed through contracts with labor recruiters who agreed to produce a fixed number of able-bodied men and women in exchange for fees. There was no guarantee of steady jobs, even for short periods of time, and in fact, layoffs in hard times were the rule. There was also a great deal of piracy in which, during occasional boom times, companies schemed to steal skilled workers away from their rivals. Those who consider lifetime employment and workplace stability to be Japanese traditions should consult the writings of Konosuke Matsushita, one of Japan's great industrial pioneers. Matsushita recalls that in 1919 employee relations were so turbulent and uncertain that he hardly ever knew whether enough men would show up for work each day to get his factory running. Matsushita was required to stand at the plant's door each morning to determine how many workers, and which ones, would arrive for work. Only then, he has recalled, could he be certain that a day of production could begin.[25]

Almost all modern scholars of Japanese labor relations agree that promises of long-term employment did not appear on the scene until the mid- or late-Taishō period, roughly about 1919 and 1920, and then only in a few large companies. Those big enterprises, rich with profits earned during World War I, saw the value of a more rational employment system, one in which the workers they had trained would stick with them. The concept was never widespread before World War II; those companies that did use it normally applied its lifetime jobs promise only to white-collar employees. It was nearly fifteen years after the war, when Japan had entered a remarkable high-growth period, before such understandings were common in the larger companies. (In 1960 only about one-fifth of the industrial work force was covered by such pledges.) "It was not until the post-war period that the principle of lifetime employment was extended to include blue-collar workers," Takeshi Inagami of Hosei University has written in a publication issued by the Japan Institute of Labor. Inagami goes on to emphasize that the other two so-called sacred jewels—company unions and the seniority wage system—also were essentially postwar institutions. "In summary," he adds, "the 'traditional' model is in fact rather new."[26]

It also seems that lifetime employment was more a consequence of economic success than the cause of it. It became widespread only in the high-growth 1960s when large companies became sufficiently profitable to afford it. And even today it is not the norm throughout all of Japanese industry. According to Professor Yasumitsu Nihei of Keio University's Institute of Management and Labor Studies, only about 25 to 30 percent of Japan's work force is covered by lifetime employment as an "institutionalized arrangement." Perhaps an additional 25 percent of the work force benefits from noninstitutionalized promises of varying degrees of reliability. At most, it is apparent, only a bit more than half of all Japanese workers are offered any type of assurances that their jobs are safe until retirement.[27]

Still, there's no doubt that Japan's labor-management system emphasizes cooperation to a degree unprecedented in the West. The roots of the system are found not in tradition and ancient history but in the postwar era, specifically the late 1940s and early 1950s. They grew in a harsh environment—the firings, strikes, and bitter hostilities that marked the late-Occupation period. The important forces in this emergence were not cultural. They were the circumstances of a fluid time and the reactions of many people. Unions, managers, the Japanese governments, and American Occupation authorities all played their hands. Had different choices been made, or had different options been presented, the result would have been different. Lifetime employment and the other important elements of Japan's new system were specific responses to specific pressures generated in a time of turbulence and rapid change.

The essential circumstance was a quick and decisive shift in the balance of power between labor and company managers. This occurred over a period of a few years, the result being that unions lost the initiative and became more vulnerable to company pressure. This did not just happen to come about. Rather, it was largely the result of the policy reversal ordered by SCAP, which by late 1947 had set out to tame the very forces it had unleashed in its early union-fostering campaign. The first sign of this sudden change in policy was MacArthur's order canceling the general strike scheduled for February 1, 1947. In the following two years SCAP sanctioned a broad-scale trimming of union power through revisions of labor laws. The revisions placed restrictions on the unions' authority to call strikes and, more important, permitted the abrogation of hundreds of union-management contracts that had been negotiated in the previous two years. All of these measures were fervently supported by Japanese governments and welcomed by business managers, all of whom felt that at last MacArthur's men were on their side.

The most shattering blow to organized labor, however, came in the so-called red purge of 1950, a series of events that weakened unions for all time. It began against the background of escalating East-West tensions and a new surge of revolutionary rhetoric from Japan's Communist leaders, who had been goaded by criticisms from both the Soviet Union and China. In June 1950 MacArthur purged twenty-four top Communist party leaders from public life and ordered the expulsion of twelve editors and managers of *Akahata*, the party newspaper. Following MacArthur's lead, Japan's government soon began purging alleged Communists from the news media and universities. Then the campaign spread into the private sector, where company after company began arbitrarily firing employees alleged to have links with the Communist movement. The targets included militant leaders in the movie, electric, transport, metal, and coal industries. By December 10, 1950, 537 companies had fired a total of 10,972 workers, and the government had discharged 1,196 from various agencies, according to Japanese records.[28]

The dismissals broke the spearhead of labor activism because those fired, whether Communist or not, were often leaders of unions pressing the strongest demands. There is little doubt that both the government and private industry used the red purge as a cover for ousting many who were not Communists. Among them were some of the very union organizers and officers whom SCAP had taught and encouraged only a short time earlier. SCAP certainly realized what was happening, because more than once it warned corporate managers not to use the red purge as a device for expelling men who were merely union activists. Theodore Cohen, who had shepherded the Japanese labor movement from infancy as head of SCAP's Labor Division, acknowledged in his memoirs that management had found the purge a handy rationale for rooting out forceful labor leaders. He wrote that companies gave "vague and flimsy grounds" for discharging workers and cared little for their real political views "as long as the 'troublemakers,' that is, the most active union people, were removed." Cohen's records showed that at least 22,000 persons were discharged in the red purges throughout 1950. "Although the reasons given for the discharges were uniformly for communist activity, the real reason is that those discharged were often the most energetic and effective union activists."[29]

Organized labor's strongest ranks were decimated by the purges. It is the belief of many students of that period that unions were permanently crippled after 1950 and that this fact had a lasting effect on the development of employment relations in Japan. The crushing of militant labor left managers free to deal with more malleable moderates in the movement and to hasten the development of "breakaway unions" more eager to settle disputes on companies' terms. Eiichi Ochiai, who had begun a labor career in a Toshiba plant, and who by 1949 had become an officer of the new *Sanbetsu* federation (see chapter 2), today regards the red-purge firings as the critical element in labor's decline as an independent force in Japan. It was not merely that the spirit of militancy disappeared, he said years later in an interview. He noted that the firings removed from the scene the first members of a professional corps of union organizers and collective bargainers. These were men who had developed skills in American-style wage bargaining. With their discharges, the labor movement in Japan lost its accumulated expertise. It was never able to rebuild that infrastructure, and this, Ochiai believes, explains why Japanese labor never developed along Western lines and was forced, in subsequent years, to settle for a system of cautious accommodation with management. He is certain that in the unraveling of labor power in the early 1950s, "the red purge was decisive."[30]

There were other reasons for the decline, of course. Unions launched a series of some of Japan's most bitter strikes—at Nissan Motor Co., Japan Iron and Steel, in the coal and metal industries, at shipping and electric companies. Virtually all were failures. Many of them were marked by the appearance of "breakaway unions" composed of members dissatisfied with the strike-prone militants. In union after union, rank-and-filers fought their own leaders, accusing them of placing leftist ideology and political goals above meat-and-potatoes issues. A widespread, although short-lived, "democratization" movement ensued, in which a few powerful union bosses either were ousted from office or deserted by their followers. Schisms in the new national labor federations reduced labor's political power. All of these were part of the overall decline. Japanese labor was crushed by SCAP's desertion, by the red purges, by the government's tough union-busting policy, and by disintegration within. When the smoke of those battles cleared, a more cautious and pragmatic movement began to take shape. It developed two overriding interests: workers' job security and promises of rising wages.

Meanwhile, management developed its own new agenda, along with a new sense of self-confidence. In their struggles with unionism, company officers were emboldened by the new support from both their government and SCAP. They were also, at last, beginning to turn a profit. For the first time, a considerable number of companies were earning money that could be reinvested in new plants and new technology, and this in turn produced exciting times for managers and technicians eager to rebuild and renew. Thousands of them were sent abroad, mostly to the United States, to learn the West's newest ways of manufacturing. They studied at American and European universities, visited the laboratories of General Electric and General Motors, and copied the "quality control" methods of the American expert, W. E. Deming. They bought patents and new technology designs and shipped home models of new products to be torn down and examined in their factories' labs. And they learned the strange new language of "productivity," which offered formulas for the steady lowering of the costs of making goods.

The new mood of excitement and anticipation in the business world came to be represented in a single word: "rationalization." In the general parlance of the day, it meant simply, "Catching up with the Western standard of efficiency."[31] But to the new technocrats of industry, it meant using modern machinery to increase the scale of production and hence to lower unit costs of each item manufactured. This was the key to future success, for if Japanese products could be marketed abroad at costs lower than those of the Western competition, the world would buy them—and would be opened to an unceasing flow of Japanese manufactures. Businessmen were swept up in the new rationalization movement as if introduced to some marvelous new religion. They embraced it with the same fervor with which the first Meiji-era entrepreneurs had adopted Western industrial styles in the 1880s.

But when it came time actually to introduce the new theory into Japanese factories, management ran into a wall of opposition from organized labor. Unions looked upon rationalization with dread. It presented fearful novelties—new machinery, new plants, even newly merged companies scaled to take advantage of cost reductions. To workers, the concept of greater productivity translated as either more work or fewer jobs or, at worst, both. Moreover, the Japanese word for rationalization—*gorika*—itself aroused old fears of massive unemployment. It had been the term applied in the early 1930s to the government's depression-era policy of forced mergers of failing companies and a general fat-trimming throughout industry, both of which meant fewer jobs. Union leaders with long memories, aware of MITI's desire to create a new wave of mergers, interpreted *gorika* to mean more of the same old bad medicine. They could find in it nothing of benefit for the working man. The fear of it was so intense and so widespread that for a time it seemed the idea of rationalization would serve to reunite the divided house of Japanese labor.

The result could have been an enormous debacle pitting labor against management in a protracted struggle. Instead, a grand compromise was fashioned. The elements of it were rather simply defined, although several years of negotiations were required before they were institutionalized into the new Japanese employment system. The fundamental step was a concession by labor to abandon its resistance to the companies' rationalization and cost-cutting plans. In exchange for that, management would offer a series of promises, all designed to preserve the security of those employed at the time. The most important: No jobs would be lost. If the new technology reduced the need for labor, excess workers would somehow be absorbed. They would be farmed out to subsidiaries or other companies or assigned jobs of lesser status but with identical pay. No one would be forced to leave the company until his normal age of retirement. Moreover, management would agree that wages would be increased gradually as the fruits of the new technology were realized in the form of higher profits. As the pie grew larger, so would the share received by employees. Each year of work would bring greater benefits. Finally, undergirding these arrangements there would be a system of continuous consultation between committees of workers and managers. Every change wrought by rationalization would be discussed in advance. Wage increases would still be determined through collective bargaining agreements, but everything else would be settled through what were called "joint consultations." Every phase of the company's business—its new machinery, investment strategies, market shares, foreign competition, and new-product planning—would be put on the table for talks. On the shop floor, workers and section chiefs would discuss each new change in the production cycle.

This coming to terms was not a sudden occurrence. It unfolded gradually over several years. It was a process pressed steadily by MITI to pave the way for Japan's industrial competitiveness and by the Japan Productivity Center, a remarkably energetic organization financed by business and government. The Center preached higher productivity as the key to progress and peace in the workplace as the key to higher productivity. It was the Center which, through thousands of indoctrination sessions, carved out the middle ground on which both labor and management could stand together. At first, old-guard business leaders bitterly opposed the cooperative ideals, insisting that the promises of lifetime employment and endless joint consultations were but preludes to socialism. Labor leaders, too, were initially hostile. Seigo Kojima, who was then a young left-wing militant in the metalworking trades, recalls that he and most of his peers suspected a Trojan Horse had pushed into their midst. "All of us were opposed at first," he said in an interview. "We all felt that higher productivity was just a phrase by management which would mean more work, harder work, and more production. We also thought it would mean losing jobs when the new machines came in. Productivity was a dirty word. We all felt it meant just exploitation of the labor force."[32] Months and even years of haggling preceded the first company agreements. It was the fear of mutual annihilation that finally produced results. As one of the participants in the haggling remembers, "Labor and management came to know gradually that they were in the same mud boat and that they had no life jackets. They just had to get along."

A return to the Yawata Steel Works, discussed in chapter 2, offers a revealing glimpse into the way in which these cooperative agreements were arrived at. Yawata's was one of the first settlements in a major Japanese industry, and it helped to set the example followed by others in the 1950s.

The early surge of radicalism had subsided in Yawata's labor movement after the aborted strike of 1947. By the following year the Communists had been routed. Yoshiji Miyata, the youthful firebrand of the 1947 debacle, left the party late in that year and took his place in the more moderate union that emerged. But relations with steel management continued to sour. The government had selected steel as a primary industry for national development and was preparing to pour its resources into rebuilding the destroyed or aging plants along modern Western lines. A major impediment was the poor state of labor relations and the ever-present threat of strikes. Bitterness over the red purge of 1950, when a thousand steel unionists across the country lost their jobs, made tensions worse. Then, in 1952, it seemed that the scene was set for a revival of all the old hostility. The National Federation of Steel Workers Unions launched a series of strikes in plants throughout Japan, seeking higher wages. Their "Autumn Wage Increase Struggle" unleashed a series of eleven strike "waves," each lasting twenty-four or forty-eight hours. The Yawata plant union joined in three of those waves in October and November. Its strikes were a near total failure. The company offered no monthly wage increases at all, only year-end bonuses, and served notice that it would maintain its position indefinitely.[33] Moreover, at this critical moment the company disclosed a new modernization plan which, using Western design and government loans, would transform its plant into the world's finest steel-making factory. The new plant would be constructed many miles from Yawata. It would mean either massive unemployment in Yawata or the uprooting and transfer of thousands of workers and their families.

It all seemed to be building toward chaos. There was an already weakened union bitter over past defeats and fearful of new job losses. There was a management determined to proceed with its modernization plan but resigned to the likelihood of violence if it did. Management seemed to blink first. It created a committee to manage the transfer of workers to the new plant site and cautiously suggested that the labor union join in the preparations. The committee moved on to broader issues and, to the surprise of almost everyone, offered its major concession: If the workers agreed to cooperate in establishing the modern factory, the company would assure them of a future share of the profits. And there would be no dismissals of those presently employed, for as long as their working life lasted. The offer was not spelled out in very specific terms, but it was enough to trigger an immediate breach within the union. Some favored it as the best that a weak union could hope for. Others opposed it as a company trick. The division was not along the old lines—radicals versus moderates. The split was now between those who wanted jobs saved at all costs and those who felt that the company's word was not to be trusted.

The leader of the first faction, those who agreed to accept the company's offering, was, surprisingly, none other than Miyata. The youthful revolutionary had shed his Marxist zeal and had risen in the new union's hierarchy. He had become a tough, disciplined bargainer whose domineering mannerisms had earned him the title of *Miyata Tenno*, or "Emperor Miyata." Miyata discussed the company's vague offer of compromise with many of his associates. He thought it worth a trial. If the company failed to deliver on its promises, retribution could come later in a massive strike. For the moment, the union had little to lose; it would be trading uncertain jobs for lifetime employment and a share of the profits their cooperation would generate. And there was something else, Miyata told his friends: Their country needed steel for its own revival. Without it, Japan would continue to wallow in third-rate status. He reminded those who supported him that Yawata had been founded as a national works to build Japan in the Meiji era. Now it was time to renew that spirit. By invoking patriotism, Miyata won over many fence-sitters, but others remained unconvinced. Dissidents argued that the company offer was fuzzy and unenforceable. Who could compel managers to share profits from greater productivity? How much sharing would there be of those fruits? The company had spelled out no percentage of the gains that would flow to workers. Why should it be trusted?

The issue came to a head in a union election for local secretary, a pivotal job. Miyata ran as the candidate of those willing to trust the company, at least for a while. A vote for him was a vote for labor peace founded on an admittedly undefined offer of jobs and future wage gains. A vote against him was a mark of distrust in the company. The whole notion of cooperation, a crossing of the class lines to test the idea of factory harmony, was in the balance. Miyata lost but managed to wheedle the local to hold a second election. He lost that one, too. Finally, in 1954, a third election was held and Miyata won. It changed the course of Yawata steel forever. Years later, Miyata, for the benefit of an interviewer, tried to recall what he had told his union peers to earn their support. He remembered his pitch as being an appeal based on both self-interest and national patriotism: "I told them that the rehabilitation of Japan was dependent on the recovery of the steel industry and that the Yawata union held an influential position in that recovery. To rebuild this industry, we had to modernize it. We had to believe that by cooperating with the company, we would also bring in more profits. And those profits would be shared with us as higher wages."

Many still distrusted him and demanded to know how he would enforce the shaky agreement. "I told them that we should give it a trial. If it developed that the company was not true to us, if it did not share the profits, we would get our share through power. We would strike for it. But we could never just strike against modernization. I said that we should allow this thing to go through and take the fruits later. If the company did not provide them, we could strike then."[34]

It was out of such conflicts as Yawata's that Japan's employment system evolved. There were three main ingredients: unions weakened by events but still strong enough to cause strife; a managerial class that had gained the upper hand but feared conflict in the plants; and an economic planning bureaucracy anxious to get on with modernization and strong enough to goad both labor and management into working out their problems in harmony. From the settlements that resulted flowed the elements of the cooperative system, primarily the guarantees of long-term jobs and wage scales rising with seniority of the workers.

6

●

The Business
Culture

When it was completed in 1968, the Kasumigaseki Building tow-
ered regally over the other office buildings in central Tokyo.
Thirty-five stories of aluminum, concrete, and steel built to sway safely
through earthquakes, it was Japan's first high-rise building, and it immediately became a source of national pride, a tan-and-cream-colored
symbol of economic success. It also became, partly in jest, a measure of
that success. People would boast that, for example, the number of
television sets exported abroad in a given month would fill so many
Kasumigaseki Buildings. Or they would ask how many Kasumigaseki
Buildings would be needed to contain one quarter's production of mo-
torbikes. Or beer. Less serious people like to calculate how many floors
of the Kasumigaseki Building would be needed to house one evening's
crowd of drunken businessmen stumbling out of Ginza bars.

The Kasumigaseki Building stands now as both a monument to
and a metaphor for Japan's era of rapid economic growth. The period

beginning in 1955 and stretching through booms and recessions into the seventies was a phenomenal one unmatched anytime, anywhere else on the globe. "The Japan Miracle" it was called, and aptly so. From an impoverished, war-battered nation, Japan transformed herself in less than a generation into an economic giant with strides so great that foreigners and Japanese alike were astonished. Famous economists flew in to examine the components of the miracle, probing and gauging like mechanics bedazzled by a daring new automobile. Photographers from foreign magazines, trying to capture the spirit of this phenomenon, shot pictures of sober-faced, earnest businessmen trooping out of Tokyo Station at 8:00 A.M. to begin their day. "Japan's New Samurai" was the inevitable caption.

The acceleration of the economy was so rapid and so unexpected that it dumbfounded even Japan's own economic planners. Bureaucrats in the Economic Planning Agency plotted out five-year plans, their growth lines edging cautiously upward on the graphs, only to find all of their estimates exceeded within two or three years. In 1955 they charted a five-year goal of 5 percent growth in the gross national product and called it a plan for "Economic Independence." When the five years were up, the GNP had risen by 9.1 percent. In 1957 they forecast a five-year growth of 6.5 percent; it actually came out to 10.1 percent. By 1960 the economy was rolling swiftly on its own momentum, growth begetting growth and still more growth, and the term "miracle" began to seem less fanciful than it had first sounded.

Rapid economic surges also established a political momentum that made heroes of a succession of prime ministers of the Liberal Democratic party, the conservative coalition formed in 1955 just in time to cash in on the era of unprecedented prosperity. There was one particular moment when politics and economics all came together. In 1960 Hayato Ikeda, then minister of International Trade and Industry, was attending a cabinet meeting on a day of national crisis. Radical students had invaded the Diet to protest Prime Minister Kishi's plan to push through the unpopular renewal of the United States–Japan Security Treaty. In the scuffling, a young girl, Michiko Kamba, had died. All knew that Kishi, his government's popularity at a low point, was finished. Ikeda looked to be the next prime minister. An aide, during a slow moment of the cabinet meeting, asked Ikeda what he would do as prime minister to regain public support. "Isn't it all a matter of economic policy?" Ikeda replied. "I'll go for income-doubling."[1]

"Income-doubling" was an audacious idea that had kicked around the bureaucracy for many months, the brainstorm principally of Osamu

Shimomura, Ikeda's economic advisor. Shimomura had calculated that, given the pace of growth since the early fifties, Japan's national income could be doubled during the sixties, and he had projected average annual growth rates of 7.2 percent to make that happen. Other economists in the government thought this plan far too optimistic, and Kishi had balked at endorsing it. But Ikeda, when he succeeded Kishi, seized it like a life raft and proclaimed it his own, calling it a policy of "virtuous growth" and hoping that it would provide his administration with a sense of stability and purpose after the nasty business over the security treaty. Others scoffed when he adopted it. Even Konosuke Matsushita, the incurably optimistic electronics pioneer, thought Ikeda rash and his plan dangerous. He felt that "people had got so carried away with the idea of rapid economic growth that they had forgotten the importance of building a healthy economy."[2] W. W. Lockwood, the noted British economist who usually marveled at Japan's achievements, was harshly skeptical. Writing when the plan was a few years old and the outcome unknown, Lockwood dismissed the idea of a decade of 7.2 percent growth, insisting that it could "hardly be more than a charting of hopes and expectations."[3] All were wrong. Growth in the sixties actually averaged 10.4 percent, and national income was more than doubled.

It was natural, then, that in this triumphant period Japanese began to define themselves in economic terms. Business became not merely a national passion but the national identity. Japanese embraced the drama of business growth with the single-mindedness that other countries devoted, for example, to newly won democracy or to a new religion. They forgot about the war, the prewar glories, and the postwar despair. Everything was "now" and "the future." It was as if Japan had no past, had been, in fact, created on some day in the 1950s. The measures of success, of national greatness, were found in economic statistics that daily dominated the main pages of newspapers—figures on production of steel, value of exports, employment rolls, business investment, productivity rates. As the fifties and sixties rolled by, a kind of national economic scoreboard kept the tally up-to-date. Japan had the world's eighth largest economy. Then the fifth. Then the third. It seems, in reading the popular articles and books that flowed forth to extol this relentless advance, that business was all that mattered. Japan had become a Business Culture.

And how it paid off. For two decades the Japanese economy raced ahead at a pace the world had never seen. Between 1951 and 1973, despite a couple of serious recessions, the economy grew at an annual average rate of 10 percent. In roughly the same period, real wages tripled. By the mid-sixties Japan was an object of marvel by foreign authorities. Japanese businessmen today still recall the thrill that passed through their circles in 1966 when *The Economist*, the British magazine that they considered a bible, awarded its world's-best-economy prize to Japan. Western economists competed with differing explanations for the astonishing success. Many kept returning to one fact: Japan was pouring more money each year into reinvestment in new machines and technology than any other country. They had built the most modern factories and crammed them with the most productive machinery, all at a rate never before recorded. It could all be traced to that fateful period of the mid-fifties when Japan's near-chaotic labor relations were replaced by the agreements that guaranteed workers' jobs in exchange for management's right to introduce the latest technology. In retrospect, nothing was more important. The largest payoff had come in the decade between the mid-sixties and mid-seventies, when the total private and public investment in business equaled an astonishing 40 percent of the gross national product. A sober analysis, one of the best foreign studies of the Japan phenomenon, was *Asia's New Giant*, published in 1976. It found the quantity of funds that businessmen had reinvested in their own plant amazing, unprecedented. "This is the most impressive investment performance ever achieved in any peacetime, democratic, market economy," its authors observed. "No other such industrialized nation has voluntarily plowed back such a high share of output into further expansion."[4]

No one seemed more surprised by the sheer scale of economic growth than the Japanese themselves. The first surprise came between December 1954 and June 1957, when there occurred the first large expansion that could not be attributed to foreign aid or the market stimulation that came with the Korean War procurements. Commentators dubbed it the *Jimmu bumu* (boom), a jesting reference to the legendary first emperor, *Jimmu*, who supposedly reigned from 660 to 585 B.C. To denote a three-and-a-half-year expansion that ended in December 1961, they reached even further back in time to call it the *Iwato bumu*, a reference to a bright period in the time of the wholly mythological sun goddess, Amaterasu. The even more remarkable five-year surge that ended in June 1970 provoked more searches for mythological heroes. It was called the *Izanagi bumu*, after one of the storybook deities who created the islands of Japan.

More pragmatically, the Japanese measured off their ascent in terms of what their enhanced salaries and twice-yearly bonuses would buy for them. For in a few short years, the nation had moved from poverty and hunger to a consumer society. The housewives who in 1950 were selling off family kimonos and rummaging in the countryside for sweet potatoes were by 1960 beginning to stock their homes with all the contrivances poured out by the country's factories. Television sets, washing machines, and refrigerators were so prized that they were inevitably called the "three sacred treasures;" by the mid-sixties they were common appliances. When the decade of the sixties began, Japan's narrow streets contained few automobiles; it was still a bicycle and subway society. When the decade ended, almost everyone who wanted one had a car. By then the "three sacred treasures" had been replaced with another phrase to describe what everyone sought. They were the "Three C's": Car, Cooler (air conditioning), and Color television. Prosperity was so widespread, so equally diffused, that once again commentators in the news media looked back in time for a historical nickname that would sum it up and lend perspective. They settled finally on the *Genroku* period (1688–1704), that time when the cities of Osaka, Kyoto, and Edo (now Tokyo) first began to bustle with commerce and townsmen began to indulge themselves in extravagances. The sixties went down in newspaper accounts as the era of *Showa Genroku* (*Showa* being the name of Emperor Hirohito's reign).

The prosperity induced by the business culture was a powerful unifying force in Japan. It tended to blur and muffle those divisions and animosities that were the hangover of fourteen years of war and nearly seven years of foreign occupation. In the late 1940s Japan had appeared at times to be on the brink of genuine class conflict, Marxism having grown so popular that the threat of revolt briefly dominated men's minds. Most of that faded with the prosperity of the sixties, as Japanese blended into a vast middle class. The Japan Socialist party declined in public approval (although, curiously, the Japan Communist party maintained the allegiance of a steady 5 percent of the public). Even the rhetoric of class conflict subsided, except on those ritualistic "strike" days when workers in red-lettered headbands marched through the streets in their perennial show of solidarity. Marxism retained its lure for academics, it is true, but outside of academia, the traces were hard to find. College radicalism was a phase to be tolerated while it lasted. As a popular saying expressed it: "Anyone who is not a Marxist in college is a fool. Anyone who is a Marxist after college is an idiot."

The business culture also interred much of the hostility generated in the fifties by Japan's acquiescence in the American security treaty. That hostility had exploded into large demonstrations in 1960, when the Diet was called upon to ratify a ten-year renewal. The near riots cost

Kishi his tenure as prime minister. But thereafter opposition to the treaty ebbed. The American presence was accepted as an essential trade-off for the new prosperity which, after all, was due in part to Washington's aid and its support of the international trading system. Many Japanese still resented the treaty and U.S. military bases, which so visibly defined their dependence on a foreign government, but the passions of the past almost disappeared. The young students who had invaded the Diet in 1960 to protest that dependence emerged as model salarymen and bureaucrats in pursuit of the Three C's. By the mid-seventies anti-Americanism was no longer a radicalizing or divisive force.

Aside from the all-smothering prosperity it wrought, the business culture succeeded as a reunifying force because it revived a sense of Japanese nationalism. The drive toward economic security and affluence was often couched in patriotic slogans reminiscent of the early Meiji period. When Yoshiji Miyata in 1954 urged reluctant steel workers to accept the bargain management was offering—job security in exchange for productivity increases—he did so in part by playing to their nationalistic feelings: Japan could not be strong again without a steel industry, he said. There was in these exhortations, too, a revival of that Japan-against-the-world sentiment that seems always to lie not far below the surface. Professor Chalmers Johnson has called attention to a period in 1961 when a sense of crisis was dominant in business circles because of Western demands that Japan liberalize her markets to allow more foreign imports. Many saw business expansion threatened and Japan reduced again to the status of a minor commercial nation. The press theatrically warned of the "Second Coming of the Black Ships" (an allusion to Commodore Perry's fleet of 1853) and wrote of the necessary "readying of the Japanese economy for a bloodstained battle between national capital and foreign capital." Even a respected MITI bureaucrat called for a "national general mobilization" similar to the militarization decrees of 1938, to ward off foreign competition.[5]

The public accepted these nationalizing appeals. Labor unions in the sixties counseled restraint in wage demands of their own members with patriotic statements: Japan's companies had to remain competitive with foreign ones, and wage rates were part of the contest. School-children learned the litany of restraint: "Japan is a small, island country without natural resources, and it must trade to survive." Even the imperial system was at times invoked to sustain support for the business culture. In 1964 an officer of *Nikkeiren*, the Japan Employers' Association, made a speech to industrial leaders. His topic was the nature of the commitment that business managers ought to bring to their jobs. His formula was a mix of patriotism and racism:

> These four islands, though narrow in their geographical expanse, are our territories. Inside these, the Japanese race alone, with an emperor as the nation's symbol, and with no mingling of other races, is making a living, the people's psychological base depending on the emperor as the nation's symbol. There is no other example of such unique nationality. This nationality must, and will, be maintained. Since it is within this framework that the economy develops and enterprises are managed, the answer to the question of what ought to be the state of enterprises and what is the right attitude of managers will become self-evident. Our task, therefore, is to write down that answer.[6]

The literature of the high-growth period and interviews with Japanese caught up in its business culture are replete with examples of people who felt they were serving a national purpose through their work or that the national purpose defined how work was to be done. To an extraordinary extent they felt that their own welfare was bound up with the nation's. A retired businessman described for me, in 1988, how he had sensed this when he set off in the fifties for his first overseas assignment as a representative of a trading company:

> I felt—we all felt then—in part that we were going abroad to help the country. Japan was very short of foreign exchange in those days. Without earning foreign currencies we could not endure. It was very hard going to Europe in the early fifties. I could not take my wife along, because the company could not afford to buy the British pounds to support us both. I was given a monthly allowance of only five hundred dollars a month to live and travel on. But we all felt that we were kind of like soldiers in the front lines. Out there earning the foreign exchange to help the country.[7]

Looking back on that remarkable period, one is struck by its absence of heroes. It was not an age of tycoons, and stories of individual achievements in the world of industry were rare. A few names stand out, like those of Konosuke Matsushita, whose personality and strong paternalistic sense are still closely identified with his electronics company's name, and Akio Morita, who built Sony's international reputation. But they are the exceptions. The public's idols were the companies themselves—Hitachi, Toshiba, Nippon Steel, Mitsubishi, Mitsui, and the rest. It was the period when the new Japanese company came into being, an organization different in many ways from what it had been in the past and in just as many ways from what the rest of the world had known. Many famous old names survived—Mitsui was a great trading and financial house a century earlier—but the structure and character of the Japanese corporation was changed forever in the postwar years.

●

The prewar *zaibatsu* were for the most part creations of strong-willed individuals whose restless energies had been unleashed by the Meiji-era's commitment to rapid industrial growth. Some resembled the "buccaneers" of a similar period in American life, and quite a few launched their enterprises under clouds of scandals involving government favors. As Japan grew and prospered, their names became legendary. Yataro Iwasaki, who came from a poor farming family, began the mighty Mitsubishi empire out of his trading company, which prospered by undercutting and bankrupting rivals. Eiichi Shibusawa personally founded more than three hundred enterprises, including the highly successful Osaka Spinning Mill, and his philosophy of business as a social institution made him famous. The electrical products giant, Hitachi, Ltd., grew out of a small repair shop started in 1910 by Namihei Odaira, who, until he was purged by SCAP in 1947, was widely known as an industrial pioneer. They were influential figures, these early bankers and industrialists, most of them known for personal, paternalistic, and authoritarian styles of management.

Gradually, the old tycoons died off, but the empires they had spawned remained in place as family-controlled corporations. Large clans owned the shares of principal companies, which in turn owned those of affiliates. The greatest of the *zaibatsu* controlled their own banks, their own trading arms, and all of the smaller affiliates that supplied them or that branched out into new fields of industry. From a central family headquarters came all of the important decisions on staff personnel, relations with labor, the use of capital, and periodic expansions. In the 1920s and 1930s the first professional staffs began to appear in the bigger houses. They were composed of men chosen not for family connections but for their education and technical expertise. But they were hired hands only. Decisions still flowed from the top and their capacity for innovation was limited. Japan went to war with a handful of family-controlled industrial and financial powerhouses drawn into the service of the imperial state.

The era of the family corporate empire ended with the Occupation, crushed under the populist crusade led by MacArthur. Viewed from SCAP headquarters as vestiges of imperial Japan, despite the fact that many of the old *zaibatsu* families had opposed the war, the companies were disestablished by sweeping edicts. Ten large clan-controlled combines were split up, along with another fifty-six family-owned enterprises. Hundreds were purged as war conspirators—by one reckoning, one out of every four top-line business executives was removed from his position. Stockholdings were dispersed and bank connections severed. As the pieces of the old empires drifted along through the tumultuous late-1940s, middle-level executives rose swiftly to fill management vacuums. They made history. For the first time, the engines of Japanese industry were controlled by professional managers. It was they who steered Japan through the first stages of economic growth, and it was they who established the new style of Japanese management. As it turned out, their ideas, like the corporate structures within which they operated, were far different from those of their predecessors. When SCAP's trust-busting fervor faded and its Anti-Monopoly Law was gutted, the fragments were regrouped into new combinations, often with the same old names. But the men who ran them and the rules by which they acted were new.

The most important difference was the large degree of freedom exercised by the new managers. They followed the old *zaibatsu* rule of choosing directors from within the company, but it was the new professional managers—not family elders—who selected them. Companies thus began to rule themselves, because the directors chosen were invariably drawn from senior management ranks. Outside stockholders had little influence. Share ownership was diffused widely at first; later, companies within the large groupings purchased one another's shares. Stockholder meetings, dominated by the inside managers, became ritualized events. For a decade or more, the new company mandarins were responsible only to themselves and to the government. MITI and the Ministry of Finance were like senior partners, forcing the companies to follow the guidelines they laid down and controlling their capital, their foreign exchange, and their acquisitions of foreign technology. But gradually the companies outgrew even them. They no longer needed government capital—their affiliated banks supplied any investment funds they could not generate themselves. Bureaucratic controls were eliminated one by one, although MITI continued to hover watchfully over one and all. Before the high-growth cycle was over, Japan's new corporations were free to do what they wanted in the marketplace, their managers responsible, in most cases of any importance, to no one but themselves.

The company, in short, became a self-contained community that largely created its own dynamics and made up its own rules as it raced along. It defined its own goals and the strategies to attain them. It resembled a Western corporation in that professional managers made key decisions, but there the similarity ended. The Japanese company operated in pursuit of the interests of those who ran it and worked in it—not in the interests of stockholders or outside directors. It could decide for itself what went on the bottom line. It became, in the classic phrase, "Our Company." As in any self-contained community, the members' benefits came first. Two guiding principles emerged to define those interests.

The first was that perpetuation and expansion of "Our Company" was the most important pursuit. It must secure its place in the competitive world, and it must organize itself for constant growth. The practical consequences of this was that vast shares of corporate profits were set aside for reinvestment and technological improvement. To that end, salaries and other forms of compensation were held to comparatively low levels. The major reward would be the fact of belonging to the company itself. Wearing the company uniform or the company lapel pin conferred great prestige. Rising through promotion within the company's ranks, not salary, was the mark of achievement.

The second principle, which flowed from the first, was that the company's internal harmony must be preserved at all costs. All must believe that their interests were those of the company, that they would prosper or suffer individually in accordance with the company's destiny. Loyalty to "Our Company" must always come first. Despite the claims of some Japanologists that "company loyalty" is an inherited trait, that it is simply an aspect of instinctive Japanese "groupism," there is little in the country's industrial history to cite as evidence. Prewar companies were authoritarian complexes; only a few endeavored to capture a worker's enduring loyalties. Internal harmony and loyalty are a part of the dynamics of the new corporate structure that arose after the war.

My first encounter with the phenomenon was in 1978 when, as an American news reporter, I set out to discover what had happened to some Kawasaki Steel Company workers who, with the industry in decline, had become redundant. I found a group of them on temporary "loan" at an auto factory, placed there by Kawasaki, which still paid most of their wages. An American worker would simply have been laid off. But Tatsuo Fujisaki, who had worked for Kawasaki for twenty-seven years, still thought of himself as a "Kawasaki man." His company even managed to see that his paychecks at the new company came in a Kawasaki envelope. I asked him if his new job on an auto assembly line had caused any personal problems. He thought deeply for several moments, then answered without a hint of artifice. He was worried, he said, that he might make mistakes in the new job that would reflect poorly on the name and prestige of his "real" company, Kawasaki Steel.

The response did not mean that Mr. Fujisaki was expressing some unique Japanese character trait, some feudal-loyalty hangover, as some Japanologists would assert. It did mean that he was emotionally committed to Kawasaki Steel. Why? Nothing puzzles foreigners more about Japan than this peculiar streak of company worship. It is often dismissed as yet another example of a Japanese "groupism" inherited at birth. Even sophisticated Japanese who scoff at popular theories of Japanese uniqueness often admit they cannot explain it. I once asked a Nissan Motor Company executive for his opinion. He confessed he had never found an entirely adequate explanation. He thought it was somehow bound up with the end of emperor worship. Japanese had been so fiercely loyal to the imperial system that when it was destroyed in 1945 they needed to transfer their intense commitment to some other institution. The company, he thought, had filled that need. An air of mystery still exists around the issue of company loyalty. But interviews with Japanese and the studies of several academic researchers suggest at least two plausible explanations. The first is that for rootless postwar Japanese, the company emerged as the strongest socializing institution, the one that gave them a new sense of belonging. The second is that loyalty was in large part deliberately engineered by company managers through education in "Our Company" values.

The genesis of both these theories lay in a demographic change of immense proportions that swept postwar Japan, especially in the period from the mid-fifties to the mid-sixties. It was the time of Japan's great urbanization, when millions of young men left farms for the cities to find jobs. The pace was extremely rapid. Between 1955 and 1965 the number of family-farm workers in the countryside decreased by 3 million persons, about one-third of the rural work force. W. W. Lockwood called this conversion from rural to urban life "a turn of revolutionary significance." The young men and boys who streamed into Tokyo, Osaka, Kawasaki, and other cities on the industrialized coast of Japan were to become the nucleus of the urban labor force that manned factories in the high-growth years. But they first arrived as country bumpkins. They had no experience in life in a vast city, no social or family ties, no friends. A large number of them were fresh from high schools and middle schools. For them the company was not merely a place of work but an all-encompassing social institution, their home away from home. The company offered to fill all their needs. It gave them a room in a company dormitory, a living wage, playgrounds for recreation, friends from similar backgrounds, even, on many occasions, wives to marry. Most of all, it gave them a place in a solid institution that structured their lives as completely as the Imperial Army had formed those of the poor farm boys adrift in the 1930s. Professor Yasumitsu Nihei of Keio University, who has studied the phenomenon extensively, believes the concept of company loyalty was born of those circumstances:

> It was in the sixties that this "groupism" really developed. Some people argue that it developed out of Japanese culture, but it actually grew out of the conditions of those times. These young men who joined companies then got their sense of identity as members of a group which was stable and long-lived. This was the company. They identified with their companies as their place in life.[9]

The young newcomers were like gifts from heaven for Japanese companies that had struggled through the years of labor militancy. They were green and malleable, searching for security and a place to put down roots and generally willing to surrender their individuality in pursuit of stable lives and decent pay. In the argot of the day, they were known as "golden eggs," so highly was their untutored talent prized. Competition to find and hire them became intense. Corporate personnel agents roamed the countryside recruiting them from high and middle schools. Sometimes they bribed teachers to recommend their firms to the most earnest students. The more remote the village, the better the recruiting grounds, because its sons were least likely to have been infected by the radical union virus of the preceding decade.

Brought to the city factories, the "golden eggs" were hatched into a community specially contrived to earn their loyalties. Rodney Clark, a British businessman who examined Japanese company life, has left a vivid description of the young recruits' reception into a Yokohama factory owned by a medium-sized corrugated box company, which he disguised under the name of "Marumaru."[10] Their arrival was treated as a cross between a coming-of-age ceremony and initiation into an American college fraternity. Three personnel executives fetched the boys from their rural villages, even paying the cost of transportation for parents who wished to come watch their sons' induction. The families were met at Tokyo Station by a gaily decorated bus that whisked them to the Yokohama plant. In a hall draped with bunting, the new *shakai-jin* (a term for anyone formally accepted into society) were greeted by the top management and given lectures on the company's proud history. Later, they were taken to their new homes, the company's dormitories, and handed over to "elder brothers"—veteran employees who would instruct them on proper company behavior and escort them on company-financed trips to Mount Fuji and tours of Tokyo's nightlife. Only after several days of such regal treatment were they introduced to the machines they would operate. (Ironically, by 1971, when Clark described this rite of passage, company loyalty already seemed a waning principle. Many of these recruits, aware of their value in a tight job market, soon left "Marumaru" for better jobs.)[11]

It was in such rites that the engineering of company loyalty began, and the process never really ceased. Throughout his life employment, the Japanese worker was admonished to look upon his company as a family and to work for its advancement accordingly. Many firms owned rustic training centers where, away from urban distractions, employees were subjected to high-voltage motivational sessions centering on their obligations to the company. In their severity some resembled cult movements like the Moonies or the Children of God, and often they provided a quasi-religious indoctrination. The most extreme programming sessions stressed the theme that the young worker was shedding his old life of freedom and frivolity for the disciplined ways of company and adult society. He was to consider himself reborn. This nearly mystical theme of rebirth, common among Western fundamentalist religions, was pounded home by company lecturers. Here is a steel company president addressing white-collar employees in the fifties:

> Not only is there the fact that our life's work is our employ-
> ment in our company, but I feel that as people in this situation
> we have two occasions that can be called "birth." The first is
> when we are born into the world as mewling infants. The
> second is when we all receive our commissions of adoption
> into the company. This is an event that has the same impor-
> tance as our crying birth.[12]

The worker's rewards for accepting this notion of rebirth were considerable. His new community was a vast social support network that replaced his lost village network of family, friends, and school. It supplied all that he needed, materially and emotionally. If single, he moved into a company dormitory where rent was low. He ate his meals at the company cafeteria, played baseball on the company's sports grounds, was treated for illness at a company clinic, and shopped at company-subsidized discount stores. His company foreman might help him find a mate, and after marriage he would move with his bride into a rent-subsidized home. His children might be educated on company loans. Small company gifts arrived on the birth of a child. It was all enormously costly to the company, but it was an investment made on the assumption that it would bind worker to company throughout his useful life. R. P. Dore, the British scholar who closely examined Hitachi in 1970, reported that the company's expenditures on such benefits amounted to 8.5 percent of its total labor costs. The comparable proportion expended by a British company was about 2.5 percent.[13]

The natural effect of all this was to fasten the employee firmly to his work group and to loosen his attachments to others. At lunch he ate with colleagues, and after work, he joined them on the recreation fields. Nights out in the bars were invariably spent with coworkers. For the woman employee, there were ikebana classes, attended in groups from her section in the company. The reborn worker's attachments to outside institutions were few and weak. Dore found that only 14 percent of Hitachi employees belonged to any social or political organizations outside those sponsored by the company. Only a fifth had not attended some kind of company social function in the previous year.[14] Even an employee's attachment to his real family became, in time, almost negligible. Work, commuting, and drinking or playing with coworkers consumed almost all of his waking hours. A common jest of the sixties was that the company man spoke only four phrases a day to his wife: *Kaita* ("I'm home"), *Meshi da* ("Meal"), *Furo da* ("Bath"), and *Neru zo* ("Sleep").

The company also took responsibility for the worker's character development. Lecturers and motivational experts exhorted him to lead an honest, productive life that would be a credit to his company's name. Dore observed that several Japanese companies financed an "Ethical Society" that developed programs of moral uplift. Part of its initiation pledge declared, "A world without kindness is grim; a world without sweat is decadent." Dore also noted that corporations preached that hard work was its own reward and that the size of the paycheck was of lesser importance. The "success books" popularized in that period disparaged the mere trophies of one's career. "Real success does not come to those who concentrate on the emoluments," Dore wrote of those themes. "These books do not dwell on the glamor and glitter of the rewards; the emphasis is all on the virtuous travelling rather than the arrival. Hard work and perseverance have a value far beyond their instrumental efficacy."[15] An enormous amount of time and preparation went into this molding of virtuous minds, especially young ones. There seemed to be constant fretting that untutored workers might stray from the right path. When, in 1965, Konosuke Matsushita introduced the five-day work week in his electronics plants, he was most concerned that the extra free time might not be used constructively. The company, he wrote, must fill this new void with still more instruction in the productive life:

> Rather than simply squandering the time on amusement, they should be encouraged to devote time to study and self-improvement—to make them better at their jobs as well as more responsible members of a democratic society. We are not "Big Brother"; but we should make an effort to give advice wherever it ought to be given—to lead them in the appropriate direction. [16]

The belief that young new employees must be treated as children being born into a new world still prevails in many of Japan's companies. Like ever-watchful grannies, personnel officers instruct, admonish, and encourage the fledgling in every aspect of his business and private life as if he were a toddler. In 1989 Fuji Bank presented its "life-learning message" to new employees in the form of a comic book based on a popular children's television cartoon character named "Ultraman." A robotlike spaceman, "Ultraman" performs his earthly feats, such as killing monsters, in spurts of activity lasting precisely three minutes. The Fuji Bank comic book urges the new recruit to model his life on "Ultraman." He should rise three minutes earlier each morning, read newspaper headlines for three minutes, limit his business phone calls to three minutes, use three minutes a day to study high-technology office equipment, stretch and relax periodically for three-minute intervals, and restrict the reading time of his office memos to three minutes. At the end of the working day, the employee should take three minutes to shift his mental gears, which means forgetting about work and preparing for an evening of sport and relaxation.

More than paternalism was involved in all this concern for the worker's virtue. In the early years especially, when memories of radical unionism still haunted management, indoctrination served a political purpose. The ideology of "Our Company" was offered as an alternative to the lure of communism still being preached by some in the labor movement. Loyalty to company and coworkers was transformed into a system of belief that could serve to insulate the "golden eggs" from Marxism. The Japan Productivity Center urged corporations and their dependent subcontractors to hold "ethics" seminars, which were explicitly designed to discourage Communist leanings. "We encouraged managers to have not just technical training but ethical training as well," recalls Kichinosuke Yamazaki, who worked for many years at the Center and, when interviewed in 1989, was its senior advisor. "We trained them in what we thought of as the true ethics of productivity, in part to help them oppose communism. We felt it was important that the companies give their employees something they could believe in."[17] Political thought in general was disparaged, and the only "ism" that was encouraged was companyism. The true brotherhood of labor lay not in socialism but in the group harmony of the workplace, where each man was loyal to his fellow workers. Inspirational sessions in the plant commonly ended with the following chant:

> Let us work together.
> Let us play together.
> Let us laugh together.
> Let us cry together.

The idea of "Our Company" became an all-embracing creed preached through hundreds of company songs, chants, and poems, most of them constructed on the intellectual level of a twelve-year-old boy. (The tone of many seems drawn from a Westerner's boy scout handbook.) A common theme was that the company itself was the source of all virtues. Hard work, loyalty, sincerity, and the like were depicted as company virtues, as if they were not to be found in the world outside. "The first principle of our firm is 'sincerity' " declared an essay entitled "The Guiding Spirit of Hitachi," published in 1959 for trainees. "To deceive neither others nor oneself, to act always in sincerity of heart, sincerity of mind—these are the fundamental moral principles for all employees to observe." Sometimes racial pride was a subtheme. It was woven together with "sincerity" in "The Hitachi Song," an inspirational call to duty:

> With a sincerity that pierces steel,
> Unflaggingly we strive.
> Difficulties we overcome, treading the thorny path.

The spirit of Hitachi carries us forward,
Conscious of the honor of our race.
Already we are world-famed Hitachi.
. . . Forward to new fields with burning zeal,
The youthful blood of Hitachi courses in our veins.[18]

Whether the Japanese employee was greatly swayed by all of these attempts to engineer his loyalty is a matter of conjecture. The official version, of course, is that he thrived on his superiors' guidance and buckled down happily to work. However, foreign researchers who studied factories and offices closely in the sixties raised many doubts. They found that many of the motivational lectures were received with disinterest or cynicism. They also observed that among young workers, especially the city-bred, the indoctrination had little effect in binding them to their companies. Turnover rates in those age groups were rather high, particularly in periods of extreme labor shortages, when many companies were bidding for their services. When the actual turnover rates of all workers were examined, the Japanese system did not seem all that different from those in the West. A study in the early sixties by the Organisation for Economic Cooperation and Development found that the turnover rate in all manufacturing enterprises in Japan was only slightly lower than that of England and West Germany. It was, however, markedly lower than that of the United States.[19]

Overall, the conventional view of the loyal Japanese worker—happily employed, immersed in company benefits, and secure for life—does not fit the facts of the time. It is in part a myth perpetuated by Japanese culturalists and foreign Japanologists. For one thing, it approximated conditions in only a part of the industrial system—namely, those large companies with deep pockets and profits great enough to pay for loyalty through the bad times. The rest of Japan's labor market was more chaotic. In medium- and small-sized firms, layoffs were common in hard times and turnover high in good ones. Benefits were few and thinly spread. There was a corresponding gap between large and small firms in the degree of employee loyalty. Robert E. Cole, an American sociologist and labor expert, conducted studies in both a large and a small firm and found substantial differences in workers' attitudes. In the smaller one, a Tokyo die-casting firm, the workers were urban born and markedly independent, prone to strikes over wages and possessed of a cynical, even hostile, view of both the company and the union. In the large auto-parts plant that Cole studied, where the labor force was rurally recruited, blue-collar workers identified closely with the company. Employees in the small company refused flatly to accept a rule mandating overtime work when the company thought it necessary. Those in the larger firm never even questioned it.[20]

Cole's and other studies that focused on what actually went on in Japanese plants found personnel complaining about the same things their counterparts overseas did. They griped about the poor quality of job training, boring work, underused abilities, and—to a striking degree—mental fatigue associated with long hours of forced overtime. (Two-thirds of all manufacturing workers registered that complaint in a 1971 government survey.) They objected to the constant transfers between company plants, which were wrecking their home lives. Promotions were unfair, too often achieved by flattering the boss. Disgruntled workers described how they were forced into humiliating demotions or subjected to pressures to quit the company entirely. Companies tried to reduce the disharmony by sponsoring "good human relations" events. Rodney Clark found those at the "Marumaru" factory to be uncomfortably strained. Despite the superficial appearance of harmony, Clark uncovered a surprising degree of distrust and jealousy among the workers:

> The contrast between the superficial impression of determined amity and the underlying contention and resentment among these . . . employees was very great. By the time I left "Marumaru," departments that had once seemed to be models of "good human relations" had been revealed to be full of animosities and spites. Sections whose members were always to be seen together in bars, and in which the senior men were continually inviting their juniors home, proved to be beset with bitter rivalries, or to contain boorish superiors or sly subordinates who caused difficulties for everyone else.[21]

Clark's observations of discontent in "Marumaru" were supported by a large number of detailed surveys conducted in the fifties, sixties, and seventies. Taken together, they suggest that the familiar theme of devotion to company has been much exaggerated and that the figure of the happy, loyal worker is more myth than fact. Most of these studies, which relied on personal interviews, registered rather high levels of worker dissatisfaction and indicated that male workers grew more dissatisfied as the high-growth period progressed. In 1971 a Ministry of Labor publication reported that 46 percent of all blue-collar workers were dissatisfied with their jobs and only 41 percent were satisfied.[22] In the same year a prime minister's office survey found 60 percent expressing either slight discontent or deep dissatisfaction, with most complaining of low wages, long working hours, and poor working conditions. Unhappiness seemed most pronounced in the very assembly-line plants that were the mainstays of Japanese manufacturing competitiveness. In an electrical appliance plant, 48 percent said they were, on the whole, dissatisfied with their jobs; the proportions were lower in a shipbuilding and a sake-making firm.[23] In general, the dissatisfaction rates were higher than in American and European factories of that era. One of the most puzzling surveys, and one that throws great doubt on the whole theory of harmony and company loyalty, was R. P. Dore's comparison of worker attitudes in a Hitachi plant and in comparable plants in England and Italy. Dore's key question was whether or not the workers believed their employers to be good ones. At Hitachi, then and now a model Japanese company, only 39 percent thought their company a good one. In contrast, the percentage approving of their employers was 71 percent and 89 percent in the Italian and English plants, respectively.[24]

Studies also exist that suggest that workers who were pleased with their employment early in their careers grew more disenchanted as time passed. And those drawn into jobs later in that period were less satisfied with their companies than those who had been in at the beginning. Four surveys were conducted in a large steel company during the period from 1952 to 1963. The percentage of workers expressing feelings of loyalty to the company declined steadily from 54 in 1952 to 26 in 1963. The proportion voicing criticism of the company increased from 18 percent to 44 percent in the same period of time. It would seem that the "golden eggs," once hatched, came to consider their new environment with less contentment.[25]

All of the positive inducements of paternalism—the promise of job security, a plenitude of benefits, efforts at plant solidarity—did not, in fact, seem to produce the devoted worker of legend. Yet these employees did work hard, eschewed strikes, and talked of spending their lives in company uniforms. There were reasons for these commitments that had nothing to do with company songs and comforting benefits. To such encouragements the companies could add an array of subtle and not-so-subtle pressures. The most obvious pressure flowed from the fact that once in the company, it was not easy to get out. Although younger workers might be able to shop around for jobs, older ones could not. The dividing line was about age thirty. Rodney Clark called the older ones the "Immobiles" because they had the least chance to move out of the company. One reason was what seems to have been a gentleman's agreement among firms not to steal competitors' workers. Another was that any worker's capacity for loyalty was suspect if he had once quit a respected enterprise. The risks of disloyalty, then, were much greater than for workers in the West. Quitting meant surrendering not only the safety and comfort of the company's paternalism but the support network of friends and associations that formed one's private life. The relatively few who attempted mid-career transfers found friendships difficult to achieve in the new company.

Large companies also worked through peer pressure to engineer both loyalty and plant productivity. Managers publicly posted the production records of each worker, so that a slacker's shortcomings would be noted by his colleagues. Small cash awards were handed out to those who took only minimal vacations or who cut their holidays short so as not to upset production schedules. It was, moreover, common practice to transfer employees from plant to plant regardless of the effect on family life. The ostensible purpose of transfers was to impress the employee with the reality of working for a large community, not merely a single factory. But the practice also compelled even greater reliance on the firm as a social institution. Transferred to a distant plant, his wife and children usually left at home, the worker could make few friends in strange surroundings, and his life was even more tightly bound to that of the company. In the firm Rodney Clark studied, 10 percent of the work force was transferred each year.

The union offered only occasional relief from these conformist pressures. Usually it worked closely with management to increase production or assure stability and was itself instrumental in reinforcing peer pressure against recalcitrant workers. I witnessed one brutalizing example of the process during a visit to the Sumitomo Heavy Industries shipyard in Yokosuka in 1979. Japanese shipyards were in a deep recession caused by Korean competition, and Sumitomo had hatched a plan to reduce wage costs by cutting older workers from the payroll. The company union had gone along with the plan because it permitted most men to stay employed, but a deep and rancorous split had emerged between younger and older workers. Seniors in the shipyard resisted the plan and were daily harassed and jeered by younger colleagues. One of the older holdouts was a man named Morita, who had adamantly refused to accept a plan that terminated his job. He had been gradually isolated by colleagues and led a solitary life in the plant. One day, Morita was seated at his lunch table, alone as usual. At a signal, a shrill blast on a whistle, nearly 150 workers filed over to his table and formed a ring around him. Over and over they shouted, "Morita—quit the company. Morita—quit the company."

Out of all of these forces—paternalistic inducements, peer pressure, constant exhortations to measure up—emerged Japan's Company Man. His company affiliation occupied almost all of his time, formed almost all of his personal identity. He called it the *uchi*, a word that literally means "house" but that in the broad social context refers to one's organization and its set of values. His *uchi* defined his place in society. Employment with a large, secure, and widely known company marked him as a man to be respected, regardless of what he did within its walls. Its size and respectability determined his social acceptance. Men with familiar lapel pins or shop uniforms found it easier to obtain home mortgages. Their daughters tried to marry into families affiliated with companies of similar status. With the uniform or lapel pin, a man drank with friends on company money (it was called "lubricating oil" because the entertainment fund supposedly reinforced on-the-job harmony) and belonged to golf clubs otherwise far beyond his means. Without those symbols, he was a poorer man, in more ways than mere wages. "The larger the organization, the more respect the person is accorded, irrespective of personal qualities," writes a Japanese economist, Iwao Nakatani. "And by the same token, a person who works for a small and weak organization is looked down upon. Such is the sad reality of Japan."[26]

The company uniform did not transform the Japanese worker of the sixties into a mindless automation. But it did instill, especially after a certain age when his mobility was restricted, a sense of dependence on the company for both his material and psychological well-being. The company could be both paternalistically generous and officiously intrusive in its engineering of employee loyalty. Both traits worked to convince the employee that his obedience was required. It was his company, right or wrong, and far more than the Western worker, he came to regard the company as the center of his life. In 1962 two researchers conducted attitudinal surveys of both American and Japanese workers and noted among the latter signs of a strong emotional dependency. Sixty-six percent of the Japanese acknowledged that they looked upon their companies as either the central concern of their lives or as a concern at least equal in importance to their personal lives. Only 23 percent of the Americans felt that way. The Japanese workers' expectations of what the company should provide were extraordinarily high. For example, 75 percent felt the company should either find them wives or at least advise them in their searches. Only 5 percent felt that the company should not be involved in the mating game. Few Americans wanted the company involved at all. One question asked what the person would do if he were on a crowded bus when his supervisor entered. More than half of the Japanese—54 percent—said they would jump up to offer him a seat. Only 4 percent of Americans said they would do so.[27] The loss of individualism inherent in such attitudes surprised and dismayed some of the scholars who investigated the "Our Company" phenomenon. The loyalties that the company demanded and induced helped produce a marvelously productive factory but left the employee eerily will-less. "Man-imbedded-in-organization has no great need to make personal choices," Dore observed. "The organization's norms set guidelines. The organization's sanctions keep him to the path of virtue."[28]

It is inaccurate to judge this dependency as the inevitable result of some inherent penchant for authority, some residue of feudal obedience. It was a product of the times. When it began to emerge in the fifties, the Japanese worker's overriding desire was for a job and a measure of security in the strange new world of postwar Japan. He was willing to surrender much to attain both. The company's approach was equally rational. It wanted loyal workers who would remain bound to the firm after receiving expensive training and who, in the interests of long-term stability and growth, would accept the corporation's goals as their own. As an engine of production, the organization that emerged from that trade-off was remarkably successful. As a social institution, it produced the perfect organization man.

The company man became an instant legend in the sixties, a folk figure of the times. Nowhere is he better portrayed than in the fiction of Keita Genji, who chronicled the white-collar employee's life in many stories and novels. Genji, whose real name was Tomio Tanaka, knew his people well. As an employee of the Sumitomo group of companies, he rose to become deputy chief of the general affairs department of the Sumitomo Real Estate Co. His short stories are in the main gentle and amusing accounts of the worker's struggle to survive and succeed in the company to which he has committed his life. Many Japanese businessmen have testified to their essential accuracy in defining how their organizations worked. But the tales also illuminate the high price paid for security in the large firm. Genji's characters have delivered not just their working hours but their souls to the company, accepting its values and personal demands in full, and in the process many of them have become oddly dehumanized. Genji defined the immense drain on a personality consecrated to the company.

His corporate presidents and directors are not kindly paternalists but tyrants of the first order. In "Private Secretary,"[29] a young employee is terrified to learn that he must accompany his president on a business trip to Hokkaido. His face reddens and his legs tremble when he realizes that his care of the boss will determine his future life in the company. Frightful adventures ensue as he tries to avert his president's liaison with a favorite geisha (a task assigned him by the president's own wife). The outcome is both comic and sad, and also very realistic. In another tale, "The Ogre," a tyrannical section chief rules subordinates by fear and pettiness. His favorite office rule prohibits junior employees from walking down a central corridor used by top executives and important visitors. Breaking the rule exposes one to angry lectures, threats, and humiliation before one's peers. Dedicated to the firm and unable to leave for other jobs, the employees meekly comply. "The Ogre" is, after all, "Our Company." The hypocrisy shines through in a scene in which the section chief, who has terrified and angered almost every worker in his charge, gathers all of them together for a lecture on company loyalty. "To put it another way," he concludes, "we all naturally look after the interests of our family. We must love our company in the same way as we love our home. You understand?"

Genji's stories show the family bound as tightly to the company as the breadwinner. "A Model Company President's Wife" presents the long-suffering spouse, Yasuko, whose good name and social status have become inextricably entwined with her husband's position and the success of his firm. Her husband is an energetic philanderer. For many years she has accepted his affairs with resignation, knowing that to protest or break up the marriage would mean a tawdry end for both of them because the company would disapprove and cast them out. She is visited one day by the wife of another officer of the company who also has strayed into infidelity. Angry and hurt, she wishes to divorce him. When she tells Yasuko her husband is sleeping with other women, Yasuko coolly replies, "Men usually do, you know." If a divorce is pressed, she explains, the husband will be forced to resign, and then both will be disgraced, left without position in society. She knows all this, Yasuko tells her friend, because she has for years faced the same dilemma. Why does she tolerate the unfaithfulness? the woman persists. Yasuko responds, "Because I'm the company president's wife and want to remain so."

The title story in one Genji collection, "The Lucky One," is the chilling account of a hapless veteran salaryman named Machida who, because of an innocent mistake early in his career, has never progressed up the corporate ladder. He is a pathetic figure around the office, where his job is to sort mail for posting or represent the company at important funerals. Machida bears his failure with stoic dignity. He is patient with sneering colleagues and obsequious to his superiors. But at home he has constructed a bizarre fantasy world in which he plays the role of a mighty company director. His room is grandly fitted with a massive desk to resemble his boss's. Seated behind it each evening, he makes meticulous notes of director's meetings, negotiations with the union, and a campaign to salvage the firm through a clever stock purchase—none of which, of course, has ever occurred. His wife plays her role as obedient secretary, calling him "Mr. Director" and rushing to fetch his tea. Machida's double life is brilliantly defined each day in brief scenes in the office-building elevator. Going up in the morning, the dignity accumulated at home is slowly shredded as the car climbs to his true fate, transforming him into the pliant, failed employee that he is. As he goes down at night, his shoulders square and he becomes, once again, the powerful company director whose lordly chamber awaits him at home. It is a compelling story of modern Japan. His devotion to the real company unrewarded, he finds solace in the fantasy of his own corporate creation. Machida is the perfect company man in both his lives.

7

●

Politics: The Game
Across the Street

I n normal times, television reports on Japanese politicians show
serious-looking men, heavy with importance and good dining, walking in and out of parliament doors or talking solemnly across tables to
one another. Bland, earnest men, these leaders of the Liberal Democratic party seem swathed in a dignity befitting managers of the non-
Communist world's longest-reigning party. But for nearly a year, from
mid-1988 until mid-1989, the scenes were different. Almost nightly,
these same men were pictured with weary, haunted looks. Hostile reporters brandishing microphones pursued them down corridors. Some
were seen apologizing as they resigned high offices. Often a familiar face
was glimpsed glaring from the rear seat of an official limousine that was
fetching him to a detention cell and a date with the public prosecutor.
Public-opinion polls registered astonishing declines in support for the
LDP and its prime minister, Noboru Takeshita; one, incredibly, found
that only 4 percent approved of his administration. Finally, Takeshita

resigned, hoping to end his days of humiliation. He was wrong. The next news cycle brought the report that his secretary, a close friend for forty years, had slashed his wrists and hanged himself.

Known as the "Recruit affair," it was the longest and most debilitating scandal in postwar politics, and for more than a year it tore through the LDP like a tsunami, or tidal wave. The Recruit Company, a fast-growing firm that became rich publishing employment magazines, had given selected politicians' aides either cash gifts or prelisted stocks in a subsidiary, Recruit Cosmos. Most of the money and profits were funneled into political war chests. The revelations, which are discussed later in this chapter, forced three ministers to resign (each was caught lying), toppled Takeshita's government, subjected several officials to criminal investigations, and forced a generation of LDP leaders into displays of penitence. It had begun as yet one more of those seamy scandals that had characterized the LDP for four decades but ended with much of the party in disgrace. Surveying the wreckage, even LDP members in the Diet were chastened. "Japan has a first-rate economic system, second-rate living standards, and a third-rate system of politics," said Masayoshi Takamura, a party regular.[1]

Within a year, however, all was nearly back to normal. Takeshita ruled the party again from behind the scenes. Others tarred by Recruit's brush slowly reemerged from privacy. The LDP did suffer loss of control of the Upper House of the Diet, in part because of scandal, but by early 1990 it had recovered enough to win an overwhelming victory in the lower-house election. All of the major party leaders retained their seats. More than $1.5 billion from party slush funds went into the victory, and few questioned where it came from. That spring the news reports again pictured portly men parading in and out, talking over the same tabletops.

One day when the storm was at its peak, I asked a Japanese friend what he thought of the Recruit affair. A retired businessman, he had followed the unfolding crisis on television. He was peeved at disclosures of bigwigs making easy money by selling government favors and taking cash from special-interest groups. But on the whole he was not shocked. Japanese, he said, look upon national politics as a world apart, an arena in which different ethics prevail. "We have a phrase about politicians— we call them *kogan muchi*," he remarked. "It means something like 'thick-skinned people without shame.' " My friend searched for an appropriate metaphor. "Politics is something different from the rest of our lives. It is like a baseball game being played across the avenue by a group of boys. I might watch for a moment if I happened to be on that side of the street, but I would not cross over to observe it. It isn't something I'd think was important in life."

The faraway baseball game is an apt metaphor. For in the postwar era, politics has evolved as something remote from normal life. It has been isolated from the mainstream of real concerns, from those pursuits of economic growth, security, and personal satisfactions. It is a puzzling phenomenon, especially for Westerners, because the superficial features of normal democratic politics are clearly visible. Elections are held, expensive campaigns mounted. People vote in large numbers and the media covers it all in stupefying detail. The Diet meets, prime ministers are chosen, budgets are enacted. But it is all oddly disconnected from matters that really concern the ordinary Japanese. When his attitudes toward politics and government are closely examined and compared with those in the West, they appear strikingly different. It is not merely a case of disenchantment, a repulsion with corruption. It is a deeply ingrained and virtually unconscious sense that politics is a distant affair somehow disconnected from the truly important affairs of life. Bradley M. Richardson and Scott C. Flanagan, two American political scientists who measured those attitudes, found the Japanese identification with politics extremely weak. "It appears that many Japanese simply do not feel that politics lies within the domain of the average citizen," they wrote.[2] To put it bluntly, the average Japanese sees politics as something so unimportant that it can safely be left to the politicians.

It was not intended to be that way. MacArthur's postwar Occupation had envisioned a lively, Western-style democracy engaging citizens in the same sense of excitement and involvement found in Europe and America. The old parliamentary framework would be retained but infused with a new spirit of grass-roots participation. Women were enfranchised and encouraged to run for office. SCAP purged nearly 35,000 prewar politicians and barred about 70 percent of the prewar Diet from public positions. Communists were released from prison and the principle of free speech enshrined in the new constitution. The initial results were gratifying. In the general election of April 1946, 363 separate parties were in operation. A multiparty system, rather evenly divided between left and right, evolved. Campaigns were robustly competitive and voting rates were high. By 1955 the two main conservative parties had merged into one, the Liberal Democratic party. On the left the Japan Socialist party offered a vigorous opposition.

Gradually the excitement died and that peculiar disconnection of citizen and politics emerged. Voting rates did remain high, and in the villages personal politics were ever popular. But across the board other forms of participation declined. Survey after survey registered a fading interest at the grass roots. Only those issues of intense personal meaning aroused serious involvement—issues like environmental pollution or the pork barrel. But the interplay of politics and broad national issues was of little consequence. Writing in the 1970s, Shunsuke Tsurumi, one of Japan's foremost cultural critics, observed that his countrymen grew more and more concerned with their private lives, less and less with public affairs. He found them best portrayed in writer Osamu Nakano's *Capsule Man,* which portrayed a Japanese as happiest and most secure "when he is shut up in his small room with his stereo, television and comic books." He emerged from his private cocoon only when stirred by an issue of personal significance. "The ordinary citizen," Tsurumi wrote, "is not concerned with politics per se, with who is premier, who is elected to parliament, the title and nature of new laws. Only when he feels his life affected by the political situation, or his life-style hampered by it, does he rouse himself from political apathy and voice his political view in public."[3]

Why this drastic change? Several obvious reasons suggest themselves. One was the decline of serious party competition over issues that mattered. The Japan Socialist party led the way by becoming almost irrelevant. From the first a strongly ideological party, the JSP was an amalgamation of left-wing unionists and intellectual Marxists committed to class struggle and a rigidly socialist view of the world. Unlike counterparts in Western Europe, it never changed. It advocated nationalization in a capitalist economy that was surging toward success. Its international program was both pro-Soviet and pro-Chinese, an awkward stance in a country committed to a security pact with the United States. Drained by ideological combat within, the JSP hardly seemed interested in fighting the LDP. Rarely has it bothered to put up enough candidates actually to control the lower house of parliament, even if all were successful. Content with its losing ways, concerned in the main with its internal ideological purity, the JSP steadily lost popularity and ceded the field to the LDP. As one of Japan's popular pundits has remarked, the socialists "have come to be too used to eating left-overs."[4]

Japan was left with a de facto one-party system, but in time the LDP, too, came to seem less relevant. It held all of the responsible positions, maintained comfortable majorities, and serviced well the needs of its constituent interest groups—farmers, shop-owners, big business. But in the important affairs of state it was curiously isolated. The pattern was established in the years of high economic growth, the era when Japan's attention was focused on the mechanisms to produce prosperity. Those mechanisms were shaped almost entirely in the bureaucracy, in the ministries of Finance and International Trade and Industry, or within the business world. Bureaucrats and businessmen were the movers and shakers. It was the bureaucracy that determined the uses of foreign exchange and decided which corporate combinations would flourish. Industrialists put these tools to work and made the economic miracle a reality. Political leaders rubber-stamped their decisions with little debate. LDP prime ministers reigned but did not rule. The name of Prime Minister Hayato Ikeda is associated with the famous "income-doubling" plan of the 1960s, but his only role was to proclaim it and reap the benefits for the LDP. The plan itself was a product of bureaucrats. In the great affairs of the state, the ruling party stood awkwardly to one side.

It was in this context that there emerged the view of politicians as a breed apart, the *kogan muchi* of my friend's description. Prime Minister Yoshida had set the stage by dismissing Diet members as monkeys playing in a zoo. In the years that followed, they were seen as irrelevant meddlers, men concerned only with their own survival and not with the serious business of government. Repeated scandals reinforced another opinion: that they were hopelessly corrupt. In 1989, with the Recruit scandal at its peak, an Asahi newspaper poll found that only 10 percent of Japanese believed that members of the Diet possessed high ethical standards;[5] a companion survey in the United States showed that 61 percent believed their congressmen had high standards. "You have this problem of social prestige," observes Takeshi Ishida, a political scientist who has written frequently on Japan's political culture. "Intellectuals look down on politics as a dirty business. There is a vast difference of social prestige between intellectuals and politicians. In the United States, if you asked a college professor about his politics it would be perfectly natural for him to say that he is a member of the Democratic party. In Japan, he would say, 'No, politics is too dirty.' "[6]

Americans, of course, often take a similarly cynical view of political leaders, but there is a big difference in the degree of disrespect, as Konosuke Matsushita, the famous electronics industrialist, discovered in 1963. He was attending a banquet sponsored in New York by *Time* magazine, at which Vice-President Lyndon Johnson and Secretary of State Dean Rusk were to speak. When those two approached the rostrum the audience rose to its feet. Puzzled at this demonstration, Matsushita asked his interpreter for an explanation. The interpreter told him it was the customary American reception for political leaders. Matsushita later recorded his thoughts:

Japan and the United States are both democracies, but one of
the most striking differences in the way democracy is practiced
in these two countries is in the attitude toward politicians.
Japanese are supposedly known for being exceedingly polite,
but the courteous attitude shown by U.S. citizens to the vice-
president and secretary of state at the *Time* party was something I found lacking among the Japanese public. Sometime
later, I attended a similar gathering in Japan at which the
prime minister, Hayato Ikeda, presented a congratulatory
speech, but not a single person rose to his feet in an expression
of respect.[7]

Venal, ineffectual, undeserving of respect—these are the harsh
judgments rendered against the Japanese politician, and they go a long
way toward explaining the popular detachment from politics. This detachment has been measured in dozens of attitudinal surveys that demonstrate Japan's differences from America and Europe. It is not a case of
skepticism or temporary disenchantment with political misbehavior. It
is something far more pervasive—the overriding sense that politics is
remote and unimportant. These surveys are puzzling, because by many
standards one would expect Japanese to be deeply involved in politics.
They are highly educated and they are prolific joiners of organizations,
two attributes that usually signify strong political attachments. But virtually every survey shows their disassociation from public affairs. A 1978
Asahi newspaper poll asked voting-age citizens if they regarded politics
as something "close to yourself." The response was unmistakably
negative—63 percent said no.[8]
    Richardson and Flanagan, two American political scientists, ana-
lyzed many academic and media surveys for their major 1984 work,
Politics in Japan. They found low levels of psychological involvement
in politics and interest in national affairs. It was, as some called it, a
"spectator culture" in which citizens deliberately distanced themselves
from politics of all sorts. Japanese, compared to other democratic citizens, had a strongly negative image of parties and politics. Rarely were
these subjects even discussed among friends and at meetings. The level
of interest was particularly low among Japanese young people. One
survey comparing Japanese youth with those in ten foreign countries
found the Japanese to be the most fatalistic in their view of politicians.
Richardson and Flanagan concluded that Japanese regarded politics as
a "distant, alien activity."[9]
    Perhaps the best gauge of such apathy is what political scientists

refer to as a person's sense of "efficacy"—the extent to which an individual feels he can influence political decisions in his society. Some feel that politics achieves what they want achieved; others see it as having little effect. In the many surveys taken in various countries, Japanese always rank near the bottom in their sense of efficacy. Politics is so remote, so far from their reach, that they hardly expect to influence it. Seventy-five percent of Americans, for example, think they can do something about an unjust law; only 42 percent of Japanese feel that way. One survey asked people whether they felt powerless to do anything about what their government did. Fifty-eight percent of Japanese say yes compared to 42 percent of Americans. Moreover, this sense of powerlessness has increased dramatically in the latter postwar years. A Japanese broadcast media survey group, *Hoso Kenkyu To Chosa*, measured political attitudes at intervals from 1973 to 1988. They repeatedly asked whether people believed in the effectiveness of elections to attain their goals. In 1973 about 40 percent declared that they did. But by 1988 only 23 percent said the same.[10]

●

Some argue that these deep-rooted attitudes by themselves explain Japanese indifference to politics and that they are the product of special character traits or Japanese culture. It is said that Japanese democracy was not something won by citizen effort; instead it was handed down to them twice, first by the Meiji oligarchy and then again by General MacArthur. Japanese therefore lack the spirit of challenge that popular democracy requires. This "cultural" explanation is widely accepted by Japanese scholars as yet another example of Japanese uniqueness, and like most of the other "cultural" arguments, it holds little water. It ignores, for example, the enormous vitality that erupted in the early postwar years when citizen interest was extremely high. It also ignores what the many surveys show—that the sense of powerlessness and detachment has developed over time, shaped by the years of experience of postwar politics.

For the fact is that the political system in Japan itself isolates the ordinary citizen and makes him feel his powerlessness. This is difficult to fathom, because the system seems superficially to resemble others in its democratic forms. In theory, it is the typical parliamentary arrangement in which members of the Diet are elected in their constituencies. The party with the most seats elects a party president, who automatically becomes prime minister and then forms a government. But in practice, it is a system packed with undemocratic features that place it beyond popular control and guarantee public indifference. Some of these features are deliberately arranged by the LDP to maintain power. Others reflect the internal factional struggles within the LDP. Altogether, they have the effect of separating people from politics.

The most obvious antidemocratic feature is a malapportionment of seats on a scale that defies any means of fair representation. It is the familiar story of rural constituencies being overrepresented and urban ones underrepresented, but the magnitude of this disparity makes Japan unique among modern democracies. Its roots are in the LDP hold on farmers' votes and its desire to maintain this hold. In the early years, that rural base was the foundation of LDP rule, and although its importance has diminished, it still is significant, sometimes crucial. According to the Ministry of Home Affairs, in 1988 there was a disparity of more than three to one in the value of votes between the most rural and most urban areas. In rural Miyazaki Prefecture, there were 105,634 voters for each seat in the Diet. Kanagawa Prefecture, on the outskirts of Tokyo, had 325,594 voters for each seat. There has been no large-scale reapportionment of Diet seats since the earliest postwar days. The LDP repeatedly promises a fair reapportionment and repeatedly neglects to do it. Japan's timid courts straddle the issue, on occasion declaring certain elections unconstitutional but refusing to invalidate them by throwing out the results.

A second feature that insulates people from politics is the manner in which prime ministers are selected. It is a case of back-room politics at its shadiest. The LDP is divided into several factions, each of which maneuvers and horse-trades for enough votes to elect the party president, who automatically becomes prime minister. Voters have no way of knowing during an election which of the factional barons will emerge on top. There is only the remotest connection between casting a vote for the local Diet candidate and choosing who will run the country. There is no assurance that the winner will represent an approach to government preferred by voters. Citizens are walled off from political results. The most startling example occurred in the selection of a prime minister in 1980. Three prominent veterans were considered leading competitors, and for weeks the media described the titanic battle for a winning majority. Large sums of money passed hands, promises of ministerial assignments were made, factional chiefs were lavishly courted—all of it out of public view, of course. When the LDP Diet members assembled for the big vote—the one that would determine who would lead the nation—none of the three was selected. The winner, by default, was a little-known politician from an obscure fishing village, a man named Zenko Suzuki. The next day, one newspaper bannered the news under a headline asking: "Zenko Who?"

Back-room manipulation is the rule in LDP politics, from the top, where premiers are chosen, to the bottom, where local candidates for the Diet are selected. The slating of candidates is all very secretive. It reminds an American journalist of the tactic employed in Chicago by the late Mayor Richard Daley, who, during election years, would emerge from rooms in the Sherman House Hotel with a list of names designating who could run as his machine's candidates. In Japan the slating evolves from private arrangements satisfying LDP headquarters in Tokyo and party committees in the prefectures. There is a small measure of public participation in that the chosen candidate must demonstrate that he enjoys the blessings of a support group, called the *koenkai*, which will furnish money and campaign assistance. Usually, a *koenkai* is composed of local business interests with a stake in their man's success and friends of the family. Personal attachments are important, and the larger the *koenkai* the better a candidate's chances of being slated. Each of the LDP national factions has a big stake in the process, too, because each would like to add a new member to its ranks in the Diet. But the general public has a minimal role. It has no chance to influence the choice of a nominee and by election day is faced with a fait accompli, a candidate selected by the bosses.

In recent years this has evolved into one of the most pernicious antidemocratic systems. It has transformed politics into an aristocratic mechanism that assures that the sons of politicians succeed their fathers in the Diet. This has less to do with family affections and desires for clan perpetuation than with the nature of the *koenkai*. Typically, this support group has been built up over many years at great cost. It sustains a politician through election after election for thirty years or more. When that politician dies or retires, the *koenkai* routinely turns to a son or grandson for a successor, realizing that the family name is important for continuity. The heir, once approved, is almost assured of the succession.

I witnessed the effects of inherited politics in 1979 on a visit to Utsunomiya, a small city about eighty minutes by train from Tokyo, where I was introduced to an aspiring politician named Hajime Funada. He did not have about him the aura of a winner. A slight wisp of a man, boyish-looking in his steel-rimmed spectacles, Funada was twenty-five years old, barely of age to stand for the Diet and the youngest of any of the 891 candidates running for seats in the lower house that year. But

Funada was a shoo-in because he possessed a single, overpowering asset—his name. His grandfather had held the seat for forty-two years, and his father had been the prefectural governor. The grandfather died in early 1979, and for a brief period seven men had toyed with the hope of succeeding him. None, however, bore the Funada name, and all were promptly eliminated once young Hajime decided to take the job. Funada, who possessed no qualifications whatsoever and who seemed to me only marginally interested in political life, was duly nominated and easily elected. No one outside the Funada *koenkai* had had anything to do with it.

The cumulative result of such affairs is a Diet in which more and more of the seats are filled by inheritance—by *nisei*, or second-generation politicians. By 1989 nearly 40 percent of the LDP lower house members were *nisei*, and a few were *sansei*, or third generation. The trend is accelerating. Shokei Arai, an LDP Diet member elected in 1986, observed that he was the only one of fourteen legislators in their thirties who was not a *nisei*.[11] Whether they are competent men is beside the point. The politics of inheritance automatically screens other aspirants out of the process and naturally expands that sense of remoteness Japanese hold toward politics. It is profoundly antidemocratic. Few people other than political scientists and a few media commentators seem to care about this. One of those who does care is Kan Ori, a professor at Sophia University in Tokyo. "It is very undemocratic," Ori says. "It is making politics a family business."[12]

In most democracies, political campaigns are thought of as vehicles that draw citizens into politics. In Japan the campaign is yet another example of how the system has come to insulate people from politics. The word *campaign* is here used advisedly, because it bears little resemblance to those in other modern democracies. It consists in large part of scenes like this: A car mounted with loudspeakers moves slowly through a neighborhood street. A smiling man, the candidate, waves at passing pedestrians, his white-gloved hand extended through an open window (the white glove being a symbol of purity). From the loudspeakers comes the shrill voice of a woman (a campaign aide) shrieking, over and over, the candidate's name and the greeting, "*Doozo Yoroshiku.*" And that is the biggest part of the political campaign in Japan.

Such an absurd scene is the product of a set of laws and customs that sharply restrict political campaigning and that, taken together, reflect a deep suspicion of democratic politics. At nearly every stage of the election process, the candidate is sealed off from the electorate. He can actively campaign in his white gloves for only a brief period—gradually shortened over the years to the current fifteen days—and his public appearances are limited by statute. He can maintain only a single campaign office and make only three street speeches. He can distribute postcards and handbills, but the messages must adhere to subjects prescribed by law. He cannot buy space in the print media to advance his ideas and is permitted only a few, brief appearances on television. Such restrictions are no accident. Their roots are in a 1925 law enacted when authorities became fearful of small radical parties. They were abolished by Occupation authorities bent on cleansing the system but revived in the 1940s and 1950s amid new concern over radicals and leftists.

The most formidable barrier is the law prohibiting home visits by a candidate or his supporters. One may not solicit votes door to door, nor even stick candidates' handbills in mailboxes. The effect is not merely to further reduce contact between candidates and voters. It also prevents politically interested supporters from involving themselves in campaigns. A foreigner is often struck by the absence of volunteer workers in Japanese elections, but the explanation is very simple. The citizen who went door to door in behalf of a candidate would be in violation of the law. There is little a volunteer can do except mail postcards or shout "*Doozo Yoroshiku*" through a microphone. Anything else places him in jeopardy. The official justification for banning home visits is comical. They would, according to the Home Ministry, lead to bribery! This in a country whose politics is shot through with high-level bribery and influence-buying.

The import of this web of restrictions and punitive laws emerged clearly in a conversation with Seiichi Tagawa. A journalist-turned-politician, Tagawa has been a member of the Diet since 1960, but by no means an ordinary one. He is the closest thing Japan has to a maverick, a fiercely independent, outspoken populist from Yokosuka who quit the LDP in disgust with corruption in 1976 and joined with several other dissidents in forming the New Liberal Club. After ten years of independence, the other defectors meekly returned to the security of the LDP, but Tagawa refused to surrender. In 1989, when I met him, he was the leader and only Diet member of the tiny *Shimpoto*, or Progressive party, an organization supported by a unique financing system that he called the *Kohi Ippai Undo*, or the "One Cup of Coffee Movement." Each member contributes the cost of one cup of coffee a month—250 yen, or 3000 yen per year. In the summer of 1989, with public revulsion growing over the Recruit scandal, membership in the movement had swelled to more than 30,000 and the party was preparing to field candidates for the upper house in five districts. Plenty of volunteer support was available, but the law prevented the use of volunteers to contact voters directly. The grass roots could not be watered.

Tagawa explained:

> It is not that Japanese people lack concern about politics. It is just a matter of not being able to transform that concern into action. The important reason is the set of restrictive laws. In the United States you are able to debate policies openly. But you cannot do that here. There are so many restrictions and many of them are subject to police investigations. Ordinary people are afraid of that and they will not get involved. There is the law against making home visits—it is a law that is very hard to disobey. The law is fifty years old and is supposed to prevent people from offering bribes. But in England and other countries people make such visits all the time during elections. In Japan, unless the law is changed and home visits are permitted, nothing will change. It is the single biggest reason why citizens do not participate. The restrictions are so severe that people think they are doing something wrong if they participate in elections. Even the police think it is a bad law and would like to get rid of it. But the Diet won't change the law. One reason is that if it were changed, Diet politicians would have to begin making home visits. And they are lazy and don't want to do that.[13]

All of these laws, rules, and customs have the effect of insulating people from politics. Each plays a part in producing the detachment and lack of interest that are such striking features of Japanese politics. But the greatest insulator is neither law nor administrative regulation. It is something far more fundamental: money.

●

The large sign hanging over the ballroom in the Okura Hotel in Tokyo explained: "A Meeting to Encourage Mr. Kondo." Tetsuo Kondo, a rising star in the LDP, had cause to feel encouraged. More than 2,000 guests representing the elite of Japan's corporate world were in attendance. The man from Mitsubishi was there. The chief of Nippon Steel delivered a speech of lavish praise. A founder of Sony signed the guest list. The line of encouragers extended down a long corridor and out the door into the hotel parking lot, where a stream of limousines deposited arriving businessmen. Before entering the ballroom to shake Mr. Kondo's hand and enjoy the sake, scotch, and tender roast beef, each guest handed over a thick bundle of yen notes with his calling card.

The transfer of corporate cash to LDP politicians, of which the "encouragement party" is but one example, is routinely practiced in Japan. It is also the most powerful instrument for insulating people from politics. It enables the party to stand alone, immune from the normal tides of citizen discontent. Almost entirely financed by handouts from big business and its several protected constituent groups, the LDP hardly needs to notice the pressures that routinely arise in other democracies. High land costs, rigged consumer prices, and limited public amenities are ugly fixtures of Japanese public life, but seldom is the ruling party compelled to act on them. As consumers or individuals, Japanese have few levers of power, and money is not one of them. The average Japanese would never think of contributing money to a politician with the expectation of winning support for an antipollution or proconsumer measure. The big money in politics flows from corporations to the Liberal Democratic party and is the main source of both that party's longevity and its insulation from popular pressures. It was Prime Minister Nobusuke Kishi who best defined Japanese politics. Beginning his Diet campaign in 1953, Kishi said, "What controls politics is power, and power lies in money."[14] His party has never lacked for it.

Since the rebirth of democracy after the war, money's corrupting influence has been a recurring plague. In 1948 a cabinet fell when it was disclosed that a leading company, Showa Denko, had bribed several high-ranking government officials to obtain a low-interest loan from a reconstruction financing agency. In 1954 large shipbuilding firms were caught bribing officials in exchange for government contracts and subsidies. Three future prime ministers were implicated in those two cases—Takeo Fukuda in Showa Denko and Eisaku Satō and Hayato Ikeda in the shipbuilding cases. None was ultimately convicted. In all, I count at least eight premiers or probable-premiers-to-be who have been tarred with money scandals. Most were collecting money for political uses. Such scandals, of course, are a feature of any government in which politicians have favors to dispense. But if the measurements of corruption are frequency of scandals, the prominence of those involved, and the amounts of money changing hands, it would seem that Japan's politics is the world's most corrupt.

Cases of individual corruption are far less important than the systematic passing of corporate money to the LDP in a form that is somehow regarded as legitimate. Like so many present-day institutions, this system was established in the early 1950s, a reaction to events of the time. Business leaders were terrified of left-wing influence. Opposition parties scored substantial gains in the Diet elections of 1952 and 1953, and the conservative Yoshida governments seemed powerless to stop them. The *zaikai*, as business and financial circles are called, determined on two measures to stem the tide: The two conservative parties must be merged into one to form a solid defense, and the new LDP required steady infusions of cash with which to campaign. Four large economic federations pooled their contributions for a committee innocuously titled the "Economic Reconstruction Council." Administering this pool were the Federation of Economic Organizations, or *Keidanren*, and the Japan Chamber of Commerce and Industry. According to political historian Chitoshi Yanaga, three business organizations contributed 30 million yen each to defray the costs of the parties' merger, most of the money coming from iron and steel manufacturers, sugar refiners, and construction firms that depended in part on government loans and subsidies for survival.[15]

This initial investment, and those that followed, have been hugely successful. The LDP has ruled without significant interruption ever since, its coffers filled annually by contributions doled out according to a fixed scale based on a company's size and importance. It is all tidily organized in the Japanese way. In general, the *zaikai* money has not been paid over in exchange for specific political favors. What the *zaikai* has always wanted for its money is stability and a general climate favoring Japanese-style capitalism. Its contributions, Yanaga writes, "have always been regarded as a form of investment, insurance, good-will expenditures, or a combination of all three." Its chits were to be cashed in when, as often happened, incompetent or unpopular LDP governments behaved so poorly that stability was threatened. When that occurred, *zaikai* pressures caused cabinets to fall and new elections to take place. Yanaga notes that business groups gave the final shoves to three prime ministers—Yoshida, Kishi, and Ichiro Hatoyama—who had failed to manage politics efficiently. "The power of life and death over the government," writes Yanaga, "has been exercised by organized business overtly and dramatically at times, but quietly on the whole, unnoticed by the casual observer."[16]

Before concluding this to be a scurrilous practice carried on by shabby figures from some corporate demimonde, one should meet with a man named Nihachiro Hanamura. He is an engaging, courteous gentleman who exudes an old-fashioned respectability. For thirty-four years he was the linchpin in the perpetual money machine. Hanamura retired as a vice-chairman of *Keidanren* in 1988, after a career spent passing large sums of money from the *zaikai* to conservative politicians. During his final years as middleman he was responsible for collecting about 90 million dollars each year from large companies and handing it over to the executive committee of the Liberal Democratic Party. At first he had operated in relative obscurity. But in 1981 the *Asahi Shimbun* described his role in a full-page article, and forever after he was known as "the keeper of the *zaikai* vault." In the West, Hanamura might have been referred to disparagingly as a high-level bag man, but in the elite Japanese circles where he operated so discreetly for so long, he was an honored figure. I found him, in 1989, to be a proud man who felt he had served his country well by supplying the LDP with enough cash to maintain its rule for a third of a century. Indeed, his services had been rewarded with one of Japan's highest honors. It explains much about the Japanese system of politics to know that this courtly gentleman who passed his life funneling money to politicians was, in 1983, presented with the First Class Order of the Sacred Treasures by Emperor Hirohito.

Hanamura's fund-raising began in the crisis year of 1954 when, as so often happened then and now, the conservatives were trapped in an ugly scandal. The future prime minister, Satō, had been caught approaching government-subsidized shipyards for campaign contributions. "That was against the law," Hanamura recalled. "Satō thought it would not be discovered, I think, but it was." The government was near collapse, left-wing parties had a chance to deadlock the Diet's upper house, and the conservatives were broke. Hanamura, then head of *Keidanren's* general affairs section, was summoned into the office of the then vice-chairman, Kogoro Uemura, who told him that a source of "clean money" must be found to support conservative candidates. By "clean money" he meant donations from businessmen who would not extract specific favors for their largesse. Small- and medium-sized firms could not be tapped because they always wanted immediate returns on their political investments—and look what had happened in the shipbuilders' case. Somehow, large companies must be convinced to contribute without seeking quid pro quos, Uemura insisted.

Hanamura dutifully began compiling the first of what became known as "the Hanamura lists"—names of large banks, insurance companies, and manufacturers. Placed alongside these names were the amounts of money each was expected to give. This time the money would go to a new organization called *Kokumin Seiji Kyokai*, or the National People's Political Association. The amounts were based on a complex formula that took into account a company's total capital, sales volume, and profits, as well as its general position in the industry. For example, Nippon Steel and Nihon Seimei were the leaders, respectively, in the steel and insurance industries and would be expected to contribute the largest sums; lesser firms would have their shares scaled accordingly. List in hand, Hanamura made the rounds of Tokyo's financial and business districts, calling on presidents and chairmen. "I would tell them," Hanamura recalled, "that they must contribute in order to preserve economic freedom in Japan. I would say that their contributions were like paying insurance premiums to guarantee that the economic system would remain free."

It was hard selling at first. Company presidents would complain that they were being touched for too much money or that they saw no reason to waste money on politicians. And there was another problem. Although *Keidanren* did avoid asking recipient politicians for specific favors, it always had a "general policy program" that it wanted Diet members to endorse. Some powerful *Keidanren* members wanted this program specifically endorsed when the politicians came to collect their money. In that way, the politicians would know they were being bought, for what, and for how much. Hanamura insisted that that would be wrong. It would smack of the old system of exchanging cash for specific political favors. He prevailed, and the practice developed of holding two separate meetings. At one, the money would be handed over. At the other, *Keidanren*'s policy program would be explained. In Hanamura's eyes, that drew the line between contributions and political payoffs, and everyone's honor was preserved. "It took seven or eight years to get all of this settled and accepted by the companies," he remembered. Businessmen were satisfied that their investments were worthy ones. The LDP was properly grateful. Buying politicians seemed so beneficial to all that *Keidanren* even extended its services to the Democratic Socialist party, a band of moderate socialists who had abandoned the leftist mainstream. "I remember that Saburo Tsukamoto [former chairman of the Democratic Socialists] would always come around to us saying, 'We are the second LDP,' " Hanamura said with a soft chuckle.

What held it all together was the perennial fear of a Socialist party election victory, especially in years when the LDP had been caught in scandals or was for some other reason unpopular. Justified or not, this fear of leftists could always be counted on to frighten business into contributing as much as the LDP said it needed. There was a period, for example, in the early 1970s when the LDP share of the total vote was declining and it seemed that the combined opposition parties might prevail. Facing a difficult election in 1974, Prime Minister Kakuei

Tanaka came running to *Keidanren* executives, frantically waving the red flag. Hanamura recalled: "Tanaka came around saying, 'If an opposition party wins, we [the LDP] won't be able to administer LDP policies. Is that allright with you?' He hit them where it hurt. People started saying, 'We cannot have that. How much money is it that you need?' Large sums of money were contributed, and the election was won. There was criticism, however, that the victory was based on financial strength."[17]

●

Kakuei Tanaka is best known abroad as Japan's supreme crook, the prime minister who carried corruption to new heights and then fell into disgrace because he accepted a bribe that was revealed in the Lockheed scandal of the mid-1970s. Such an accounting does the man an injustice, however, because his career amounted to far more. He dominated his political times as no other Japanese premier has ever done. He was an artist of politics, one of those rare figures who seizes on a common theme the way a great musician takes hold of his instrument and compels it to produce a higher form of music. His work embraced the best and the worst of democratic politics, a grand vision for social change coupled with an immense personal greed for money and power. He brought a taste of prosperity to many of Japan's forgotten people. He also enriched himself and his grasping friends. In his prime, he was a man of enormous energies and (to his friends) great personal magnetism. He was a Japanese version of such men as Huey Long and Lyndon B. Johnson.

Postwar prime ministers have been, with the exception of Yoshida, bland organization men of little personal distinction. The traditional path to power runs through the national bureaucracy and the LDP ranks, neither of which admires individualism. Caution, patience, and an instinct for compromise are the characteristics most valued. Those, coupled with an acceptable college degree and a socially advantageous marriage, may move an ordinary man up the path, and good fortune can carry him to the top. Tanaka possessed none of these. He never even got a college education. Brilliance, hard work, and a capacity for managing other men propelled him upward. Unlike his postwar peers, he arrived in the premier's office by using his own native talents. Brusque where the others were bland, belligerent where they sought to avoid confrontation, at times crass, at other times warm and almost too human, Tanaka was a bulldog in a kennel of pedigreed spaniels. Unaccustomed to finding giants at work in those years, Japanese frequently compared Kakuei Tanaka to Hideyoshi Toyotomi, the sixteenth-century warlord who, despite humble beginnings, rose to rule the country.

Tanaka grew up in Niigata, one of Japan's least blessed prefectures. A region of hills and mountains facing the Sea of Japan, Niigata is today only two hours from Tokyo, thanks to the *shinkansen* train line that Tanaka himself caused to be built. When Tanaka was a child, it might as well have been on a different planet. Cursed with the highest snowfall in the nation, Niigata was virtually isolated from the rest of Japan throughout the long, bitter winters. There were few roads to begin with and they were rarely plowed open. The acute sense of isolation and alienation engendered by fifteen feet of snow was brilliantly captured in *Snow Country*, the finest novel written by Yasunari Kawabata, who won the Nobel Prize for literature in 1968. It was set in a Niigata village totally enveloped by snow. In Niigata, the snow dominated everything, from commerce to family life. Children left home for the winter to live in dormitories so they might go to school, there being no open roads for school buses. Men lived in company lodgings in Tokyo or Osaka in order to earn the family living. Only women, the aged, and small children lived at home. There was, naturally, considerable jealousy of those more fortunate Japanese who lived in the east. There was resentment, too, that the political system afforded few rewards, not even snow plows, for the people of Niigata.

The poor boy from the snow country emerged on the national scene in 1947 when he was elected to the Diet. He quickly got into trouble. In 1948 he was arrested for accepting a bribe from coal company owners opposed to a government plan to nationalize their mines. Cleared of the charge, he set about building a personal political machine in Niigata that would enable him to withstand any assaults from outside. "Politics is numbers," Tanaka frequently said, and his special creation was a numerical advantage in local elections so great that for years no serious candidate ran against him or his favorites. First, he organized the poorest farmers and the most snowbound hill people, promising that in Tokyo he would obtain the public works and infrastructure improvements they deserved. Later, he organized businessmen and the more affluent, incorporating them into his machine with contracts and subsidies. Years of promising and delivering on promises created for Tanaka the largest local machine in Japanese politics. Known as the *Etsuzankai*, it dominated politics in every municipality in the constituency, numbering nearly 100,000 supporters at its peak in the 1980s. The *Etsuzankai* was so large and so powerful that it became almost a branch of government. It selected the public-works projects Tanaka would then supply and made sure that they went first to those villages where the Tanaka vote was greatest. It was the simplest sort of pork-barrel politics, but it also served a populist purpose. Snow plows and much, much more found their way to Niigata.

It very early became clear that Tanaka was no mere hayseed trading in political pork. Before winning the premiership, he was known as a man who could fix anything. His contacts within business and government were extraordinarily varied, especially for one who had begun as an outsider, and other politicians found that his tentacles seemed to reach everywhere. A minor but illustrative example is provided by Hirotatsu Fujiwara, one of those Japanese media figures who by saying things colorfully rise to rank of "commentator" and who are thus often favored by politicians. In 1969 Fujiwara had written a scathing attack on *Soka Gakkai*, the Buddhist-oriented social organization out of which grew a popular opposition party, *Komeito*. *Komeito* wanted the book banned and brought extraordinary pressures on publishers and bookstores. Tanaka was both a friend of Fujiwara and a secret influence in *Komeito*, even though that party was nominally opposed to his own LDP. Tanaka called Fujiwara and said the resolution of the conflict was simple: The book would be published and *Komeito*'s friends would buy up most of the copies. "Give me the numbers and the price and it will all be paid for," Tanaka promised, according to Fujiwara's subsequent account. "You won't suffer any loss."[18]

It was his manipulation of the national bureaucracy that made Tanaka truly special. He held three ministerial portfolios before being chosen prime minister in 1972, and he left his mark on each. The typical Japanese cabinet minister has little control over or even influence on the bureaus under him. It is usually they who manipulate him. Tanaka reversed the process simply by learning everything useful to know about a ministry's inner workings. He would bark in his gravelly voice and senior bureaucrats would hop. If they pleased him, they often found themselves handsomely rewarded, usually with promotions but often with cash gifts to boot. Some were offended by his intervention in their turf, but others admired his extensive knowledge and boundless energies—"the computerized bulldozer," they called him. Tanaka's mastery of the bureaucracy made him a credible national leader and helped him reach the top. It also enabled him to revolutionize the collection of political money in Japan.

Until Tanaka came along, the Hanamura system had served the LDP nicely. The annual "Hanamura list" of political donors had by then become institutionalized, and the large sums of money enabled the party to win election after election. But it was not enough to satisfy the demand for cash that the increased factionalization of the LDP induced. Each of the four to six major factions of the party needed money to attract followers in the Diet. It was in that way that faction members had the chance of seeing one of their own elected prime minister. The normal flows of money arranged by Hanamura were never intended to appease that craving. The business donors wanted to finance stability, not factional warfare. As the perpetual outsider, Tanaka was the leader most in need of raw cash to build his faction. In pursuit of that goal, he relied very heavily on his bureaucratic influence.

His method was a form of high-level, systematic influence-peddling that connected those who wanted favors with those in the bureaucracy who could provide them. Very often Tanaka's clients were companies and entrepreneurs who, like himself, were outsiders. They were not privileged members of the *zaikai* network. They needed access to the power over economic life that was held within the ministries in the form of permits, licenses, information, protection from competition, controlled bidding, and dozens of other practices. But how to gain that access? Bribing bureaucrats is a very risky business in Japan. Tanaka supplied the entree. The client might want clearance to operate some unusual form of machinery on the job. Some ministerial regulation blocked him. A phone call from Tanaka cleared the way. If a road contractor found his firm barred from an established bid-rigging scheme, Tanaka saw that he was counted in. His faction got the fee for such services, and the money was used to enlarge the faction. These were not isolated, incidental practices; they were systematic. In time, the Tanaka faction came to offer itself as a "supermarket" that provided connections into any ministry. The client merely had to find the right shelf in the store. The money poured in and Tanaka's faction grew larger and larger. Finally it was the largest and he became prime minister. The press honored its power by calling it not the "Tanaka faction" but the "Tanaka *gundan*," or the "Tanaka corps." Those who were offended by such pervasive peddling of influence had another name for it all: "structural corruption."

Tanaka's downfall was as spectacular as his ascent. In 1974 an influential magazine, *Bungei Shunju*, published two detailed articles on Tanaka's "money politics." At first, as usual, the mainstream Japanese media ignored the articles. But Tanaka was questioned on them during a luncheon appearance at the Foreign Correspondents Club of Japan, and the international repercussions transformed them into a sensational issue at home. Tanaka was forced to resign. Two years later a report by a United States Senate subcommittee described how Lockheed paid him a 500-million-yen fee to fix the sale of its passenger jets to All Nippon Airways. He was indicted and, after a long trial, convicted. His system survived him, and for a long time afterward he was still the inner boss of the LDP, the "Shadow Shogun," in the media's new argot. From the seclusion of his compound in Tokyo's Mejiro-Dai he raised money for his faction, selected prime ministers, and bulldozed government ministries.

Tanaka never discussed his misfortunes publicly, but from all evidence available, he never considered himself guilty of doing wrong. He seemed genuinely perplexed that his system of raising political money was deemed corrupt. And he also seemed to feel that he was somehow a victim of irrational pressures mounted from abroad. I interviewed him one day in 1981 at his Mejiro-Dai estate, where he was waiting out his trial, feeding his carp, and entertaining the dozens of friends and favor-seekers who still came to call. The terms of our interview proscribed questions about his legal problems, but at the end he talked briefly about the fateful events that had brought him low. What he seemed to want to say was that the Lockheed case came about not because of suspicions aroused in Japan but by the investigations in Washington that had prompted criminal charges against him. With a very thin smile, Tanaka said, "What happened, I think, was that I caught an American cold."

●

Tanaka suffered a stroke and at last relinquished his personal power, but his brand of money-politics survived and has become institutionalized in all factions of the party. Factions routinely tap individual businesses for the cash needed to fight their wars. Money for favors is now endemic, despite the cosmetic reforms promised by the LDP after each new scandal erupts. After the Lockheed mess, limits were placed on individual contributions. Politicians circumvented the limits by devices such as the aforementioned "encouragement parties," at which bundles of yen were handed over by company executives and not counted as political contributions. Each of these new channels existed side by side with the old Hanamura system, which still funneled large packages of money from the traditional *zaikai* to the LDP as a whole. By the late 1980s the original purpose of the "Hanamura list"—providing financial support without demanding specific favors—had been defeated.

How routine it had all become was revealed in the Recruit scandal of 1988–89. At the core of it was a polite, boyish-faced entrepreneur named Hiromasa Ezoe, chairman of the Recruit Company, an immensely successful firm that started as a publisher of magazines for young graduates seeking jobs. Like Tanaka, Ezoe was an outsider who lacked connections in the cozy world of Japanese business and government. Like Tanaka, he appreciated the role that money could play in establishing such connections. Before the scandal he caused had run its course, it was revealed that Ezoe's company had bought its way into prominence by passing money or shares to dozens of politicians, a number of high-level bureaucrats, and even executives at two leading newspapers.

The main route consisted of passing them shares of stock in Recruit Cosmos in the months before those shares were made available to the public. Recruit Cosmos was a real estate subsidiary that had also become hugely successful. Once its shares were publicly traded they would inevitably rise in value. They were then like pieces of solid gold for the favored recipients. Large numbers of them were sold secretly to aides or relatives of men at the pinnacle of Japanese politics, including the major faction leaders. Twenty-nine thousand shares went to aides of Yasuhiro Nakasone, the former prime minister. Another 13,000 shares were pressed upon an aide and a relative of Prime Minister Noboru Takeshita. Other bundles went to aides of faction bosses Kiichi Miyazawa, the finance minister, and Shintaro Abe, who was the LDP secretary general. Ezoe scattered his largesse widely, and the revelations that dribbled out smashed a number of Japan's myths. For example, the notion that career bureaucrats were above reproach was demolished when senior men in the Education and Labor ministries were found to have accepted favors intended to help Recruit's publishing ventures.

As disclosure followed disclosure, as more and more politicians were compelled to reveal their finances, a picture of Japanese politics emerged that astonished even hardened cynics. It was the sheer size of the cash flow that amazed them most. The records of receipts by Prime Minister Takeshita's organizations were most staggering. In a two-year period (1985–1987), Takeshita's support groups had accepted 151 million yen (more than a million dollars) from the Recruit companies alone, apparently as funds to be used in his campaign for premier. This was not, of course, a public campaign that might require election expenses; this was an internal LDP effort to win Diet members' support in the intraparty contest. Most likely, Takeshita's people handed the money out under the table to Diet members willing to pledge him their votes. Recruit was only one of the many donors to the Takeshita cause. In May

1987 Takeshita held a lavish "encouragement party" to raise more funds. Recruit was but one of the encouragers. In all, something like 60,000 tickets were sold for that single party, raising a grand total of nearly $14 million. When yet another Recruit loan was disclosed, one he had earlier denied knowing about, the prime minister was forced to resign.

●

The large sums of money raised by all of these methods—the *zaikai* flow handled by Hanamura, the favor-peddling streams systematized by Tanaka, the odd new devices like "encouragement parties"—amount to far more than corrupt influences. They are the greatest source of the Japanese public's insulation from politics. The money flow forms a broad moat between politics and ordinary Japanese. It makes politics a self-financing world unto itself, a thing apart from real life. It makes possible the view of my friend who looked upon politics as a distant baseball game, something of only casual interest to him. Politicians play their games, which have no relation to his world of business and private life. No politicians would think of approaching the ordinary citizen for financial support and asking for his views on what government should do. Indeed, the money flows the other way, from the politicians and their business allies down to the people. The notion of grass-roots politics is now almost unknown in Japan. It is the politicians who water the grass roots. With cash.

A man well qualified to explain this top-down process is a tubby, middle-aged politician with thinning hair who has been near the center of LDP politics for two decades. Michio Watanabe, a member of the lower house from Tochigi Prefecture, is a former finance minister who at the time of the Recruit scandal held the important party position of chairman of the LDP Policy Research Council. He is a blunt and candid man, as are many Diet members from rural districts, and lacks the artifices by which other politicians screen their activities. Once, some disgruntled farmers expressed displeasure at hints that the LDP might cease protecting them from foreign food exporters. If they didn't like what the LDP was doing, Watanabe retorted, they should look for another party to support. Charges of corruption and influence-peddling in the LDP bring no apologies from his mouth. If ethical purity is the test of a good politician, Watanabe has said, perhaps politics should be left to the clergy and scientists. Spoken like a good Boston pol.

At the peak of the Recruit affair, with his party reeling under the daily revelations, Watanabe was asked to explain the apparently insatiable need for political money in Japan. "It costs a lot of money to run for office," he said simply. The demands for money were incessant and growing worse. Once, when he was a young politician, the needs could be met from the fund that big business provided the LDP (the Hana-mura system). No longer. Today, politicians had to throw "encour-agement parties" for themselves to bring in extra yen. Or they made funds-begging visits directly to corporate offices for special handouts. Or they engaged in what he called "financial engineering"—obtaining shares of company stocks certain to rise in value. All this Watanabe explained to a large group of journalists without apology or embarrass-ment. If he regretted anything, it seemed to be only that modern times had changed the trusted patterns of the past.

Most revealing, however, was Watanabe's description of how the average politician spent what he collected. It seemed that very little was expended on electioneering. (How could there be when laws ban tele-vision ads, door-to-door visits by campaign workers, and most of the other bits of election paraphernalia common in the West?) Almost all went toward watering the grass roots—the direct or indirect buying of allegiance from constituents. Asking them for contributions was out of the question; the money passed down from him to them. People from back home make trips to the capital and must be dined and given tours. A politician must attend every wedding and funeral, at heavy personal cost—the cash gift and flowers typically run to 50,000 yen ($333) each. Sometimes there are four or five weddings a day and an equal number of funerals. The chores are exhausting, expensive, and time-consuming. "Some days," said Watanabe, "you do nothing but ride around in your limousine in a black suit, with a white tie (for weddings) in one pocket and a black tie (for funerals) in the other." He must attend between 200 and 300 year-end and new-year parties every season in Tokyo, each costing 10,000 ($67) to 20,000 yen ($133) in gifts. Requests from tem-ples, shrines, local festivals, and schools are endless. "These days, when-ever a new school opens in your district, you get a stream of requests for cash gifts. They want you to buy the school a new piano, a statue, or even a library. And you cannot be the only one not to donate. So politics costs more and more money."[19]

It is a system far removed from the hopes of those who modeled postwar politics. Politics is a field for politicians and their contributors, not for the people. To the extent that real people are involved at all it is as recipients, not participants. The politicians themselves are satisfied with this lack of citizen involvement. They do not appear to think that what they do should be of any concern to the ordinary man. Watanabe said it best when, one day, he was asked by a reporter about the meaning for the LDP of the Recruit scandal. He seemed bewildered by the question. Why, he seemed to be wondering, should anyone outside of political circles care about such things as scandal. In exasperation, Watanabe said, "The newspapers make a fuss, and even at the Diet they talk about nothing other than those things [the Recruit affair]. But what in the world have they got to do with national life? Just because of those things, have people become poorer or have they been unable to get a pay raise? Has the business community had hard times?"[20]

8

●

"Rich Nation, Poor People"

As befits the headquarters of the world's largest securities corporation, the Nomura Building is a proud tower of restrained elegance that exudes a sense of power and money, from the grand lobby paneled in granite squares (*mikageishi*) to the fiftieth floor where expensive restaurants overlook the panorama of modern Tokyo. It stands in a cluster of skyscrapers shooting up from the Shinjuku district a few miles west of Tokyo center. Only three decades before it was built (in 1978) the area still bore the marks of end-of-the-war devastation—blackened homes and shops, a train station where thieves lingered, and the bustling black market where the daughters of proud families sold their kimonos for food money.

From the glass observation windows, the visitor looks out upon other sleek towers bearing the names of companies known around the world—Fuji Ginko, the globe's third largest bank, Sumitomo, Yasuda, Mitsui, Dai Ichi Seimei, KDD. They loom like guardian pillars over the heartland of the world's richest and most productive country, and standing atop one of them is a good way of measuring how far that country has come. As eloquently as anything does, the towers of Shinjuku speak for modern Japan. Their message is far different even from that of the older Kasumigaseki Building, that marvel of 1960s' Japan that was home for corporate headquarters when success was first being tasted. The Kasumigaseki Building spoke for an era of hopefulness but also of doubt, a time when Japanese were not at all certain they had arrived. Its pragmatic, solid-block contours suggest a kind of fortress mentality of people working grimly to keep the wolves of poverty and depression at bay. "We are earnest and hard-working," it seems to say, "but we cannot rest for a moment lest disaster strike." The Shinjuku towers speak in a confident tone, and their message to the world is far different: "We are rich, strong, and powerful, and we shall be here forever."

They also testify to the durability of that national equation formed in the immediate postwar years. The pieces of that equation were the subject of the first half of this book. They include the bargain that Prime Minister Yoshida struck, which won independence and linked Japan to the prosperous West; the accommodations reached by labor and management, which produced high productivity and few strikes; the dominance of bureaucrats in directing the economy; the fostering of a business culture that concentrated energies on advancing the corporation; and the molding of a political system that did not interfere with the pursuit of national wealth.

From abroad this equation all seemed so peculiar: an energetic and enormously successful country that played no part in the world's events. A nation in which, contrary to the principles of capitalism, central planning produced a roaring economy. A political system of great stability in which politicians were hardly more than bit actors. It all made sense only in the context of the times of a nation with only one goal: commercial success. All was submerged in the culture of business, the immense drive to revive and rebuild. All that might detract from economic achievement was simply ignored. What did it matter that politicians were playfully impotent, or that labor unions were lifeless extensions of company management, or that the national ambition did not extend to foreign power plays like Vietnam or the Middle East? All that the West found so odd in these arrangements seemed perfectly natural to Japanese who, after all, had set it up that way in the early postwar years to achieve the goal of economic power.

The strength of that commitment was proven again and again in the 1970s and 1980s, when Japan's economy was forced for survival into repeated transformations. The early successes had been built on top of three pillars—a cheap yen, cheap oil, and an open trading system in the world's biggest market, the United States. So long as the yen was undervalued, Japanese exports encountered little resistance abroad. They were cheap and of high quality and the world snapped them up. So long as oil prices were low, Japan, which imports virtually all of its petroleum, could keep manufacturing costs down and invade foreign markets. So long as the American trading doors remained open, the flood of cars, television sets, synthetic textiles, and other products would continue. By the eighties, none of those pillars was intact. The yen was no longer cheap and neither was oil, and the American doors for imports were closing.

The traumas began with the shocks of the early 1970s. President Nixon forced a revaluation of the dollar against the yen, and exporters panicked, foreseeing the end of Japan's recovery. The government reacted by stimulating the economy with a public-works boom and increased welfare payments, which sparked the first serious wave of inflation in a decade. Then came the first oil shock when the Organization of Petroleum Exporting Countries (OPEC) succeeded in quadrupling oil prices. That sent inflation raging higher. Growth rates plummeted in the seventies, convincing many businessmen that the long postwar flowering was at an end. They cut payrolls fiercely, prescribed a new wave of "rationalizations" within their plants, and introduced yet another round of machinery investments to cut labor costs and conserve energy. The adjustments worked, exports rebounded, and the second oil shock passed without serious damage.

It was the erosion of that third pillar, the open American marketplace, that seemed to signal the final disaster. Until the 1980s Japan had never run significant trade surpluses with her favorite partner. But in the "go-go" 1980s of Ronald Reagan, the American consumer developed an enormous craving for Japanese products. The trade gap widened and would reach an unsustainable $50 billion a year. Almost every American industry was threatened by the torrent. Predictably, many of them screamed for protection. Steel quotas took effect against Japanese producers in 1978 and were followed in three years by the so-called voluntary restraints on Japanese automobiles. Machine tools and computer chips soon fell under similar restrictions. Before long, economists calculated, approximately 30 percent of the items Japan exported to the United States were in some way restricted by protectionist measures. When by 1985 the trade gap had not narrowed significantly, Washington engineered its most stunning reprisal. With the approval of Tokyo and European capitals, the yen was pushed up against the dollar in the most forceful revaluation of the postwar era. The era of *endaka* had arrived.

Endaka means simply a "high yen," and it is almost impossible to recall now the sense of near terror that it spread through the business community and government. The remaining third pillar of Japanese economic growth—the advantage of selling abroad in countries with more powerful currencies—was finally smashed. As the yen rose, so did the cost of Japan's exports. Central banks combined in the ferocious drive to appreciate the yen higher and higher. Within a year-and-a-half after the 1985 agreement by five leading industrial powers, the yen was twice as strong against the American dollar. For the rest of the world, it was perhaps a striking currency realignment. In Tokyo it meant dooms-day, the end of an era. The age of exports was over, the newspapers said, and Japan would have to accept it. What loomed ahead were years, perhaps decades, of slow growth, lower wages, and a declining standard of living. Japan had reached her limits and there was nothing she could do. *Endaka*, said a *Keidanren* official in February 1987, was a crisis "unprecedented in severity" in the postwar era. A few months later a ministerial conference report declared that "the domestic economic situation in Japan remains grim in light of the continuing sluggishness . . . and the difficult employment picture." An American author, then writing a book on Japan's economic strength, swept postwar history aside in a single sentence: "The strong yen seems destined to shatter forever Japan's export-based economy."[1]

Once again, the fears were proved exaggerated, the trauma short-lived. Doomsday was not, after all, at hand. Within two years of the currency realignment, Japan's economy was off and running, stronger than ever. The turnaround was a complex affair engineered by both government and the big companies. The bureaucracy launched a 6-trillion-yen public-works program to stimulate the economy and lowered interest rates to promote one of the great building booms of postwar Japan. The result was the creation almost overnight of what might be called a "second economy," one fueled not by exports but by domestic demand. Personal savings poured out of banks and into new homes, cars, and home electronics. Simultaneously, industries underwent yet another siege of restructuring and rationalization. They cut payrolls to the bone, moved older workers out of their jobs, built factories overseas where labor was cheap, and reduced business expenses so severely that, to cite one instance, executives at Nissan could be issued new pencils only after turning in inch-long stubs of old ones. Most important, they discovered the reverse side of the high-yen coin, which showed that a powerful currency made buying things overseas cheap. That discovery unleashed a sudden and enormous wave of overseas conquests. Japanese investors bought up foreign companies almost as if they were consumer items and began building even more new plants on foreign soil. An investment in America, for example, cost only half as much in yen as it would have before the great realignment. The combination of all these produced a recovery so swift that even the word *endaka* disappeared from newspapers. The year 1987, which had begun with such pessimism, produced a respectable growth rate of 5.2 percent. In the first quarter of 1988 the economy grew at a rate of 11.3 percent, the highest in the industrial world and the largest increase in Japan in a decade.

●

To someone looking down from atop the Nomura Building in the 1980s, the fruits of Japan's economic success stories are stunningly visible. The view encompasses the surrounding towers, the commercial and financial centers of downtown Tokyo, and the start of that broad coastal plain stretching to the south and west, through Yokohama and Kawasaki, on to Nagoya and Osaka and Kobe. Japan today accounts for 10 percent of the entire world's gross national product, and most of it is the work of people in this coastal empire. Nowhere on the globe is so much industrial and financial power concentrated in such a small land area.

The manufacturing giants based here have successively dominated all but a few of the world's most important industries. Supremacy in steel and shipbuilding had come early in the high-growth days and was quickly followed by command of cars, television sets, videotape recorders, and all of the other electronic playthings the world was yearning to buy. Profits fueled the steady sweep upstream into more sophisticated fields. In 1979 a machine-tool industry leader explained to me that although Americans dominated the field he thought that, perhaps, just perhaps, Japanese had reached a level of technology that could challenge them. A decade later Japan's producers were nearing control of half the market in the United States. Japan had learned to make cars, according to the conventional wisdom of 1979, but in fields like computers she lacked the creative edge to succeed. Ten years later Japanese manufacturers were flooding the West with laptops and work stations and aiming at the supercomputers that were the last American refuge.

Industrial robots were Western inventions, but by the late 1980s Japan's companies had installed four times as many as America's, eight times as many as West Germany's. Innovation was not the Japanese strong point, Westerners kept repeating. But as early as 1982 Japanese were registering twice as many patents as the Americans, four times as many as inventors in the United Kingdom.

The same sort of dominance appeared in the field of finance. Well into the 1970s Japan's banks and financial markets were justifiably regarded as primitive. People piled up savings in banks, which in turn loaned their money to corporations affiliated with their industrial groups. Stock offerings were timid affairs, and no Japanese institution even thought of international investments or loans. Tokyo was small change, American and European bankers believed. By the mid-1980s Tokyo challenged London and New York as an international financial center and in sheer money power overwhelmed both. When the world's fifteen largest banks were ranked by total assets at the end of 1988, the top ten were all Japanese. Only one American bank was ranked at all, at Number 12. The strongest on the list, Dai-Ichi Kangyo, held total assets nearly double that of Citicorp, the largest in the United States. Overall, Japan became the world's largest creditor nation in the 1980s, passing the United States, which slid down into net debtor status. Only twenty years earlier, the Tokyo Stock Exchange had been of minor importance; securities trading was a faintly shady business. By the late 1980s Nomura Securities own stock's value on the Tokyo Stock Exchange was greater than the value of all American securities companies combined. And in 1987 there occurred one of those benchmark occasions by which knowledgable Japanese love to measure their country's ascent: In terms of the total capitalization of listed companies, the Tokyo Stock Exchange became the world's largest, finally topping New York's. The value of shares listed on the Tokyo board represented 40 percent of the entire world's stock values.

•

The view from atop the Nomura Building was one of great national wealth. But the view from ground level was considerably different. Down where the average Tokyoite lived, life was a world of little luxury, a world so different from the one of corporate success and glitter that it hardly seemed a part of the same nation. There was no real poverty there, and it is true that most of the appurtenances of modern comfort were available in profusion. But by almost any standards of comparative analysis, the average Japanese family lacked the advantages that had accrued to Western ones similarly blessed with national economic gain. In the 1980s the contrasts between national affluence and personal welfare became harshly evident, and Japanese began to wonder seriously if they had been denied the fruits of their labor. In all of the industrialized world of free economies, they worked the longest hours, commuted the longest distances, enjoyed the fewest public amenities, and paid the highest prices for what they consumed. And the question began to be heard: "For what?"

The issue was often posed in comparisons of the middle-class office worker's life at home and in his company. His home was a tiny apartment or house crammed with television, stereo, expensive furniture, and all manner of kitchen gadgetry, but with little space for living. Off to work he went, dodging cars and bicycles in the tiny winding streets, while his children headed for classes in schools that resembled World War II army barracks. For the two-hour commute, he was packed into trains so crowded that shifting to turn a page of his newspaper was almost painful. But at the other end lay a world of corporate opulence stunning in its contrasts. In the wealthy Aoyama district of Tokyo, the C. Itoh trading company headquarters was a monument to success and worldly achievement. On arriving, employees passed through an immense lobby decorated in tasteful grays and beiges and rose in a nearly silent, computerized elevator to an executive floor where huge glass panels afforded a breathtaking glimpse of the city. All around the neighborhood were similar commercial palaces, interspersed with elegant restaurants and gleaming shops packed with the most expensive imports—Gucci, Yves St. Laurent, Burberry—a cornucopia of luxury goods.

Although the Japanese lived in the world's second most powerful economy, the relative drabness of their livelihood became a subject of a painful national debate in the 1980s. It may have begun with a European bureaucrat's sarcastic observation that the ordinary Japanese were workaholics who lived in homes no better than "rabbit hutches." His comment at first stung even those Japanese accustomed to foreign criticism of their economic life. But the kernel of truth it contained was difficult to deny, and by the end of the decade its essential accuracy had become a part of the political discussion. "Japanese live in what look like pigeon cages and commute over long distances like carrier pigeons," Takako Doi, the Socialist party leader, said during a Diet debate in 1989. People hardly noticed her remark, so common had its point become in the public dialogue. A political scientist and popular commentator, Kuniko Inoguchi, observed in an essay that the richness of

Japanese life was concentrated in lavish displays that had little to do with a person's daily life:

> Japan's riches are to be seen not in people's homes but in the luxurious office buildings at the hub of its economy, in the glittering row of fashionable shops, the spanking new factories, the latest fully-computerized "intelligent buildings," elegant hotels and sprawling airports, the auditoriums with their painstakingly calculated accoustics, or the facilities of the recent Tsukuba Science Expo before they were demolished.[2]

●

The disparity reflected the central fact that the Japanese system as it had developed worked brilliantly to achieve commercial success but that all else was subordinated to that achievement. Work, people's savings, government capital, corporate profits—all were devoted to manufacturing goods that foreigners wished to buy. Economists took to calling Japan a "production-first country" to distinguish it from those countries that existed to meet the needs of their people, the consumers. Market expansion and ever-higher rates of manufacturing productivity were the only measures by which Japan's success was judged. In the course of industrial development, the Japanese system did spin off extremely desirable by-products. It lifted people out of poverty, provided a steadily rising standard of living, permanently reduced unemployment, and filled homes with consumer goods.

But at some level the system seems to have ceased advancing the public good and became solely the vehicle for corporate expansion. The human, everyday costs of this leveling off were considerable. They were measured in such crucial areas as declining rates of wage increases, continued long working hours, extremely high prices, poor housing, and the persistent failure of government to provide the public amenities that other modern nations took for granted. Perhaps it was only coincidence, but a number of these failures to progress occurred, or at least became apparent, in the late 1970s and early 1980s. It was as if the system had reached its capacity to produce change that enhanced public well-being. By the mid-1980s this fact was being recognized even by government bureaucrats. A special commission headed by Haruo Maekawa, a prominent businessman, lamented the shortcomings and called for "revolutionary improvement in the quality of life." Ordinary people, too, were clearly aware of the system's diminishing ability to improve their daily lives. A succession of officially sponsored public-opinion polls found people in a mood of growing disgruntlement.

Several Japanese premiers had acknowledged that the formula for national economic growth somehow did not translate into the enhancement of living conditions, and they had promised far-reaching corrections. Kakuei Tanaka's plan in the early 1970s to "remodel" the Japanese archipelago was a design for increasing welfare payments and moving jobs from crowded cities to regional centers. Later, Masayoshi Ohira's "Garden Cities" scheme proposed to ease the strains of living in huge urban areas offering few amenities. Noboru Takeshita's "*Furusato*" plan was a similar vision of life-enhancing measures that would supposedly double the citizens' level of happiness just as the high-growth plans had doubled income in the 1960s. All were quickly forgotten almost as soon as they were presented. None was in harmony with a system that seemed hell-bent on "production first." The demands of corporate expansion had precedence. Ms. Inoguchi's essay noted that while in the United States wealth was seen as a way of improving the quality of life for citizens, the same was not true in Japan. Japan had many paved roads where no one lived and futuristic infrastructures everywhere except in homes. Inoguchi noted that

> in Japan . . . better economic performance does not enrich people's lives. Rather we live as we do in order that the economy may prosper even more. Long working hours, family members being forced to live apart, discrimination against women: all such practices that distort and devalue our lives have been foisted upon the people in the name of the propagation of wealth. And the impression is inescapable that the wealth so accumulated has functioned only to further strengthen the economy, not to give people better lives.[3]

Inoguchi's essay attracted wide attention in Japan and abroad because it expressed in painfully explicit language what scholars and statisticians had long known. More than any other modern nation Japan had plowed its wealth into business investment and industrial infrastructure and ignored the sort of improvements that make ordinary life easier. That concentration was perhaps understandable when Japan was poor, its economic underpinnings fragile. But the imbalance continued even into the 1980s, when its economic power was proven beyond doubt. Japanese saved their money at extremely high rates, but their frugality benefited primarily the national wealth. Public spending in general remained surprisingly low. In 1987 government disbursements of all kinds represented only 27 percent of the gross domestic product, the lowest of all the OECD nations. Japan spent (proportionately) what other countries did for the education and health of her citizens, but the overall level of public spending ranked her with poorly developed countries. Her total expenditures on social needs was only 16 percent of the national product, lower than all other OECD countries except Spain.[4] The production-first ethic controlled all public planning, even when it came to such obvious needs as national pensions and care for the elderly. The official guide to welfare planning for the 1980s, drafted in 1979, decreed that those burdens should continue to be borne by individuals and companies, not the state. The government social planners explained that hard work and a longer working life, not welfare support, were the proper answers. They would protect Japan from such dangers as "the British disease," which induced only indifference to work and low productivity.[5]

The result was a country rich in production and corporate wealth but oddly resembling a struggling third-world nation in public amenities. Japan had fewer public libraries per person than any modern nation. In the United States there were four public libraries for every 100,000 people; in Japan there was only one. West Germany had three public museums for each 100,000 of its citizens; Japan had less than one. A country whose people talk incessantly of their love of nature provided few public urban parks. Tokyo in 1980 had 1.9 square meters of park space per inhabitant; New York had 19.4 and West Berlin had 26.1.[6] Japan built fewer expressways than other nations, and most of them were constructed to serve industry, not people. By 1988 she had constructed less than half the expressway mileage that West Germany had to serve only two-thirds as much land space. Even undeveloped countries endeavor to provide such elementary services as flood control and public sewage. Japan virtually ignored both. In 1988 half of all Tokyoites lived in areas liable to suffer flooding. One would expect that the world's greatest creditor nation, a country adept in all areas of high technology, could supply its citizens with rudimentary sewerage and drainage systems. But in 1989 only about one-third of Japanese lived in homes served by flush toilets and sewerage systems. In all other modern countries, about nine out of ten persons had such basic amenities.[7] Most Japanese seemed unaware of the shabbiness of their public life until the 1980s, when its shortcomings were pinpointed in a series of government and private reports. Compared to foreigners, they had profited little from their country's success, and their discontent began to register. An international survey conducted in 1987 found that Japanese were more dissatisfied with their living environment than people in both the West and in Southeast Asia.[8]

●

The production-first ethic that restricted ordinary public services also served to limit the gains achieved by working men and women in their jobs. The great bargain struck between labor and management in the 1950s began to unravel in the 1970s. That bargain had set the stage for years of peace in the factory and provided the lift-off for the high-growth era. It assured workers in large companies that they had jobs for life and large annual wage increases. In exchange, management had the right to introduce all of the technology it could buy. All would prosper as higher and higher rates of productivity produced greater earnings. Throughout the high-growth period, the trade-off worked marvels for the workers. Wage increases in major companies soared in the 1960s, ranging from 8.7 to 18.5 percent. The rising tide did indeed raise all boats.

Then came the slow-growth 1970s, and the bargain began to come apart. The two oil shocks were the major cause. Frightened by the rapid increase in oil prices, company managers looked around for costs to cut and settled with a vengeance on the labor force. There were two waves of "rationalizations," the euphemism for restructuring plants, which labor had always dreaded. Wage increases were held to a bare minimum after 1974, prime jobs were replaced with automated machinery, and part-timers and casual workers were hired at low wages to fill jobs formerly held by full-time workers. Early retirements were urged on highly paid employees who thought they had been hired for life; many who resisted were shuffled off to subsidiaries and affiliated companies.

The severe cutbacks made macroeconomic sense in the tough times of the 1970s, and unions did not resist. But in the 1980s the companies held to the hard line despite rising productivity and profits. At some point, around 1983, the old bargain collapsed. The rate of nominal annual wage increases fell below that of productivity gains and stayed below throughout the decade, while corporate profits soared. The key feature of the bargain—that labor should share equally in the rewards of higher productivity—was essentially abandoned. Labor was by then too weak to protect itself. Proof of the changed equation came in the spring of 1989, when unions mounted their annual campaign for wage increases. Corporations' 1988 profits had been the highest in history, and the table seemed set for solid raises. Even an official of the government's Economic Planning Agency said that an increase of at least 6 percent was justified. Instead it was barely 5 percent. Following their production-first instincts, companies poured their profits into research, grasping for even higher levels of technological advances. Labor was powerless.

Atsushi Seike, assistant professor of economics at Keio University, has closely watched this deterioration of labor's power and the concomitant decline in wage increases. He believes it represents a fundamental retreat from the old bargain with management. "There had been this implicit contract back in the fifties and sixties," he said in an interview. He continued:

> Workers would get good jobs at high wages and were promised lifetime employment. In return, unions would not object to the management leadership. It worked well at first, but after the oil shocks these two pillars of the contract were weakened. Labor was unhappy, but it went along. It had compromised too much and could not regain the old bargaining position with management. The lower wage increases may have made good sense in the 1970s, because of the threat of inflation, but it is no longer reasonable in the 1980s. Companies have regained their power and their profits, but labor has not and it is losing ground. It no longer receives fair compensation.

His verdict is borne out by the statistical evidence, which shows that Japan's production workers—those credited with making Japan the world's most productive country—were rewarded poorly in comparison to workers in other developed countries. In 1985 wages paid to Japan's manufacturing production workers were far lower than those in the West at prevailing currency exchange rates. On a scale in which Japan's wages were 100, wages in the United States were 190 and those in West Germany 139. Total labor costs for those workers, including benefits, were precisely half of those paid out by companies in America. Japan's workers, under the bargain struck in the 1950s, had expected to receive a larger share of the pie as the economy grew. They did so well into the 1970s. But since 1977 the labor share of Japan's national income has been declining. By 1982 that share was considerably below the share of national income enjoyed by workers in the United States and West Germany.[9] After the large-scale currency realignment of the mid-1980s, when the yen's value appreciated, the comparisons made Japan's wages look more respectable. But in terms of what the wages could buy, the huge gaps remained. In 1986 if the purchasing power of a Japanese wage was figured at 100, the American wage was worth 184 and the West

German was worth 153. *The Economist* magazine calculated in 1990 that although Japan's per capita income was the world's highest, its average hourly wage rate of $8.15 was among the lowest in the industrialized world. It was the long working hours and overtime, not good wages, that made the Japanese worker well off. [10]

●

The pattern was much the same in management's derailment of campaigns to give workers more time off for leisure. Throughout the 1960s and early 1970s the time spent at work declined sharply from the peak, when a sixty-hour workweek was not exceptional. The first oil shock of 1973 put an end to that trend. Since 1975 the number of hours worked annually has remained at the same high levels, and in the manufacturing industry alone, the number has actually tended to increase. Panicked by soaring oil costs, companies replaced dismissed or retired workers with more overtime for those whom they retained and halted the movement toward five-day workweeks. Late into the 1980s, with profits climbing rapidly, companies only grudgingly reduced working hours marginally. This was despite clear signals that the nation wanted more breathing time off the job. Every one of the many surveys of public opinion taken in the 1980s disclosed a clear preference for more leisure. The stereotype of "Japanese workaholics" has always been exaggerated; polls taken since the mid-1960s show convincingly that employees want to work less and play more. A survey in 1988 by the General Council of Trade Unions (*Sohyo*) found that two-thirds of Japanese workers feel they work too hard. More than three-fourths of them said they did not enjoy a comfortable life, mainly because of low wages and high tax burdens. Even the government pressed industry to relent and cut work-weeks. It was a clear case of corporate power resisting public pressure.

Little changed. When the Economic Planning Agency in 1988 compared Japan's working hours with those in the rest of the industrial world, the gap was startlingly wide. The average Japanese worked 2,150 hours a year, 500 hours longer than his counterpart in West Germany. The employee in a Japanese company was permitted 112 days off each year; the German got 144 days off. [11] On the average, a Japanese was working 360 hours a year longer than his counterparts in five Western countries. [12] He took hardly more than a week of paid holiday time—6.2 days—in 1989, compared to 19 in the United States and 29 in West Germany. [13]

The same system that eventually worked to hold wages down and keep working hours long also served the corporate interest of keeping prices high. Throughout the postwar period, Japanese seemed vaguely aware that they paid more for everything than people in other advanced countries. They resorted to a variety of myths to justify these differences. Japanese enjoyed the prestige value of higher priced goods, it was said. Or they maintained that Japanese demanded higher quality and better service than foreigners. Or they believed the explanation that high prices were an essential cost of self-sufficiency for an isolated, insular country that was poor in natural resources. It was not until the late 1980s that they began to suspect they had been duped and that exorbitant prices were the inevitable by-product of a production-first country where the companies could rig anything for their own benefit.

The turning point came with the publication in 1989 of the Economic Planning Agency's survey of consumer prices in Japan and abroad. It was an instant best seller—the first edition of 20,000 copies was sold out in a month. Everything, even products made or grown in Japan, was far more expensive in Tokyo than in New York or Hamburg. Ten kilograms of rice cost 3,780 yen ($25) in Tokyo. In New York, far from the rice fields, it cost only $8.95. An ordinary man's suit cost 57,420 yen ($383) in Tokyo, only $242 in New York dollars. A color television set, pioneered if not actually manufactured in Japan, cost 104,400 yen ($696) in Tokyo, about twice as much as the same set in New York. Every public service a homeowner needed for survival—gas, electricity, water, and sewerage—cost him more than it did his counterpart in the United States or Europe. Even the mailing of a simple postcard cost the Tokyoite twice what the New Yorker paid. Across the board, the EPA reported, the level of prices in Tokyo was 40 percent higher than in New York.[14]

The contrasts illuminated in the EPA document held an importance far greater than their shock value to the Tokyo consumer. They called into question many facets of the system that presumably had conferred such blessings on a hard-working people. In a broad economic context, Japan appeared to be not entirely the affluent country everyone had been taught to believe in. It was one thing to take comfort in the relatively high nominal wages the Japanese workers enjoyed. It was another to realize that the wage bought 40 percent less than the New Yorker's. Economists had long been aware of the enormous disparity and packaged it concisely in a formula known as "purchasing power parity"—a comparison of the value of a currency with those of other countries in terms of what money could actually buy. For example, the

OECD calculated that in 1988 Japan's gross domestic product per capita amounted to $16,136, an amount second only to that of the United States among major industrial countries. But when the purchasing-power-parity formula was applied to that figure, the GDP per capita in Japan was only $12,332. Instead of ranking a proud second, Japan was a mediocre ninth.[15] What the Japanese system had granted in terms of nominal prosperity it had in part taken away through the device of higher prices.

It often happens in Japan that the appearance at the right moment of a government document unleashes the usually tame news media. Properly sanctioned from above, the press can be turned into a formidable agitator. Such was the case with the EPA report. Newspapers like *Nihon Keizai Shimbun* and the *Asahi Shimbun* pounced on the official numbers as if suddenly struck by a great light beamed from heaven. Reporters raced around Tokyo discovering that prices were indeed extraordinarily high. They found, to the surprise of no one who had ever been overseas, that Japanese travelers could buy almost anything at reduced prices when they stepped off the plane in Honolulu or Paris or Rome. Breathlessly interviewing returning Japanese at Narita Airport, a *Nihon Keizai Shimbun* reporter found a university professor coming back from the United States with a personal computer purchased for the equivalent of 540,000 yen. It would have cost 868,000 yen in a Tokyo retail shop. A certain Mr. Noji told reporters this shocking tale: In Rome, he had purchased a pair of cotton socks for the equivalent of 1,000 yen. Later, in a Tokyo shop, he had spotted an identical pair costing 11,000 yen. One newspaper calculated that if every traveler spent as much overseas as the ones it had interviewed, the total spent would exceed annual sales of the Seibu department-store chain.[16]

All of these disparities were the result of a commercial system that was at its heart uncompetitive and that conferred on businesses the ability to control prices and hence profits. Clear proof was evident in the years following 1985, when the Japanese currency appreciated sharply because of an agreement among major countries to force a de facto revaluation. The yen's appreciation meant that importers of foreign goods could buy much more cheaply abroad. They did so but passed only a fraction of the savings on to consumers in Japan. Importers, wholesalers and retailers, even regulated public utilities simply kept their prices high and gobbled up the profits. Between October 1985 and January 1988 the EPA calculated that the rising value of the yen and lower oil prices should have reduced the prices of goods in Japan by 29 trillion yen. Only about a third of that, however, was actually passed on to consumers. Businesses simply kept the rest.

All of this quite legal extortion was a legacy of the same production-first ethic that had brought the appearance of prosperity to Japan. Almost from the first, the government had sanctioned wholesale collusion among companies large and small. MITI itself had led the charge against the Anti-Monopoly Law and the Fair Trade Commission bequeathed by the Occupation, which had envisioned a populist model of competitiveness. Bid-rigging, price-fixing, and controlled retailing had been as much a part of the economic miracle machine as the government-induced importation of technology. They were merely the other side of the coin. Gutting the antimonopoly law enabled new cartels to form and lift industrial production to ever-new heights. It also permitted such practices as the notorious *dango* system in which construction companies rigged bids in order to divide up building contracts. Major manufacturers were given free rein to fix retail prices by the process of establishing their own outlets and refusing to sell to any other shops. Japanese paid the price, literally, for their country's economic accomplishments.

It was not only the businessmen who conspired against the consumer. Perhaps the most appalling cases of price-fixing involved the behavior of government itself in its maze of restrictions that impeded competition and in its indifference to private collusion. The EPA report made it clear that prices for commodities directly or indirectly under government control were among the most exorbitant. To protect its farming constituents, LDP governments defended import restrictions that maintained the prices of beef, rice, sugar, and other foods at levels far higher than world prices. Those governments in the 1960s also erected legislation that in effect virtually prohibited large supermarkets and retail stores from operating in local neighborhoods, a device to serve another constituency, the association representing thousands of "mom and pop" shops who would be injured by large competitors. (It took the Izumiya supermarket chain thirteen years to open a store in the Tokyo suburb of Shiroume because of opposition from local shopowners, whom it eventually bought off for several hundred million yen.) Some of the greatest price disparities reported by the EPA were among those public services in theory regulated by government but in fact left to set their own prices. The cost of natural gas for heating and cooking was twice as high as in the United States. Electric rates were much higher. American rates for long-distance telephone service were one-third the comparable rates in Japan. In most foreign countries, the ostensible purpose of regulating public utilities is to control prices on behalf of the consumer. In Japan it served only to keep them high.

Commercial transactions directly regulated by government ministries were among the most costly. The standard charge for a single bank remittance was 800 yen, although studies showed it really cost a bank only about 40 yen. The charges were sanctioned by the Ministry of Finance. Taxi fares were twice those in New York and London, thanks to the Ministry of Transportation's regulation of cabs. The disparities in public-service charges were so great that companies went abroad to avoid them. Telexes were routed through Hong Kong because international rates there were far cheaper than those in Tokyo, which were regulated by the Ministry of Posts and Communications. When the A-One Bakery in Osaka wanted to send New Year's greetings cards to some 3,000 customers, it flew them to Hong Kong and mailed them back to Japan, thus saving 53,000 yen ($353) in postage. [17]

The dream of the typical salaryman in the 1960s and 1970s was often summed up in a simple phrase: "A 20-million-yen home one hour from work." The boom times of those years turned the dream into reality for millions of Japanese. By the early 1980s home-ownership in Japan compared favorably with that in Western countries. Japanese homes were smaller to be sure—floor space on the average was about four-fifths as large as in Western homes, and the residential lots were tiny by comparison. But a nation that had begun the postwar era with entire cities demolished had made it possible in three decades for nearly two-thirds of her families to purchase homes of their own.

In the 1980s the dream collapsed. First in Tokyo, then in Osaka, Nagoya, and other cities, housing prices soared out of sight. The 20-million-yen house an hour from work now cost 80 million yen. In 1988 the successful salaryman earned 5 million yen a year, and to obtain a standard thirty-five-year mortgage he could be allowed to spend no more than six times his annual income, or 30 million yen. Neither a house nor an apartment could be purchased for that amount anywhere in central or suburban Tokyo. The dream house was to be found, if at all, at a distance from his office that required four hours of commuting each day. The Tokai Bank estimated that in London or Paris a wage earner could buy a home for three times his annual income. The average Tokyoite paid twelve times his income.

The usual explanation—that Japan is an overpopulated island country with little flat space for housing—could no longer suffice in explaining such inflated prices. The answer lay in corporate expansionism, greedy speculation, and most of all in the policies of government at all levels. The escalation of land prices began in 1984 when it became clear that Tokyo, because of a liberalization of the financial system, was destined to become an international center for banks and investment houses. Office space in the central city became desirable, and Japanese companies began buying it up. Price increases spread quickly, first in the business districts and then into residential neighborhoods. Rents and land costs doubled in a year and then doubled again. A luxury apartment in a new building cost $17,000 a month to rent; a rather average piece of residential property one hour from downtown cost $500,000. A buying panic spread deep into the Tokyo suburbs and then to Yokohama, Nagoya, and Osaka. To cope with the demands for home loans, banks introduced an unusual new feature—a two-generation mortgage that bound both the buyer and his first son to monthly payments for as long as seventy years. Speculators descended on small-property owners throughout the urban areas, begging them to sell out quickly so that apartments could be constructed. Many who resisted were subjected to heavy pressures. The *jiageya*, which translates roughly as "land-price boosters," were notorious for their tenant-removal tactics. They called in gangsters who harassed, intimidated, and often physically abused those who refused to move. In one neighborhood the thugs simply ripped down an old wooden house, leaving the renters no choice but to move on.

The salaryman's dream dissipated because he was suddenly competing with corporate capital to own a bit of land and stood no chance of matching it. But behind that obvious catastrophe were layers of government policies that worked to escalate land prices and keep rents high. The concentration of all central government agencies in Tokyo—despite twenty years of plans to decentralize—was one of them. Another was the antiwelfare bias which held low-rent public housing to a minimum, despite the obvious demand.

But the major reason urban housing became unbuyable was the political system's currying of votes among Japan's owners of small farms. The visitor to Tokyo is amazed to find hundreds of small vegetable plots sandwiched in among apartments and homes. They exist because the LDP has cosseted farmers everywhere with tax breaks and subsidies. Agricultural land, even in densely crowded urban areas, is virtually untaxed, its tillers subsidized with price supports and other benefits. The owners, most of whom farm only on weekends, quite naturally settle back to enjoy the appreciation of land prices, knowing that eventually they can harvest millions of dollars from their rows of radishes. It is estimated that nearly 20 percent of land in the Tokyo megalopolis consists of such plots. Removing props from the farmers and converting the land to apartments would solve most of the urbanites' housing problems.

●

The sum of all of these economic distortions was a Japan oddly mis-shapen and somehow out of balance, as if a majestic new palace had been constructed with its girders askew. There was something funda-mentally and unfairly amiss in a country that stacked up piles of national wealth while its people worked longer than any other for far fewer gains. "Rich nation, poor people," one pundit observed, and although the word "poor" was an exaggeration, it was not a great one. Japan in the 1990s is stable and overwhelmingly middle-class, but its middle-class citizen is hardly better off in the ordinary amenities of life than his counterpart in Manila, the capital of a country that Japanese regard as an economic basket case. In a ten-part series unusual for its incisive criticism, the *Asahi Shimbun* in 1989 described an economy in which goods were extraordinarily expensive because of government restrictions and the rigged bids of entire industries. It was an economy in which companies were rich but ordinary people could not buy a house. Ev-erything seemed devoted to keeping companies prosperous. While the average salaryman abandoned all hope of home-ownership, the *Asahi Shimbun* noted, Hitachi would spend $50 million to house employees considered vital for its expansion. It was, said the *Asahi Shimbun* team, a *yuganda* ("distorted") economy.[18]

Japanese became acutely aware of the distortions. Dozens of public-opinion polls reflected both their awareness and their disenchantment. "There is a discrepancy between the country's growing economic power and the quality of Japanese life," the Economic Planning Agency stated with rare directness. They continued:

> This can be attributed to long working hours, living-related social infrastructure which needs to be improved in some aspects (compared with industrialized Western countries), a high cost of living, the soaring of . . . land prices and insuf-ficient quality of housing in the metropolitan areas and, in general, a sense of unfairness with various aspects. . . . Fu-ture economic management needs to return some of the fruits

of economic development to the further improvement in the quality of life.[19]

It was an unusual turnabout for an agency that for three decades had been concerned only with higher growth rates for the national economy. But the frustrations had crept into the agency's own polls of public opinion in the 1980s. Between the early and late years of that decade there had been a remarkable decline in public approval of the way things were run. A standard question on EPA polls for years had asked Japanese if they were satisfied with their lives as a whole. As late as 1984, nearly two-thirds expressed general satisfaction. By 1987 slightly less than half—49.9 percent—said they were satisfied.[20] The difference represented in those two surveys reflects a stunning decline in confidence in the postwar system.

Because the evidence lay all around, recognizing the distortions and injustices was easy. Removing them was far more difficult because they were the product of the very system that had produced Japan's national economic power. Nor could there be any recourse to politics, as there often is in other democracies. Indeed, the politicians of Japan survived on the benefits they received from keeping things as they were. It was not a macroeconomic fluke that reduced a Japanese worker's buying power to three-quarters of an American worker's or made rents the world's highest or kept the price of the simplest staple, rice, at the highest level of any country on earth. These and all of the rest of the inequities were the results of the arrangements of three decades, arrangements that had been the source of national pride. In the 1990s Japanese looked around and discovered themselves the victims of their own success.

9

Old Values, New Money

Noboru Takeshita rose from the ranks of a modest merchant family in a poor region to become a prime minister of Japan in the 1980s. Like successful politicians everywhere, he is fond of reminding people of his humble beginnings. As a young boy, he has recalled, he carried his lunch to school in a *bento*, the traditional box for the frugal traveler's food. Waste nothing, his parents admonished him, so young Noboru observed a strict regimen in eating his lunches. When the *bento* was opened, a few grains of boiled rice would stick to the inner lid. Using chopsticks, he would meticulously pick off each grain, one by one. Not until each stray grain was eaten would he allow himself the luxury of digging into the bed of rice, pickles, and bits of fish packed into the *bento*. It was not a peculiar habit. Waste was a sin for his generation and for several to follow. "If you waste rice, you will go blind," mothers warned their children.

Frugality was a trait deeply ingrained in the Japanese mentality, a trait so honored that it became, over the years, a part of the moral code. It was in part a matter of making a virtue of necessity, for most Japanese had always been poor. Even the well-to-do paid obeisance—Takeshita's family, for example, was in fact far from poor. Wealth was obscured in dress and personal belongings. Somewhere along the line, a certain refined drabness became the standard of fashion. The older the kimono, the more stylish. Men might wear silk shirts at home, but they wore cotton in public. Loud and flashy colors were the mark of parvenus, pale ones the sign of gentility. The proper businessman of the Meiji period might show a glint of gold chain disappearing into his watch pocket, but that was the limit of tolerable ostentation.

Depression, war, and the poverty of defeat etched the trait more deeply. Plainness remained the necessary fashion, even when the economic recovery was far advanced. People might pack their small homes with all the modern gadgets, but in public, drab remained good, even when it had become incredibly expensive. The successful businessman clothed himself in tailored $2,000 suits that to an American looked like $100 specials whipped off the racks at Sears. The old habits of frugality were reinforced by the preachings of postwar governments, which encouraged personal savings as the highest virtue. The admired models of that period of fantastic economic growth were men who made practical things for public consumption but who also saved or hid their great wealth. Konosuke Matsushita, the postwar paragon of commercial success, made several fortunes and saved them all. He died in 1989, leaving an estate worth nearly 2 billion dollars. Perhaps the most revered figure of the age was Toshiwo Doko, the president of Toshiba (which he rebuilt from ruins) and for years the acknowledged dean of the business community. On a typical business day, Doko rose at 4:00 A.M., shaved with a fifty-year-old razor, exercised, weeded his garden, recited Buddhist sutras, and read the morning papers. Then he took a public bus to the train station for the commute to work. Matsushita and Doko personified the Japanese version of the puritan ethic: Life was a grim struggle in which the fruits of victory must remain concealed. And the *bento* lid must be picked clean.

But in truth Matsushita and Doko were, by the time they died, priests of a dying religion. A stroll through the Ginza department stores in the week that Matsushita died confirmed the flowering of a shocking new faith, a conspicuous consumption ethic that mocked all that he and Doko represented. On display at the famous Mitsukoshi store that Christmas season were the baubles of opulence. For the gentleman golfer of the postpuritan Japan there was a solid gold putter for $9,000, a jade one for only $1,040. A plain golf bag cost $3,750. For the stylish new Japanese woman—the daughter, perhaps, of one who begged for potatoes four decades earlier—there was an ordinary-looking leather purse for $2,200. The really smart might choose a crocodile purse for $14,000.

If anyone understood the spirit of the new age it was Hirobumi Kato, a young man who that season was in charge of Mitsukoshi's toilet accessories department. Japanese rarely entertain at home and so hardly bother to spruce up bathrooms, a pattern that left Kato with a humdrum business. Sales had been so discouraging that his floor space had been reduced by two-thirds. Bright and ambitious, he searched for something unusual to brighten his corner in the Christmas season of 1989 and decided that luxury was the coming thing, the more expensive the better. What, he wondered, would Japanese shoppers consider the height of luxury? He searched his memory and recalled an American movie that had featured an automobile lined with mink. Mink bathrooms would certainly catch the eye, he decided. So on a table he arranged the following items: a mink toilet seat cover ($1,500); a mink-covered roll of toilet paper ($950); a mink doorknob cover ($660); a mink bathmat ($2,640). Total mink-accessoried bathroom: $5,750. Kato had conceived it as a clever attention-getter. He privately wondered if anyone would actually buy such an outfit, and Mitsukoshi's fur department thought him daffy. He quickly sold twenty sets and his season was made. Emboldened, he added a simple toilet-cleaning brush with a gold-plated handle for $265. Fifty of them were snatched up in a few days. Beaming proudly over his display of mink and gold plate, Kato expressed the theme of the dawning new age: "The more expensive it is, it seems, the better it sells."[1]

Kato's triumph reflected an enormous transformation in Japanese life during the 1980s, a leap from earnest abstinence to conspicuous consumption on a grand scale. Drab was out. Flash was in. The old puritanism had given way to an age of lavish spending. It was as if the secret yearnings of Japanese had been suddenly unbottled and had bubbled forth in great gushings of consumerism. The greed for expensive trifles was at times frivolous, at times vulgar. There was both silliness and arrogance in this wild pursuit of the previously forbidden, and old-fashioned Japanese privately sneered at the ostentation. The accumulation of great wealth had always been quite respectable, of course, but its excessive display ran against the moral code. Simplicity and restraint had been the aesthetic guides, at least since the Meiji Restoration 120 years earlier. Their endurance as national values had been regarded as further proof that Japanese were in many ways superior to the gross foreigners.

And so it was that in the great spending spree of the 1980s yet another of Japan's popular myths came tumbling down. Gold, for example, had for centuries been a respectable treasure best kept out of sight. In 1989 Japan went on a gold-buying binge, its big spenders competing for the most garish display. At Mitsukoshi they bought gold-plated refrigerators for $6,000 each. They ordered calling cards engraved in gold print, bought house keys made of gold, paid more than $200,000 for golf clubs plated in copper and gold. Sales of golden accessories doubled in five years. The truly vulgar ordered personalized gold busts of their heads and shoulders for $140,000 or a single solid-gold nail, of no practical value, for $625. On Valentine's Day the flashy lover could pay $12,150 for a single heart-shaped chocolate candy containing a small gold ingot. For the most conspicuous consumers, finely ground shavings of pure gold could be scattered over dishes in restaurants to produce gold curry, gold omelettes, gold coffee. Even sushi—the dish that more than any other is supposed to represent spareness in cookery—could be ordered with sprinklings of gold flake on top.

In the old culture of restraint, weddings were simple affairs. A plain Shinto ceremony and the exchange of cash gifts in small denominations were sufficient to launch bride and groom into marital harmony. Only the rich and chic used diamonds to seal engagements, and honeymoons were overnight visits to nearby spas. In the 1980s, however, simplicity was abandoned in the great stampede toward showiness. In 1967, for example, only 6 percent of engaged women received diamond engagement rings. Two decades later 77 percent of them had diamonds. The import of diamonds quintupled between 1978 and 1988. The new ethic of lavish display was so entrenched by 1989 that the average cost of ceremony, reception, and honeymoon soared to nearly $30,000, a sum roughly equal to a worker's annual salary. Ingenious marital matchmaking agencies offered the prospective bridegroom a complete package of bride, wedding, reception, and honeymoon for up to $70,000. Some even rented wedding "guests"—distinguished looking men who masqueraded as important bureaucrats or celebrities—to add tone to an otherwise undistinguished reception. The need to display wealth began to invade even funerals. For a price, the bereaved could close out the solemn rite with a pageant in which ten white doves flew out of a cage.

Inevitably, the great spending surge induced a new and different form of Westernization in Japan. The buying of things Western had always been regarded as somehow gauche, unless the things bought had practical value. Machines and technology were, of course, ever popular for their usefulness in building the economy. And of course the young had their peculiar tastes in music, hamburgers, and Coca-Cola. But in the years of severity after the war, buying foreign goods was frowned upon, considered to be either unpatriotic or in bad taste. Western art could not compare with the clean, simple lines of classic Japanese paintings. Foreign cars were big and ostentatious, and the ownership of one marked a person as at best frivolous and at worst criminal. (Only the *yakuza*, Japanese gangsters, drove around in large American sedans, usually Lincoln Continentals.) Since very few Japanese could afford such foreign luxuries, they once again made virtue of necessity and pronounced things Japanese to be superior in all ways.

But native pride faded in the 1980s, weakened by the currency alignments that made things priced in dollars suddenly cheap. In the shifting ethics of the time, the new rich could best show their status by buying symbols of Western affluence. Purchasing one more Hiroshige print would do nothing for the parvenu businessman, but snapping up the work of famous Western painters would stamp him as culturally advanced. So the Yasuda Fire and Marine Insurance Co., previously one of Japan's stodgier firms, paid $40 million for Vincent van Gogh's *Sunflowers* in 1987 to celebrate a corporate birthday. That was three times the amount ever paid at auction for a van Gogh. Nippon Autopolis Co., a motor-car-racing company, paid $52 million for a Picasso masterpiece and hung it in a theme-park museum designed to boost attendance at auto races. The bias against foreign cars was dissipated; Tokyo's narrow streets were soon clogged with Mercedes, Jaguars, and BMWs. The strong yen made foreign real estate cheap, especially when compared to Japan's inflated prices, and the new smart set turned to foreign shores in pursuit of condos and homes. Half-million-dollar condos in Honolulu were bought like dresses at a fire sale—one Japanese couple paid that much and returned home not sure whether they had bought or only leased the ocean-side condo. Japanese realtors drove through the swank neighborhoods of Honolulu with cashier's checks at the ready, buying on the spot for clients back in Tokyo. For some, a trek abroad to buy real estate was considered onerous. For them, creative brokers set up televised showings in Tokyo of properties for sale in America and France. The buyer could pick off a Los Angeles mansion with a flick of his credit card. A regular weekend television show marketed, among other properties, a fifteenth-century French chateau priced, complete with family furnishings, at only $2 million. An average of 4 million Japanese watched the show each week.

There was, in this 1980s' splurge, a change of values so startling and unanticipated that it sometimes seemed that a totally new public culture had been superimposed on the old. It was as if an entire nation had leapt from poverty-induced frugality to wanton self-indulgence in a mere two generations. In the late 1970s credit cards were few and frowned upon, symbols of wastrelism found only in the decadent West. The better-off still went around the streets with pockets and briefcases stuffed with cash. By 1989 120 million credit cards were in circulation, enough to supply every Japanese with one card. Predictably, bad debts rose swiftly. No matter. Money seemed to flow so easily and endlessly that Japanese often seemed to be in competition for the prize of silliest spender. When the British liner *Queen Elizabeth II* berthed in Yokohama one morning in 1989 for a two-month visit, its choicest cabins were priced at $2,600 per night—not for a luxury cruise, merely for the bragging rights to having been aboard. Anything with a famous Western name pulled yen out of wallets and purses. It did not matter much that products labeled Gucci, Yves St. Laurent, or Christian Dior cost five to ten times more in Tokyo than abroad. The name counted for everything. The secretary-general of the Tokyo Fashion Designer Council, Noboyuki Ota, estimated that only 1 percent of Parisians and 10 percent of New Yorkers actually ever bought clothes bearing top designers' names. But 60 percent of Tokyoites did, he said.

The pattern of spending was so much a reversal of past consumption mores that it almost seemed to be un-Japanese. Dozens of essays and news columns deplored the new habits as wasteful and even unpatriotic. Parents reminded their credit-card-laden children sternly of their own hard times, when family treasures were sold to put rice on the table—but to no avail. The style-setters of the age were people in Jaguars and designer dresses who flew to Honolulu on weekends to shop and glance at their condos. There seemed to be few words in the Japanese vocabulary to describe the new pursuit of status. A new suburban residential development, where homes cost $1 million and up, was named "Exceed," as if there existed no proper Japanese name to describe adequately its dwellers' station in life. One academic writer, in an essay protesting the new age of indulgence, observed that many Japanese had ceased using the Japanese word *"kane"* and had adopted the English word "money" in boasting of wealth.[2]

The spending had almost nothing to do with traditional values. Things were bought not for investment or future returns, nor for making one's life more productive or comfortable. Toshiaki Izeki, a Keio University sociologist and marketing consultant, observed that the overriding purpose of the new lavishness was the visible enhancement of one's "life-style." He noted:

> They buy jewels and paintings to upgrade their life-style, not to hold and sell for profit. A few years ago, one could do that with a one-carat diamond. Now it takes two carats. If they entertain at home, they buy twelve-piece dinner sets, imported. They will buy complete sets of Italian furnishings— furniture, carpets, sofa, even the wallpaper. I know of one man who recently built a new home and bought all of the furnishings he thought he needed in one trip to Takashimaya [an expensive department store]. It cost him 50 million yen [about $350,000]. Then he decided he still did not have enough, and so he hired a professional buyer and went to Europe to buy more.[3]

●

Who were Japan's nouveau riche? The people responsible for this decisive break with the old frugality ethic represented a small proportion of the population. The average salaried worker reacted with surprise and disbelief when told he was living in the world's most affluent society. Seventy percent of middle-aged men questioned in a newspaper survey in 1988 said they did not lead affluent life-styles.[4] The spending binge of the 1980s was not a mass phenomenon but a movement centered in certain specific groups. Broadly speaking, these could be lumped into two separate categories. There were those who were not really rich at all but who bought their affluent styles of living with monthly earnings and corporate expense accounts. Their buying habits reflected new attitudes, not new wealth. And then there were those who became really rich because of the radical economic changes that swept over Japan in the decade.

The not-really-rich who fueled Japan's spending boom were usually the young or couples on the brink of middle age. Young, unmarried women with modest working incomes could spend lavishly on designer clothes and exotic holidays because they still lived with parents and had no ordinary living expenses to meet. They could afford frivolity for a time before married life reduced their freedom. Then there were the married couples in their thirties who simply chose to spend what they earned and to worry about tomorrow tomorrow. It was these sons and daughters of postwar bureaucrats and businessmen who most strikingly turned away from frugality and toward consumption. In a curious twist, their spend-now habits were reinforced by the enormous inflation of housing prices in the 1980s. The average price of a house was 80 million yen (about $530,000)—well beyond the means of ordinary wage earn- ers. They surrendered that dream and began to spend current income instead of saving it. Wandering around Tokyo in the late 1980s, one encountered vivid evidence of this change. Middle-class neighborhoods were still populated by families living in small houses and tiny apart- ments, but the streets were jammed with Mercedes, BMWs, and Jag- uars. Living for the moment, that most un-Japanese of traits, became the creed for their age.

Hikoharu Kure and his wife, Motoko, were in many ways typical of the new breed—comfortable in income but lacking in real wealth. At forty, Hikoharu was a fifteen-year veteran with the Ministry of Trade and Industry. He had followed the usual career path into the upper reaches of the bureaucracy after graduating from Tokyo University. But there the resemblance to his father's generation ended. He liked dining out with his wife and enjoyed membership in three clubs that met weekly for intellectual discussions. He took full vacations at fashionable coastal resorts and bought books, records, and household appliances as he wished. Motoko, meanwhile, indulged her preference for expensive pottery and metalworking classes. Their style was not lavish, but neither was it the nose-to-the-grindstone frugality of their parents. Hikoharu made a conscious decision not to save money. He set aside only enough for his son's education and resolved to spend the rest. "I feel that 1,000 yen now is equal to 50,000 yen for what I will want in my fifties," he said one afternoon in his office, where he agreed to discuss his spending plans with a reporter. "Now, I feel that I have energy and many inter- ests. I can enjoy it more now. Some people want to save their money for their old age, but that is not my attitude."[5]

A second type of not-really-rich were the corporate executives. Their affluence depended entirely on an affiliation with one of Japan's large, prosperous companies. They dined at expensive restaurants, drank at posh Ginza bars, and were driven to and fro in limousines—all at company expense. Every modern economy has its expense-account rich. Japan's were different because of the sheer scale of their spending. In 1988 total corporate expenditures on entertainment actually reported to tax authorities amounted to more than $34 billion, three times that in the United States and a sum equal to the gross national product of New Zealand. This new breed was given the nickname "*shayozoku*"— literally, "a tribe that flourishes off corporate beneficence." Japanese companies had long subsidized housing for those in the lower ranks who were unable to pay Tokyo's high costs of living. In the 1980s they enabled executives to live lavishly by paying most of their rent in apartments few others could ever afford. A new residential building in Shibaura, near the waterfront, became home to dozens of the subsidized wealthy. Tokyo Electric Co. bought up eighty-seven of its luxury suites for more than $700,000 each and rented them to selected executives for a nominal sum of $200 a month. They were, of course, merely Cinderella-style rich. Once retirement age came they were literally out on the streets, facing the harsh reality of Tokyo's unsubsidized housing market.

Japan's "really rich" were those who had benefited from the 1980s' booms in real estate and corporate securities. The scale of those surges was unprecedented anywhere else in the world. Although the precise number of suddenly rich investors and speculators is difficult to measure, it is probably true that never before in human history had so many become so rich so swiftly. Between 1980 and 1987, *The Economist* calculated, the total value of Japanese personal and corporate assets— primarily land and securities—nearly doubled in yen terms and quadrupled in dollars.[6] Residential land in Tokyo more than doubled in value in six years and commercial land prices tripled. Between 1980 and 1987, according to the Misawa Homes Institute of Research and Development, the number of people who owned land valued at more than $2 million tripled. The increase in company stock values was even more phenomenal. In 1978, just before the greatest of all booms began, the Nikkei stock average index stood at about 4,000. By 1989 it had soared to more than 38,000, and the value of stocks listed in Tokyo was greater than anywhere in the world. Although the already rich benefited most, people in ordinary circumstances found themselves hurtling into the highest income brackets. The vegetable-shop owner who lived with his family in two tiny rooms above their shop in Mejiro, for example, found himself worth $5 million when the neighborhood went trendy in the late 1980s. To be sure, much of the new wealth existed only on paper. Relatively few could cash in their real estate gains, for instance, because there were no modestly priced lodgings to buy elsewhere. In 1986 only about 1 percent of Tokyo's land-rich actually sold for profit. And Tokyoites began joking about the new class of "ghost millionaires." These were people, often retired businessmen, who lived in modest homes suddenly priced at $1 million dollars and up but whose small incomes allowed no room for frills or expensive habits.

The most important of the new "really rich" were the successful entrepreneurs who made fortunes great and small in the 1980s. They were largely a product of a major change that overtook the Japanese economy, perhaps the most important since the economic landscape was refashioned in the 1950s. Japan's successes were built by large corporations, great bureaucratic organizations that were sanctioned and protected by big government. The Hitachis, Toshibas, and Mitsubishis employed tens of thousands of people and managed them with an almost military style of organization. Many smaller companies did, in fact, flourish on the fringes of that landscape, and many entrepreneurs became wealthy owners of their own companies. But many also went bankrupt and others survived only as suppliers to the corporate giants. Shoestring businesses had their place, but not a very big one.

The sweeping changes of the 1970s and 1980s created a golden age for a new breed of entrepreneur. A primarily manufacturing economy was transformed into a service economy—that is, one in which the production of goods became less important in the total economy than the supplying of services of all kinds. This was a natural phenomenon that had already occurred in other advanced economies, but in Japan the transformation came about very rapidly. New construction companies sprang up to build homes for the affluent. Entirely new business-service companies—marketing consultants, financial advisory firms, office-supply shops—began growing swiftly. The Recruit Company, before its political scandal (see chapter 7), was the epitome of entrepreneurial spirit; it provided job-finding information to high school and college graduates and quickly made a fortune. A new economic animal called the "leisure industry" was born to reap profits off those with higher incomes. Travel agents, restaurateurs, and entertainment specialists of all kinds went into business for themselves and flourished. It was an age when the quick and daring could amass legal fortunes in businesses that the Toshibas of Japan spurned. In 1977 a salaried employee of Japan Air Lines, Hanunori Takahashi, quit his boring job to work for a small electronics company in Tokyo. In eleven years he transformed the stodgy little firm into a leisure-world giant with assets worth $6 billion and a string of South Seas resorts stretching to Tahiti.

The arrival of a new-rich class and its lavish consumption habits did much to erase the notion of Japan as a country culture-bound to frugality. Given high incomes and bundles of cash, it seemed, Japanese behaved pretty much as nouveau riche anywhere else in the world. They spent for momentary pleasure and for those trophies that could visibly mark them as owners of new wealth. Many deplored the new ostentation, and there was much talk of Japan sinking into the sort of degenerate frivolity that had ruined other nations. Foreigners grew angry at the sight of Japan's new real estate barons snapping up the best of Western art. But for those with a sense of history, it was all very familiar. Britains of the empire and turn-of-the-century American arrivistes had behaved much the same.

●

A more serious result of the "wealth explosion" was the dissipation of another Japanese postwar characteristic: social equality. One of the nation's great strengths in the relentless drive for economic success had been the widespread assumption that all would benefit more or less equally. The great vision of the times was of an entire people moving together as a nation, reaping similar rewards from their hard work. It was in some ways reminiscent of the compelling ethic that united Japanese during the harsh war years when they were inspired by the slogan, "One hundred million Japanese hearts beating as one." Just as in the war period, sacrifice would be equally shared and so would the fruits. The ideal of social homogeneity was a vital adhesive in the years when Japanese were struggling to lift their standard of living. They were one nation, one race, one class. From the mid-1960s on, almost every public-opinion poll found 90 percent of Japanese declaring they were members of the middle class.

The genesis of this ideal lay in the initial postwar years, for prewar Japan had been far from a model of social equality. In the years between the Meiji Restoration and the Pacific War, the amassing of great wealth by rural landlords and rich industrial and financial families was an accepted fact of life. Two forces prevailing in 1945 changed all that. First, the Occupation reforms were powerful levelers. They broke up the great land holdings and virtually eliminated the peasant class of tenant farmers. The giant *zaibatsu* were dismantled, stripping the richest families of their wealth, and an American-inspired tax code introduced progressive taxation. The Occupation's initial support for organized labor gave workers a strong hand in bargaining for wages. The second propelling force was the wave of Japanese radicalism that swept over the country in the early postwar years. This was more than a revival of socialist theory suppressed in the war years. Young men released from the army were just as radical as the old leftists and just as inclined to break down the old social structure they held responsible for war and devastation. It all combined to produce an egalitarian spirit that was totally at odds with the prewar way of life. Underpinning it, too, was the fact that the crushing defeat had rendered Japan a near-classless society, one in which nearly all were equally poor.

Nothing reflected the leveling movement better than the first series of labor contracts negotiated under Occupation supervision. They assumed the principle of equal pay for equal work, with little regard for education, status, or skill. A settlement reached in 1946 by the electric power workers' union provided for a basic "livelihood wage" for all employees, regardless of position. Pay raises would be based on need— the number of an employee's dependents, for example, or the scale of living costs in a given area. For a time, the "livelihood wage" pattern was accepted by the government and spread to other industries.

This inclination toward almost communal equality dissipated rather quickly as the Occupation shifted its weight against labor and toward business managers, but it left its mark on much of Japanese life for four decades. Unions usually included both white- and blue-collar members, and the differences in their pay, at least in the first years of employment, were only marginal. Indeed, employees coming straight from college were among the most avid unionists, intent on applying the leftist theories then taught in virtually all branches of higher education. Class divisions based on job and position were small. A poll of white-collar workers in 1963 found that a substantial majority thought of themselves as aligned more with workers than with management, and a substantial number identified themselves as socialists.[7] Schools preached an unrelenting egalitarianism, in part because of Occupation reforms and in part because most teachers were members of a proselytizing socialist union. From the lowest grades on, pupils were taught that all had equal talents and that hard work and perseverance could move all up the education ladder in equal steps. Tests that might divide school classes according to intelligence were spurned. What mattered were the repeated achievement tests, which measured work, not innate talent.

Those who grew up in the old Japan and lived through the postwar transformation recall the drive toward social equality as an enormous and lasting change. Jinnosuke Miyai, a Shell Oil-Japan executive, believes:

> [I]t was a revolution as big as the French Revolution or the Meiji Restoration. The war and the Occupation completely destroyed class distinctions. The country was flattened socially as well as physically. The effects were everywhere. I can remember that in the late 1940s my first task at Shell was to

eliminate almost all of the distinctions between [white-collar] staff and workers. The rich old *zaibatsu* families had been destroyed, and most of our companies were being run by middle-level managers, people who had come up through the ranks. It was our practice at Shell to start all new employees at the bottom—our company leaders in Europe were very unhappy with that idea. We made few distinctions, at first, between university graduates and workers. Our practice was for even university graduates to remain union members for fifteen years. Getting rid of distinctions was just part of the times. I can remember that my son was a close friend and schoolmate of my driver's son. They always played together.[8]

A great deal of that workplace egalitarianism survived, and most authorities agree that it helped produce the long period of relative harmony in Japanese factories. It is true that workers in large companies, where productivity rates were higher, were paid much more than those in small ones. But within each company, wage differentials were—and still are—small. Throughout most of his working life, the blue-collar worker receives only slightly less in salary than the white-collar employee who is nominally part of management. By Western standards, the gap in salaries paid to top-level managers and lowly shop-floor workers is very small. A *bucho*, or department head, earns only about three times as much as his lowliest employee. Japanese company presidents, according to several surveys, earn, on the average, about six or seven times the salaries paid to new recruits in the same firms. One study often cited estimates that company presidents in the late 1980s received 7.5 times the income paid to the newest of workers. In Europe and the United States they received between 30 and 50 times as much.[9] In late 1988 the average Japanese company president received only about $240,000 a year in salary and bonuses—about 10 percent of the compensation paid to chief executive officers in American companies evaluated by *Fortune* magazine. The same small differentials exist in the government bureaucracy, which has traditionally attracted graduates of the most prestigious universities. A deputy minister, the highest rank attainable by a career civil servant in Japan, is paid about five or six times as much as a newcomer at the bottom.

Primarily because of these narrow wage differentials, class distinctions based purely on income were smaller in Japan than in almost any other industrialized country. The large class gaps that emerged in Europe and America as postwar prosperity raised incomes did not exist in

Japan. This relative equality has been reflected in several studies conducted by the Organization for Economic Cooperation and Development (OECD) that measure the incomes of people in each of ten deciles of the populations of member countries. In general, they show that Japanese in the bottom 10-percent income bracket have more of the total income than the lowest 10 percent of other OECD nations. And the top bracket of Japanese have less of the total income than do the richest in other countries. A detailed OECD survey in 1976 found, for example, that the bottom 10 percent of Japan's population received twice as much of the total post-tax income as the comparable group in America. The leveling of incomes in Japan began in the late 1950s, continued through the high-growth years, and grew even more pronounced in the 1970s. In the same years, the American trend was toward less and less income equality. [10]

Relative equality in Japan was reinforced by several other factors, some stemming from deliberate policy, others from traditional practices in Japanese society. The progressive tax code bequeathed by the Occupation was largely maintained, although much unearned income escaped taxation because of the absence of a capital gains tax on securities until 1989. The rich pay a greater share of taxes in Japan than in the United States. The absence of widespread real poverty at the bottom of the scale in part reflects the refusal of a racially exclusivist country to accept foreigners and refugees as Western nations have done since World War II. One social characteristic that adds to the appearance of equality is the family system. More of the elderly live at home with their children than do so in the West. That practice reduces the number of single-person poor households, a large reservoir of poverty in countries like the United States. For all of these reasons, Japan entered the 1980s boasting of the most egalitarian social system in the industrialized non-Communist world. It had few impoverished minorities and no real underclass to speak of. There was relatively little segregation by income. Urban neighborhoods tended to be little mixing bowls of classes, with shabby old wooden houses tilting against modern new ones, all of them small by Western standards. Equality of education remained a great leveler, opening the highest career tracks to the worthiest of students. Low rates of unemployment throughout the 1960s and 1970s had meant that only the laziest could not find jobs. It all encouraged the notion that Japan had escaped the perils of modernization that marked other developing countries and had emerged a far more cohesive nation than, for example, the United States, with its sprawling slums, urban riots, and impoverished minorities. Japan had mastered both growth and social equality, Prime Minister Noboru Takeshita asserted. In a book extolling postwar progress, he observed that the income of Japan's wealthiest one-fifth was only 2.9 times that of the poorest fifth. In the United States, the gap was three times as great. "Seen overall, we have succeeded in achieving an equitable distribution of wealth," Takeshita wrote.[11]

Takeshita had a genius for bad timing. His book appeared just as Japan was discovering that events of the 1980s were demolishing much of this cherished egalitarianism and that some Japanese were, in fact, much more equal than others. The prosperity they had imagined as being fairly shared by all turned out to be much less equally distributed, and the leveling effects of more than three decades were being erased. It appeared that the rich did indeed get richer and that this transformation could occur at a dizzying pace in an economy as dynamic as Japan's. By the end of the 1980s, Japan's postwar society no longer seemed blissfully classless.

Two events—the rapid rise of land values and a soaring stock market—lay behind the change. In the mid-1980s land prices soared, first in Tokyo, then in other eastern urban centers, and finally in lesser cities around the country. Residential land prices in Tokyo rose 95 percent in 1987 alone. Much of Japan became a speculator's paradise where quick profits were made overnight. Cheap money borrowed one week was plowed into parcels that were valued 20 percent higher the next. Already flush with cash and with few places to lend it, banks encouraged the speculation, granting large loans using properties at suddenly inflated values as collateral. There were two effects of the dazzling boom: Middle-class families in Tokyo and other eastern cities were priced out of the housing market; and many landowners suddenly became very rich. Much of the new wealth lay only on paper, but that paper could be churned into other types of profit by using it to borrow cash. In a matter of only two years, Tokyo, and to a lesser extent other cities, had been transformed into a realm of the haves and the have-nots—those who had owned land and those who had not and never would.

Much of the real estate profit was poured into Tokyo's stock market, which had been booming since the late 1970s. Stock prices as measured by the leading index were ten times higher when the 1980s ended than when it began. The enormous gains in wealth from playing stocks were nearly clean profit, since Japan had never bothered to tax capital gains on securities. New wealth engendered in the financial markets was concentrated in the highest brackets. In 1988 the Eco-

nomic Planning Agency underscored this tilt in wealth by calculating
how much stock value increases had accrued to each one-fifth of the
population. Stocks owned by the lowest fifth had risen only from 0.4
trillion yen to 2.8 trillion yen. For the richest fifth, the gain was from
3.4 trillion yen to 24.4 trillion yen. [12]

The "asset gap," as the land and stock-price inflation was termed,
was not in itself a surprising phenomenon. People with money tend to
make more, and clever risk-takers profit in every country moving up the
economic scale. What was stunning about Japan's asset gap was the
suddenness and size of it all. The land of the vast middle class had
hurtled into a two-class society within only a few years. One government
economist measured the change by combining the value of all assets
owned by the most middle-class segment and by the richest. In 1980 the
middle fifth of Japanese (by income) owned 7 million yen worth of
assets of all kinds and saw this grow by 1987 to only 10 million yen. The
top fifth, on the other hand, watched their assets rise from 30 million
yen to a staggering 100 million yen. The study made the asset gap stand
out starkly: The richest fifth of the population owned ten times as much
in assets as did the middle-class fifth, and that enormous gap had grown,
for the most part, in a mere seven years. [13] At first it had appeared that
the widening gap referred only to assets, like stocks and land holdings.
But another government study found that between 1982 and 1986 a
considerable difference had arisen in household incomes, a category
that consisted mostly of earned income, not capital gains on land and
stocks. It was alarming because inequality in income had been declining
for the previous twenty years.

The sober and irrefutable government studies were quickly translated into press accounts of a growing unfairness, and both underscored
what the ordinary citizen could see happening all around him. A kind
of inequality fever began to run through the social system, and well-
known facts came to assume ominous proportions. It had long been
known that doctors got rich faster than others. Then came the report
that doctors earned nearly seven times more than average workers and
that this gap was larger than in any other modern nation. It was also
noted that wealth and position could be passed on to children to a far
greater extent than previously believed. Doctors inherited their doctor-
fathers' rich practices. Politicians bequeathed their Diet seats and money
sources to their sons. New-rich entrepreneurs sent their sons to college
abroad and wrote off the costs as business expenses on the pretext that it
was for business training. In the midst of it all came the great Recruit
scandal (see chapter 7) with its shocking accounts of bribery and stock

manipulation, a tale of ill-gotten gains and favoritism for the rich and powerful that dominated the press for a year. Finally, as if driven by some perverse instinct to maximize public outrage, the LDP forced through the parliament a package of tax revisions that could only exacerbate the sense of unfairness—it lowered rates on the highest incomes and socked the average householder with a 3 percent tax on almost everything he bought at retail. As the British magazine *The Economist* summed up these added assaults on the Japanese public: "While they were sweating to save for a house or to find the right stock for their savings, up popped the politicians bearing a consumption tax for them while trousering a nice capital gain courtesy of Recruit."[14]

The result of all these changes in the 1980s was not merely a threat to a lower class suddenly dumped while everyone else headed upstream. It was a challenge to the vast Japanese middle class that had long been comforted by the notion that the rising tide would raise all boats. A majority of the people felt stranded when the great tidal wave raised about one-fifth of the population to sudden, unthinkable richness. Most people were left to rethink their stations in life. When the decade began about 60 percent of all Japanese felt they were in the center of the middle class. By 1987 only 52 percent felt so.[15] For the first time, more than 20 percent of Japanese looked upon themselves as lower class. Ironically, the popular pessimism grew most rapidly between 1985 and 1989, on the whole a very prosperous period. In those years the proportion of Japanese expressing satisfaction with their livelihood fell from 71 to 63 percent. The year 1988 was one of recovery for business in Japan. It left nearly a third of the people stating that they felt worse off economically than the year before.[16] The Economic Planning Agency published an extensive examination of both the widening gaps and what people thought of them. The results revealed how out of date was the notion that Japan was a fair and equal country. Three-fourths of the people looked upon the new differences in income with a sense that society had become unequal and unfair. Eighty percent felt the tax system was unfair. Most were willing to accept differentials that arose from hard work. What aroused their wrath was the unfairness that stemmed from luck in the stock market and real estate bonanzas.

As previous chapters have shown, there was always more disenchantment with the system than that which appeared on the surface. The surprisingly high levels of job dissatisfaction and the dislike of job regimentation were examples of that. Millions of Japanese had benefited little from the business culture. But the malaise of the 1980s was something different; it touched on the core of the system itself. It was, in fact, people at the center who were stung most by the appearance of great new wealth. Some of the strongest criticism of the new-rich was centered in the ranks of salarymen and middle-level bureaucrats. The values they had supported were those of study, hard work, and rewards for honest endeavor. They had spent their youth studying for college exams, and they had pushed open the doors of success by diligence. Becoming rich was never in their dreams. Advancement was its own reward. In the 1980s they looked up from their desks and found to their astonishment that the old value system had been overturned. Salaries in the suddenly fashionable securities companies were twice their own, and men of little talent (they felt) were ripping down shacks to build lavish new homes while they remained in tiny apartments, having abandoned all hope of owning houses.

The abrupt shifts in status and class divisions alarmed Japan's conservative press most of all. Its editorials, normally bland and reassuring, boomed forth in outrage at the new cleavages, once the respected EPA had certified them as true. "The widening gap in assets is clearly to be blamed for the creation of a two-class society—the New Rich and the New Poor," declared the *Japan Economic Journal*, published by the staid house of Nihon Keizai Shimbun, a sort of *Wall Street Journal* of Japan. A magazine of equally conservative credentials, *Tokyo Business Today*, found the nation heading for ruin, its work force demoralized. "Japan's uniquely equal society has . . . already started crumbling from within and there is every possibility that a new class will come out of the ruins," it lamented. "If all these developments are allowed to go unchecked, the worker morale which has so far held Japanese society and economy together is bound to disintegrate."

This new sense of unfairness—a sense of wealth growing from greedy speculation and the manipulation of markets—was an especially bitter experience for Sen Koga. When I met Koga in 1989, he was eighty years old and a respected elder statesman of Japan's labor movement. He had begun organizing workers in the 1920s, when unionism had enjoyed a brief respite from government repression, and had returned to the union halls in the 1940s, when Occupation-sponsored reforms gave labor its greatest opportunity. A radical at first, he had mellowed during the period of strikes and finally had come to terms with the idea of company-dominated enterprise unions. What changed him was the promise offered by the productivity movement of the early 1950s. Its formula for labor-management cooperation provided that the worker would share equally in the fruits of higher productivity. Hard work would have its fair rewards. Wages and benefits would rise as the com-

pany produced and sold more goods. Koga joined the new Japan Productivity Center because its formula for sharing seemed fair. "Fairness"
was an important concept to him, had guided him through stormy,
dangerous days on the picket lines. "Never by afraid of being poor, but
always be afraid of being unfair"—that had been his personal motto
throughout life, he said.

Now, in January 1989, he saw the principle of a lifetime eroded.
People made fortunes by manipulating stocks and selling land at inflated
values. It was *furo shotoku*, or "profit without work." *Furo shotoku*—he
hurled the phrase around like a curse. It was all summed up, he said,
in the Recruit affair, where politicians amassed riches through shady
stock transactions. It was "unfair," Koga said over and over. The government would not act to stop it, and it was beyond the power of
organized labor to curb such grand-scale corruption. "Who would dare
to talk today about the principles of the productivity movement?" he
asked. No one could claim that rewards were shared equally when
hustlers grew wealthy overnight and workers struggled on their modest
incomes. The appeal of the productivity argument was meaningless,
dead, buried now in the debris of *furo shotoku*.

10
●

Touches of Rebellion

Looked at from outside, the Spiral Building, in the trendy Aoyama section of Tokyo, appears to be a beguiling monument to modernism, a pastiche of aluminum, glass, panels, and jutting beams, all fitted together irregularly into a nine-story structure that is both eye-catching and puzzling. Its true message, in fact, is inside. There is a spacious lobby containing nothing but a piece of modern sculpture and an information booth. On one side stretches a long, broad corridor that serves as an art gallery and leads to a carpeted ramp that curves in a swooping, graceful spiral to a second-floor shop. In the center of the ramp stands a large square platform painted Chinese red. On a day in 1990 there was nothing on the red platform except mounds of a powdery substance shaped like mountains and volcanic craters. The effect is one of grand spaciousness, a pleasant change from the cramped and crowded jumble of most Tokyo buildings, where each precious square meter must be utilized to sell people things. There is something utterly un-

Japanese about the Spiral Building in its almost willful "wasting" of expensive space. In a café off the lobby, the tables are placed wide apart, affording privacy and elbow room, features foreign to all but a few Japanese restaurants.

The Kasumigaseki Building is a monument to the 1960s, a rather grim fortress well suited to the ideals of maximized efficiency and hard work that characterized Japan's high-growth years. The 1970s, when Japan first began to achieve world-class financial strength, are expressed in the Nomura Building in Shinjuku. Its message is one of great and lasting power. The Spiral Building, which opened in 1985, is a much different kind of symbol. It speaks of an age when Japan became less concerned with making a living and forging ahead, when she began to slough off some of the old rigid habits and began to enjoy herself. It says that Japan has reached the stage of appreciating diversions and capriciousness, that Japan is so rich it can waste even her most precious commodity, space.

For in the 1980s Japan began to reinvent herself once again. She emerged in that decade secure and confident from a long era of scarcity and fear, a period that in fact stretched back a half-century to the depression and the beginnings of war. Money is a liberating commodity, and for the first time in history a large number of Japanese had a great amount of it. It underwrote a new freedom to experiment, a license to question and even mock things that had long been accepted. Attitudes toward old habits and institutions changed remarkably, even radically, in the 1980s. Work and its rewards, politics, the place of women, even the economy itself—all of these began to be questioned and criticized in ways that Japanese had foresworn during the grim struggle for revival after the war.

That struggle had imposed on Japanese a rigid set of values. Hard work, economic growth, and above all social stability were the principal values of the age, and the great national consensus insisted that they be observed. There were moments of rebellion, such as the radical protests against the military alliance with America and the Vietnam war. These gradually waned, however, and the fierce radicals went off to work in the successful new companies. For the most part, Japanese willingly submitted to the orthodoxy of views and rules that reinforced the struggle for that overarching goal of "stable growth." Japanese worked so hard for national economic goals, dissented so rarely, insisted on such modest rewards that they seemed citizens of some authoritarian regime. Foreigners joked: "Japan is the only Communist system that works." But the true ideology of the age was not capitalism or socialism or even democratic liberalism. It was an age of what one wise observer called "economism," one in which ". . . the tendency to give priority to economic values strikes deeply into the individual consciousness of each citizen and affects his daily life-style. . . . People rarely use any yardstick other than profit and loss."[1]

"Economism" was a demanding creed requiring submission to strict rules. In working life, the needs of the company took precedence over family, friends, and even personal health. Nowhere was conformity more rigidly enforced than in public schools. From kindergarten through high school, the student was subjected to the most extraordinary discipline. The length of his hair, the shape of his trousers, the color of his socks—all were defined by school rule books. Waywardness meant discipline and most schools winked at corporal punishment. It was news, but not really shocking news, when Gifu Prefecture junior high schools enforced a code of silence to assure conformity. Students were forbidden to make sounds, even in class, where they responded by hand signals signifying "Yes," "No," or "I don't know." Learning was almost always accomplished through rote and recitation, the student giving back word for word what his books or teachers had given. Critics, even many who were part of the national education bureaucracy, pointed out repeatedly that such strictness produced dull people, uninteresting and unquestioning. But the system also produced high levels of achievement in math and literacy, and the criticisms were usually ignored. The tyranny of achievement tests followed the student everywhere. Scores might determine which high school he could enter, and more scores decided which college he would attend.

Rigidity and discipline had been features of Japanese education since the dawn of the Meiji era, but they had been redoubled after the war. "Economism" played its role here, too. Schools were expected to provide literate, numerate workers and not much else. Naohiro Amaya, an ex-MITI official who served on one of the many education reform commissions in the 1980s, once noted that universities adopted the role of ranking graduates through test scores so that corporate recruiters could hire the best. It had gotten to the point, he said, that "Japanese universities have become in effect subcontractors for the major companies."[2]

Despite all of the criticism and demands for change, the system rolled on because it served the purpose of a society geared to business success. One of the most searing indictments of the system came from an unexpected source, Prime Minister Noboru Takeshita, himself a former middle-school teacher. Takeshita observed that even the supposedly liberated education system of the Occupation years had quickly resorted to standardized practices that produced a homogenized student body and homogenized graduates. This resulted in good workers for the skilled labor pool needed by industry and good consumers of mass-produced merchandise, Takeshita wrote. But it also produced people short on creativity and individual initiative. "If we continue the kind of conformist education we have to date, focusing primarily on stuffing children with a set body of knowledge, we risk destroying their individuality," Takeshita declared in 1987.[3]

The result of "economism" was a stifling consensus that permeated Japanese life in the 1960s and 1970s—a disposition not to challenge the established view of things lest the good times cease to roll. The organs of state and business, of course, did much to reinforce this disposition, but the real source of the consensus was voluntary. Japanese deeply believed that their success might be transient, that what had been built up with such extraordinary work and patience might be swept away on a wave of social instability. Organized labor meekly accepted its diminishing share of the economic pie because its leaders believed in "stable growth" as much as company executives. The salaryman and his wife grumbled about high prices, their wretched housing, the absence of public amenities readily available in other modern countries. Rarely was the discontent translated into organized opposition, however. The boat must not be rocked lest the engine be swamped.

In the 1980s the great fog of "economism" began to lift, and attitudes toward all of these rigid institutions began to change. As always in Japan the changes came slowly and circumspectly, more with a murmur than a roar. No institutions crumbled. But with the dawning of economic security, many of the old inhibitions dropped away and a new habit of questioning took hold, not merely among the young and the outsiders but among people at the core of the postwar system. Politics, social practices, work and careers, women's role, even the economic system itself—all of these were subjected to examination and criticism in ways that would have been considered vaguely unpatriotic in the 1960s and 1970s. There occurred an enlivening in social affairs that contrasted markedly with the grim, nose-to-the-grindstone behavior of the period of high economic growth. People began to say quite freely that they wanted more from life than hard work, saving money for disaster, and devotion to company.

Japanese delight in measuring their own attitudes, and the 1980s produced dozens of public-opinion surveys that recorded this shift in values. For many years, cross-sections of Japanese had been asked whether they placed emphasis on preparing for the future or living a fuller life at the moment. Throughout most of the 1960s and 1970s, when "economism" was in full flower, they had stressed preparing for the future, a sign that memories of hard times past were very vivid. In 1985 a survey recorded a watershed: More said they preferred to live a full life at the moment than prepare for the future. Another series of surveys had attempted to gauge Japanese feelings about the sort of affluence they preferred. Did they want "material affluence," which meant secure incomes, or did they want "spiritual affluence," which meant opportunity to experience pleasure or enjoy cultural pursuits. Before 1979 a majority had always preferred material affluence. But the 1980s recorded a fast-growing majority who preferred spiritual affluence.[4]

Most of all there was a new desire for diversity, an interest in creating individual values as opposed to those of the group. "Groupism," the herdlike instinct that sociologists had supposed to be an essential cultural ingredient of "Japaneseness," began to wane in the 1980s. Survey after survey found, especially among the young, growing preferences for individual life-styles. Careers that provided opportunities for individual expression were becoming preferred to those that offered merely organizational prestige and assured incomes. Bosses began complaining that they could no longer induce office workers to drink with them after hours; the young wanted to enjoy their own friends. Individual tastes in consumption, leisure activities, and travel were perhaps the most conspicuous signs of the enlivening of Japan in the 1980s. To appear to be independent, to seem to be cultivating one's own interests, to display a sort of capriciousness—these were the self-images it was fashionable to present. Even the government bureaucracies snapped to attention. In 1987 the Economic Planning Agency officially deplored "the Japanese value system which does not allow diversity" and advocated a shift to one which "accepts various life styles," one in which "it is fundamental that everyone has his own value system."[5]

It was fitting, then, that one of the first widely popular novels of the decade celebrated this new spirit of self-centeredness in the young. The publication in early 1981 of a slim volume entitled *Nanto-naku Kuristaru* (*Somewhat Crystal*), by Yasuo Tanaka, was less a literary event than a revelation of how swiftly mores were changing in the time of economic plenty. Its characters were the rich and easily bored students in fashionable but not prestigious colleges like Aoyama Gakuin and Rikkyo. They roamed the cafés and discos of Roppongi and Akasaka, enjoying one another's light-hearted company, or hopped into bed with a casual partner at one of the "love hotels" for a round of quick sex. They wore brand-name clothes of foreign make, sang and danced to Western music, and spent their parents' money with credit cards. To be "Crystal" was to be cheerful and untroubled by ordinary cares, aloof, for a period of time in college, from discipline and work. A young heroine in the novel describes life with her boyfriend: "Junichi and I live without anything bothering us. We buy or wear or eat something that makes us happy. We listen to pleasant music or take a walk somewhere or do something that makes us feel good."[6]

The "Crystals" were, to be sure, but a part of their time, but their popularity among young readers was a signal that old values were crumbling. If they were in revolt against anything it was the extreme seriousness of their parents' generation. Work and saving money had been the core of life for their fathers and mothers, who had lived in dread that prosperity might disappear. The "Crystals" took prosperity for granted. Economic deprivation, war, politics of any sort simply did not figure in their lives. As the young author of the novel, a college student, explained to an interviewer:

> There's no war, no emergency, no demonstrations. There are no serious problems. In older times young people talked passionately about love or friendship. Now we don't bother. We act by mood, not pragmatically, by feeling, not logic. . . . Let me explain that slowly. There is no fear of death or war or hunger. There will be no change in the near future. Japan is peaceful and stable. We are rich.[7]

This affable novelist, true to his characters, did not even seem to take seriously the writing of literature. After graduation, he thought, he would become a salesman for an oil company. By mid-decade Tanaka's "Crystals" had entered the mainstream of work and marriage, but their indifference to serious matters lived on to define a generation. In 1986 the most popular new word of the year was *shinjinrui*, which translates roughly as the "new human breed." The new breed were like the old "Crystals": young, hedonistic, and given totally to temporary pleasure.

Most Japanese obviously could not afford such pleasurable idleness. Work and careers were still central to their lives. But in the 1980s attitudes toward work underwent a profound change. The older generation had held work sacred. Devoted to job and company, they had brought to their offices and factories a dedication matched only by the prewar attachment to the imperial state. We have seen that a good deal of this devotion had been engineered by skillful managers who transformed the young "golden eggs" into pliant workers, but much of it, too, was the result of genuine commitment. In the 1980s this commitment declined substantially. From the many surveys of that decade there emerges the picture of an employee who cherished free time more than work time, who preferred family and friends to company life, and who above all wished to assert his independence—and was deeply unhappy when he could not. The pervasive theme was a desire to place private pursuits, not work, at the core of one's life.

The most striking expression of this was the changed attitude toward the company itself. The coercive paternalism that had been tolerated and even admired in the early postwar decades began, in the 1980s, to seem intolerably intrusive. The company demanded too much of both the employee and his family. It transferred him at will to strange towns, required him to work long hours, and insisted to an oppressive degree on regulating his nonworking life. A hint of dissatisfaction with this system had begun to appear in the early 1970s, when the expression *mai-homuism*, or "my-homism," swept into the public consciousness. It basically denoted a preference for one's own home life and private interests, and authorities have written that it was a modest rebellion not only against the demands of "companyism" but against commitment to public concerns in general. It was often associated with political indifference and social detachment.

In the 1980s this attitude was revived as a defense against the all-encompassing embrace of the company, and poll after poll recorded its spread. Each year more new employees entering the job market said they would stress private pursuits, not devotion to the company. In 1988 85 percent of college graduates awaiting corporate recruiters said they would put family first, work and company second, according to the Recruit Research Co.[8] Even the view of the company as an institution changed sharply. No longer was it worshiped as the benevolent benefactor deserving eternal loyalty. It was now a place where one went to earn money. Each year recruits were asked in surveys what working in a company meant to them. A way to develop their own abilities? A way to serve society? Or merely a source of income? In 1977 about 21 percent had regarded the company as merely a place to earn money. That figure had more than doubled—to 44 percent—by 1984.[9] By 1987 61 percent of all company newcomers said they regarded the company merely as a place to make a living.[10]

It is not surprising, then, that that great pillar of company loyalty called "lifetime employment" began to crumble. As noted earlier, lifetime employment was more a slogan than a reality for most Japanese workers because it was actual policy only in a minority of companies. What changed was the attitude among employees toward the policy itself. It ceased to be the ideal among younger workers, whether it existed or not. A survey by the Economic Planning Agency in 1985 found that a bare majority of workers, about 54 percent, agreed with the notion that it was best to work for one company as long as possible. But only a minority—41 percent—of workers in the twenty-five- to thirty-four-year age group believed that.[11] Several Japanese authorities have pointed out that this lack of interest in lifetime employment was probably not merely a matter of personal preference. Companies themselves, in the late 1970s and early 1980s, were disentangling themselves as fast as possible from lifetime commitments. This chiefly meant getting rid of unwanted employees in their fifties. Ironically, corporations were under government pressure to raise the retirement age from roughly fifty-five to sixty and dutifully declared this to be their policy. In fact, it became customary to push men toward retirement starting at age fifty—either by offering bonuses as inducements or threatening transfers to remote branches if they refused. In the new scheme of things, lifetime employment clearly was to be applied only to a small core of valued executives whose skills were considered essential.

The shift in attitudes toward the company and long-term employment was reflected in a surge of voluntary job-switching that was abnormally high by Japanese standards. Previously, despite the evidence of widespread job dissatisfaction, relatively few tried to seek greener pastures. Changing companies, except for the very young, had been both a mark of disloyalty and an act of futility, the latter because few companies would break the corporate line to hire switchers. Jumping from Toshiba to Hitachi would have been unethical had it been possible, which of course it was not. But in 1987 about 4.4 percent of the work force switched companies—not a large number by Western standards, but, nevertheless an 80 percent increase in five years.[12] Another 6 million said they were thinking of switching. They switched for reasons familiar to all workers anywhere: a bad boss, low pay, commuting problems. The most authoritative survey, performed by the Labor Ministry in questionnaires to 10,000 workers, found that 45 percent of them would change jobs if a better one were available.[13] Company loyalty in the treasured old-fashioned sense had become meaningful only to Japan's older workers, those trained in the early days of hardship when any job was a blessing. This casual disregard for "companyism" was perhaps best illustrated by a perfectly serious insurance company report that surveyed the secret dreams of the average Tokyo salaryman. What would he most like to do but knew he could not? Thirty-seven percent of these dutiful workers said they would choose first to have love affairs with women in their offices. A close second, at 36 percent, said they would change jobs.[14]

The new spirit of independence was to some degree made possible by rapid economic changes in the 1980s. In many small ways the changes encouraged individualistic behavior. The major shift to a service economy opened up thousands of new jobs in new companies started by entrepreneurs uninterested in the old, rigid company pattern. They demanded skill more than loyalty. Computer operators and programmers could switch jobs with ease in search of better wages. Banks, security companies, and insurance firms that expanded rapidly when the financial sector was liberalized needed new skills quickly, and the old promotion-through-the-ranks formula was outdated. They began bidding against one another for the qualified. American-style "headhunters" appeared on the scene, filling jobs for a fee and stealing experienced specialists for their clients. Raiding companies for top brains became common, a major break from the old gentlemen's agreements on employment cartels. In several surveys, up to 70 percent of Japanese companies acknowledged that they recruited from other firms. Japan's new economic reality loosened the old ties and made independent movement possible.

But the driving force was the spirit of independence itself. The old pattern—study hard, pass college entrance exams, and bury one's life in the company—lost much of its appeal for the new generation. Its members believed in work, to be sure, but in work that satisfied their personal goals, not the company's. Privacy and personal time were important to them. Throughout the late 1980s business leaders lamented the new balkiness of salarymen—they spurned company dormitories, refused to drink after hours with their section chiefs, and sped home to family and television sets when the normal workday ended. The willingness to break old rules was displayed in countless small rebellions—revolts against family pressures, school restrictions, entrance exams—but it was at work that it received its most eager expression.

●

A few moments at lunch with Kozo Hasegawa tells one that he is not the businessman of Japan's postwar legend. At the age of forty he dresses in tailored suits of a Continental style, orders Perrier instead of sake, and speaks bluntly and without embarrassment in fluent English. When I met him in late 1989 he was already a successful restaurateur with two chains of dining spots operating in Tokyo and Yokohama, both catering to the trendy young set of people who might have stepped from the pages of *Nanto-naku Kuristaru*. He was as free of conventions as any Japanese businessman I had ever encountered. He drove a Jaguar, owned a condo near Manhattan's Columbus Circle, and traveled frequently to New York, which he loved for its sheer exuberance and sense of liberation. Hasegawa is a man of his times. He became successful in the 1980s by flouting every rule of well-ordered Japanese society and by capitalizing on the free-spiritedness of the new generation. He was a maverick as a child at home, in school, at college, and in the business world. He was the spirit of the 1980s wrapped in one well-tailored package.

Hasegawa was born in Yokohama in 1950, the son of a stern tyrant who ran the family's liquor-and-rice store, and his first rebellion began as a child. His father called him stupid and lazy and ridiculed his every minor mistake. Their violent scenes—the father also fought constantly with his mother—made home a torment. Kozo became an early television addict, and his favorite programs were American family sitcoms, which in those days usually featured heart-warming scenes in happy homes. Parents cherished children, love was reciprocated. "I can remember watching those and crying every time," Hasegawa recalled years later. "It was so much what I wanted." Throughout his teens he spoke not one word to his father, and in a climactic encounter he knocked the man unconscious.

School was his next revolt. He had few friends, despised the strict teachers, and hated to study. Teachers, like his father, called him dumb. "I could always tell by their eyes they despised me," he remarked. In junior high school he was ranked fifty-eighth in achievement out of a class of sixty—"The two below me were retarded children." He thought often of suicide and once went to the roof of a tall apartment building but drew back at the last moment. That night he sat down alone and, drawing on some inner conviction, determined to take charge of his own life. First he would earn self-respect at school. He bought an English-language book on self-hypnosis and memorized its methods. Each night he would press his fingers to his forehead and repeat fifty times to himself "I love studying." His achievement scores improved markedly, and within one year he had climbed from the rank of fifty-eight to that of twelve. His reward was to be accused of cheating by the teacher, who also vowed to prevent his entry into the affiliated high school. Kozo screamed back: He would pass the entrance exams for the best high school in the prefecture. He did, and never since has he known such deep satisfaction. "It was simply ecstasy, the dream come true," he recalled. After high school, he stood exams for Waseda, a prestigious private university, and was accepted.

Once inside Waseda's gates, it would seem, Hasegawa was well placed to enjoy the rewards of his labors. The future stretched before him like an open road to the successful life, Japanese style. He could enjoy four pleasurable years of drinking, sports, and girlfriends, and then he would surely be selected by one of Japan's prestige corporations for a lifetime of secure employment. Within two years, however, he had rejected it all. College was boring, unchallenging. He imagined the rest of his life flowing in a placid stream where he would be required to do nothing more than drift mindlessly along. He looked back nostalgically on his early days of self-accomplishment, when he had buckled down to studies and passed exams by personal struggle and discipline. The company life, Hasegawa concluded, would be worse than college. "In college it was well understood that we were merely resting for the big race of life, in which all of our energies would be devoted to doing what the companies would expect of us." In a world of personal freedoms the company, with its strict rules of behavior and loyalty, loomed as an island of "feudalism." "It is so strange," he recalled thinking. "In Japan we are free to do as we please, to speak what we want. But the company life is still like feudalism."

Abandoning the comfortable Waseda life, and with it the promise of the best Japan could offer, he fled to Sweden with $700 in savings in his pocket and began a new life as a dishwasher in a restaurant. There followed twenty glorious months of freedom—washing dishes, traveling around Europe with friends in a used Volkswagen, courting and marrying a blond Scandinavian girl. Returning to Japan with his bride, he found mother, father, and grandfather pressing him—with all of the tactics of guilt and obligation—to take over the family liquor-and-rice shop. Another bout with his father ended in near violence. Hasegawa began his own business on borrowed money, a small coffee shop called "Scandinavia House" in the Takadanobaba section of Tokyo. Another struggle with the system ensued. In exchange for a small loan to decorate the shop's interior, the bank insisted that he maintain a savings deposit of at least 200,000 yen. He thought of telling the bank to keep its loan but instead pressed his fingers to forehead as he had done in junior high school and forced himself to concentrate: "This is a bank, I need it. This is a bank, I need it." His instinctive rebellion quelled, he made the deposit and got the loan. With his blond wife as an extra attraction, the shop succeeded, and within two years Hasegawa had saved 10 million yen. The savings financed his first restaurant, a bar and snack shop in fashionable Roppongi. He called it "Zest," a name he chose from a dictionary because it was easily memorized by customers and expressed the free-spiritedness he hoped to convey.

As his restaurant empire expanded, Hasegawa turned against the grain once more. His management style is determinedly un-Japanese. He expects a blunt outspokenness from all employees. Obsequiousness is seen as a sign of weakness, if not incompetence. Despite their supposed concern for workers' welfare, Japanese bosses are traditionally tough and unyielding, especially those in small businesses such as restaurants. Hasegawa insisted on precisely the reverse. Once he discovered that a Zest manager—one of his early favorites—was browbeating waiters and the kitchen help, to the extent of demanding sexual favors from the young women. He promptly fired him. The pattern of automatic promotions and identical annual wage increases—the norm in traditional Japanese firms—was abandoned. Ability, almost alone, determines wages and positions, and a rigorous achievement scale measures everyone, separating the adept from the poor performers. A waiter with ten years of experience may earn little more than a newcomer. Western-style competitiveness is rewarded with large annual bonuses for the most successful.

By 1989 Hasegawa's venture embraced twelve restaurants, half named Zest and half named La Boheme, which grossed $13 million a year. Their popularity owed much to his determination to break with Japanese traditions. There is nothing about them that is remotely Japanese in either menu or decor. The Zests are roomy Southwestern American *cantinas* that serve tacos and hamburgers. The La Bohemes are lively Italian pasta parlors. The styles of both are almost eccentrically whimsical. One Zest features a stuffed vulture hanging from the ceiling. The newest La Boheme is dominated by an original oil painting of a bare-breasted woman holding a man's bloody head on a platter. All are spacious in size and casual in atmosphere, the antithesis of most Japanese eateries, even those serving foreign cuisine. The regular customers are models of their generation's "Crystals"—young men and women seeking diversity and the offbeat. It is a curious and revealing communion, Hasegawa and his young clientele, a kind of conspiracy to leave the old, well-ordered life outside.

In his drive for success, Kozo Hasegawa broke with almost all of the conventions that held postwar Japan together. He rejected his parents, married a foreigner, abandoned a good college, spurned the security of company life, and devised a way of managing business that was the precise opposite of Japanese "companyism." The mark of each stage was his desire to lead life as an individual, to experience personal challenge, and to put his own stamp on his affairs. These traits are supposedly foreign to the Japanese. Huge tomes have been written to prove that Japanese prosper only in communal settings where rules of the group are clear and conventions are clearly described. The 1980s showed that this pattern is far from immutable. The trend of the decade in all fields was toward individualism in the Western style and away from group constraints. Hasegawa was perhaps an unusual example, but his experience was far more common than one might expect. Many of the 1980s' business-success stories featured young entrepreneurs who tired of company routine and branched out on their own. A weekly staple in popular magazines was the feature story on some maverick in his thirties or forties who fled security to create his own little patch. Job-switching, in the public mind, became not treasonous but admirable.

Nothing underscored this shift in values more than the consumption patterns and life-styles favored by Japanese in that decade. The old pattern, which became fixed in the first flush of steady incomes, was one of undeviating uniformity in purchasing. One bought what one's neighbor bought, sometimes within hours. Keeping up with the Joneses is a universal phenomenon, but keeping up with the Satos was a passion. In the stage of mass-consumption that began in the 1960s, everyone acquired the "Three C's" (car, cooler, and color TV) as quickly as possible. They looked exactly like the "Three C's" next door because they were exactly the same models. If a product achieved a certain level of popularity, if it came to be accepted as the sort of thing one ought to buy, its success was guaranteed. The most exaggerated case of mass-purchasing was perhaps that of Louis Vuitton handbags. No woman could be without a Louis Vuitton—not a Louis Vuitton lookalike or some casual variation, but an authentic Louis Vuitton with distinctive styling and a French label to prove its source. A group-tour flight from Honolulu to Tokyo in the late 1970s presented the almost eerie scene of row after row of young Japanese women hugging their new Teddy Bears and Mickey Mouse dolls, each one identical to the one in the next seat. Status meant doing almost precisely the same thing as the next person on the block.

In the eighties the pattern changed. One wanted what others did not, because the greater goal of purchasing was to own things that enhanced one's own specialness. Analysts in the advertising and marketing industries called it the age of "segmented masses," one in which mass-consumption gave way to individual tastes and companies were forced to diversify products to cater to many different and very personal aspirations. The trick was to attract the buyer with goods that lifted him out of the crowd, precisely the reverse of the 1960s' pattern. Americans would recognize this as buying goods that "make a personal statement," goods that portray the owner as a person of distinct tastes. Advertising posters in the late 1980s did not stress a product's durability or even good taste but sought in ingenious ways to suggest its capacity to show one's uniqueness. For one period in 1989 it seemed that every poster contained the word *jibun*, which means "oneself," regardless of whether the product advertised was a car, a holiday, or a school for studying the art of pottery. A subway poster that year described a new car made by Mitsubishi Motors Corporation as "the individual four-door Galant," which was specially designed "for the new person." Foreign travel was one of the boom industries of the 1980s and it was hawked by advertisers as a totally new leisure concept. Gone were pictures of Japanese, cameras in hand, trudging through Rome in large parades behind a flag-bearing group-tour leader. In their place were photos of couples enjoying tourist spots by themselves.

The arbiter of economic change in Japan is the government's Economic Planning Agency, and its annual reports are regarded as official guides to new trends and the proper responses to them. Its 1988 survey depicted Japanese as having shifted rapidly from seeking "material affluence" to "mental affluence." That meant putting rising disposable incomes into purchases that enhanced one's sense of personal satisfaction. Producers responded to this change by providing diversity and sophistication. Proportionately less of a family's money went for food, durable goods, and savings. Larger shares were put into travel, leisure, education, and cultural pursuits. According to the survey, "each person has his own idea of mental affluence and life style. It is . . . sophisticated because consumers concentrate their investment in things important for the realization of life style."[15] People spent less on furniture, more on art, jewelry, and gold, in part because these were considered sound investments but also because it was hoped that they marked one as a person of good taste.

One of Japan's most prominent purchasing-habit gurus is Toshiaki Izeki, a Keio University sociology professor and marketing consultant to several large companies. He sees the enjoyment of diversity as the greatest consumerist change of the postwar years. Coffee offers a good example of this phenomenon. The same person might buy instant coffee for breakfast, order regular coffee for lunch or the afternoon break, and select espresso after a good dinner. Izeki observed that this new desire for goods that fit momentary expectations had created enormous demand for rentals. The new consumer often refused to purchase an automobile, which required regular polishing and expensive garaging. Instead, he rented when he needed a car—often a Mercedes for special nights out in the city and a four-wheel-drive vehicle for weekends in the country. He spurned as conformist such once-popular group entertainments as *karaoke* singing in bars. His self-image was better served by spending $275 on a fashionable Bordeaux for dinner.[16]

Izeki also believes the new individualistic consumption pattern has had ripple effects that go far beyond the mere buying of goods to affect the way people, especially the young, look at their lives. Buying things to assert one's own persona assumes having the time to enjoy and display them. That means more and more leisure time, less and less time spent at work. When choosing a career, he found, young men increasingly were prone to opt for work that allowed a maximum of free time—not because they were lazy but because free time was necessary to present themselves as individuals. In an interview, Izeki commented:

> This is largely why the young men I teach [at Keio] do not follow the normal path into company life. It is too restrictive. The company's restraints and rules do not permit them to have more than two or three weeks of vacation. The big company is a heavy burden on them. They are more likely now to quit the large company to open their own small firms, or to choose the smaller one at graduation. They want personal freedom and independence, and this is especially true in the past ten years. This is an enormous social change.

●

One of the most striking aspects of the period of "economism" was its lack of social protest and generalized criticism. The tide of postwar radicalism was spent by the mid-1950s, and for thirty years it was as if a moratorium had been declared on serious domestic debate. The only broad-scale protest throughout those years was motivated by anti-Americanism—the student demonstrations against the security treaty and the war in Vietnam—and anger at Japanese officials who colluded with Americans. On domestic issues, the public was generally silent, an exception being the localized assaults on polluting industries. Socialists and Communists, of course, assailed oligopoly capitalism from entrenched ideological positions, but fewer and fewer people listened. Political corruption within the LDP "money factory" was soberly deplored and then quickly forgotten. No strong consumers' movement arose to challenge the structure that rigged prices at high levels. People fretted about the dearth of public amenities—roads, libraries, parks, sewerage—but rarely formed public organizations to demand them. There seemed to be a consensus that Japan's miraculous economic system was, in fact, a fragile structure that might collapse under pressure, undoing what decades of hard work had wrought. No one could risk being accused of pricking the bubble.

In the 1980s Japanese found their voices again. The decade was marked by rising dissatisfaction with almost everything—corruption, the company work ethic, high land prices, shady new fortunes, and miserable housing for the middle class, all of which had been tolerated before. By rowdy Western standards, it was genteel protest. Much of it was launched from within Japan's bureaucracy, a fact that gave it great credibility, for the old structure had to a large extent been built by older bureaucrats. The great affluence of the 1980s had a good deal to do with it. It became clear that the structure was not so fragile after all, that well-intended criticism would not bring it toppling down. The new sense of confidence opened many areas of social concern to probing, even incisive, critiques from intellectuals, the press, and people who worked at the core of the system itself.

Perhaps the best bellwether of both the decline and revival of social concern is Japanese film-making. Japan's cinema in the late 1940s and 1950s was among the world's finest and, as we have seen, it was largely devoted to social-reform causes such as labor's rights, the evils of monopoly capitalism, and the plight of underdogs. By the mid-1950s it was in retreat, and the following three decades were a desert of cinematic inanity, the most famous creation being a monster called *Godzilla*. Disaster movies, teenage love stories, and sword-clanking samurai dramas became the standard fare. Satire and social commentary virtually disappeared from the screen. This demise perhaps illustrates better than anything else the deadening influence of Japan's rigid economic system. The movie industry had become an oligopoly of four large companies that totally controlled the market. They not only produced movies but also owned the distribution channels and the major film theaters, leaving the independent producer only a few small houses in which to show films. To pack their own with paying customers, the major studios targeted the teenage market and catered almost exclusively to its taste. The result was the *Godzilla* genre. Japan's authentic film giants, including the world-renowned Akira Kurosawa, kept producing only by obtaining funds from American financiers. Even the great Kurosawa largely abandoned social concerns in favor of historical drama.

The 1980s' revival was remarkable for its breadth. Independent film-makers, whose works were often shown first in seedy second-run houses, somehow found the resources to produce movies that gently mocked Japanese life and pilloried many of the previously sacrosanct institutions. One of the most popular was *Kazoku Geemu* (*The Family Game*), which speared many of the pretensions of middle-class life, including the all-encompassing campaign to get a son into a good college. The corruptive character of politics was assailed in *Zennin no Joken* (*Requirements of a Virtuous Man*), which featured the trials of a scholarly professor who attempts to remain unsullied in the money-logged world of a Diet election, only to discover that the real corrupters are the people themselves, who expect, and bluntly demand, that the candidate in effect buy their votes. *Mitsuyaku* (*Secret Agreement*) targeted government secrecy and oppressiveness in a screenplay based on a true-life scandal of 1971, featuring a tough *Mainichi Shimbun* reporter who obtained Foreign Ministry documents through a love affair. A touching story of a fifty-seven-year-old businessman nearing retirement emerged from another film, *Kaisha Monogatari* (*Company Story*), which bared the sad truth of how a lifetime of serving the company drains the individual, leaving him, in the end, with nothing of value except memories.

Political themes—especially those that recalled the war and Japan's military conquests in Asia—had for years been considered taboo. But in the new era of experimentation, even Japan's old imperial venture could be hauled up for criticism if it was the work of a genuine master like Shohei Imamura. His 1987 film *Zegen* (*The Flesh Trader*) described the early-century doings of a Japanese man who was both a government spy and brothel owner in Southeast Asia, and who used both careers to advance the cause of Japan's future imperial adventure. His sad end was a commentary on the fate awaiting men who do imperialism's work.

Sudden affluence and shifting social values made Japan's 1980s an era ripe for satire, a genre in decline for thirty years, during which Japanese took themselves and their hard work far too seriously to enjoy jokes at their own expense. As if on schedule there emerged a cinema satirist of great skill. Juzo Itami, an actor turned director, became the Balzac of Japanese filmdom during a decade when people finally relaxed and began looking at their lives, as if suddenly curious to see what sort of society they had created. Itami had the answers ready, and he provided them in three marvelous movies that brought him international acclaim. He produced his first film in 1984, and a mere five years later Vincent Canby of the *New York Times* was calling him "the man who is possibly the only true social satirist at work in movies today."[17]

The son of a prominent prewar director, Mansaku Itami, Juzo Itami had had a satisfying career as a screen actor when, in the early 1980s, he turned to directing. As an independent, he faced all of the obstacles presented by an industry devoted to mass entertainment and in control of most of the houses where first-run movies were shown. Itami dodged them, first by borrowing from friends and mortgaging his own home to obtain financing, and then by opening his first feature in a second-run theater. His subsequent productions were financed by profits from the first ones, and he never became dependent either on the big Japanese houses or on foreign capital. As a result, Itami has been free to poke his cameras into whatever themes personally interest him. There is a kind of logical progression in his work. His first instinct was to jab lightly at the realities of Japanese life with a warm good humor. By the end of the decade he had moved to an attitude of passionate disgust.

His first movie, *Ososhiki* (*The Funeral*), concerned an upper-middle-class family's confrontation with the death of the family patriarch. The family, naturally, must provide a funeral, but in the new Japan this is no simple matter. No one knows how to do it. To find out, they memorize scenes from a handy videotape guide to proper burials and proceed to stage the funeral much as one learns to sail by reading books and hiring professional guidance. It is an amusing, warm-hearted movie, but the message is sharp: In their pursuit of the rich life, Japanese have lost touch with old traditions. Itami once summed up *Ososhiki's* meaning: "Japan has left behind old values to accomplish economic success. We live in a consumer-oriented society, but some things don't change. At death, the old values grab you."[18] Along the way, the director skewered many Japanese habits, especially the worship of money and the compulsion to perform proper rites in proper forms. These become intertwined in a modern Japan where propriety comes with a high price tag. In every area of life, experts on form have found ways to make large fortunes by teaching those fearful of breaking some unknown rule. It is a truism of every institution from flower arranging to sushi making. In *Ososhiki*, Itami revealed its power in the funeral business. The Shinto priest arrives in a white Rolls Royce. The family must spend large sums to bury the old man, money that is recouped in the obligatory gifts of the invited mourners. The climactic scene is a famous one. The mourners' cash is blown off the ritual gifts table by a sudden gust, provoking a panicky scuffle to retrieve it. Even in death the money chase continues.

From family ritual Itami progressed in his next film to bigger targets. He was in an angrier mood this time. *Marusa No Onna* (*A Taxing Woman*) was a less gentle, more biting satire than *Ososhiki*. It delved into such subjects as gangsters, corrupt politicians, and tax evasion, unsavory practices that were, however, as much a part of the 1980s' Japanese scene as kabuki and sumo. Evil emerges in the form of Gondo, an immensely rich racketeer with connections in the *yakuza*, Japan's underworld. To avoid taxes, much of his wealth has been cached away in hidden bank accounts and a secret safe packed with gold bullion. Public virtue and indignation come in the person of a woman tax inspector (portrayed brilliantly by Nobuko Miyamoto, who is Itami's wife in real life), who tenaciously tracks down the hidden riches and nails Gondo. Along the way are peripheral glimpses of corruption—a deceptive banker and a venal Diet member among others. It is a grim movie saved from tediousness by Itami's odd touches of understanding and even sympathy. He discovers human warmth even in the villainous tax evader, and there are moments when the viewer is torn between respect for the pursuer and admiration for the pursued. Villainous he may be, but Gondo is also part of the comic human scene.

Itami's third satire was very different from the first two. It depicted a Japanese society saturated by sinister and savage forces, the veins of corruption reaching everywhere, the little man reduced to helpless victim. *Marusa No Onna 2*, a sequel to *A Taxing Woman*, pitted the same tax inspector against tax evaders, but there the similarity ended. She was at war with an unscrupulous property developer who hired thugs to frighten poor tenants, crooked politicians, scheming religious cult leaders who fleeced followers, and vicious gangsters who unleashed dogs on ordinary people. By 1988 Itami was concerned not with human frailty but with social corruption on a grand scale. Onizawa, the sinister businessman, is no mere crook. He schemes to evict tenants, poses as a Buddhist miracle worker, and even seduces a young girl who has been handed to him as collateral on a loan. To make the point that Onizawa symbolizes a national trait, Itami has him seek refuge in patriotism: "I do what I do for the sake of the country," Onizawa says, trying to justify his wreckage of people's homes to build commercial skyscrapers. "If no one ever did the dirty work, how could Japan ever be great?"

It may seem that tax evasion and real estate schemes are not the stuff of great drama. But Itami had a grasp of what rankled Japanese in the 1980s as the great boom continued and quick fortunes were made overnight. Tax evasion by entrepreneurs was a major issue for middle-class salaried workers who had no chance to cheat. And real estate fortunes topped the list of grievances against the nouveau riche. Itami made the prosaic scheming of such venturers stand for all that was unpleasant about the 1980s: greed, speculation, the gap between rich and poor. The obsession with money, he once said, was essential to understanding Japan in that decade: "Money represents a kind of future. Previously the gods sustained people. But in the present age, it seems like money has taken the place of the gods."[19] In Onizawa, that monstrous crook, the director went far past satire to the level of pure outrage. "Money is a living thing," says this evil old man, who is meant to be a voice of his times. "It grows with time. Money is my child, my future life. When I am at one with money, I am immortal."

●

As the decade neared its end, the LDP suffered its greatest national defeat since its formation in 1955. Its candidates lost a series of local elections in 1989 and then lost so many seats in the Upper House election that the party no longer held a majority and was forced to cede control of that chamber to a coalition of the Japan Socialist party and several minor parties. An entire generation of older LDP leaders— Yasuhiro Nakasone, Noboru Takeshita, Shintaro Abe, and Kiichi Miyazawa—were forced off the political stage. The events shattered all of the old assumptions—that is, that the people were so satisfied with the LDP and so skeptical of the opposition parties that they would never switch. Throughout 1989 Japanese were treated to unimaginable scenes on television news shows. Prime Minister Takeshita resigned, his public approval rating having fallen below 10 percent. He was replaced by Sousuke Uno, who himself resigned a few days later in a sex scandal. One after another, trying their best to appear contrite and promising sweeping reforms, the party's elder statesmen resigned high positions and abandoned their ambitions. They were victims of the highest tide of political protest to strike Japan in thirty-four years.

The cause of this revolt was not a leftward tilt in which Japanese re-embraced socialism. Two immediate reasons lay behind the public's sudden uprising. The first was the Recruit scandal, with its series of revelations of how politicians and their aides made large piles of money from favor-seekers. The second was a consumption tax on almost all purchases of goods that the LDP forced through the Diet after having pledged not to introduce one. It was the intermingling of these two issues at a peculiar moment in history that compelled the public, at last, to react. The impact of each was heightened by the general mood of discontent that had arisen in that somewhat tawdry decade. The making of quick fortunes in stocks and real estate, the growing gap between rich and poor, the failure of labor to make significant wage gains—all of these were the background of the unprecedented political revolt. The rebellion did not reshape the political system. The new men who took power were cut from same conservative cloth as those who were deposed. But it did reveal the fact that public pressure from below could destroy careers and force a change of faces.

There was another factor, too, one that underscored the new acceptability of criticism in the 1980s. That was the press. The Japanese media had for so long been an adjunct of the political system that it rarely did more than wink at scandal. It had been part of that general public conspiracy to avoid sustained probing of malfeasance lest the economic bubble burst. Bribery and the selling of favors, that mixing of public service with private gain that some called "structural corruption," were routinely noted and passed over in the pages of major newspapers. But the new tolerance of criticism infected even this bastion of rigidity. Just as in the case of cinema, where new themes could be explored, the press felt encouraged to probe issues previously deemed out of bounds. The tip-off that new breezes were blowing was the media's handling of the Recruit scandal. It began when a young *Asahi* newspaper reporter in Kawasaki exposed the first traces of the company's cash deals with politicians. The press never let up. Each night for nearly a year television presented accounts of Recruit stock and cash finding their way into politicians' accounts. Under the glare, the LDP beneficiaries of Recruit's favors gave up and resigned.

Some naturally compared the events to the downfall of former Prime Minister Kakuei Tanaka, but there was one all-important difference. Tanaka was brought down by events that originated abroad, and without them he would probably have remained in office. His resignation in 1974 stemmed from the publication in a monthly magazine of his political money dealings. That story was ignored by the establishment newspapers until Tanaka was grilled about it by reporters of the Foreign Correspondents Club of Japan. Foreign reporters, not Japanese ones, did Tanaka in by publicizing abroad the seamy record ignored by the Japanese press. And Tanaka's subsequent indictment in the Lockheed scandal was propelled not by the Japanese press or prosecutors but by revelations in Washington by a subcommittee of the U.S. Senate Foreign Relations Committee. In neither case were the Japanese media the initial pursuers. That had changed by 1989. The Recruit affair was the first in modern times to wreck a conservative government because of the vigilance of the Japanese media. It was a homegrown scandal pursued to the end by the hometown press.

●

The role of bureaucrats is an esteemed one in postwar Japan, not merely because of the political power they wield, which is considerable. They are looked to for philosophical guidance as well. Their thoughts on what is right and wrong with society count for a good deal, and even junior members in several ministries have easy access to the news media and opinion magazines. In the 1980s much of the important social criticism came from these young mandarins. From the middle ranks of the Economic Planning Agency came the definitive analyses of the widening gap between rich and poor. From the powerful MITI flowed reports assailing high prices, the rigged distribution system, and the long working hours forced on company employees. It was natural that they felt a personal irritation at the sight of Japan's nouveau riche indulging their taste for luxuries while they, the supposed elite, remained stuck with their families in tiny rented apartments. Their own status was diminished in a society that regarded money, not education and dedication to public welfare, as the goal of life. One day in 1989 a government economist in his midthirties interrupted an explanation of the growing social imbalance with a sudden explosion of personal anger: "The newest recruit in one of the securities houses earns twice as much as I do!" Some of the most thoughtful dissent of the decade emerged in what might be called a minirevolt of the young mandarin class.

Nobuaki Takahashi was a typical rebel. He was thirty-six years old when I met him in 1989, and he had marched steadily up the proper rungs on the success ladder. He was perhaps a perfect example of the postwar meritocratic system, which permitted Japan's diligent males to rise as high as their talents and hard work could take them. Takahashi grew up in the bleak coal-mining town of Yubari, on the northernmost main island of Hokkaido, in a region devastated by the coal industry's decline. He passed the tough entrance exams for Waseda, the prestigious private university in Tokyo. After graduation in 1976 he became a policy researcher for MITI and did a stint at the Japan Economic Research Center. The mid-1980s found him in planning research at the Japan Development Bank, and it was there, in 1989, that he produced a magazine article that elevated him to instant celebrity in a nation that had learned to tolerate and even value mavericks.

"*Tai Koku Nihon No Uchinaru Mazushisa*," which can be translated as "Poverty in Superpower Japan," appeared in the February 1989 issue of *Chuo Koron*, the country's most prestigious intellectual and literary journal. It was a broadside directed at the current working of Japan's economy, which Takahashi saw in part as a failure. Japan boasted of producing 15 percent of the world's gross national product and of being the largest creditor nation. Japan was indeed a successful country, Takahashi agreed, but its power was overstated. Much of the exaggeration arose simply from the 1985 appreciation of the yen against the dollar, an arrangement that on paper made Japan's assets, credit, and external buying power seem much larger overnight. Japan's economic power was partly a myth, and by bragging endlessly about it, Japan was beginning to appear as "an ass in a lion's skin."

According to Takahashi, half of Japan's economic system was not working, or at least not working to benefit ordinary people. The productive half was working well, rising to higher and higher levels of efficiency. The distributive half was a failure. It failed to distribute the fruits of success in a fair manner. This was a failure of government, because it is government that has the duty of seeing that rewards are passed around with some degree of fairness. "The improvement of economic efficiency and reinforcement of productive power will make the country and the businesses rich and prosperous, but not the life of the individual," Takahashi concluded. "The fairy tale of economic growth and people's confidence are now fading away." Japan's postwar success was indeed admirable, he noted. "But what can we leave in history? Industrial waste and stacks of bonds and security papers?"[20]

Had Takahashi been a doctrinaire socialist, his views would have been little noted. But because he was firmly settled in the core of Japan's establishment, his views sparked little blazes everywhere. He had been interviewed by television and his *Chuo Koron* article was being expanded into a book. Other famous periodicals asked him for articles, and he had written one, for the *Asahi Journal*, which said that banks and securities firms made too much money and that they had to be "made to bleed." In person, he seemed anything but a firebrand. Careful research was his forte. At lunch one day he was amiable and witty in quick wry bursts, but once he launched into his thoughts on Japan's economic failures and the screwing of the little man, he changed remarkably. His eyes grew stony with a hard determination, the stare of a man not to be taken lightly. He reminded one most of Ralph Nader, the American consumer activist, in his cold conviction. What did his coworkers think of his articles? They did not take him seriously, he said. "They say they would just like to be rich, too." There was considerable criticism of his views at the conservative Japan Development Bank, where he worked. Does his boss criticize him, too? "Of course," said the maverick mandarin. A pause. "But I am willing to be fired. I will say what I feel."

11

●

The Myths of
Nationalism

Yasukuni Shrine stands amid cherry trees in central Tokyo, a memorial to Japan's dead soldiers and sailors, whose spirits are said to hover about on occasion. It is also the center of a peculiar controversy, one that obscures more than it explains about modern Japan. To the political Left, Yasukuni is a symbol of militarism and a vestige of a shameful imperial past. The Right sees it as a national shrine to old glories, dead heroes, and a divine emperor. Neither commands a great deal of attention in apolitical postwar Japan. But together they have managed to make of Yasukuni a symbolic test of patriotic loyalties, one that mainstream politicians find difficult to ignore.

Each August 15 renews the test. That is the official date for commemorating the end of World War II, and politicians high and low are required to make some gesture to dead veterans enshrined at Yasukuni. But how to do it? Paying respect as a government official angers the Left, which considers such an act an official sanctioning of the Shinto religion. That not only violates the spirit of the constitution but smacks of neoimperialism, since Shinto was the state religion in the war years. But to appear at Yasukuni merely as a private citizen would irritate the Right, which seeks a revival of state Shintoism and insists on official endorsements.

In the late 1970s this conflict was elevated to high comedy as Japan's leading politicians sought to bridge the gap by alienating the fewest people. One prime minister refused to state whether he went to Yasukuni as a public official or a private citizen. But, the press noted, he had traveled in an official limousine. A succession of premiers were watched closely as they signed the shrine visitors' book. Did they sign merely their names? Or did they include their ministerial titles? Each annual visit became a farcical parade of politicians and reporters scurrying toward the shrine's entrance, reporters grilling ministers, ministers scuffing along looking solemn, or angry, or both. Finally, in 1985, Prime Minister Nakasone tried to end the show by letting the world know he was attending as prime minister—and so what? The next year, humbled by criticism, he didn't go at all.

One would suspect from all this fuss that a great national debate was being waged over fundamental issues, such as peace and war, fascism and modern democracy, imperialism and pacifism. In fact, nothing of the sort was happening. Most Japanese cared little for Yasukuni, were ignorant of the last war, thought of Emperor Hirohito as a quaint fatherly figure, and regarded Shintoism as a faith suitable for marriage ceremonies and little else. If they visited the Yasukuni grounds at all it was probably to get tipsy on sake under the cherry blossoms each April. The notion that Yasukuni was a burning national issue was a fiction nursed by the press and professional leftists and rightists in Japan. It is the same with several other symbolic issues gathered under the rubric of "Japanese nationalism." Whether to fly the national flag at schools is one. So is singing the national anthem. In history textbooks, phrases describing Japan's role in the Pacific War are fought over furiously. For a few combatants, these "nationalist" issues are battlegrounds. For most Japanese, they are virtually meaningless.

Yet they remain at the core of one of the serious misperceptions of postwar Japan—that she is a fervently nationalistic country bent on reviving her past. Japanese in the 1990s are in fact one of the least nationalistic peoples on the globe. Ethnocentric, yes. Unthinkingly convinced of the superiority of their own culture, certainly. They are smug about their racial homogeneity, suspicious of foreigners, and alternately enticed and repelled by outsiders' ways. But nationalists they are not. There is no consensus in postwar Japan on national mission, no acknowledged sense of the country's place in the world, no settled conviction that Japanese have a role, as a nation, to play outside their borders. They display a vague aspiration to gain the world's respect but have not thought much about how to win it. There is little personal commitment to the national state. A series of public-opinion polls stretching back into the 1950s have asked Japanese citizens each year whether they prefer to contribute more to society or to their own self-interests; each year registers a declining interest in serving society as a whole.

Japanese nationalism—if defined as a sense of national identity and purpose—died a victim of World War II and was all but forgotten in the crusade to escape poverty. Not until that struggle was clearly won in the late 1970s was much thought bestowed on the idea of Japan as a nation. Many had, in those years, tried to revive that powerful political nationalism that had bound Japanese since the Meiji Restoration. The results were paltry because the old ingredients no longer existed. In postwar Japan the emperor was a man, not a god, the constitution had been written by foreigners, and even the national anthem carried an odor of shame. The debate over Yasukuni was not a signal of renascent nationalism. It was a revealing measure of how deeply the old nationalism had been interred.

●

The demise of nationalism had begun with the emperor's surrender broadcast on August 15, 1945. In the grueling years that followed, even the word "nationalism" took on a nasty connotation. It became somehow synonymous with prewar militarism, which most Japanese—when they thought about it at all—blamed for the great disaster. At first, the Occupation authorities had tried to bury it completely. Display of the national flag was banned. Kimigayo, the national anthem, disappeared from public gatherings. MacArthur's officers erased much Japanese history from school textbooks, barred productions of nationalistic Kabuki dramas, and censored out of the press any innocuous references likely to incite old feelings of patriotism. The submergence of nationalism continued long after the Occupation had ended. Talk of national destiny, even of national pride, remained suppressed by an unspoken consensus that it was dangerous. Patriotism became a furtive emotion, one best left in the shadows. It was appropriated by right-wing gangs whose activities often mixed it with common thuggery and extortion. A wisp of nation-

alist spirit emerged briefly in the anti-American demonstrations of the
late 1950s, when the U.S.-Japan security treaty was being revised and
extended. It disappeared with the resignation of Prime Minister Kishi.
The demonstrating students, except for the most radical, folded away
their banners, washed behind their ears, and went back to classes. Never
since has the idea of nationalism had an appeal for the young.

A few intellectuals of the time did try to grapple with the question
of national identity, but they were usually outside the mainstream.
College faculties were dominated by orthodox Marxists who viewed
nationalism in any form as an extension of the old imperialism, which
had brought on the war. Attempts to disentangle normal feelings of
national pride from imperialism were futile. It was as if a century of
Japan's history that began with the Meiji Restoration had been casually
displaced. The writer Kai Oi lamented in 1963 that a sense of national
cohesion had been irrevocably severed by the war and the public's
acceptance of war guilt. Both the Occupation and the Marxists had
reinforced the separation.

"This relentless severing of all ties between the old Japanese Empire and post-war Japan caused the Japanese people to lose their national
consciousness which had been fostered since the Meiji Restoration in
1868," Oi wrote in *Chuo Koron,* in one of the more serious examina-
tions to appear in a mainstream intellectual journal. He listed several
instances in which national feelings might have been expected to rise up
but did not:

> Even though Japan was used as a strategic base during the
> Korean War, the people had no feeling of national crisis.
> Even though Okinawa has not been returned to Japan, there
> has been no heightening of national concern. . . . The op-
> position to the ratification of the revised mutual security agree-
> ment with the United States did no more than force the
> resignation of Premier Kishi. Now that the new agreement has
> been ratified and the country has returned to normal, the
> people hardly give it a second thought. [1]

The war was indeed the key. No one seemed to want to talk of it.
Whatever their private thoughts, and these were actually quite varied,
Japanese for nearly thirty years tacitly agreed that it should not become
a public issue. The conquests in China, the invasion of Southeast Asia,
the war with the United States—all of these were deemed unfit for
public debate. The war years seemed to disappear into a mist, abandoned to private memories and unread archives. History stopped with

the Manchurian Incident of 1931 and began again with August 15, 1945. Rokuro Hidaka, a professor and writer, remembered that his students in Kyoto seemed to know nothing of the entire Showa period, the years of Emperor Hirohito's reign, which began in 1926. In high school they had studied nothing of the years after the Manchurian Incident. They faced almost no questioning of that period in their college entrance exams, and they arrived in college having memorized certain dates, the names of prime ministers, and not much else. "As for the 'causes' of the wars," wrote Hidaka, "all they remember are meaningless fragments such as that the cause of the Sino-Japanese War was the [fact] that the armies of Japan and China clashed on Marco Polo Bridge in the suburbs of Peking in 1937.[2]

Growing up in the postwar years, children were confronted with a stupefying void. Parents told them horrendous stories of sacrifice, hardship, and death, and so their personal images of the catastrophe were keen. But it all seemed to make no sense. They were left with no explanation of what it had all been about. Michiko Hasegawa was born in 1945, studied at Tokyo University, and went on to become a college professor. In an essay looking back on her youth, she remembers her parents' vivid stories of B-29 raids, searchlights crisscrossing the skies, and incendiary bombs falling at their gate. But at school, she recalled, those years were officially treated as a kind of "dark age," one in which "the very light of reason had been abandoned":

> We were taught that for inexplicable reasons the entire country had gone mad, thinking it could achieve the impossible and convinced that wrong was right. . . . We imagined that those responsible for the creation of the dark age had been punished and that the rest had repented and exorcised the darkness from themselves. The period, in short, was obliterated. Instead of seeing ourselves as children of a darkness, accordingly, we became accustomed to the idea that we were born of nothingness.[3]

This void of unrecollected history did more than cut Japanese off from their own past. It separated them almost totally from other Asians, those whose countries had been ravaged by the last expression of Japanese nationalism. School texts rarely touched on the atrocities committed in China, Singapore, or the Philippines. The Rape of Nanking, as the rest of the world knew it, was merely another "incident" in that hazy conflict. When confronted abroad with accounts of wartime barbarity, the average Japanese could only express his confusion. Asians thought him devious; in fact, he was merely uninformed. This veil of official ignorance was perhaps the greatest burden carried by Japan's diplomats as they tried to revive relations with the countries their fathers had pillaged. To attempt to clear the slate with apologies was impossible, because apologies would lift the veil and revive all of the unpleasantness at home, which had been buried by time and obfuscation. The results were often ridiculous. In 1972, when he went to Peking to begin the process of normalizing relations with China, Prime Minister Kakuei Tanaka inserted into his banquet speech the strongest wording of apology that politics at home would permit: "During the war, Japan caused great troubles for the Chinese peoples." When this was greeted with stony silence, Tanaka quickly amended his remark: "There were many cases in which Japan caused great troubles." Later, according to reporters present, an infuriated Chinese leader, Chou En-lai, said that Tanaka's "apology" had been suitable for one who had spilled a cup of tea.

For the average Japanese, Japanese atrocities were the rumors of war. The facts of the war, those that they knew to be true, were all on the other side. The atomic bombings of Hiroshima and Nagasaki, the incendiary raids on Tokyo and other cities—these were indisputable. When looked at from the perspective of those terrible events alone, the war made sense only if Japan were a victim, and that is how a great many people remembered it. The sense of victimization was reinforced by accounts of the Tokyo War Crimes Trial, in which seven wartime leaders had been sentenced to death. One of the most memorable books of the 1970s was Saburo Shiroyama's *Rakujitsu Moyu (The Sunset Aglow)*, which depicted the life and death of Koki Hirota, a wartime prime minister and foreign minister. Hirota was the only civilian among the seven hanged, and the book presented him as a solitary hero railroaded to death by a vengeful judge and a hapless American defense attorney. The book was enormously popular and was transformed into an even more popular television series by NHK, the national TV network. Many studies had pictured the War Crimes Trial as a travesty, and some of them were written by Americans who had participated in the court proceedings. But the saga of Koki Hirota was something special in the lives of Japanese, a heartrending account of a stoic and a rather ordinary man who was a victim of "victor's justice." Few who saw it have ever forgotten it.[4]

Sympathetically treated, Hirota's case was reinforcement for the sense of victimization, but it did nothing to explain the war itself. Who caused it and why were questions left unanswered for decades, except by Marxists, who blamed Japan's imperialism, and right-wingers, who fingered foreigners as the culprits. There is still no comprehensive popular work that attempts to sort it all out. Perhaps the strongest candidate for the role was a book published in 1964, *Dai Toa Senso Kotei Ron (In Affirmation of the Greater East Asian War)*. It was the work of Fusao Hayashi, a novelist and critic who had been a Marxist in the 1920s, shifted to ultranationalism after the war, and engaged in tart polemics against the Left in the 1960s. Its thesis had first appeared in a series of articles in 1964–65 in *Chuo Koron*, where it had caught the attention of a few intellectuals. Hayashi explained World War II as the last stage of a hundred-year war by Japan to ward off Western colonization of Asia. The first shots had been fired in 1863, when the British had shelled the southern port of Kagoshima, and in 1864, when a combined foreign fleet bombarded Japanese forces at Shimonoseki. All subsequent history was in some way a repetition of those dramatic encounters on the eve of the Meiji Restoration. Japan's war with Russia, her first defeat of the Chinese, and her later interventions in Manchuria and China had to be seen in the light of a grand purpose—to expel the barbarians—according to Hayashi. And it was not merely a war to protect Japan. Japan fought to defend all of Asia, to release her from the shackles of Western colonization. It was, Hayashi said, a hopeless fight, but one that had to be fought. His book aroused little interest outside of intellectual circles, in part because it echoed a bit of the wartime propaganda military leaders used to justify the invasions of Southeast Asia. But its arguments are still revived occasionally. It fits quite neatly with the vision of Japan as the noble, inevitably failing victim.[5]

Because there was so little intellectual interest in reexamining Japan's prewar past, the idea of nationalism remained well below the surface of postwar life. It was frequently used by right-wing groups, which were often linked with prominent politicians but which had little general support. Their major weapon was the sound truck, which hurried through urban streets broadcasting patriotic songs and warlike chants. The divinity of the emperor, reinstatement of Shintoism as a state religion, and respect for the armed forces were their principal planks, none of which had great appeal. Their strength, such as it was, lay in stealthy acts against leftists and the occasional assassination. In 1960, for example, a right-wing assassin strode into an auditorium and, with a short sword, killed the speaker, Inejiro Asanuma, leader of the Socialist party.

One incident in 1978 perfectly illustrated the furtive quality of that type of nationalism. The Right had for years attempted to revive respect for the fourteen war criminals, including Premier Hideki Tōjō, who had been tried in the late 1940s by the allied tribunal. Their rehabilitation in the public mind, it was thought, would go far toward erasing Japan's war guilt. The first stage in such a restoration would be the enshrinement of their names in Yasukuni Shrine. This would serve to link, once again, the notion of an official state religion and the officers who had directed Japanese armies in the lost war. Directors of the large shrine had made the decision to enshrine the fourteen names in the late 1950s but had never dared to carry it out because of the controversy sure to follow. One night in October 1978, without any public announcement, the shrine's priests inscribed the names on pieces of parchment, stealthily completing the enshrinement. No one outside Yasukuni knew anything about it until the following April, when it was disclosed by a newspaper acting on a tip.

There are many, foreigners and Japanese alike, who look into these shadowy activities and see a menacing resurgence of militaristic nationalism. To them, Japan seems forever on the brink of reverting to prewar ultranationalism. It is an illusion. What is striking is the public indifference to displays of nationalism and nationalist symbols of any sort. This indifference is one of the most enduring traits of the era. It is perhaps best revealed in the life and death of one of Japan's finest postwar writers, Yukio Mishima. It may seem demeaning to dismiss so great a writer in this fashion, but we are here concerned not with Mishima the novelist but Mishima the political activist. In the last decade of his life he set himself the task of single-handedly reigniting the flame of Japanese nationalism. His astounding and at times bizarre crusade accomplished nothing for his cause and transformed Mishima himself into something of a political freak. But it also revealed a good deal about the Japanese and their feelings.

With his enormous literary talent and an equally enormous talent for making his own life dramatic and meaningful, Yukio Mishima was one of the most dazzling figures of his age. He lit up that age with a stream of novels, plays, Noh dramas, essays, and poetry, some of them of such quality that he won an international reputation rare for a Japanese writer and was periodically mentioned as a candidate for the Nobel Prize in literature. He was a teenaged prodigy at the Peers School, where he was adopted into an influential literary coterie and marked for fame. This achievement was particularly remarkable, as Mishima had a punishing childhood. His father, a tyrant of the first order, had ridiculed his literary bent and on occasion ripped apart his manuscripts as soon as they were written.

Mishima's reputation was made by 1948 when, at the age of twenty-three, he published *Confessions of a Mask*, an autobiographical novel. Almost all of his novels reveal a penchant for fantasy and a worship of physical beauty. They also disclose a morbid fascination with death, especially suicide. In Mishima's dark world the taking of one's own life was the one act of "purity," a word he used often.

Until the 1960s Mishima seemed to have little interest in politics of any sort. In pursuing his aesthetic truths, he had all but ignored the political confrontations and lively debates that occupied many of his generation. The left-wing utopianism of many postwar writers simply bored him. If he was attracted to anything, it was the Right, and in a 1959 novel, *Kyoko's House*, he made what was perhaps his first political commentary. A central figure in the novel is a boxer who, his career in the ring ruined by an accident, turns to a group of right-wing extremists to find a new validation for his life. But there is nothing in the novel to suggest a philosophy of politics. Mishima remained aloof from the riotous student demonstrations that preceded the extension of the U.S.-Japan Security Treaty in 1960. One evening in June of that year, tens of thousands surrounded Prime Minister Kishi's residence, demanding repeal of the treaty. It was a dangerous, threatening mob, marking the emotional high point of postwar protest in Japan. Mishima watched it all coolly from a distant rooftop and later, in an essay, seemed concerned only to the extent of wondering exactly why the demonstrators hated Kishi so much.[6]

In the early 1960s Mishima began to look around him and to examine what sort of country Japan had become, as if noticing it for the first time. He found it a soft, materialistic, and spiritually suffocating society devoted to work and play and not much else. Nothing about what he called that era of "languid peace" appealed to man's loftier instincts. In one essay he wrote: "Although it is true that we are living in a period of languid peace, we do not have an appropriate ideology or philosophy of life that enables us to live with a sense of spiritual satisfaction. People in this country do not know how to live in an age of peace; their lives seem to be floating along without direction." Pacifism, he went on, could never satisfy man's thirst for higher meaning. And he added, ominously: "An ideology that is to provide spiritual satisfaction must contain the kind of dangerous allure for which men are willing to die."[7]

The idea of death as the cure for a society turned shallow was extended at some length in Mishima's nonfiction book, *On Hagakure*. The original *Hagakure* was the work of a samurai-turned-priest named Jocho Yamamoto (1659–1719), who had sought to revive the warrior tradition in an age he considered to be soft and sybaritic. Its central teaching was that man must be willing to die, indeed must use his life consciously as a preparation for death. Yamamoto packaged his message in a succinct line: "I found that the way of the samurai is death." *Hagakure* enjoyed a popular revival in the militaristic climate of the 1930s, especially among Japan's kamikaze pilots, but was ignored in the era of postwar pacifism. Mishima disinterred it once again to illuminate his disgust with his own age. He compared postwar Japan to Yamamoto's complacent period of Tokugawa rule. In both were the signs of moral rot. Yamamoto's Genroku era was peopled with pseudowarriors concerned merely with the ornate style of their clothing and swords. Japan in the 1960s suffered the same unmanly ostentation. "Today," wrote Mishima, "if you go to a jazz coffeehouse and speak with teenagers or young people in their twenties, you will find that they talk of absolutely nothing but how to dress smartly and cut a stylish figure."[8] Modern "expense-account aristocrats" were the reincarnation of the Genroku samurai who wallowed in borrowed luxury through debt to their *daimyo*. Worse, modern Japanese were cursed with a fear of death. "Ours is an age," he wrote sarcastically, "in which everything is based on the premise that it is best to live as long as possible." Yamamoto's theme had been the reverse. *Hagakure*, declared Mishima, was "an attempt to cure the peaceful character of modern society by the potent medicine of death."[9]

In *On Hagakure*, Mishima had married the themes of death and national honor. A short story entitled "Patriotism" is a shocking and morbid account of the double suicide of a soldier and his young wife. Mishima thought it a masterpiece; it is written with an austerity of language he used on works he considered very important. The story is based on the abortive rebellion of February 1936, when a group of officers, imagining themselves agents of the emperor, took arms against their superior officers. The emperor never came to their support and they were overwhelmed. In Mishima's tale, his hero, Lieutenant Shinji Takehama, is sympathetic to the rebels' patriotism but is summoned by superiors to lead the force that will destroy them. Despondent, he tells his wife, Reiko, that he cannot do it. The scene that follows is Mishima's view of how a model couple should respond in a tragic circumstance:

SHINJI: "Well then . . . tonight I shall cut my stomach."
REIKO: "I am ready. I ask permission to accompany you."
SHINJI: "Good. We'll go together."

Their pledge induces ecstasy:

> With happiness welling almost too abundantly in their hearts, they could not help smiling at each other. Reiko felt as if she had returned to her wedding night. Before her eyes was neither pain nor death. She seemed to see only a free and limitless expanse opening out into vast distances.

Then:

> REIKO: "The water is hot. Will you take your bath now?"[10]

Almost all of what Mishima had come to believe in during his final decade is in "Patriotism"—noble love, honor, the decisive act, purification through death. It synthesizes the truth of his latter-day politics, which was essentially personal and aesthetic. Politics was the stage upon which Mishima could play out his fantasies and perform the glorious act of death, thereby bringing value to his own life. Nationalism was the politics he preferred, although one imagines that he might have been just as satisfied with any other handy ideology. He had little in common with the right-wingers who glorified the emperor; Mishima once regarded Hirohito as something of a traitor for having proclaimed himself a mere mortal after the war had ended. Armies of psychologists could argue forever about what brought a famous writer to such madness.

The purpose of Mishima's final drama was to ignite the old flames of passionate nationalism, and he prepared for it with his customary zeal and diligence. He managed to be commissioned an officer in the Ground Self-Defense Force (GSDF) and trained in its camps, racing through drills with young men half his age. He seems to have hoped his act would revive respect for a military that suffered the indignity of being banned by the constitution it was sworn to uphold. Finding little enthusiasm among the soldiers, Mishima formed his own private army from among young right-wing students. (He was introduced to them by Fusao Hayashi, author of the book *In Affirmation of the Greater East Asian War*.) He called it *Tate no Kai*, or "The Shield Society," and provided its members with money and uniforms. Periodically he arranged for them to train with the GSDF, an exercise he called, inevitably, "an experiment in purity." The public seemed to think it was an experiment in silliness. His "Shield Society" was dubbed by the press "Captain Mishima's Toy Army," and his own brother scoffed that he was merely "playing war."[11] The society's formal goals were protecting the emperor, fighting Communists, and rousing regular soldiers to act with patriotism against unidentified enemies.

At first, the finale took shape in Mishima's mind as a fantasy battle in the streets of Tokyo: Leftist mobs overwhelm the police and threaten the emperor, who is saved by the "Shield Society's" heroic intervention. Dismissing that scenario as unlikely, he settled on one equally fantastic. He wrote the script in minute detail, placed himself in the final death scene, and brought four young Shield cadets into the act. And so, at 11:00 A.M. on November 25, 1970, at the Self-Defense headquarters in Ichigaya, an astonishing denouement unfolded. Mishima and his cadets seized the commandant in his office, bound him to a chair, and barricaded the doors. Brandishing a razor-sharp sword and threatening to kill the commandant if his orders were not followed, Mishima demanded that the 32nd Regiment be assembled in front of the headquarters to hear a speech. When the soldiers had gathered, Mishima stood on a balcony thirty feet above them, clad in the society's uniform, wearing a white headband, his white-gloved hands on his hips. His manifesto called on the men to rise up against the constitution, to abandon liberal democracy and revive the samurai spirit. "Rise with us and, for righteousness and honor, die with us," he pleaded.

It is doubtful that Mishima had ever anticipated success. But he must have thought that if the glorious spirit of nationalism lingered anywhere in Japan, it must be within the military. Possibly he had expected gestures of sympathy. But the young soldiers proved just as apathetic as any in the postwar generation. No one paid attention to his words. There were jeers and hisses, shouts for him to come down off the balcony, to free the commandant still imprisoned inside. Mishima had expected to speak for thirty minutes but gave up after only seven. He and a cadet named Morita, side by side, shouted three times, *"Tenno Heika banzai!"* ("Long live the emperor!") and then moved quickly inside. Seated on the floor, Mishima thrust his short sword into his stomach and drew it across. As he slumped forward, Morita brought the long sword down on his neck to complete the seppuku, but in a final grotesque failure was unable to sever the head. Another cadet stepped forward and finished the final act.

●

In a society as enthralled with the mass media as Japan's, the role of "commentator" is a lofty one. He or she is a person gifted with words and ideas on almost every subject. He or she appears regularly on television talk shows and writes frequently for both mass-circulation and prestige magazines. A generalist, the commentator is not expected to know a great deal about any single topic. His talent lies in translating complex issues into simple statements that the average reader can comprehend. As a group, commentators transmit the approved wisdom of the moment, spreading the consensus on Japan's positions. They are extremely important figures in the molding of public opinion, especially opinion having to do with the nation's role in the world.

One of the most prominent commentators in the 1980s was Taichi Sakaiya, a former MITI bureaucrat turned writer and critic. In August 1985 his interview with a member of the Diet appeared in the prestigious magazine *Bungei Shunju*, the subject being the incessant American demands that Japan contribute more to the defense of the non-Communist world. Sakaiya was cast as the interviewer but typically answered his own questions in the snappy, anecdotal manner that was his trademark. What the world needed to understand, said Sakaiya, was that Japan was simply not a warlike nation. This was because Japanese had a greater reverence for human life than others and could not easily comprehend the Western concept of willing people to die for abstract causes. He asserted that Switzerland, for example, promoted the construction of bomb shelters and sanctioned the killing of a neighbor who tried to enter anyone's cave in the ground. That people had "an obligation to die" was an idea traceable to Christianity and Judaism and hence totally unknown in Japan.

Warming to his theme, Sakaiya went on to other examples. Noah had packed his ark with animals but permitted only two humans aboard. Japanese would never tolerate such a choice. Japan's long history as a peace-loving nation was proven by the absence in any period of cities built within walls. In foreign countries, cities were always built inside of walls. Furthermore, Japan had never endured wars in which rulers killed or enslaved those people captured from other clans. This certainly proved his point, Sakaiya thought. "Because Japan has not experienced truly severe wars of that sort, it is very difficult for the people as a whole to spend large sums of money on defense. . . . We must have foreign countries understand this point when they make requests on defense."[12]

It mattered not that each of these assertions was demonstrably false or that Japan in 1985 was engaged in a very formidable defense buildup of its own. For Sakaiya was engaged in the practice of a logically undemanding form of pop-art known as *Nihonjinron*. It means "theories of the Japanese," and its purpose is to demonstrate what makes Japan both different from other countries and unique on the face of the globe. At the core of all *Nihonjinron* are two assumptions: 1. Japan's culture and traditions are unique and owe nothing to those of any other country;

2. Japan's modern practices are drawn exclusively from her culture and tradition. The result of these assumptions is obvious: Modern Japan cannot be judged by standards produced by alien culture and cannot be expected to behave as other countries behave.

The propagation of Nihonjinron has been an immense industry in postwar Japan and has employed the labor of thousands of practitioners—college professors, commentators, and writers of both popular and serious dissertations. It was by no means a formal academic discipline, but a number of important intellectuals enhanced their careers by employing it in their essays. By thinking up new examples to support it, dozens of popular media figures made their names. It seems to have become a widespread form of philosophizing in the 1970s. One study has estimated that between 1946 and 1978 at least 700 titles were published dealing in some way or another with the Japanese identity, 25 percent of them appearing between 1976 and 1978.[13] Some scholars have noted that the nature of Nihonjinron changed over the years. In the early postwar years, with Japan in deepest despair, the works often expressed a sense of national inferiority. Later, after the economic recovery, they turned to stressing Japan's superior ways of doing things.

The modern Nihonjinron is inherently nationalistic, and it appeals to a people wanting proof of their moral and cultural superiority. One way it provides this is by asserting that fundamental character traits differentiate Japanese from others. Among the most common examples are these: Westerners are coldly rational; Japanese are warmly intuitive. The West is aggressive, masculine; Japan is peaceful, feminine. Foreigners insist on precision; Japanese prefer a certain fuzziness. Westerners act from abstract principles; Japanese distrust dogma and like to muddle through life's problems. Rough confrontation delights the foreigner; a Japanese regards head-on argument as shameful. And on and on.

These are not merely theoretical differences. In practice, they confer on Japanese a moral superiority. Sakaiya's assertion that Japanese possess a greater reverence for human life crops up in many other Nihonjinron samples drawn from everyday events. In 1977 a Japanese airliner was hijacked in Dacca and a huge ransom was demanded. Japan hastened to pay up, despite the international campaign to prevent deals with hijackers. It was justified in many editorials and semiofficial comments as evidence that Japan valued lives over money, unlike the West. Love of nature is often cited as a trait dividing Japanese from foreigners. An eminent writer-scholar, Shozaburo Kimura of Tokyo University, has concluded that love of nature is somehow one of the major reasons that Japanese reject Christianity. Westerners have a compulsion to re-shape nature, the Japanese don't, he has written. Because they are at one with nature, they need not look to man-made religions to find internal peace. According to Kimura, "In this Japanese climate of har-mony between man and nature and between man and man, it is nearly impossible to foster cults or individuals capable of commanding abso-lute obedience in body and soul."[14]

The market for examples of Japanese uniqueness is a lucrative one. Locating these samples is like mining for gold, and some of the richest lodes are discovered not in character traits but in physical distinctions. The most famous miner, undoubtedly, was Dr. Tadanobu Tsunoda, a nose-ear-throat specialist who discovered that the Japanese brain func-tions in a manner different from a foreigner's. He reported that the Japanese brain perceives sounds in a manner different from that of the Westerner's brain. Tsunoda wrote:

> My findings seem to provide an explanation of the unique and universal aspects of Japanese culture. . . . Why do Japanese people behave in their characteristic manner? How has Japa-nese culture developed its distinctive features? I believe the key to these questions lies in the Japanese language. That is, "the Japanese are Japanese because they speak Japanese." My investigations have suggested that the Japanese language shapes the Japanese brain function pattern, which in turn serves as a basis for the formation of the Japanese culture.[15]

This astounding revelation was solemnly accepted by millions of Japa-nese readers. Indeed, much of *Nihonjinron* goes uncontested in Japan, although it causes much amusement when exported abroad. A classic example was the testimony in Washington in 1987 by the former min-ister of Agriculture, Forestry, and Fisheries, Tsutomu Hata. It was Hata's mission to explain to American congressmen why Japan could not lower its import barriers to permit more American beef to be sold. The reason, he said, was because Japanese have larger digestive tracts than foreigners and thus have a physiological aversion to red meat.

The quest for samplings of Japanese uniqueness occupies those at the pinnacle of their professions, especially academics. History is ran-sacked for proofs of specialness. One of the country's most honored academics, Professor Takeo Kuwabara of Kyoto University, expressed delight in the fact that large numbers of Japanese children go on school excursions together, even venturing as far as Tokyo to see the nation's capital. It is of course a practice common in most other countries, but

Kuwabara thought it uniquely Japanese. "It is quite an achievement," he wrote. "In France, how many of its people have seen Paris? In the United States, how many people have been to Washington?" Everything that passed his eye stirred Kuwabara to admiration for his country's inventive culture. For example: "Japanese coffee shops are also unique." No evidence was offered to support this notion, nor any of his other conclusions, such as this one: "The weekly magazine is another uniquely Japanese invention."[16]

Any foreigner who grapples with learning the Japanese language is surprised to discover the large number of "loan words," or foreign words imported into Japan's vocabulary. Such words as *computer* or *word processor* are used daily in the press and in advertisements. It often seems that Japanese would be unable to converse about modern life without these borrowings. Ironically, even the word to describe the country's supposedly "unique" culture is borrowed from English, appearing in Japanese texts as *yuniiku*. The basic written language is derived from the Chinese. German, French, and most of all English have infiltrated for more than a century. Yet a primary industry of Japanese linguists is certifying Japanese to be free of foreign influence. Despite all of the evidence to the contrary, *Nihongo* (the Japanese language) is relentlessly depicted as a "pure" language. The most influential of the linguistic purists in the postwar period was Haruhiko Kindaichi, a professor at Sophia University and star of many *Nihonjinron* radio and television discussions. He began his work in 1957 with the publication of *Nihongo*. It was in large part designed to refute the work of other postwar intellectuals who, in their effort to eradicate all vestiges of nationalism, had found Japanese a less-than-suitable language; one prominent writer had even proposed abandoning it for French. Kindaichi was not content merely to endorse *Nihongo* as a tradition worth continuing. It was, he claimed, a language uniquely pure. "The Japanese language has a unique position among the languages of civilized countries," he wrote. "That is, there is absolutely no other language of a similar nature." He went on to explain that it had endured no other influences than that of Chinese long ago. A generation of foreign linguists has enjoyed destroying Kindaichi's thesis in remorseless attacks, pointing out that Japanese is no more or less distinctive than other languages and in fact borrows many foreign terms. Yet Kindaichi's disciples continue touting its essential purity to this day.[17]

The *Nihonjinron* movement was an often comic, even ludicrous, undertaking, but it was not without meaning. It was the surface sign of a deeper search for a national identity in the social and cultural debris left over from World War II. It had begun in earnest in the late 1960s and early 1970s, those years when Japan's economic recovery was an accepted fact and when people were at last reviving their confidence. For the first time in a quarter-century, they had an opportunity to look around them and be concerned with something larger than the immediate struggle to earn a living.

What they saw, beyond the billowing smokestacks and handsome new buildings, was not a pleasant sight. They seemed to have no past, no roots. In the years after the defeat they had been taught that what had gone before was tawdry, even evil in the eyes of the rest of the world. What was good was Western—the songs they sang, the styles they adopted, the technology they borrowed, the operas, movies, and discos to which they flocked. For more than two decades nothing that was traditionally Japanese seemed of much value.

They were charged, then, with reinventing their own past, and the materials at hand were not inspiring. Nationalism, before the war, had been defined as devotion to the emperor and other symbols of state, such as the flag and anthem, and to ideas of empire that had been coined a hundred years earlier. This political nationalism would not do. All of the old symbols were tainted with catastrophe and defeat, were casualties of the war, and Japanese were uninterested in reviving them. Hayashi's apology for the war, Mishima's pathetic attempt to revive the old military spirit, and other efforts to build on the past were doomed to irrelevance.

In their stead, Japanese settled for a form of cultural nationalism of which the Nihonjinron writings were a revealing element. They had the value of reaching back past the war and the Occupation to bits and pieces of Japanese culture that were untainted, still pristine. The fact that many of them were pure myth mattered not at all. Each in its way was a soothing reminder of better times. The noble samurai could be reincarnated as the dedicated businessman, not the warrior Mishima preferred. There was much moral comfort in the notion that Japanese excelled not just in building cars but also in reverence for nature and human life. True or not, it was certainly uplifting, for it satisfied a deep longing for a past worth remembering. Economic success had freed them for the search. One perceptive student of Nihonjinron, Winston Davis, has observed that the movement was so broad, so embracing, that it amounted almost to a "civil religion," one that replaced the discredited version that had brought defeat.

"The self images we see emerging in it," Davis wrote, "are not the finished products of a new ideology, but an on-going search for a new national identity by a people whose economic enterprise has recouped what generals, gods and a divine emperor previously lost."[18]

●

The *Nihonjinron* essays were comforting because they helped to fill the vacuum created by the war defeat and the Occupation. They did so for the most part without touching on the most painful memories of the war-and-Occupation period. They harked back to culture and tradition, not to politics, and they dealt with aspects of the Japanese people, not of their former leaders who wrought nothing but catastrophe. Most of the *Nihonjinron* endeavors, in fact, fit quite comfortably with the notion that prewar nationalism, the war, and submission to foreigners were all aberrations caused by a foolish military class. Whatever had happened in those days—and the postwar generation knew little of what had, in fact, happened—it was not a product of Japanese popular tradition. Cultural nationalism and political nationalism did not mix. Was that not the message of the Mishima fiasco and the scorn with which the public had greeted his bizarre suicide scene?

But this did not satisfy a substantial number of postwar nationalists who chose to struggle in the political arena. For them, the rejection of prewar nationalism still rankled. For them, the question of national identity was still bound up with the war era and all of its powerful symbols: Shinto, the emperor-as-god, the flag, the national anthem, the foreign-imposed constitution, the Tokyo war-crimes trials, and many others. Most of all, they despised the fact that postwar Japanese had so easily accepted the notion of war guilt. Expunging that guilt and making Japanese see that their war had been not sordid but rather noble, not aggressive but defensive, was perhaps the one mission on which the political nationalists found themselves in agreement.

They were a disparate lot, not the centrally guided right-wing conspiracy that many Japanese and foreigners imagined. Some were hardly more than gangsters who, supplied with funds by rich superpatriots, patrolled the streets with sound trucks blaring military songs and threatened left-wing groups like the Japan Teachers Union. Others were prominent intellectuals whose writings, like Hayashi's in the 1960s, sought to justify the conquest of Asia. The hierarchy of the Shinto religion, barred by the constitution from public roles, was another faction. A sporadically influential mass lobby was centered in organizations representing surviving families of those killed in the war. Within the LDP, a group of young right-wingers in 1973 founded an anti-

Communist coalition called *Seirankai*. Like young military hotheads in the 1930s, they sealed their allegiance in a blood oath.

In the 1970s and early 1980s the political nationalists' platform often dominated the news, creating the impression that prewar imperialism was renascent. Its planks were invariably linked to World War II. Diet members were quietly pressured to honor the war dead by attending ceremonies at Yasukuni Shrine. Campaigns to revise the American-written constitution were launched. The Ministry of Education, upon which much of the pressure was focused, insisted that schools require daily displays of the national flag and singing of the national anthem.

The crusaders went on to attempt a broad rewriting of the history of the Pacific War. The Nanking massacre became an "incident" involving few deaths, for example. Even the annexation of Korea back in 1910 became an act of friendship to save that country from the Russians and Chinese. For years a struggle wound on in courts over revisionists' attempts to describe the invasion of China in the 1930s not as aggression but merely as an "advance." The effect of all their pressures and lobbying, taken together, was to convince many that Japanese were seized anew with a rampant militarism. They lacked an important national leader, because no one with high political ambitions wanted to risk association with unpleasant memories of the war and its aftermath. But in Yasuhiro Nakasone they seemed to have found their man.

Nakasone was the most complex and perplexing prime minister since Yoshida, one of the few in his generation to demonstrate a grasp of the idea of personal leadership in Japan's democracy. Like Kakuei Tanaka, who was to make him prime minister in 1982, he began political life as an independent outsider, forcing his way to the top rather than inching toward it from within the bureaucracy. Compared to his colleagues, who, with the exception of Tanaka, made blandness a virtue, Nakasone had charisma. Tall and solidly built, he had a deep, rolling baritone voice that he used to great effect in local campaigns. He built a rapport with an audience similar to that of the best American orators. When he spoke, listeners murmured back words of approval and encouragement, very much like Southern blacks once responded to Martin Luther King. He had ideas of his own and liked to express them, traits not much admired in Japan's consensual politics. He frequently changed his mind, so much so that the hostile Japanese press early labeled him a "weathervane," but in truth he was far less likely to run with the crowd than his rivals, the leaders of other LDP factions.

Nakasone is best remembered as the "internationalist" prime minister, in part because of certain policies he adopted but also because of the way he could put them forward. One foreign diplomat with many years of experience in Japan called him "the only prime minister who ever uttered a complete sentence." He spoke a fair amount of English and even managed to establish a personal rapport with foreign leaders such as President Ronald Reagan. At annual summit meetings, his predecessors had always seemed out of the flow, unable to chat and mix with Western heads of state; official summit photographs invariably showed the Japanese representative staring vaguely into space. Nakasone managed to appear in the center of the pack, where he seemed to gossip casually with a Thatcher, Reagan, or Kohl. With Americans he was relaxed and ever cooperative. He could even use the word "alliance" to describe the Japan-America relationship; his predecessors dreaded the term. Nakasone worked hard to open Japan's markets to the West, endorsed American arms control measures, and substantially increased Japan's foreign aid. He was, to most Westerners, "Mr. International-ism."

The other side to Nakasone was a strident nationalism that was far outside of the political mainstream. He had been a young naval officer in World War II and returned to civilian life in the Home Ministry, which in prewar years had been the enforcer of civilian patriotism. By his own account, he was appalled at Japan's flagging spirits during the Occupation period and entered politics in 1947 partly to try to revive them. His campaign style was particularly out of step with the times. Nakasone wore an old Imperial Navy uniform, which he stripped of its epaulets, and rode through his constituency on a bicycle bearing the Japanese Rising Sun flag, which MacArthur had banned.

His positions on issues were most unconventional for someone with high ambitions, but had strong emotional appeal to the right wing. He urged revision of the constitution MacArthur had imposed, con-tending that it had stripped Japan of her nationhood. He also advocated a large, strong, and independent military devoted to defending Japan, not merely to sharing America's role in Asia. He insisted that Japan's schooling problems had begun with American-imposed liberal ideas that left students lacking in "moral education" and love of country. He publicly blamed the West's bullying of Japan for having caused the Pacific War. The West, he would say on the stump, practiced *fukuro dataki*, an emotion-laden phrase that means "forcing someone into a bag and then beating him with sticks." He talked frequently of Japan's lost "spiritual culture" and sense of national purpose, and in moments when he thought his words would not be quoted, he could be implicitly racist. Once, in the countryside, he deprecated foreign countries that contain a mixture of races, describing them as nations of "*Omajiri*"—a thin mixed rice gruel lacking in substance. "Persons of unclear nationality like '*Omajiri*' cannot be respected," he said. [19] He diligently courted groups of war veterans whose professional associations were devoted to making prewar military life respectable.

Nakasone did not become prime minister because of his rightist views. The LDP is conservative, but political views are of little importance in selecting its leaders. He won the prize in the usual way—by manipulating factional strength and, most of all, by earning the support of Kakuei Tanaka, still the king-maker. But he was the natural hero of nationalists and attempted to validate their causes. The Yasukuni Shrine in Tokyo, the memorial to the war dead, was at the top of the list. Other prime ministers had waffled about appearing there on August 15, hoping to avoid criticism by going merely as private citizens. Nakasone went openly as head of state. His first cabinet had a distinctly right-wing cast. It included so many former police and Home Ministry officials that it was known in the press as the "police cabinet." He called for a far-reaching study of educational reform, which he intended to be the vehicle for reintroducing "moral education" in the schools, a way of reviving prewar values like patriotism and respect for the authority of elders. He clung to his belief that the "MacArthur constitution" must be revised if Japan were to have a fundamental law reflecting her own traditions. He rewarded the right wing by appointmenting to high office those who shared the right's political nationalism. For the first time, a cabinet minister publicly argued Japan's case for waging World War II. The taboo against such public statements was broken by Nakasone's education minister, Masayuki Fujio, who contended that Japan was not the aggressor, that the Nanking "massacre" may never have happened, and that the war crimes trial in Tokyo was "a kind of kangaroo court."

None of these had much to do with running a modern nation. But each was a piece in that symbolic reconstruction dear to the nationalists' hearts. Taken together, they offered official respect for Shintoism, encouraged patriotism in the young, eased the old war guilt, and erased vestiges of the Occupation period. In short, they would appease those who traced Japan's faults to scars left unhealed since the defeat of 1945. That is apparently what Nakasone had in mind, for he spoke frequently in the early 1980s of wanting to settle the accounts left pending by Japan's surrender and the Occupation. Had he succeeded, the nationalists would have seen their agenda of political symbols substantially advanced, and their brand of nationalism might today count for something.

Instead, the agenda failed. Nakasone made his official visit to Yasukuni Shrine in 1985, evoking enormous protest from other Asian
countries victimized by Japan's armies. He abandoned the visits in
1986. He gave up his hope of revising the "MacArthur constitution,"
recognizing that this would prove too divisive. His plan to revive "moral
education" in public schools wilted in the hands of several study commissions, which could agree on very little. Dreams of making Japan's
aggressions in World War II respectable faded—Education Minister
Fujio was forced to resign for his defense of Nanking. Nothing much
came of the government's efforts to rewrite school history books to
sanitize the Japanese military.

Publicity given to these various causes created the impression that
Japanese in the 1980s were embarked on a new right-wing crusade to
restore prewar values and practices. Other Asian nations that still remembered the period of conquest—China, the Koreas, Singapore, and
the Philippines—protested loudly at each supposed example of renascent superpatriotism. In fact, nothing like that was happening in Japan.
Public-opinion surveys of the time registered not an increase in nationalist sentiments but a widespread indifference to causes associated with
the nation or society at large. When asked whether they wanted to do
something for their country or hoped the country would so something
for them, Japanese answered overwhelmingly in favor of the latter. Polls
of the prime minister's office between 1971 and 1986 consistently found
only 13 or 14 percent wanting to serve the state in any capacity. Older
people in a 1988 survey expressed strong feelings of patriotism; but only
20 to 30 percent of men in their twenties acknowledged being patriotic.
Over the same period there was no perceptible increase in the number
of people who felt it was necessary to foster patriotism. Compared to
their cohorts in other nations, young Japanese adults were conspicuously low in devotion to their nation. A survey of the Management and
Coordination Agency in early 1988 measured their devotion to national
interests against those of young adults in ten other countries. Only 5.5
percent of the Japanese would sacrifice their personal interests for the
sake of society's interests, a rate far lower than in the other nations.
About 40 percent of the young Japanese expressed a willingness to serve
their country under some circumstances. The rate was twice as high in
the other countries.[20]

The most conclusive evidence of Japanese indifference to nationalist causes was a series of annual surveys conducted by a broadcasting
research firm between 1973 and 1988, the period when nationalism was
supposedly on the rise. They registered no significant change in nation-

alist sentiment throughout the period. And the proportion of people wanting to make some contribution to the nation actually declined by seven points. Much of the nationalist agenda had revolved around attempts to increase reverence for the old imperial institutions, and it was sometimes presumed that a return of emperor worship was a rising threat to democracy in Japan. It did not happen. The broadcast company's research found that indifference to Emperor Hirohito was widespread. The number professing respect for him actually declined between 1973 and 1988 (from 33 to 28 percent), and almost half of all Japanese said they had no feeling whatsoever toward him. Only the oldest generation—those with emotional memories of prewar imperialism—expressed strong support. Among the young adults, Japan's future leaders, Hirohito was, if anything, a peripheral figure.[21]

The nationalists' agenda failed despite Nakasone's earnest efforts because it was hopelessly out of touch with the times. It had always had more to do with symbols than substance, but its symbols were those for which few Japanese cared to trouble themselves. It was a backward-looking agenda in a country obsessed with the present and the future. If its symbols appealed to anyone, it was to older Japanese for whom the old militarism had been a momentous phenomenon. Their generation was dying out. Young and middle-aged Japanese in the 1980s knew little and cared less about the war period and the Occupation. They could not be much concerned with revising their country's war history because they had been taught almost nothing about that history in the first place. The emperor was a dim figure hidden in the Imperial Palace. Yasukuni Shrine was merely a fine place to drink oneself silly under the cherry trees in April.

12
•

The Odd Man Out

I t was July 1978, and the leaders of the non-Communist industrialized nations were gathered in Bonn for the annual economic
summit. The meetings had been cordial and apparently productive, for
as the seven heads of state posed for the official photograph, they exuded
a sense of relaxed informality and might have been mistaken for old
fraternity boys brought together at a college reunion. Only one seemed
out of place. Off at the end, Prime Minister Takeo Fukuda of Japan
wasn't chatting with anyone. Instead, he stood slightly apart, his eyes
turned skyward as if following the flight of some interesting bird.

The photo was an unintended expression of a central truth. In the
arenas of postwar foreign policy, Japan has ever been the odd man out.
She has been a member of all the important institutions—United Nations, World Bank, General Agreements on Tariffs and Trade, International Monetary Fund, and Organisation for Economic Cooperation
and Development. Her role in each has rarely been significant. In all

the Western councils, she has been nominally a participant but in deed a cipher, a partner but always a remote one. The great trials of the times somehow unfold with Japan on the sidelines, distracted, gazing into the distance at a bird in flight. This almost eerie detachment from the affairs of state has often been summed up in a phrase: Japan is in but not of the world.

Not until the mid-1980s did Japan care to grapple with the thought of playing an international role. Until then, she carried the weight of a middling nation—an Asian Portugal, perhaps. By treaty, she was a member of the "Western bloc" but a reluctant one, managing almost to ignore the cold war that raged on her perimeters. The fires in the Middle East seemed remote to Japanese, except on those occasions when they threatened to cut the flow of oil. Revolutions and civil wars tore old civilizations apart, but even those in Southeast Asia ignited only flickers of interest in Tokyo. This unworldly detachment sometimes caused even Japanese to wonder. A popular psychiatrist, Keigo Okonogi, diagnosed it as an adolescent phenomenon akin to the teenager who never grows up to accept responsibility for anything, not even his own fate. Japan, he wrote, had become a "moratorium state" incapable of acting, immobile even in the face of threats to its own obvious interests.[1]

In a crisis, Japan seemed always out of step. The late 1970s witnessed a worldwide series of terrorist hijackings of civilian jetliners. To curb them, the major target countries agreed that there should be no surrender to terrorism. Storm the captive airliners or wait out the siege was the international code. Germany, Israel, and France had followed the code and successfully freed hostages. Then, in September 1977, a Japan Air Lines jet and 140 crew and passengers were taken hostage at Dacca, Bangladesh. The hijackers, members of the radical Japan Red Army, demanded not only ransom money but the immediate release of friends held in Japanese prisons for brutal crimes. Into Tokyo came international pleas for Japan to hold fast. Ten nations refused to allow the jet to land on their soil if, as threatened, the hijackers tried to move elsewhere. The Japanese government waited only briefly to make its decision. A plane carrying $6 million in ransom and six released radicals was dispatched to Dacca, and the passengers were released. Prime Minister Fukuda explained that "human life is more precious than the earth."

I arrived in Tokyo that fall as a correspondent fresh from Washington. The contrast in capitals was extraordinary. Washington was the center of the world, a place where global decisions were made daily. Affairs in the Middle East, Moscow, and Indochina had been the stuff of page-one news for decades. For better or worse, the United States and its friends in Europe took sides, debated, and fussed with one another about the cold war, the Gaza Strip, nuclear missiles on the continent, and guerilla wars in Latin America. In Tokyo I felt that I had somehow wandered off the planet. On a day that saw the world whipped closer to war in the Middle East, the nightly television news might feature the northward creep of the cherry-blossom season. How did Japan fit into the cold war in those days when East-West detente was slipping? One day I was informed that the principle of the Fukuda government was one of "omnidirectional diplomacy." Puzzled, I asked if that meant Japan saw no distinctions between East and West, that Moscow and Washington looked much the same from Tokyo. "Omnidirectional," I was told, "does not necessarily mean equidistant."

Such nonexplanations baffled foreigners. They puzzled even many Japanese, who were hard-pressed to account for the passivity of their country. "The Japanese policy has been to avoid entanglements in international politics," wrote one scholar, Jun-ichi Kyogaku. Japan talked unceasingly about world peace but did little to help bring it about. Kyogaku noted that Japan never committed its soldiers to United Nations peace-keeping forces, and she granted refugees and defectors only temporary sanctuary. When it came to matters of greater moment, Japanese seemed somehow immobilized. "Being inconspicuous and passive has been the Japanese approach to international affairs," Kyogaku continued. "Thus, when Japan, which today is an economic superpower, is asked to assume global leadership and responsibility in a world that is threatened by trade friction and economic conflict, the Japanese do not know how to act."[2]

Explaining their country's disengagement, many Japanese inevitably fall back on cultural definitions. Japan historically had been aloof from the world. In ancient times she had been a "peripheral" state, never really involved with the continent. The Tokugawa shogunate had shut the world out for a quarter of a millennium. Thus, goes the argument, postwar Japan's withdrawal from the world was a mere return to tradition. Like most of the cultural uniqueness theories dredged up to explain Japan's modern behavior, this one, too, ignores the facts. Since the Meiji Restoration Japan had been deeply—and belligerently— engaged in Asia. She was an expansionist nation, determined, like Western imperialist powers, to conquer colonies and expand economic influence. Only superior arms forced her to retire. The postwar disengagement was abnormal, not a reversion to type. For the first time in fifty years, as the economist W. W. Lockwood observed, Japan walked softly and lacked a big stick.[3] Japan's peculiar international behavior was a product of the times, just as were her political and economic systems. It was a reaction to war and defeat, the mood of a weary people, and most of all the special pressures that arose in the immediate postwar years. Her isolation and seeming indifference to events of the world grew from those forces that pummeled her in the crucial years following the war.

The setting was a nation weary not merely of war but of the world. That world was a hostile place. Japan's closest neighbors were a historic enemy, the Soviet Union, an embittered former colony, Korea, and a soon-to-be-communized China whose people had suffered greatly from Japanese military brutality. Southeast Asia seethed with resentment of its former invaders, and from every point on the globe came demands for war reparations. Japan was the criminal. In a sense there was no world from which Japan could withdraw; the world had withdrawn from Japan. Her people were entombed in a deep sense of national inferiority and self-hate. Ironically, only the United States, the conqueror, took any interest in her at all, and who knew which way that interest would push the country? "Foreign policy" was an almost laughable phrase. Whenever pollsters asked the Japanese what sort of foreign policy they wanted, most shrugged and said they favored a vague neutrality.

By default and the force of circumstances, Japan handed foreign policy over to the United States. The Americans pushed her in totally different directions. At first, Japan was to be an unarmed neutral. Then she was to be an ally in the cold war. The United States did not hand back the power of independent foreign relations with the signing of the peace treaty in 1951. Instead, it used that treaty to circumscribe Japan in almost every way. It determined what nations Japan would be friendly with, which it should oppose or favor, how and where it would trade.

What the United States wanted in Japan was an obedient client state, a stable pillar in the house of anticommunism. It largely succeeded. In the security treaty signed in 1951, Washington preserved the right to place troops and bases on Japanese soil and even to intervene militarily inside Japan in the event of domestic turmoil. This was the price of independence for Japan. But it was a limited independence. The security treaty attached Japan to the non-Communist side in the cold war and ended any thoughts of autonomy or neutrality. It also established a pattern of foreign relations that has endured, with many rough patches, ever since. Japan, today, still looks first to Washington to determine what she can or can't do in relations with the world. She does not always follow instructions, but American approval or disapproval sets the framework for how Japan will act. For years, Japanese diplomats have used a rueful joke to explain their sensitivity to signals from Washington: "It is the ghost of John Foster Dulles." Sometimes this kowtowing to Washington is said to be merely another "cultural" trait. Japan, it is said, has always followed the lead of some foreign power, preferring, as some Japanese intellectuals like to put it, to trail in the path of "the strongest horse." Again, the cultural argument holds no water.

This dependence on the United States brought with it many advantages, almost all of them economic. For dependency was the key to prosperity. With it, Japan was ushered into the non-Communist economic system on which her success is based. Guided by Uncle Sam, Japan was allowed to join GATT, the World Bank, the IMF, and the OECD. It got credits from the U.S. Import-Export Bank, procurement contracts from the Korean War, and military assistance. Most important of all, it was granted nearly total access for many years to the greatest prize of all, the American market. It could export without restraint to the world's richest consumer mart, all the while maintaining strict controls on merchandise imports and direct investment in its own markets.

The price of these benefits was high in other terms, because the United States insisted on choosing Japan's friends and enemies. From the first, Dulles and others in Washington viewed the peace treaty as a mechanism for aligning Japan against America's foes; it would, he promised, bring Japan ". . . within the framework of the larger United States strategy in the Far East." Even after the treaty was signed, Dulles seemed to be obsessed with the notion that Japan was unreliable and that she might either join the Communist bloc or cut a deal with it that would undermine American hegemony in the Pacific. American insistence that Japan sign a separate peace treaty with non-Communist nations—not the comprehensive treaty that most Japanese appeared to favor—was the first stage in sealing Japan off from the Soviet Union.

Sealing Japan off from China was more difficult, requiring constant U.S. vigilance and pressure. The American refusal to permit diplomatic normalization or, for a decade, official trade with Communist China, was very unpopular in Japan. Even conservative politicians and most businessmen regarded China as a potential friend and trading partner, and there was pressure from both groups on governments in Tokyo to disregard the American policy of quarantining the Communist state. Yoshida never considered Red China a threat. Nevertheless, to please Washington he signed the fateful letter recognizing Taiwan as another cost of winning independence, and for years Japan dutifully marched to American instructions. It reluctantly joined the American crusade to block China's entry into the United Nations in 1961. Its obedience was sustained until, to their great surprise, Japanese discovered that President Nixon himself had moved secretly to break the quarantine.

But in one area, militarization, Japan refused to follow the line marked out by the United States. From the 1950s on, the United States pleaded with Japan to rearm and contribute to the non-Communist alliance. It asked for a radical increase in military manpower, insisted that Japan take part in collective defense, and urged her to revise her American-written constitution to permit Japanese troops to be sent into combat overseas. Japan persistently refused to budge. Not until the late 1970s did she begin a significant arms buildup, and she has never reached the manpower levels that Dulles was insisting upon in the 1950s. She has never sent armed forces overseas, not even in peace-keeping missions sponsored by the United Nations. Her responses to American pressure have usually taken the form of procrastination and evasions, but they have been uniformly negative. Historian John Dower has recorded a revealing episode of Yoshida's refusal to buckle when Washington was pressing hard for help in the Korean War.

It is a conversation between Colonel Frank Kowalski, an American military advisor in Japan, and a Japanese official. Americans wanted defense forces increased from 110,000 to 300,000, and Kowalski explained why Japan should see that as being in her own interests. Kowalski recalled this exchange:

> "Ah, so," responded my friend, "we will strengthen our forces, but not until 1955."
> "Why 1955?" I asked.
> "By then the Korean war will be over."
> "But why must you wait until the war is ended?" I persisted.
> "Because Mr. Yoshida does not want Japan to become involved in the Korean War. If we organize 300,000 troops as your Mr. Dulles wants us, your government will insist that we send some of these troops to Korea. That is why the Prime Minister agreed to expand our forces only to 110,000."[4]

●

The issue seemed settled in 1960 when, after enormous protests and a riot at the Diet, the security treaty was renewed. The renewal cost Prime

Minister Kishi his job, but it settled for good the question of Japan's foreign policy. Thereafter, foreign policy would be essentially fixed in Washington. Japan had but to follow, moved not by her own design but by nudges and threats from the United States. In 1964 Masataka Kosaka recorded this development in an essay entitled "Japan: A Nation Without a Foreign Policy." Neither political party was concerned with Japan's independent role in the world, wrote Kosaka, a Kyoto University professor and a popular author. Neither bothered to have a foreign policy. The LDP was obsessed with purely local interests and its constituent pressures. The Socialist party was concerned only with the purity of its ideological positions, and its only policy was to continue to oppose the security treaty.[5]

Settlement of the security treaty issue ushered in the period of "economism" when nothing mattered but hard work and economic growth. Kishi was succeeded by Prime Minister Ikeda, who launched the decade of "income doubling" that was to bring Japan abreast of the other industrial powers in economic development. It was an era in which international standing was measured not by political influence but by annual increments of GNP. Before 1960 the question of Japan's relations with other countries had been loudly debated. Relations with China, the Soviet Union, Taiwan, and the United States were issues that divided people and rocked governments. After 1960 they were eclipsed in the great crusade for growth. Japan came to define herself by economic terms alone. A poll conducted by the *Yomiuri Shimbun* in 1970 was revealing. It asked people what they thought Japan should do to become a "big power" in the world. The responses recorded only domestic concerns. Thirty-seven percent said Japan should expand its economic strength, 33 percent favored raising living standards at home, and 23 percent opted for improving social welfare. Few of the respondents mentioned anything having to do with foreign countries per se.[6]

For Japan, this pursuit of economic gain essentially rested on exporting goods abroad and buying natural resources. A foreign policy to sustain those activities seemed the natural course. Curiously, Japan officially did little—compared to what other mercantilistic nations in the past had done—to create one. She did not embark on a naval buildup to protect her shipping lanes, vital both for exporting goods and acquiring materials. Rarely did she exert political influence on other nations to obtain markets, protect investments, or assure raw materials. As a government, Japan stood idly by. Trade and investment were the domain of trading companies and the giant manufacturing companies, which on occasion carried out foreign policies of their own. Japan's government did service them with a strenuous export-promotion policy but rarely indulged in displays of muscle or overt influence on their behalf. Issues of security, for sea-lanes and markets alike, were handled by the United States, and Tokyo had only to see that the bilateral boat was not rocked. Donald C. Hellman, an American expert on Japan's foreign policy, has observed that she hardly acted like a nation at all in pursuing her own economic security. She had carefully divided politics and economics into two compartments and had not tried to link economic interests with military power. "Japan's approach to the issue of security," he wrote, "has been that of an expanding international trading company, not that of a nation-state."[7]

In at least one area, the Japanese government did in fact turn foreign policy over to private enterprise. Foreign-aid programs in other modern countries are a tool of foreign policy. They are used to bolster friends, create spheres of influence, and cement alliances. Japan's foreign-aid programs grew steadily in the 1970s and then mushroomed into the world's largest in the late 1980s. But there was a difference. Japan's loans and grants to developing nations were organized to benefit Japanese manufacturers and trading companies almost without regard to national interest. A large percentage of the funds was "tied"—in other words, they were to be used to purchase goods and services from Japanese firms. Government money was being sent abroad not to advance a coherent national interest but to increase the profits of large companies.

Moreover, those companies were the actual organizers of most of the foreign-aid programs. The government in Tokyo had little voice in selecting projects in the recipient countries. Trading companies did that. They decided where it might be worthwhile to build a dam, a harbor, a power plant. Then they talked the local country into requesting money from Japan to build it. Approval was usually routine. "We don't have enough staff even for planning," the head of Japan's Overseas Economic Cooperation Fund (OECF), Takashi Hosomi, told me in 1987. "We have no employees in our embassies overseas. So the trading company gets approval for a project in the donee country. They do the engineering work and they get most of the contracts."[8] When, in the late 1980s, the Japanese government reformed the system to reduce the amount of "tied" aid, it still relied on the large trading and construction companies to select projects. Because those companies also got the engineering contracts, they were the likely ones to build the projects as well. As late as 1989, when Japanese foreign aid exceeded that of any other country, Japanese firms were being awarded three out of every four engineering contracts. And most of the aid was being delivered to

Asian countries where the Japanese firms had large existing interests. Foreign aid, then and now, was not an instrument of government foreign policy but a tool for enriching private enterprise.

●

For most of the postwar years, then, Japan did not have a foreign policy, except in the limited sense of encouraging exports and otherwise ser- vicing the business community. Keeping a low profile in an interna- tional setting managed by the United States was sufficient. Economics governed everything. The world in those years was torn with every imaginable upheaval—racial wars, religious conflict, national liberation movements, great-power confrontations. Japan simply sat them out, or tried to. Inevitably, however, she was occasionally drawn in. Even the most passive foreign policy had its tensions. Japan's involved the in- stances in which her economic interests, as defined by big business, conflicted with the larger purposes of maintaining a stable relationship with the United States and getting along with the Western community of nations with which she had cast her lot.

Often, she was badly out of step. This usually happened when Western countries set out to discipline lesser nations for behavior of which they disapproved on moral or strategic grounds. The West had gradually developed codes of conduct, usually involving human rights or national sovereignty, which it sometimes sought to enforce through sanctions, embargoes, or other such quarantines. Inevitably, it insisted on Japan's participation. Also inevitably, these cases would place Japan's economic interests in peril. It was then that Japan's remoteness from the world community would become especially apparent. For her natural instincts were to ignore such inconveniences and get on with doing business. The West would them stomp its feet impatiently, and Japan would eventually go along, but grudgingly.

The situation in South Africa was an example of this pattern. When the United States and Europe established economic sanctions in protest of South Africa's system of apartheid, Japan at first passed. In Tokyo, a familiar bureaucratic stalemate set in. The Foreign Ministry, whose mission is getting along with Western countries, favored sanc- tions. MITI, charged with defending economic interests, did not. Trade with South Africa was indispensable, MITI contended, because of that country's production of chromium and platinum, which are used in industrial processes. As the stalemate persisted, Japan's trade with South Africa suddenly blossomed, growing by 25 percent in 1986 and another

15 percent in 1987, in dollar terms. (Part of the increase represented only yen appreciation.) Japan suddenly found herself in the awkward position of becoming South Africa's leading trading country.

In such cases, Japan's actions clearly reflected her remoteness from Western concerns. In a system organized primarily to promote business interests, questions having to do with democracy or government oppression are of little consequence. The Foreign Ministry on occasion would strive for policies more in line with those of the Western democracies. It usually failed. There is, too, in Japan a strong feeling that the West is often hypocritical in applying its moral codes. A Japanese diplomat once asked me sarcastically when the United States would begin applying its moral sanctions to the Philippines, which at the time was a quasi-police state ruled by President Marcos. Taiwan and South Korea, two other American allies, were, in the 1970s, governed by authoritarian regimes. Why not punish them? How, the diplomat wondered, could China be at one moment a repressive Communist empire and the next a trade-favored friend?

But the habit of letting corporate interests dominate her foreign-policy choices carried a price. In case after case, Japan seemed to place narrow economic advantage above ethical considerations. To avoid angering China, she was virtually alone among major nations in declining to criticize the suppression of dissent by Chinese forces in Tibet. She was among the first nations to recognize the regime of General Saw Maung in Burma after its brutal crackdown on democratic insurgents in 1989. In several cases, Japan moved two ways at once. She faithfully followed the United States' embargo of aid to Vietnam in the 1980s, while allowing her businessmen to open offices and begin unofficial trade. After the killing of students in Beijing in June 1989, Japan again copied American sanctions, but her traders were quick to reestablish their own relations. As *The Economist* noted: "First out when the shooting started. First back in as soon as the People's Liberation Army had finished mowing down the pro-democracy demonstrators in Tiananmen Square."[9]

These were short-lived embarrassments, quickly forgotten when other events caught the world's attention. The situation in the Middle East was altogether different. Japan's endorsement, for nearly two decades, of the Arab cause revealed her deep division with the West and produced the only major instance of a definitive, long-term break with American policy around the globe. It was not a complicated matter: Japan needed Arab oil. She relied on it for two-thirds or more of her vital petroleum supplies. For most of the postwar period the cheap oil

came easily and few choices had to be made. But the 1973 oil shock—
when prices soared and Arab states tried to embargo sales to friends of
Israel—ended a cozy era. Japan had to make choices.

The de facto Japanese ostracism of Israel began then, although in
the usual manner, no pronouncements were ever issued. Japanese companies simply did not import from or export to Israel—not until 1988
did her automobile industry sell the first Japanese-made car in that
country. The political ostracism was nearly as complete. Not until 1988
did a Japanese cabinet minister visit Israel. Despite American pressure,
Japan welcomed the Palestine Liberation Organization when most of
the West was still trying to quarantine it, only stopping short of formal
recognition. She was among the first to support Palestinians' rights to
establish a separate state. There was more involved in all this than oil.
Japan was never interested in the Middle East, never considered its wars
and religious conflicts part of her concerns. At times, in fact, Japanese
leaders indicated that they thought the Middle East was a bad job
botched by the British and Americans. "Japan is interested in maintaining close ties with the Middle East for our own reasons, and these are
not shaped by political or ideological motives," a foreign minister,
Sunao Sonoda, once said, in a classic expression of Japanese aloofness.
"Close ties," of course, referred only to the Arab states. Other countries
had mucked up the region, not Japan. Sonoda added, "Japan has left no
political stain on the history of its relations with the region and this
makes it possible for our Middle East policy to be unique and
independent."[10]

Japan's insensitivity when clear-cut ethical crises emerged was perhaps best illustrated by her reaction to an Iranian mob's seizure of
American embassy hostages in 1979. The act posed no ambiguous
challenge; it was an extreme violation of fundamental international law.
It involved not a single, isolated individual, but the diplomats of Japan's
closest friend, the United States. While protests were sounded in virtually every non-Arab capital, Japan at first remained silent. The government struggled to find words that would censure the deed without
offending an Arab state that supplied 10 percent of Japan's oil. American
emissaries flew to Tokyo to demand a condemnation. Even American
diplomats in Tokyo, normally solicitous of Japan's "oil problem," were
outraged. Finally, Prime Minister Masayoshi Ohira muttered a gentle
rebuke, objecting to the hostage-taking on "humanitarian" grounds—he
had at first, I was told, objected even to the use of the word "humanitarian." Only American pressure moved him to speak at all.

The episode, once the pressure eased, provoked no great soul-searching in Tokyo. It had been a painful choice between Japan's only real international friend, the United States, and an important oil supplier. There was regret that things had come to such a pass but also resentment that Japan had been forced to choose at all. Other nations pursued economic advantage without bowing to international law. Why was Japan being treated differently? Japan was always to blame, her diplomats objected. One of her most effective diplomats, a lifetime admirer of the United States, Nobuhiko Ushiba, summed it up during an interview: "We are always somehow in the dock."

●

If any nation had cause to fear the advance of international communism in the postwar years, it would certainly seem to be Japan. She was a poor and devastated island country only a short missile hop from the two great Communist powers. To the north and west loomed a hostile Soviet Union bent, so it was said, on world domination. South and west lay China, a Communist empire under Mao Zedong after 1949. Both converged in North Korea, only a few hours by boat across the Sea of Japan. It was in Asia, moreover, that Communist expansionism was a genuine fact. The borders of Europe were settled in 1945 and remained fixed for nearly a half-century, but Asia was a battleground. Mao's triumph was followed by Chinese attempts to export revolution into Southeast Asia—to Indonesia, Malaysia, and the Philippines—while the Soviets secured their foothold in Indochina's independence movements. Much of Asia seemed up for grabs, the arena of real combat in a cold war that elsewhere was, in fact, a stalemate. By all of the conventional modes of reasoning, Japan should have been terrified.

She was not. Throughout that period, Japan behaved as though the cold war was a remote affair that need little trouble her, a distraction but not a danger. She seemed to regard it as a distant struggle between two powerful camps that ought not involve her, should not divert her from the goal of economic recovery and the achievement of prosperity. She was, of course, aligned with the Western camp, the one that called itself the "free world." But that was an accident of history, Japan seemed to believe, one of those random fates that can befall a country that allows itself to be beaten and occupied. Time and again, with monotonous regularity, Americans arrived in Tokyo to warn Japan of the dangers and to beg her to rearm swiftly and join the forces of resistance. Just as monotonously, Japan refused. Within the government there raged for years an Alice-in-Wonderland argument over the degree of danger posed by the Soviet Union. Should she be regarded, officially, as a "threat" to Japan? A "potential threat?" Or "no threat at all?" When the cold war unofficially ended in 1990, Japan could not, by herself, have resisted a Soviet invasion for more than a few days. The intrigues of the West, with their episodes of espionage, defection, and infiltration, seemed alien games to successive Japanese governments. Not until the 1980s, when the great confrontation appeared to be all but over, did Japan notice that it had never enacted an antiespionage law to protect her state secrets. It had hardly occurred to her that one might be necessary.

It was this attitude toward the cold war that more than anything else illuminated the aloofness of Japan's foreign policy, or the absence of one. It was simply not Japan's business. She refused to become entangled in America's crusade in Vietnam, chafed under the American quarantine of Communist China, and objected quietly to Western restrictions on trade with the Soviet Union. When prodded, she grudgingly followed the American line but wished most of all to be left alone and unnoticed in international conflicts. When the Soviet Union invaded Afghanistan, the West rushed to punish her by organizing a boycott of the 1980 Olympic games in Moscow. Japan's initial response was ambiguous, and her own Olympic committee tried quietly to participate. Only when Western pressure became overwhelming and she saw herself as an outcast did Japan join the boycott. During the period of indecision, I asked a Japanese diplomat to explain his country's reluctance to join the movement. He seemed unperplexed. It was not simply to avoid irritating the Russians, he said, but to avoid attracting any attention whatsoever from Moscow. Japan had coasted quietly along in the cold war, comforted by the Soviet preoccupation with Europe. She wanted that to continue: "The bear has her nose pointed toward Europe," the diplomat said. "We do not want her to turn around and notice us."

Being in but not of the Western camp was a position that plagued almost every Japanese government in the postwar era. Japan accepted the security treaty with the United States—that had been the price of independence—and she prospered under American protection. Her instincts were to go with the West without alienating Communist governments, and as a result she was forever caught in the squeeze. In 1981 Prime Minister Zenko Suzuki made the visit to Washington that is required of any Japanese premier. Its purpose was to demonstrate solidarity with the West, to assure an American president that Japan was in the fold. Casually, Suzuki agreed to a joint communiqué that spoke of the "alliance" between Japan and the United States. Back in Tokyo, and facing opposition from pacifist members of the Diet, Suzuki just as casually stated that "alliance" did not mean military cooperation. To any neutral observer, it would seem that the two countries had been in an "alliance" for thirty years that had obvious military significance. Suzuki simply willed it away.

This casual disregard for what other nations saw as imminent danger was the Japanese approach to the cold war for decades. It was not the sole property of the Japan Socialist party and the other professional neutralists. It was the belief of most conservatives, too, that international communism was not a great menace. Prime Minister Yoshida, whose pronouncements guided the ruling party on international issues, was no pacifist and was far from ignorant of strains in the world. Although steadfastly resisting Western pleas for rearmament, he never thought that Japan would remain defenseless forever. Publicly he justified his opposition to a large military on financial grounds—Japan was too poor to rearm—but the real reason lay in his inner conviction that communism's threat was a minor one. He detested both the Soviet Union and communism in general but never thought a Soviet invasion a reasonable concern of his government. The USSR, he said, was weak and poor and totally absorbed in the affairs of Europe. He thought China too sensible to embrace communism for long. Most important, Yoshida believed that the alliance of those two countries under a red banner was a transitory affair, and he predicted the Sino-Soviet split long before it occurred. He wrote in his final years that he had always considered the two powers "basically incompatible" and ultimately bound to come into conflict.[11] Once, as a prime minister defending his views on military matters in the Diet, Yoshida even denounced the notion that Japan should prepare for a "just war" of self-defense. "I considered it harmful to accept such an argument," he explained later. "Recognition of a right to self-defense can provoke a war [under the excuse] of a just war." When pressed, he would fall back on that old, reliable belief in the Japanese spirit for national survival: "The safety and independence of a nation rests not exclusively on armaments, but on a people's passion for independence and freedom."[12]

A generation of American officials steeped in the cold-war logic was alternately puzzled and angered by Japan's lackadaisical attitude. John Foster Dulles had fumed and fussed at Yoshida about rearmament and loyalty to the Western alliance so many times that the prime minister came to dread their encounters. Official Washington could not understand a state of affairs that found American lives and treasure pledged to defend a country that did not seem to recognize that it was in danger. U. Alexis Johnson, then the undersecretary of state, was asked by members of the Senate Foreign Relations Committee in 1971 why the American bases in Japan were more unpopular than those in West Germany and South Korea. He was direct in his answer: "The Japanese do not feel the immediate menace and do not recognize the importance of the United States bases to the security of the entire Far East."[13]

One of the shrewdest analysts of Japanese cold-war attitudes was William H. Jorden, a former news correspondent. In a book published in 1957, he noted Japan's proximity to the USSR, China, and North Korea. These three bellicose Communist powers were the most likely military threats. But Japan did not seem especially worried, he said. "It would be misleading to assume that the Japanese are as aware of this threat or as concerned by it as others, particularly Americans, think they should be. The Korean War and the almost studied disregard the Japanese displayed toward it showed how little real concern was felt among Japanese that their country might suddenly be invaded." Then Jorden put his finger on a larger truth: Japanese were far less worried about a Communist invasion than they were of being drawn into a war caused by misjudgments of either the Soviet Union or the United States. Instead of protecting them, the U.S. bases could be the magnet attracting Soviet attacks—the cause of war, not a defense against one. Jorden wrote: "As far as its own safety is affected, Japan's primary concern is that it may be caught between the power of the United States and that of the communists and thus come to serve as an unwilling battleground."[14]

Prime Minister Kishi was forced to resign after pushing through the Diet in 1960 the bitterly contested revision of the security treaty with the United States. The furious protests over that episode, when thousands rushed the parliament building and brought Japan to the brink of chaos, are remembered as the climactic events in Japan's cold-war debate. When Kishi finally won by dubious means, the debate was ended and Japan settled in as the permanent ally of the West. On the surface, the battle had been between leftists and neutralists on one side and a pro-Western, anti-Communist alliance on the other. The American view of the cold war, with its necessary commitment to collective security and freedom, had prevailed. Japan had irrevocably joined the "free world." Or so those events were interpreted.

A clear-eyed American observer of that stormy trial saw it differently. George Packard, a student of Japanese politics, had followed the debates and dissected the motives and arguments of both contestants. What he found and recorded in a book *Protest in Tokyo*, is one of the most illuminating examples of Japan's essential uninterestedness in the cold war. Both sides were motivated not by international considerations but by notions of Japan's self-interests, Packard wrote. The Left had fought the treaty as an invasion of Japan's sovereignty. The conservatives favored it on balance as serving the national interest—what was good for the American relationship was good for business. Neither, Packard concluded, cared much for international solidarity, however it might be defined. "The concept of collective security in which a country fights from its own shores to preserve world peace and thus its own security was alien to all wisdom and common sense in Japan." Packard observed that one of the treaty's most influential academic supporters, Professor Zengo Ohira, was actually advocating "moral neutrality" between East and West and urging a nonideological choice based on what would best serve Japan's national cause. The treaty's friends never expressed support in terms of moral conviction, Packard noted. Throughout it all, he said, there was a notable lack "of the accompanying view heard in NATO countries that the treaty contributed to the strength of the free world, to freedom, to democracy." Such arguments simply held no interest for the Japanese people.[15]

That indifference to the ideological and moral struggles of the world characterized Japanese opinion throughout the cold war and explains well enough the government's wariness at choosing sides. Isolationism is an inexact description of the mood. Japan never wished to withdraw from the world. She simply refused to see the events of the time through an ideological lens, as the Americans insisted she should. This was reflected in one way or another in many public-opinion surveys that probed attitudes toward the cold war. A 1954 survey of leaders in business, labor, the bureaucracy, and universities forecast the views that Japanese clung to throughout the era. An analysis of that survey by the American Lloyd Free found that only 17 percent of those leaders— the people who most influenced Japanese public opinion—showed any awareness whatsoever of the ideologies and political systems competing for world supremacy.[16]

In Washington, this behavior always seemed a sign of unfaithfulness, a lack of appreciation for American leadership in the moral crusade. The comfortable distance Japan was able to establish between herself and the warring world was paid for with American protection. That is the view of countless politicians who have accused Japan of accepting a "free ride" on American defense budgets. The reality was different—Japanese never really felt they needed protection. A poll conducted in October 1969 was typical: Only 5 percent said they thought an attack on Japan was likely, and only 35 percent thought it a possibility. The great majority either dismissed the idea or said they had never considered it.[17]

The presence of American bases in Japan has been widely viewed not as protection for Japan but as an instrument of self-serving American strategy. In 1955 those bases were looked upon more as a threat to Japan's security than as a shield against Communist aggression—they might provoke an attack by the Soviet Union. Only 19 percent believed the bases enhanced Japanese security; 43 percent thought they endangered it.[18] Over the years, the bases came to be accepted (except in Okinawa, where they are still enormously unpopular). But the notion that the American security blanket is important to Japan has never found many true believers. In August 1989 a national survey asked Japanese to identify those factors that had enabled the nation to maintain peace without being invaded since the end of World War II. The largest proportion, nearly 40 percent, singled out the existence of Japan's "peace constitution" as the most important single factor. Only 18 percent named the security arrangements between Japan and the United States.[19]

The Westerner who suffered cold-war anxieties for forty years may find such views uninformed, even escapist. A people who seem to believe that their nation enjoys peace simply because it has a "peace constitution" do not seem very realistic. Surely, their leaders know better. But for the most part, those who have set defense policy in Japan, at least into the 1980s, share at least the opinion that Communist aggression is an exaggerated threat. There are both hawks and doves in Japan's defense establishment, but the notion that an expansionist Soviet Union or China imperils the islands has never been fully accepted— witness the continuing argument over whether to designate the Soviet Union a "threat" or merely a "potential threat."

Masamichi Inoki is perhaps best qualified to express that establishment's dominant view. A former professor at Kyoto University, he has been writing on foreign affairs and Communist strategy since 1940 and has studied in Germany, England, and the United States. From 1970 until 1978 he was superintendent of the National Defense Academy, Japan's West Point. For many years he has been head of the Peace and Security Studies Research Institute, a think tank in the Roppongi section of Tokyo that conducts research for the Self-Defense Agency, Japan's Pentagon, a few blocks away. Inoki has been familiar with his nation's international concerns for four decades and speaks with the authority of one who has been at the center of the national security mainstream.

"At no time since 1945 has Japan ever been afraid of a Communist invasion," he said one day in his Roppongi office. "I remember one day in 1960 when [former prime minister] Yoshida said that it would not happen. He said that both China and the Soviet Union would continue to be very noisy but that they would never try to invade Japan. I think that showed his wisdom."

Like Yoshida, Inoki believes that the American security presence was a helpful deterrent, a kind of insurance policy. But he also believes that the Soviet threat was exaggerated. Soviet policy in the Far East was always defensive, even the military buildup of the 1970s culminating in the placing of Soviet forces in the Northern Islands, a few miles north of Hokkaido. Inoki remarked, "I have always believed that Russia could be very strong in defending its own country but that it was not very good in invading other countries. Look at Finland, in 1939—it took the Russian army months to subdue a tiny country." After the war the Soviets were far too concerned with controlling Eastern Europe to spend time planning incursions in Asia, Inoki said. "She has suffered too much indigestion trying to absorb Czechoslovakia, Hungary, and Poland." Japan has looked on postwar Russia as economically weak and technologically backward, too anemic internally to contemplate invasions and occupations in Asia, Inoki went on. The rest of the world, including NATO, had been excessively worried about a Soviet menace. Never, Inoki repeated, had Japan feared the prospect of a Soviet invasion.[20]

13
●

The Odd Couple

On the face of it, the relationship between the United States and Japan is one of the world's most curious bilateral arrangements. They are in part rivals, in part friends, and they are forever quarreling with each other like spouses in any marriage of convenience. For forty-five years the United States has played the role of dominant partner, attempting to lead and attempting to get Japan to follow. The pattern has frequently broken down, only to be reinstated by compromise, and this odd-couple relationship has somehow endured and flourished, a testament to the practice of muddling through.

Japan has, to herself, often justified her role of weak-spouse follower by depicting it as a historically natural one. In this explanation, she has always sought alliance with stronger partners to avoid isolation. "Do not be an orphan of the world" was a common prescription in the Meiji period as Japan groped for a footing in the world, and one of her proudest moments was her alliance with England early in this century.

Her most disastrous moment was when she decided to follow Nazi Germany in the 1930s. This habit of following in the wake of powerful friends is often described in Japan as an example of *senpai*, the common practice in which a young man seeks out an older mentor to further his career. Seizaburo Sato, a leading foreign-policy academic, fits it all into a cultural pattern with a homely description: "The desire to conform with the trend of the times leads to the practical diplomacy of betting on the 'winning horse.' "[1], In fact, this cultural explanation has little to do with how the Japan–United States relationship got underway or with why it has endured. It was born in the exigencies of the early postwar period when Japan wanted independence and economic help. Prime Minister Yoshida put the pieces of it together to end the Occupation, and it has lasted for similarly pragmatic reasons. Japan chose America as the "winning horse" not for cultural reasons but because there was no other way to turn.

In this relationship there was never a great deal of affection or natural trust. The two countries shared no cultural history or common language. In the twentieth century they had been wary rivals and then bitter enemies. During World War II each had regarded the other as subhuman. Historian John Dower has described how both Japan and the United States had depicted the other in propaganda as scarcely better than animals.[2] Americans had been taught that Germany had merely been led astray by a gang of Nazi thugs, a temporary aberration that would be corrected by their defeat in the war. But they had been taught that Japanese were a despicable race of people. And to Japanese, Americans were barbarians of a lower order.

So the relationship that followed the war was built on no special affinity but on mutual national interests so strong that neither side could see profit in abandoning them. The American interest was strategic and military. It wanted a stable host country that would provide a home for the air and naval bases that were the keystones of American forward defense strategy in Asia. Nothing else much mattered, and the perennial fear of American policy makers was that Japan might bolt the alliance and sink into neutralism. There was much talk over the years in Tokyo and Washington about the increasing trust and warm human relations between the two countries, and leaders of both insisted that there was more to the relationship than money and arms. But for years the United States expected little more of Japan that that she be a passive military ally, and at bottom the Japanese recognized this. Prime Minister Nakasone knew his audience well when, in a 1983 interview with Washington newspaper editors, he promised that under his guidance Japan would serve as an "unsinkable aircraft carrier" for American forces in Asia.

For its part, Japan had one overriding interest in America, and it was economic. In the immediate postwar years this interest was primitive in that it was defined as food and financial assistance. Later, it came to be centered on access to the American consumer market. And just as Washington would do almost anything for Japan to keep its military bases safe, so Japan would perform almost any act of friendship to maintain that market access. In Tokyo one frequently heard voices insisting that Japan must diversify her markets to lessen her dependence on the American consumer's desire for her cars, television sets, and VCRs. But for four decades Japan's economy was dependent for growth and stability on those customers. With them, she was a prosperous, growing country, the envy of economists everywhere. Without them, she was a country of middling means. To maintain them she must be deferential to Washington. An official of MITI, Hajime Tamura, once candidly explained this habitual deference: "Japan depends on the United States for 40 percent of her exports and this is why we cannot speak to Americans as freely as we like."[3]

Despite these mutual addictions and all the talk of an "equal partnership," the relationship was never one of genuine parity—Japan was always Number Two. Even in the 1980s, when her economy was the world's largest on a population basis, when her citizens' per capita income exceeded that of Americans', Japanese leaders shunned the Number One label as though it were a fatal mystic sign. It was always understood that America held the ultimate upper hand. Throughout the 1970s and 1980s the United States made persistent demands on Japan to open up her markets to foreign imports. It extracted concession after concession by threatening to deny her a piece of the American market. Never did a responsible Japanese leader retaliate in kind by suggesting that American access to bases be diminished. Japanese did from time to time remonstrate against Washington for playing the bully and demanding too great a concession. They stalled endlessly in trade negotiations to minimize the supposed damage that would result and complained about overbearing Americans ordering them around. But never did they propose to break off the relationship.

It is fashionable today to say that in all of these dealings Japan made no concessions whatsoever, that she had stonewalled the Americans at every turn. The relationship so cherished by State Department diplomats, it is said, is a one-way street, and its benefits flow in only one direction, to Tokyo. Japan refused to increase her defense budget to help the non-Communist world, maintained a high wall against imports of foreign goods, structured her economy to take advantage of the global trading system, and cooperated in no international ventures that did not enrich her companies. Many Americans accepted these charges as true in 1990. The record is rather different.

I arrived in Tokyo in 1977 as a correspondent with an American wish-list, a compilation of those demands that Washington was pressing on Japan. It was based on interviews I had before leaving Washington with the Treasury, State Department, and Pentagon. The notes were a record of where the relationship stood that year in terms of major issues. The most important items on the list were:

1. An increase in the Japanese defense budget, beginning with repeal of the ceiling that restricted military spending to 1 percent of the gross national product.
2. An expansion of Japan's domestic demand in order to increase the purchase of foreign goods. (The United States was with much publicity insisting that Japan purchase more goods like beef and oranges, but its basic preference was for a fundamental restructuring that would enable Japanese to spend more money for what the world produced.)
3. An appreciation of the yen to a more realistic level, which would tend to reduce Japan's exports and increase America's.
4. A deregulation of the Japanese financial system, giving foreigners access to capital and markets.
5. An increase in Japanese foreign aid to assist developing countries.

When I reexamined the list in the mid-1980s, in all major respects the demands had been met:

1. The 1 percent ceiling on defense spending had been lifted. Japan ranked sixth in the world among nations in military expenditures (third by some comparisons). Washington was saying that Japan had gone far enough in that direction.
2. A huge pump-priming plan launched in 1985 by Prime Minister Nakasone led to a greatly increased domestic demand that was pulling in foreign imports in record amounts, including cars and other manufactured goods previously considered unsalable in Japan.
3. The yen had approximately doubled in value against the American dollar under an international agreement that the Japanese

government had supported in spite of enormous business pressure at home.

4. Japan's financial system had been substantially deregulated in accord with international demands by the Ministry of Finance, usually considered the most intractable of Japanese institutions.
5. By a series of budget increases, Japan had become the world's largest donor of foreign aid to undeveloped countries and was transferring to the Third World twice the share of national wealth that the United States was sending.

All of these sweeping concessions were accomplished only after a great deal of wrangling among Japanese bureaucrats, politicians, and business leaders. All were instituted under persistent American pressure. Washington pointed fingers, twisted arms, and lectured Tokyo at every stage. Japan eventually would give in, not because of some sudden affection for the United States but because she became convinced that her overriding national interests were best served by doing so. To be permanently at odds with America was unthinkable because it would be bad for business. Japanese businessmen were horrified at the rapid government-induced appreciation of the yen in the mid-1980s. But they were made to realize that the overall health of the American economy was more vital to their exports than the short-term advantages of a cheap yen. The American market counted for everything. When, in 1981, Japanese car makers grudgingly agreed to restrain exports of automobiles to the United States, they were merely recognizing a higher balancing of interests. Worse things would happen to them if they did not.

Forty years of such reactive behavior produced a peculiar effect on the Japanese system. It gradually came to be institutionalized into the day-by-day governance of Japan. On any important issue beyond purely domestic politics, the Japanese ear was always cocked toward Washington. "What would the Americans think and do if we . . . ?" "Managing" the American relationship became the first challenge of any man elected prime minister. To be trusted at home, he must first demonstrate that he could perform well in Washington. This fact became institutionalized in the form of carrying *miyage*, or gifts, to the seat of power there. It might consist of a promised trade concession or a pledge to increase the defense budget. The purpose was to elicit praise from the chiefs in Washington, which could then be transformed into political capital back home. Critics might quibble that the practice of giving *miyage* was demeaning and smacked of the ancient Asian custom of offering tribute to the emperors of China. But prime ministers knew what counted most among their ruling blocs.

Even more peculiar was the practice known as *gaiatsu*, which means "foreign pressure." It was discovered that pressures from Washington could be harnessed to produce desirable results back home. Political resistance could be tamed, public opinion swayed, and bureaucratic programs shaped by pointing to words emanating from across the Pacific. Perhaps the longest-running example of this involved the Japan Defense Agency (JDA). For years, its professional warriors were inhibited by the national antimilitary sentiments and had to settle for only modest increases in arms budgets. But in 1979 their fortunes changed as administrations in Washington began clamoring for greater defense buildups among allies and accusing Japan of enjoying a "free ride" in the military arena. The JDA, allied with a small but growing military-industrial network, played these criticisms skillfully into the public debate, and its budgets soared while domestic spending languished. The Foreign Ministry inevitably became the master practitioner of *gaiatsu*, using Washington's demands and criticisms in bureaucratic infighting to achieve what it wanted within Japan. The Foreign Ministry, lacking a powerful domestic constituency, is the weakest of Japanese ministries. But *gaiatsu* gave it clout. Throughout the bureaucracy, indeed throughout the Japanese establishment, the American influence is either courted or feared. America is, some say in jest, the only real opposition party in Japan.

The smooth flow of this mutually serviceable relationship was on occasion interrupted by some unanticipated jolt. The most jarring, to Japan, were the two "Nixon shocks" of 1971. Without warning, Nixon suspended convertibility of the dollar to gold, thus forcing the yen and other currencies to float freely on the market, ending two decades of rates fixed in Japan's favor. His sudden opening to China, after two decades of forcing Japan to isolate that Communist nation, followed weeks of assurances that no such overture was thinkable. The two secretive acts underscored the one-sided nature of the relationship and angered those who had believed that it had been one of equal partners.

But the structure endured, in part because so many Japanese, both prominent and ordinary, had so large a stake in it. At a very personal level, a large number of Japanese benefited enormously from the relationship. Many became rich through it and many had their careers advanced by it. It was not unlike the typical colonial relationship in which those natives who are clever and diligent rise in life by courting the ruling powers or satisfying their needs. An incident on August 15, 1945, the day the war ended, foretold what was to come. A publisher named Kikumatsu Ogawa learned of the surrender while buying sweet potatoes on a farm outside Tokyo. He immediately dashed back to his office and overnight completed a small manuscript entitled *Handbook of Japanese-American Conversation*. It sold 4 million copies in one month.[4] Those who worked with the Occupation laid the foundation of successful careers. Some were in demand by Japanese firms wanting to sell goods to the military authorities. Women who scrubbed floors at SCAP were rewarded with the right to scavenge garbage, no small privilege in days of starvation. Wangling scholarships to study at American colleges was a certain path to upward mobility. Postwar history is littered with accounts of Japan prospering while serving their new masters.

On a grander scale are the biographies of those who rose to power by earning the solicitude of Americans, both during and after the Occupation. Prime Minister Yoshida was selected and nurtured by the Occupation, which obligingly purged one prominent politician so that Yoshida could become premier. Prime Minister Kishi had been a certified major war criminal until released and rehabilitated by the Americans, who deemed him newly purified. Ordinary politicians quickly learned that their careers were enhanced by evidence of American approval. Two generations of them have flown to Washington to appear at the side of bigwigs in the Congress and have photographs sent home to constituents as proof of their acceptance. All of these examples in various ways testify to the power of American influence and the manner in which Japanese accepted that influence as perfectly natural. In the Philippines, by contrast, the politician who too openly curried American favor risked the opprobrious label of "Amboy," or "America's boy." What might seem obsequious behavior in another country was calmly accepted in Japan. Wits might refer to the Foreign Ministry as "a branch of the U.S. State Department," but they did so in jest. Curiously, diplomats who fawned too much or who were too obliging sometimes irritated Americans more than their countrymen. Ambassador Edwin O. Reischauer was known to be frequently miffed by Foreign Ministry minions who ran to him for advice on any step they intended to take: "That's something you will have to decide on your own," he would snap.[5]

The equation began to change in the 1980s. In rhetoric if not in deed, Japan and the United States began to treat each other almost as hostile forces. Washington demanded from Japan not just trade concessions but a wholesale restructuring of her economic system. Japan's trade surplus had grown to more than $50 billion, and as Americans watched industry after industry decline under the Japanese export surges, they concluded that only extraordinary resistance would block them. Congress sanctioned retaliatory measures of broad scope. Japanese companies recycled their overseas profits by purchasing American firms and expensive real estate, touching off the fear that Japan was "buying up America." An American public-opinion poll in 1989 recorded an alarming notion that would have been unthinkable a few years earlier: A majority of Americans (52 percent) considered Japanese economic might more of a threat than Soviet military.[6]

The Japanese responded to all this at first with bewilderment, then with anger. Japan, said people in high places, was being made the scapegoat for America's own shortcomings—her inability to control her budget, her decline in manufacturing competitiveness, her ruthless dismemberment of her own companies. Washington's own failures, it was said, had cost America the right to order Japan around. America was full of crybabies. When Japan felt ready to develop her own air-force fighter plane, the FSX, America said no. When Japan sought more power in the World Bank and the IMF, Washington blocked her out of pettiness and jealousy. When Japan refused on constitutional grounds to commit forces to the Persian Gulf, Americans called her indifferent. All of these complaints were lodged by Japanese who held important positions and were framed in language rarely heard in Tokyo. It began to seem on both sides of the Pacific that four decades of mutual restraint and a muting of frictions would end in temper tantrums.

This fractious debate was based on specific disagreements, but it had its roots in a subtle change that was undermining the entire relationship. That relationship was based on the assumption of mutual interests: America needed bases in Japan and Japan needed markets in the United States. For reasons not quickly recognized in the late 1980s, that mutuality of interests began to founder. Neither needed the other, at least not to the same degree and not in the same ways that had prevailed in the past. The old justifications for treating each other respectfully and delicately simply no longer applied.

One pillar—Japan's usefulness in the American strategic design for Asia—began crumbling with the winding down of the cold war. The American bases still scattered around Japan had been key bricks in the wall constructed in the early 1950s to deter Communist aggression from both China and the USSR. But by the late 1980s the United States had become friendly with both Communist powers. In 1990 reports published by the Pentagon suggested that Soviet power in East Asia was diminishing, as was the threat of aggression. What, then, was the value of the air and naval bases in Japan? In part, of course, it was to defend South Korea against the still-dangerous Communist North. But it grew obvious that the massive American defensive screen could no longer be justified—or financed—as a post–cold-war instrument. In recognition of this, the United States in 1990 proposed the withdrawal of about 15,000 troops in the region, including some from Japan.

At the same time, a change took place in Washington's attitude toward Japan's own military capabilities. From the days of John Foster Dulles, there had been unrelenting pressure on Japan to strengthen her armed forces to join in the anti-Communist resistance. Until the early 1980s Japan largely resisted that pressure and kept her military budget at modest levels. This greatly irritated the United States. In 1977 an American military attaché scoffed at Japan's military contribution. Her forces could not defend the island of Hokkaido for even a few days, he said, and her sea patrols were unable to spot Soviet submarines. There was no coordination at the top of even these meager resources. I recall the attaché saying scornfully, "Their idea of a command center is to push two desks together and put a phone on them."

In little more than a decade, the American attitude had been reversed. The arms buildup promoted by Prime Minister Nakasone gave Japan one of the strongest sea and air forces in Asia. It would be but a short time before Japan outranked all but the two superpowers in total military spending, climbing over both France and Great Britain. One began to notice that American representatives no longer pounded desks in Tokyo demanding bigger military budgets. The year 1987 was a pivotal time, one of those unnoticed moments that when looked back upon signify a seismic change in the U.S.-Japan relationship. For the first time in the postwar era, Japan increased its defense budget without being formally asked to do so by Washington.

Indeed, it appeared that by 1990 the United States had become concerned not with the weakness of Japan's military but with its potential strength. An important Pentagon document, designed to guide American strategic thinking in the Pacific for decades to come, stated that one objective in connection with Japan should be "discouraging any destabilizing development of a power projection capability.[7] In other words, the United States should prevent Japan from becoming the wielder of an offensive force. That perception was strengthened when a top U.S. Marine general in Japan told an interviewer that American forces ought to remain at bases there because "no one wants a rearmed, resurgent Japan. So we are a cap in the bottle, if you will."[8] The defense relationship had become almost absurd. Washington was on the one hand asking Japan to pay more of the costs of basing American troops and on the other hand planning to use the presence of those bases to discourage further Japanese rearmament.

This was a remarkable turnabout, and it produced one of the finer ironies of the postwar relationship. Instead of issuing warnings about Soviet threats and urging bigger arms budgets, the United States, by 1990, was recording a diminished threat and implying that Japan should curb its military spending. This shift occurred almost simultaneously with a reverse shift on Japan's part. The Japan Defense Agency, by 1989, had concluded that the Soviet Union was indeed a "threat," or at least a "potential threat," and was seeking to continue the large budget increases first begun under American pressure. The two countries had almost precisely reversed their courses. The irony was amusing, and it underscored the fact that the old anti-Communist pillar no longer stood firmly in place. The United States did not need it, or not, at least, as much as it once had. An important part of the relationship was slowly withering away.

The second pillar—Japan's need for the American markets—was also weakened. From the first, they had been kept accessible despite the lack of reciprocity on Japan's part. Japan's industrial strategy of shutting the door to any foreign products that might endanger her own budding industries violated American free-trade rules, but for two decades the United States overlooked the transgressions. She did not want to endanger Japan's economic recovery and, more important, did not want to risk an assault on trade barriers that would ignite a nationalist reaction in Japan. The latter concern was very real. Threats to open Japan's markets invariably produced strong protests from her business community. When, in the early 1960s, the demands to liberalize tariffs mounted, Tokyo businessmen erupted in loud complaints that the dreaded "Black Ships" were returning. The United States backed off. It was official government policy that America needed strategic bases more than it needed Japan's buying power.

The peace was not difficult to keep until the 1970s, when Japan's export stream became a torrent and several key American industries were threatened. Japan was accused of dumping goods at artificially low prices into the American market as her companies pursued their goal of winning market shares at any price. The American dilemma was severe. She did not want to abandon her free-trade image by resorting to overtly protectionist quotas and tariffs. But somehow the exports had to be slowed to reasonable levels. The result was a fudging compromise in which the United States forced Japan to limit exports in those goods that were causing the most distress.

The device for accomplishing this was the "voluntary restraint agreement," a misnomer for a practice that in fact violated free-trade precepts but had the value of ending the most dangerous trade disputes. This was the pattern: The United States, under pressure from endangered industries, would insist that Japan's companies "voluntarily" limit their exports to an agreed percentage of the American markets. Japan's companies naturally objected but eventually would bow under pressure from their own government, which realized that the alternative would be worse—America might shut out exports with tariffs, quotas, or import surcharges. Voluntary agreements covered exports of steel, automobiles, machine tools, and semiconductors. They invariably caused serious distortions—higher prices in America and the formation of export cartels in Japan—but they did prevent trade disputes from getting out of hand. Ironically, the idea of "managed trade" is today anathema in Washington, which persists in acting as though trade imbalances will be straightened out by the free play of the markets. In fact, the United States has been managing trade with Japan for well over a decade.

Restraining Japan's exports by such artificial means had a further impact. It compelled Japanese companies to open new plants and begin producing in the United States. Limited to a certain share of markets accessible by exports, they did the next best thing and simply moved inside the markets. Such major auto companies as Honda and Nissan moved inside about the time that the voluntary restraints were imposed on their exports. The biggest breakthrough came when mighty Toyota, always averse to manufacturing outside its home country, followed suit. Other industries followed, and soon the American Midwest and South were dotted with Japanese factories, all employing American labor making things to sell within the American market. Their success surprised even the Japanese. When the auto restraints were being negotiated in the early 1980s, American trade representatives warned that Japan should limit herself to about 22 percent of the American market. By 1990 the combination of Japanese autos exported and those made in America equaled 35 percent of the American market.

The overall effect of these changes, although not foreseen, was to guarantee for Japan's manufacturers a large and growing share of the

American market for her principal export products, the large money makers. That market was now locked in. By 1989 38 percent of all Japan's exports were going to the United States, and market shares there were being increased monthly by the production of goods at Japanese plants in Ohio, Michigan, Tennessee, and many other states. The most popular Japanese goods in the American markets were automobiles and consumer electronics. Both were safe. A voluntary restraint agreement assured that a certain percentage of Japanese autos could enter the American market. Japanese transplants could make as many as they could sell in America. In the field of consumer electronics—television sets, VCRs, fax machines, and the like—there was no real competition. American companies had either been driven from the field or, as in the case of VCRs, had never seriously entered it. Because it no longer had to worry about the market that was most profitable. Japan could afford to relax. There would be struggles ahead for the newer high-technology products in which America held leads, but most of the old ones had been settled. One of the great anxieties of the postwar years—Japan's fear that her economy could be devastated by an American protectionist movement—was fading. And with it was disappearing that second pillar that held up the Pacific alliance: the need to sell in America. Japan's economic dependency was still great, but it was no longer in danger. The pillar was becoming irrelevant.

●

Throughout these twists and turns, Japan's fundamental view of the United States had altered very little. Japan's leaders remained conspicuously deferential in their dealings with Washington and cautious in their pronouncements, even when they felt in their bones that Washington had done Japan wrong. Pure economics explained a good deal of this deference. But there was more than profits and market share to this. For all her many faults and arrogant habits, America remained Japan's only good friend among nations. Without her, Japan was indeed an orphan in the world.

In the late 1980s this attitude changed. A testiness, even hostility, replaced the habitual deference. American diplomats could sense it when they carried the latest in a chain of trade demands to Tokyo. No longer were they received pleasantly with promises that Japan would do her best to satisfy them. Blunt-spoken officials at MITI simply told them they were being unreasonable. A flood of Japanese books and articles described the United States as haughty and irrational and called upon

the country's political leaders to cease their kowtowing. The new mood
was explicit in a series of essays that Shintaro Ishihara, a neo-nationalist
member of the Diet and sometime novelist, contributed to a book
entitled A *Japan That Can Say "No."* Ishihara's message was that Japan
should no longer bow and scrape before American politicians and should
assert her own foreign policies. The book was immensely popular and
lent support to those in government who were most weary of being
lectured by Americans. A certain style, or set of mannerisms, was noted
in the bureaucrats whose job it was to manage the endless disputes
between the two countries. Formerly obliging and apologetic, they now
became assertive and almost painfully direct. By late 1990 it was acceptable, even praiseworthy, to snap back at Washington.

This was no mere matter of atmospherics. For behind the new
mood lay a vivid change in the basic Japanese perception of her postwar
mentor. No longer was America the strong power that shepherded Japan
through her infancy. Now, suddenly, she had become the pitiful giant.
America was the world's greatest debtor, her factories were not competitive in world markets, her dynamism was withering away. Her trade and
budget deficits had crippled her. She was going the way of Greece,
Rome, and the British Empire, a victim of global overreach. America
was dependent on Japan now for investment funds to plug her budget
gaps and begged her to pay half the costs of maintaining U.S. bases.
How could she pose as Japan's protector when she had to plead with
Japan to finance her own troops abroad? The *Asahi Shimbun* summed
up the change in attitudes with a telling commentary:

> In Japan, there is a saying, "Look for a large tree when seeking
> shelter." In diplomacy, Japan has always followed this adage,
> remaining smug and safe under a big tree called America.
> Lately, however, the Japanese have begun to notice signs of
> decay on this once virile and verdant tree. The tree has lost
> some of its branches and no longer offers total protection from
> the elements. It is about time Japan started walking its own
> path of diplomacy without constantly running to shelter. And,
> actually, Japan should go even one step further and be pre-
> pared to act as a "prop" for the United States.[9]

When examined closely, the individual components of this disenchantment were neither new nor startling. What the Japanese of the late
1980s were saying had all been said in the United States. Her decline in
industrial competitiveness was documented by many American studies.
The falling value of the dollar merely reflected an industrial and finan-

cial decay. The view of the United States as a fading empire driven to bankruptcy by a bloated military budget echoed the opinion of a Harvard scholar, Paul M. Kennedy, whose book, *The Rise and Fall of the Great Powers,* was a best seller in Japan. If a Japanese businessman cared to compare American competence invidiously with his own, he had only to quote from David Halberstam's *The Reckoning,* which portrayed the rise of Nissan and the decline of Ford. True to form, Japan was importing its most modern view of the world from across the Pacific. What was new was its willingness to espouse that view in assertive, even hostile terms.

The change was in part generational, and nowhere was this more apparent than in Japan's conservative business establishment. The core of that establishment is *Keidanren,* or the Federation of Economic Organizations. Since 1950 *Keidanren's* leaders have been the powers and spokesmen of Japanese business, and their views on the United States have been the accepted standards. For most of that period it was led by veterans of the postwar recovery, men who had performed the restructuring of basic industries, like steel and electric power. They were, to a man, "American-firsters" who appreciated the boosts given by American aid and open markets. Chief among them for more than three decades was Yoshihiro Inayama, the head of Nippon Steel and the most powerful of all *Keidanren* leaders. America had saved Japan after the war, he was fond of saying, and Japan should be grateful. In the bitter 1981 campaign to force Japanese auto makers to restrain exports to America, he insisted that Japan should oblige.

In the late 1980s Inayama had vanished from the scene, along with his entire generation. *Keidanren* had become the bastion of what was called "GNP nationalism," the belief that Japan's successes were home-made and that, in a phrase often heard, "Japan had nothing more to learn from the United States." It was composed of business leaders who had come of age not in poverty and American-induced recovery but in the boom times when Japan's growth led the world. Ken Otani, a veteran reporter for the *Asahi Shimbun,* chronicled *Keidanren's* doings for years and has written widely on the new nationalism and suspicions of the United States. "The present-day leaders of *Keidanren* established their positions in the days of high economic growth, and they have a sense of equality with businessmen in the United States," he said. "They do not remember, as Inayama did, the American money and technology. They came to power after Japan's success was established, and they feel they are equal to Americans."[10]

Their view now, overwhelmingly, is that Japanese management

and methods are superior, that American businessmen are incompetents, and that Japan should do nothing to bail the United States out of its self-induced collapse. They reject arguments that Japan's markets are closed or manipulated. That is all nonsense from the whining Americans. Japan has won her markets fairly by working harder and planning better. They express little of the deference shown to Americans by the business leaders they replaced. Susumu Ohara of the *Nihon Keizai Shimbun*, Japan's leading business newspaper, summarized the feelings of the "GNP nationalists" in a perceptive 1987 editorial comment:

> These individuals are strongly critical of those Japanese who continue to subordinate themselves, retaining the postwar mentality nurtured during the rule of the U.S. Occupation forces. They also point out and underscore, in an un-Japanese way, the many facets of Japanese superiority and its ability to produce superb industrial products. . . . It is their strong feeling that it is now time for Japan to lift itself out of the cocoon of its postwar mentality, its servile feeling of inferiority, and instead become more acutely aware of our nation's vitality, its strength, its prowess."[11]

If anyone could sum up the business world's changed mood it would be Hajime Karatsu. His career reflected in precise stages the progression from extreme admiration of the United States to contempt. In 1948 he was a young engineer with the Nippon Telegraph and Telephone Public Corporation, working to rebuild a collapsed communications system. Equipment was in such dismal condition that long-distance telephoning was virtually impossible. If a Tokyoite wished to make a call to someone in Osaka, he routed it through Los Angeles. An angry Occupation official summoned Karatsu one day and ordered him to study American ways of manufacturing telephone switching equipment to improve the quality. It was the beginning of a love affair with American engineering methods. Karatsu studied the works of the American high priest of quality control, W. E. Deming, and became a convert. Later, as a systems planner for Matsushita, he introduced the marvels he had learned to Japan's premiere electronics firm. His enthusiasm for America was unbounded.

The year 1980 found Karatsu a managing director of the Matsushita Communication Industrial Co., and his views of American industrial skills had been shaken. The old masters were turning out shoddy products, and productivity was slipping. The American manufacturing system was creaky and losing market share in goods to foreign companies, chiefly Japanese. Karatsu and a group from the Japan Productivity Center set out to help repay the old debts. They planned a series of instructional films and seminars with American businessmen pointing out how Japanese had borrowed methods in the 1950s, improved on them, and made them work in Japan. Karatsu's group approached the task a bit timidly, not wanting to appear too presumptuous. The group's first title was "The Association to Rescue the United States," but that was abandoned as immodest. When I interviewed Karatsu and his friends in 1980, their mood was that of people who wanted to help a temporarily slipshod friend who had helped them much in the past.

A decade later the mood of Karatsu and his business world had changed radically. America was a sinking power whose day was almost done. Its companies were lazy, their managers egocentrics who cared for nothing but their own salaries and the bottom line, he wrote. Nothing could be done for them any longer. Americans were habitual whiners who blamed their losses on a convenient scapegoat, Japan. American industry was being slowly dismantled as companies sought cheap labor and higher profits by manufacturing overseas. Thousands of manufacturing jobs were lost each year. Each month in America the equivalent of one Japanese corporation's work force was being dismissed or laid off. The new jobs that were being created in America were mostly in Japanese firms that had moved there to build factories. The sun was setting on the American empire. Japan could no longer help her. "Japan thus will certainly become the world's No. 1 economic power," Karatsu wrote in 1990. "The U.S. will then be protected by Japan rather than being its protector as some people believe."[12]

The same anti-American noises were to be heard in the corridors of the Kasumigaseki Building, where Japan's major national bureaucracies are located. In the past many of these bureaucrats had played the role of buffers, seeking to ease tensions that arose in trade and military disputes. Their instinctive role had been one of accommodation. No longer. An American diplomat with years of experience dealing with them observed in 1990 that the mood had changed perceptibly from one of accommodation to one of confrontation. Younger officials, especially, were eager to challenge the dominant American leadership role, he said. "They are quick to bristle when we launch some new demand against Japan." Even in the Foreign Ministry, traditionally friendly— some would say obsequious—to American views, younger diplomats stated quite bluntly that they were fed up with American arrogance and clumsiness. They no longer regarded Washington as the superpower to be blindly followed. A vice-minister of the Foreign Ministry, Takakazu

Kuriyama, made the point with unusual directness in a magazine article: "The time when Japan could take for granted an international order
sustained by U.S. strength and unilaterally depend on it is long past."[13]
The elders in the LDP were still instinctively receptive when Americans
called on them for help in settling disputes, but not the younger ones,
the American diplomat said. A generation gap was notable there, just as
in the business community. The newcomers were defensive, fearing
repercussions if they appeared too open to Americans. "To a man, they
have a fear of being maneuvered by arrogant Americans," the diplomat
said. "They cannot let it appear that they are being pushed around by
us." As a result, they tended to dodge issues on which their elders in the
LDP had been willing to help.

The new bureaucratic resistance was particularly noticeable in Japan's military. Relations between it and the Pentagon had been extraordinarily warm throughout the 1980s as military budgets soared and as
Japan looked more and more like a true ally. Their interests were identical, and Japan's military leaders looked to America's for the sort of
gaiatsu ("outside pressure") that would help them in their budget fights.
If the Pentagon demanded that Japan raise its defense budgets by 7
percent, then the Japan Defense Agency could translate that into pressure on the tight-fisted Ministry of Finance.

That cozy relationship of mutual back-scratching diminished as
the United States charted a military reverse course. By 1990 the Pentagon was no longer pressing Japan for a bigger defense outlay and was
hinting confusingly that she had gone far enough. What America now
wanted was more of Japan's defense budget spent to defray the costs of
maintaining U.S. bases on her soil. The military bureaucracy resented
the demands, which would mean fewer yen to spend on Japan's own
tanks and planes. Japan was once again being asked to twist and turn to
the American mood, and the anger in military headquarters in Tokyo
was extraordinary. It boiled over one day in 1990 when the U.S. Senate
passed an amendment calling for the withdrawal of 10,000 American
troops a year unless Japan paid 100 percent of the basing costs. Coolly,
displaying a resentment that would have been unthinkable a few years
earlier, the Defense Agency's top civilian leader retorted that if such a
line were insisted upon, the troops should just go home. Japan had
never asked for American forces to be stationed there in the first place,
he said.

In the souring of U.S.-Japan defense relations, nothing angered
the Japanese military more than the FSX affair. The FSX was to be
Japan's self-built support fighter plane, the first to be designed and

constructed by Japanese alone without American help. The Japan Defense Agency and four large companies saw it as the opportunity not only to build an independent warplane but to lay the groundwork for a national aerospace industry. Washington balked, insisting first that the two countries coproduce the aircraft and, later, that approximately one-third of the production be guaranteed to American manufacturers. A fierce high-level political shoving match went on for months until, grudgingly, Japan acceded to the coproduction plan in 1989.

The bitterness over the FSX was intense within the Japan defense community, the alliance of weapons manufacturers and military officials that had become powerful in the 1980s. One American diplomat required to deal with its members said privately that the whole defense dialogue had been severely diminished. For the Japanese saw the affair not as a minor money dispute rigged to save American jobs but as a strategically planned crusade both to curb Japan's defense power and to curtail her move into the aerospace industry, one of the few in which America still held a competitive advantage. The mood was best described by Ichiro Naito, a former official of the Defense Agency's Technical Research and Development Institute, which had planned to develop Japan's own FSX in collaboration with four companies. The United States, he said in a magazine interview, had "smashed" the independent FSX because it greatly feared what such a technological coup could mean for Japan in the aerospace field. It reminded him of Japan's enormous breakthrough in developing the famous Zero fighter plane on the eve of World War II. The FSX, he said, was a case of the Zero brought up to date. The reason that America crushed the plan, he said, is "that the FSX is a fearful fighter plane for the U.S. I mean technologically. . . . If the U.S. were to approve the [independent production] plan, Japan will make a big leap forward, the same as in the prewar days. Therefore, it was impossible to approve it, by any means."[14] The anger spread beyond the military complex, with many articles and editorials denouncing the American interference. Businessmen saw it as one more sorry case of a supine government catering to American economic demands, selling out Japan's interests in the process. "The United States pressured Japan despite the fact that such a move was tantamount to interfering in the formulation of defense policies and jeopardized Japanese national sovereignty," wrote the *Japan Economic Journal.*[15]

In support of the new anti-Americanism, many Japanese intellectuals weighed in with books and articles echoing these themes. A disparate group, they were classified informally as a neo-nationalist school, signifying that they were not associated with the old nationalism, which revered the emperor and defended Japan's part in the Pacific War. They assailed American arrogance and interference in Japanese affairs and generally attributed the deteriorating relationship to the United States' economic problems. *A Japan That Can Say "No,"* coauthored by Diet member Shintaro Ishihara, was the book best known abroad—a pirate version circulated widely in Washington before it was even talked of in Japan. A former diplomat, Motofumi Asai, called upon Japan to cancel the U.S. security treaty because it no longer served the interests of either country. Osamu Shimomura, a former bureaucrat who had been the architect of the income-doubling economic plan for the 1960s, analyzed American decline in *Japan Is Not to Blame—It Is America's Fault*. Other provocative titles were *Japan in Danger* by Hideo Itokawa and *The Downfall of America* by Seiki Sha.

The neo-nationalists mixed their contempt for America with an equally forceful assault on their own government, which they depicted as cowardly and inept in acceding to demands from Washington. This view was quite widespread in academia. Takeshi Igarashi, professor of American political history and diplomacy at Tokyo University, believed that most of his colleagues, especially the young ones, resented the Japanese government's craven behavior more than American overbearingness:

> What we Japanese most dislike is the way our own government deals with the United States. It is never prepared for today's issues and is forever trying to postpone decisions. The demands are always coming from the United States [in trade and defense matters], and our government just tries to be passive. It has no ideas of its own. This is a matter of national pride for us. We have recovered our self-respect and would like to be respected by a foreign country. Among our young people, this feeling is very strong."[16]

In 1987 a thunderbolt of a book on the United States descended from the pinnacle of the Japanese intellectual establishment. Its author, Jun Eto, was a sophisticated scholar, critic, and novelist who had won many of the nation's principal literary awards, and his many articles were coveted by the important journals of ideas. He could argue his case against the United States from the perspective of one-time admirer and student—Eto had studied and taught at Princeton University in the early 1960s and had returned as a visiting scholar at the Woodrow Wilson Center in Washington in 1979. He joined the neo-nationalist crusade with a bang. His book, entitled *The Japan-U.S. War Is Not Over: Fatal Conflict*, became a best seller and established Eto as one of the harshest critics of the United States. His theme was that the United States and Japan had been at "war" in various guises since 1905, when Japan demonstrated her power by defeating imperial Russia. Ever since, the United States had viewed Japan as a threat to her power in Asia. Americans under MacArthur had at first sought to eliminate that threat by disarming Japan in the Occupation and forcing on her the "peace constitution." Needing help against communism, the United States had sponsored a defense force but had always intended it to be a supplement to American armies in Asia, not an independent military. America, Eto wrote, had for eight decades viewed the relationship with Japan as "confrontational" and was determined to keep her in her place. In his eyes, the economic friction of the 1970s and 1980s was simply war by other means, and the only new element was that, this time, Japan was winning. Japan's economic might would prevail. "Without Japanese investment," wrote Eto, "the American economy would collapse."[17]

Japanese public opinion can change with great rapidity when leaders begin signaling that it is acceptable. So with businessmen, intellectuals, and bureaucrats all downgrading America and picturing her as the new enemy, it was not too surprising to watch public opinion follow suit with a blink of the eye. An American living in Tokyo could easily sense the new drift. Television talk shows were crammed with scenes mocking America. A once-friendly businessman would cut off a conversation with the dismissive remark, "Japan has nothing more to learn from the United States"—as if there were no more reason to talk. American economic influence once was discussed with respect, even fear. Now the attitude was patronizing. In 1987 an eminently respectable research group, the Social and Economic Congress of Japan, suggested that the United States might solve its budget problems by defaulting on Treasury bonds and pleading bankruptcy. It seemed, oddly, that the most patronizing were those who had considerable experience in dealing with American issues. While discussing the slings and arrows of trade politics with me, a Yale-educated college professor abruptly ceased defending Japan with this line: "The United States has nothing to sell that we Japanese want to buy. Except perhaps wood. You do make good houses." Her contemptuous remark caught the new mood precisely. America's role was henceforth to be that of the hewer of wood, the drawer of water, like some third-world colony.

This was the period when across the Pacific foolish American congressmen were smashing a Toshiba television set and Detroit workers were crushing a Toyota automobile. Japanese watched the childish behavior and wrote it off as another sign of American decline. But at the level where they lived and worked and were vulnerable to economic pressures, the Japanese grew equally childish and on occasion vicious. In 1988 a film prepared by agricultural and consumer groups melodramatically warned Japanese not to buy foodstuffs imported from the United States. It pictured spoiled vegetables on a wharf, rotten American wheat spilling from open bags, and American crop-spraying planes dumping tons of allegedly carcinogenic pesticides in fields. There were shots of deformed test monkeys and even deformed fetuses in bottles. To a background of ominous music, a man asked, "Are you still going to eat these foods?" For the dense viewers who missed the message, there was a scene of American planes dive-bombing children in Vietnam.

The sum of all this translated into decisive shifts of public opinion against the United States. Ever since the 1960s opinion polls registered the fact that America was for the Japanese the most admired nation in the world. No other country was comparable. But in the late 1980s the polls changed direction radically. A Louis Harris poll for *Business Week* asked Japanese how much admiration and fondness they felt toward the United States as a nation. A majority, 54 percent, replied either "not very much" or "none at all."[18] In a *New York Times*–CBS News poll in 1987, 55 percent described relations between the two countries as unfriendly. Only one-third had felt that way just a year earlier.[19]

The winds had changed direction and had all but blown away the comfortable notion that Japan could forever plod along behind the United States. Washington, for so long the center of Japan's attentions, had grown hostile. Under a new trade bill an American president officially designated her a protectionist country, along, incredibly, with Brazil and India. A government that had coddled her and claimed to have protected her through the cold war now seemed to have little use for her except as a whipping boy, a scapegoat for what had gone wrong in America. It was all very bewildering. Americans fretted each time a Japanese firm bought out an American one or opened some new plant to make cars or machine tools. Yet in Tokyo there were offices of forty-five American state governments begging for greater investments. What did they want, these Americans? What could Japan do to satisfy them? In1989 an article in *The Atlantic Monthly* staggered the Japanese. Japan was so different from the rest of the world, it played by such different economic rules, the article argued, that there was only one solution. Japan had to be dealt with differently—had, in fact, to be "contained." What did "contain" mean? Japanese intellectuals pointed out that it was a cold-war word, a description of how to treat aggressive enemies.[20]

Among the Japanese writers who attempted to capture the new mood, the sense of being relentlessly picked on by Americans, Kenichi Ohmae was perhaps the most incisive. Ohmae was chairman of the Japanese branch of an American firm, McKinsey and Co., and the author of many books and articles that touched on the deteriorating relationship. In 1989 he wrote an article for *Chuo Koron* comparing Japan to a familiar figure in Japanese life, the strong, competent wife who, despite her outstanding abilities, is treated by her husband as a serf. Ohmae wrote:

> Japan is like a strong wife who is being scolded. While pretending to being scolded, she has made big savings from the household accounts, and in a time of emergency the husband is of no use at all. Japan is like such a wife. When the husband calls for tea, she takes a cup of tea to him. When he says, "Dinner!" she serves dinner. America, the husband, is feeling pleased with himself. However, in actual fact authority and money are gradually shifting to the wife. If the husband tells the wife to leave, it will be the husband who will be unable to support himself. They [America and Japan] are like such a husband and wife.[21]

And then came the biggest change of all. Until late in the decade, the barrages from abroad had been reckoned to be an unpleasant part of economic conflict. The West was jealous and naturally inclined to lash out. Japan could take her lumps. But at last she began to perceive something more ominous in the maligning remarks. The West, many important people began to complain, would never tolerate an economic threat from an Asian country. The West was racist, had always been, would always be. The issue was not economic competition. It was racism. A flood of books, articles, and public commentary by respected individuals made the point again and again. Each separate conflict over trade or defense or foreign investment was seen as an example of racism, of Americans looking down their noses at an Asian people. Washington talked of Japan's being an equal partner, wrote Shintaro Ishihara, but in fact looked upon Japanese as an inferior. "At the root of all the present frictions between Japan and the United States," he concluded, "there is their prejudice toward a non-white people."[22] When the U.S. House of Representatives passed a trade bill aimed almost exclusively at Japan, Hajime Tamura of MITI called it the result of "racial discrimination" and the "self-conceit of a superpower." When in 1989 Sony bought out Columbia Pictures, *Newsweek* magazine, in an emotional assault, charged that Japan had purchased "a piece of the American soul." A Foreign Ministry spokesman, Taizo Watanabe, observed wryly that many other countries bought properties in America without being accused of purchasing part of "the American soul."

Finally, to a good many Japanese the fractious times began to remind them of the dark period on the eve of World War II. The parallels they drew were far from exact, but the repetition of them in the popular and intellectual media revealed just how much Japanese had come to feel threatened. In the thirties Japan's war-minded militarists had frightened people with the warning that they were being "encircled" by Western colonial powers. And today a respected American journal was calling for the "containment" of Japan. Even sober, thoughtful men found the comparison with prewar days irresistible. A U.S. Senate resolution calling for direct retaliation against Japanese exports appalled Saburo Okita, an eminent economist and former foreign minister who was not normally given to incendiary comments. It reminded him, he said, of "the mood before the outbreak of war."

And so Japan entered the 1990s more confident than ever of her own powers but deeply pessimistic about relations with America. Those whose duty it was to nurture that linkage were the most pessimistic. Something had to give, they said. The old assumptions about mutual interests no longer held. A parting of some sort was inevitable. America saw Japan as an economic threat, they said, and Japan saw America as arrogant, racist. Younger Japanese in the corridors of the important bureaucracies and large companies seemed especially aware of the change to come and even eager to see it happen. They would lead Japan into the 1990s, and they were not mesmerized, as their elders had been, by the fear of severing the unequal partnership. All that was in the past. Japan was too strong now ever to be an "orphan of the world."

14

●

Japan Adrift

Ａll journalists like to imagine that they constantly stand on the brink of history. This is especially true of foreign correspondents, who are disposed by their craft to see important transformations wherever they are called upon to travel. The ends of old eras and the beginnings of new ones are seen and recorded with great frequency. Immensely significant turning points pop up almost as soon as the correspondent's plane arrives in some new country. Much of this is egotism, a state of mind summed up in the saying, "I am here and so there must be a big story to file." All this is said partly as an apology and partly as a warning for what is to follow as this book winds down. For in 1990, living in Tokyo, I thought I discerned the end of something, though not, I admit, any new beginning.

A theme of this book has been that Japan is what she is because of what occurred in the first years after the war. She was shaped by the shifting turns of the Occupation, by the conflicting ideas of her own postwar leaders, and often by the sheer quirkiness of events. The first ten years were a giant mixing bowl of ideas and pressures out of which eventually flowed certain arrangements and accommodations that determined what Japan would become. I believe Japan would have been a much different country had all of this not taken place. Her economic organization, her sense of place in the world, and the living styles of her people were all shaped by those events. Earlier history and culture, I think, had little to do with any of these, and they endured fundamentally to the present time.

In 1990 I suspected that those arrangements had played themselves out and that Japan was ready for something new. They had made Japan a rich country but not an important one, except in the narrowly commercial sense—and not a particularly appealing one if judged by the public-opinion surveys, which recorded large areas of dissatisfaction with daily life. There seemed to be a general understanding that what had transpired in the formative years was no longer serviceable. Yet there was no agreement on how change could be brought about. Japan wanted very much, in 1990, to be viewed by the world as an important and respected country but had no idea of how to become one. Japanese wanted an easier, more modern life in which to enjoy the fruits of their successes, and more personal freedom in the Western sense. But the country's institutions, shaped in the early postwar years, seemed incapable of permitting those things to happen. Japan seemed to me to be curiously paralyzed—eager to change, although certainly not in any revolutionary sense, but unable to do so. She seemed frozen in time by the commitments of her early postwar days.

●

It sometimes seems that Japanese leaders—in business, the media, politics, and the bureaucracy—are all reading from the same script. An idea takes hold and is expressed by everyone of importance in almost identical words, as though the gods have handed down a litany that all are charged with repeating. In 1990 one litany had to do with Japan's role in the world. It went something like this: "The postwar era is over and Japan has won. She must now play an important part in creating a New World Order. America is too weak, her economy sliding, her military power fading. Japan must join America and Europe in shaping the new age. Japan's power must be committed to that end." The litany was always uttered in profound tones and with the vaguest of generalizations, but constant repetition raised it to the level of a national consensus. Japan must guide and form the world waiting to be born. In moments of immodesty, some of the seers envisioned something grander. *Pax Britannica* had come and gone, and now the time of *Pax Americana* was passing, too. Why not *Pax Nipponica?*

The rest of the world also expected Japan to take her place as a world power and to act in ways commensurate with her economic might. It seemed only natural that she would do so. No commercial power in history had been satisfied merely to exploit markets and buy up raw materials. They had backed their power with force of arms or the threat of it. Japan would certainly follow suit and learn the old lesson that national interests had to be protected by military means. Foreigners had expected this of Japan for years. In the 1960s the American futurologist Herman Kahn had discovered Japan, pronounced her a nation destined to shake the world, and had predicted confidently that by 1975 she would become a nuclear power. He was dead wrong, of course, but that did not unsettle the world's opinion of Japan as a superpower-to-be. By 1990 she was edging her way into third place in the world's military race. It was, said the analysts abroad, but a matter of time.

In fact, Japan had no idea where she was heading. There was no consensus on doing anything at all, certainly not those things that other economic powers had done in the past. Her great corporations pushed on relentlessly, grabbing market shares in every corner of the globe. Her government was the world's largest donor of aid to the Third World. Beyond this, however, Japan was incapable of deciding what it should do, and so she did nothing. Once the litany had been uttered—"Japan-must-play-a-role-commensurate-with-her-economic-power"—little else happened. Japan was gripped with a peculiar paralysis of political will, much like a person whose brain commands arms and legs to move but finds them ever immobile. It was not merely that Japan could find no role to play in the great global stability drama. She could not act even when her most obvious interests were at stake.

Her immobility was illuminated by an episode that occurred in 1990, and it is worth examining in some detail. On August 2 Iraq invaded Kuwait, occupied the country in a rush of arms, and proclaimed it an Iraqi province. There was no doubt that this was a global threat, because by seizing Kuwait, Iraq could bully its neighbor, Saudi Arabia, and gain influence over nearly one-half of the oil shipped from the Persian Gulf. With that power, Iraq could virtually control oil prices throughout the world, and it had already indicated that it would demand far higher prices than were being paid before the invasion. Oil prices soared to more than $40 a barrel and put pressure on every country, rich or poor, including Japan.

In a rare display of unity, the world responded by word and deed. The United Nations condemned the invasion and put in place an embargo that cut Iraq off from the world. The United States, Europe, and several Arab countries formed a large multinational army, began stopping vessels bound to and from Iraq, and demanded that Iraqi troops be pulled out of Kuwait. Most of the ground troops were American, but many other countries contributed sizable units. Rich Arab nations agreed to pick up most of the cost of military operations. Each of those countries risked a great deal. The Western countries risked heavy casualties, and the Arab countries risked popular uprisings by Arab nationalist groups that were angered by the sight of foreign powers lined up on Arab soil prepared to fight an Arab country. And then the world looked at Japan to see what role she would play.

Her instincts were to do nothing because the history of such confrontations inevitably had found Japan on the sidelines, reluctant to move in any direction. In the past she had developed a distaste for global embargoes and had had to be pushed mightily by the United States to join in them. She had pretended to avoid choosing sides but for many years had avoided direct trade with Israel in order to appease the oil-producing states. (She had remained friendly with both Iran and Iraq throughout their eight-year war.) She had steadfastly refrained from engaging in any perilous adventure that might require military exertion abroad. Her constitution, which renounced war making as a right of the government, would not permit it.

But if ever a case could be made for joining the world in collective action, the Iraqi invasion was it. This was neither a symbolic censuring of a country that the United States wanted censured nor a faint-hearted international attempt at doing good. Japan's vital interests were at stake, and more than at any other time in the postwar era, she had cause to act. The accessibility and cost of Gulf oil were crucial to her industry—she imported almost all she used. The United States pressed her hard to react, and she could not yet resist American pressure on a vital issue. More than three hundred of her own people were being held hostage by the Iraqis, who were using them, along with other foreign nationals, as human shields to deter air strikes against Baghdad. Finally, the United Nations had voted the embargo and was preparing to sanction the multinational army gathered in Saudi Arabia. Not to act in conjunction with the United Nations would have been to ridicule the main line of Japanese foreign policy since the war. Support for the UN had been a pillar of diplomacy—the only one except for following American signals—and Japan would look foolish to ignore it when the UN had at last acted decisively. For a change, Japan had almost no reason not to act.

The first hurdle was easily bounded over. Japan announced that it would support the UN embargo. The second one was not so easy. Her "peace constitution" prevented her from joining an international military force, she said. But because she sympathized with its worthy goal, Japan would contribute money. How much? One billion dollars. The rest of the world scoffed at the promise. The world's richest country putting up only $1 billion of her treasures in a venture that would preserve her energy lifeline? Embarrassed, Japan's leaders regrouped and came up with the more respectable figure of $4 billion. And the world asked, "What else?" To which Japan answered only that her troops could not be sent to the Middle East because of the constitution. But, asked the world, was that not the same war-renouncing constitution that had enabled Japan to spend more money on arms than any nation except the two superpowers? In every Western capital Japan was accused anew of dodging responsibilities, allowing friends to take risks while she sat back to await the outcome. *Risk* was the key word in this mostly secret diplomatic exchange. As usual, it was the United States that put the point most precisely. Japan must risk lives and take a chance in this instance, or she would be scorned by the world for years as the international artful dodger who gained much but paid back little.

Into this dilemma stepped Prime Minister Toshiki Kaifu with the sort of bizarre compromise to which Japan resorts when caught in conflicting pressures. He introduced the United Nations Peace Cooperation Bill, providing that members of Japan's Self-Defense Forces (SDF) could be dispatched overseas for operations sanctioned by the UN—but not for combat. Socialists and members of other opposition parties denounced it as violating the constitution. The Diet debate revealed all of the elements of Japan's unworldliness. Kaifu earnestly attempted to defend the measure and managed only to make it seem ludicrous. The SDF troops would not engage in the use of armed force, he said. They would not be sent to "dangerous" areas. They would be armed only with pistols and rifles for self-defense, not for attack. They would take orders from him, back in Tokyo. What if the troops were attacked? They would not be, he replied, because they would be in the back lines, not at the front. But Iraq had long-range missiles that could reach anywhere, did it not? No answer. The debate sputtered on for weeks in that autumn of 1990. As it did, and as the issue became crystal clear, the public turned

against Kaifu's bill. Only one-quarter or less of the Japanese supported
it. Then Kaifu's own Liberal Democratic party wavered. Veterans like
Shin Kanemaru publicly opposed it. The government plan was left in
tatters, and in the Middle East Japan once again did nothing. Finally,
on November 8, the bill was abandoned.

By any conventional analysis, the fiasco could be written off as a
monumental error by an inept government. Kaifu was one of the weakest of prime ministers, lacking a sufficient power base. His bill was not
well thought out, was poorly drafted, and was ultimately indefensible in
debate. Or the sorry episode could be explained by the theory, then
fashionable abroad, that Japan really had no effective government. In
the thesis advanced by Karel van Wolferen, whose book *The Enigma of
Japanese Power* was extremely popular overseas, there was no center of
power that could make decisions and respond to events in the world.
The government in Tokyo was not really a modern democracy. It was
a web of special interests without the capacity to govern as other democracies did. According to this theory, the Persian Gulf crisis revealed
Japan as structurally incompetent to act even in her own interest.

A third explanation, one that had currency in Western capitals,
was that Japan had merely dodged responsibility once again. Japan cared
little about events far from her shores and selfishly sought to avoid them.
Japan cared only for markets and profits, and when they were not
directly at stake, the world could go hang. She would risk nothing but
money and even that with reluctance. Japan was a bystander by choice,
willing to abandon the concept of collective defense at the first whiff of
gunpowder.

All of these explanations, it seems to me, missed the point. In such
matters as sending forces overseas, Japan was paralyzed by her postwar
history, by those accommodations and arrangements that were made in
the years immediately after the defeat. She had accepted, far more
earnestly than foreigners suspected, the restrictions of the constitution.
Article 9, which forbids the making of war, was indeed imposed by
foreigners on a subject people, but it quickly came to be accepted as part
of the national fabric. Japan has been subjected to enormous pressure
over the years to change that view but could not bring herself to do so,
not even when the United States brought pressure and not even when
important national issues were at stake. Pacifism had been ingrained in
the postwar era, first by orders of the Occupation and then by a tacit
public agreement too strong for any force to break. The fiasco over
Prime Minister Kaifu's UN peace-keeping bill was simply a measure of
how deep those feelings run.

What it showed was that Japanese are not ready for foreign military adventures of any sort. American pressures, obvious national interests, and the ill will of the rest of the world are not sufficient to budge her. If she seriously envisions playing some larger role in world affairs, it will not be in the form of collective military action to deter aggression. Until the episode of Iraq revealed her true feelings on the matter, she had not seriously considered the question of risking lives abroad to attain any goals, least of all those of the world community.

The difference between Japan and the West in that regard is very great, and it has been best explained by Kiichi Miyazawa. Miyazawa has been at the center of policy and politics from the beginning of the postwar era, first as a bureaucrat and then as a politician. He was on that crucial mission to Washington that set the stage for Prime Minister Yoshida to win independence. No one, I think, understands better the postwar history that restrains Japan from such international ventures involving arms. In 1990 he was asked about the UN peace-keeping bill when its failure was almost certain. Since the war, he replied, Japan had not faced the issue of endangering soldiers' lives for some abstract cause considered important elsewhere in the world. "People in Christian cultures and Western European democracies," Miyazawa said, "have had such discussions among themselves and it is clear to them that peace and freedom should be achieved at any cost, even blood. For the Japanese, the question has been taboo. . . . Now we are asked [that question]. We haven't found an answer."[1]

●

Early in each postwar decade the Ministry of International Trade and Industry has produced a document exploring the years ahead and charting the paths for Japan's next economic advances. These "MITI visions," as they are called, are considered enormously important. Businessmen and bureaucrats read them closely for clues as to where the nation should concentrate its resources. The vision for the 1960s called for the targeting of heavy industry and chemicals as the next step up on the economic scale. For the 1970s MITI selected the "knowledge-intensive industries" such as electronics and computers. The 1980 version pointed to development of even higher technologies. The visions proved to be remarkably accurate forecasts. What MITI said should be done was in large part done.

In 1990 MITI stunned Tokyo by producing a vision that differed radically from earlier ones. Subtitled "Toward Creating Human Values in the Global Age," it hardly dealt with industrial progress at all and opened with the heretical thought that economic growth per se was not necessarily a boon for Japanese. What was needed, it said, was the organization of "human-oriented international trade and industrial policies" that were aimed at happiness, not merely expansion, and the ultimate objective was to be "the improvement of the daily lives of citizens." The paper went on to propose a list of specific goals: consumer protection and help in buying higher value for less money; shorter working hours for employed people; improved status for women wishing to enter the work force; more meaningful lives for the elderly; better, bigger homes at reasonable costs; fewer hours spent commuting to work; and enlargement of the social infrastructure, including sewers, roads, and parks.[2] In business circles the paper was greeted with puzzlement and skepticism. MITI, it was said, had crossed the line into dreamland. In what everyone was now calling the "postindustrial age," MITI was pictured as desperately seeking some new bureaucratic role to play.

But, for whatever motive, MITI had tapped into the current of the times. The mood of Japanese in 1990 was precisely as the paper described. In almost all reaches of society, people talked of striving for the same goals. Just as there had been a special litany urging Japan to become a powerful, respected nation playing a role in the world, so too there was a litany that encompassed domestic hopes. It went like this: "Japan has reached a new postwar plateau. Her people have worked long and hard enough and are entitled to enjoy the fruits of her success. Rapid economic growth has raised the status of the nation and enriched the mighty corporations, but her citizens have not shared fairly in the prosperity. Somehow the new age dawning must provide the realities of affluence for Japanese, who want to work less, play more, and above all live comfortable lives. The economy must be redirected toward that purpose."

In the late 1980s there was no dearth of plans for this age of "human-oriented" reform. From the core of the influential bureaucracies, MITI and the Economic Planning Agency, flowed a stream of ideas, plans, targets, and policies. Working hours could be cut to 1,800 a year, bringing Japan into line with the United States. A land-use tax policy was designed to free more urban space for housing, thus forcing down the cost of apartments. Task forces churned out yet another round of papers proposing that new development be dispersed to regional centers. This would ease crowding in Tokyo and Osaka and help to revive the outlying regions, which were being rapidly depopulated. Rice could be imported from abroad to bring down domestic prices, which were five times the international market level. It was a time for thinking daring thoughts, and some of them bordered on the fanciful. From the bureaucrats at MITI came a dazzling scheme for coping with the problems of the aged population, which was growing at a rate faster than in any other country. The "Silver Columbia Plan" envisioned establishing colonies abroad for Japanese seniors to live out their lives basking in the sun.

But the deluge of paper plans produced very little in the way of actual reform. The MITI vision of 1990 itself admitted that the campaigns for fewer working hours had "stalled." Land prices remained at extraordinary high levels, and the dream of home buying receded for even the highly paid. Regional dispersal plans were filed away on dusty shelves where they joined those of the previous twenty years. Prices of everything that consumers bought—including rice—stayed in the stratosphere. People wondered what had ever happened to the "Silver Columbia Plan."

For Japan in 1990 was as immobilized in the area of domestic reform as she was in her dream of advancing onto the world stage. The brain thought, but the arms and legs did not move. A society that for forty years had been pragmatic and flexible in reordering itself seemed somehow incapable of even modest alterations. In the 1970s, for example, Japan had become alarmed at the rate of industrial pollution, which was making urban air unbreathable and streams too dirty for fish. In a few years she had mobilized a consensus for reform. Bureaucrats, businessmen, and politicians had been prodded into one of the most successful antipollution crusades the world had then witnessed. It had been a proud moment for it had revealed a side of Japan that was often hidden behind a conservative exterior—an ability to achieve change when change was called for. In 1990 the mood for change on other issues was there. But next to nothing was achieved.

This immobility, too, was a legacy of the early postwar years, the period when Japan's future was determined. The course that had been fixed then was a strenuous one that required the loyalties of all parts of society. It called for hard work, low wages, and a bare minimum of those public amenities that made life pleasurable in nations that had not been destroyed by war. For better or worse, but mainly out of necessity, Japanese had sanctioned the new economic ethic giving priority in all things to the needs of industrial development and high growth. They had acquiesced in the new business culture because it promised jobs and rising living standards. The rewards had been great and visible, and they had produced the miracle of which all were proud.

But those same arrangements confined as well as freed. They tended to block off avenues of change that might have challenged the business culture and made it in later years more appealing. Perhaps the most glaring problem was the absence of an independent labor union movement. The compromises of the late 1940s and early 1950s had smothered the notion of truly independent unions and transformed the infant organizations first sponsored by the Occupation into agencies of the big corporations. They grew up by no means powerless, but they lacked the influence to bargain successfully over such goals as higher wages, reduced working hours, and more holidays. In these fields, they accepted what the companies thought fitting to dole out. More important, company unionism had negated the concept of a national union movement, which might have become an engine of reform on broader social issues. It is instructive to consider the differences between Japan and West Germany, two defeated and crushed nations. The West German labor movement became strong in every sense that Japan's was weak, and it proved not only better at bargaining for ordinary gains but far more influential in setting the priorities for social welfare on a national scale.

In many other ways it seemed that the very conditions of economic success were coming back to haunt Japanese in 1990. They had acquiesced in a set of government policies that had seemed sensible in the 1950s because they lent encouragement to protected industries and assured jobs. Their government had formed cartels, sanctioned price-fixing, and created hundreds of regulations that favored farmers, businessmen, and bankers. But by 1990 these chickens had come home to roost. They were at the root of the high prices and limited choices a Japanese faced on every shopping trip. Low returns on savings and high interest rates for consumer loans were not the result of bad luck or greedy shysters. They were the direct result of government policies that favored bankers and loan sharks. In accepting the business culture that levied such penalties, the Japanese had also forfeited the habits of dissent and reform. Japan never developed one of the fixtures of postwar society elsewhere: a forceful consumers' movement that could expose unfairness and inform citizens of the precise ways in which they were being disadvantaged. Nowhere in Japan today are to be found strong, general-purpose watchdog groups that can blow the whistle on corruption or bid-rigging or harmful chemicals. A Ralph Nader would be scorned in Japan.

The institutions that might have mounted some challenge to the status quo were incapable of doing so. None seemed more ineffectual in this respect than the universities. College days in the 1950s and 1960s had been a time of great ferment and debate in Japan. Issues such as the American security alliance, socialism, the emperor system, and the war in Vietnam could be raised on the campuses even though they might not be elsewhere in society. By 1990 the Japanese university was a playground, a place to enjoy one's last days of youth before being absorbed into the rigid institutions of the business culture. Government studies lamented this fact, but no one sought to change it. Almost everyone acknowledged that the college years were a waste—teachers taught little and the students studied even less. Task force after task force sought to modify the entrance exams, which tested only the amount of memorization accomplished by students in prep schools. Nothing of any consequence was altered.

In their efforts to weed out the injustices that had crept into their private and public lives, Japanese had increasingly turned to the courts. One of the common misperceptions of Japan is that legal actions are unpopular for cultural reasons—one does not air dirty linen in public. In fact, the 1970s and 1980s had seen virtually every national issue, from pollution to divorce to the emperor system, tested in suits brought before courts of law. By 1990 there were even cases alleging that corporate working rules caused death and illness from acute exhaustion. The litigants got little help from the legal system. Judges presided but seemed to dislike deciding. Cases dragged on for years, even decades, often ending in nondecisions. The courts refused to rule in any definitive way on the most obvious contradiction of postwar life, the existence, under a constitution that banned war, of a large military force. They occasionally found that a grossly malapportioned Diet violated the law but refused to order any changes in the political map. Irresolution was the guiding spirit of even the highest courts. The most prominent examples were the cases seeking compensation for sufferers of mercury poisoning, the famous "Minamata disease," which had first been identified in 1956. Demands by many victims for compensation had remained unsettled, despite a number of legal suits. By 1990 1,211 of the victims had died and others were nearing death, their suits still unresolved. That year the courts ruled that the cases should be settled out of court, on the grounds that final appeals might carry on into the twenty-first century, when all litigants would be dead.

Japanese had acquiesced, too, to a system of politics that people came to recognize as almost meaningless. Since the early 1950s politics had been subordinated to the goal of economic growth. The duty of politicians was to assist in attaining that goal, and the long ascension of the conservative LDP was justified entirely by the interests of "stability." After the great debates of the 1950s had petered out, the LDP was dominant, and the country was seen to be able to get on with its real business, which was business. The only opposition party of any strength, the Socialist party, degenerated into an ideological debating club that was as far removed from political reality in Japan as was the Communist party in the United States. The LDP was left free to represent the interests of business and farmers and those small merchants willing to pay the price of protection. Bribery of politicians was annoying, but it was tacitly recognized as an essential part of the system, a small price to pay for their cooperation in the quest for stability. Each time a seriously contested general election appeared on the horizon, the media framed it in only one overriding question: Would the LDP maintain a "stable majority?" That was, after all, the only question that mattered.

The notion that politicians should play a progressive role in addressing the matter of reform seemed, in this context, an alien idea. Indeed, reform of any serious kind was a threat to the LDP. Policies aimed at lowering land prices, dickering with working hours, loosening petty regulations, reducing the prices of rice and other commodities and goods, raising taxes to provide public amenities—any of these would have antagonized the corporations and interest groups that maintained LDP Diet members in their comfortable tenures. People distrusted the LDP, but they distrusted the Socialist party and the minor parties even more. The sterility of the political system had been all but guaranteed by the system established in the 1950s, when it had been tacitly agreed that politics was too important to be left to the politicians and power had been vested in business and the bureaucracy. By 1990 it was too late to turn to politics as an agent of social reform.

The 1980s had been a decade of doubt and questioning, a time when a new generation had begun to ask where Japan was headed. It was by no means a revolutionary period when what was old was discarded, but it did reveal the Japanese in a challenging mood. Almost everything that had seemed fixed since the earliest postwar years was examined to determine if it was worth preserving. People, especially the young, questioned the old work ethic, the role of women, the importance of family, the system of politics, corporate wealth and personal privation— almost everything, up to and including the place Japan would hold in the world. For the first time there was serious and occasionally angry criticism of each of these. In reviewing the public-opinion surveys of that time, one cannot avoid being struck by the large gaps that existed between public attitudes and the reality that persisted, between what Japanese wanted and what actually was. People wanted change.

But their energies seemed oddly paralyzed. There were no engines of reform at hand. Looking around Tokyo in 1990, one encountered rigid institutions that had served admirably in the past to achieve immense change but that now seemed mostly impediments. In the forty-five years since the war ended, Japanese had met and conquered almost every challenge and had brought order and prosperity out of chaos. In 1991 the assumptions that had led them to this peak seemed of limited value in coping with new challenges. Forward movement seemed to have ceased, replaced by drift and immobility and a sense of not knowing how to change the habits of nearly a half-century.

Notes

●

Preface

1. Edwin O. Reischauer, in Harry Wray and Hilary Conroy, eds., *Japan Examined: Perspectives on Modern Japanese History* (Honolulu: University of Hawaii Press, 1983), 336.

2. Kazuo Kawai, *Japan's American Interlude* (Chicago: University of Chicago Press, 1960), 49.

Chapter One

1. Kiyohisa Mikanagi, interview.

2. Fukuo Izawa, interview.

3. Kawai, *Japan's American Interlude*, 4.

4. Masataka Kosaka, *100 Million Japanese: The Post-war Experience* (Tokyo: Kodansha International Ltd., 1972), 12.

5. Christine Chapman, *International Herald Tribune*, February 28, 1984.

6. Walt Sheldon, *The Honorable Conquerors: The Occupation of Japan, 1945–1952* (New York: The Macmillan Co., 1965), 81.

7. Isamu Togawa, *Sengo Fuzokushi* (Tokyo: Sekkasha, 1960).

8. Theodore Cohen, *Remaking Japan: The American Occupation As New Deal* (New York: The Free Press, 1987), 195.

9. Robert A. Scalapino, *The Japanese Communist Movement, 1920–1966* (Berkeley and Los Angeles: University of California Press, 1967).

10. Cohen, *Remaking Japan*, 297.

11. Ibid., 57.

12. Mark Gayn, *Japan Diary* (Rutland, Vt., and Tokyo: Charles E. Tuttle Co., 1981), 84–92.

Chapter Two

1. Douglas MacArthur, *A Soldier Speaks* (New York: Frederick A. Praeger, 1965), 182.

2. Kosaka, *100 Million Japanese*, 92.

3. Ibid., 87.

4. Shigeru Yoshida, *The Yoshida Memoirs* (London; William Heinemann Ltd., 1961), 148.

5. Meirion and Susie Harries, *Sheathing the Sword: The Demilitarisation of Japan* (London: Hamish Hamilton, 1987), 203.

6. Cohen, *Remaking Japan*, 197–202.

7. Eiichi Ochiai, interview.

8. Miriam S. Farley, *Aspects of Japan's Labor Problems* (New York: The John Day Co., 1950), 82.

9. Ibid., 88–89.

10. The story of the Yawata steel union was pieced together from several lengthy interviews with Yoshiji Miyata and from a book of recollections he edited—*Yawata Seitetsu No Rodo Kumiai Shi* (The Yawata Steel Labor Union) (Tokyo: The Yawata Steel Labor Union, 1957).

Chapter Three

1. Akitsugu Yamazaki, *Korigashi No Jukkai* (Memoirs of a Loan Shark) (Tokyo: Seinen Shobo, 1950).

2. Jean Stoetzel, *Without the Chrysanthemum and the Sword* (New York: Columbia University Press, 1955), 256.

3. Yoshida, *The Yoshida Memoirs*, 124.

4. Edward Seidensticker, in a preface to Jared Taylor, *Shadows of the Rising Sun* (New York: William Morrow and Co., Inc., 1983), 9.

5. Yoshida, *The Yoshida Memoirs*, 171.

6. Kawai, *Japan's American Interlude*, 196.

7. Stoetzel, *Without the Chrysanthemum*, 255.

8. Ibid., 162.

9. Shintaro Ishihara, *Taiyo No Kisetsu*, (Season of Violence) (Rutland, Vt.: Charles E. Tuttle Co. Inc., 1966), 27.

10. Ibid., 51.

11. Ibid., 55.

12. Ibid., 57.

13. An excellent history of this cinema era, from which I have borrowed, is Joseph I. Anderson and Donald Richie, *The Japanese Film: Art and Industry* (Rutland, Vt. and Tokyo: Charles E. Tuttle Co., 1959).

14. Ibid., 191.

15. Details of Dazai's life are drawn from Phyllis I. Lyons, *The Saga of Dazai Osamu: A Critical Study with Translations* (Stanford: Stanford University Press, 1985).

16. Osamu Dazai, *The Setting Sun*, trans. Donald Keene (London: Peter Owen Limited, 1956), 166.

17. Jiro Osaragi, *Homecoming*, trans. Brewster Horwitz (New York: Alfred A. Knopf, Inc., 1954), 112.

18. Ibid., 125–26.

19. Jiro Osaragi, *The Journey*, trans. Ivan Morris (Rutland, Vt., and Tokyo: Charles E. Tuttle Co., 1967), 307.

20. Osaragi, *Homecoming*, 214.

21. Osaragi, *The Journey*, 155.

22. Osaragi, *Homecoming*, 215.

23. Ibid., 287.

Chapter Four

1. John W. Dower, *Empire and Aftermath: Yoshida Shigeru and the Japanese Experience, 1878–1954.* (Cambridge and London: Harvard University Press, 1979), 18. I am indebted to Dower's marvelous biography for the details of Yoshida's early career.

2. Yoshida, *The Yoshida Memoirs*, 278.

3. Ibid., 9.

4. Ibid., 14.

5. The Kempeitai, or Military Police, had been watching Yoshida for six years.

6. Kiyohisa Mikanagi, interview.

7. Akira Matsui, interview.

8. Ibid.

9. Yoshida, *The Yoshida Memoirs*, 106.

10. Mikanagi, interview.

11. Takaaki Kagawa, interview. Kagawa was Yoshida's personal secretary for four-and-a-half years.

12. Dower, *Empire and Aftermath*, 311.

13. Kosaka, *100 Million Japanese,* 130.

14. Yoshida, *The Yoshida Memoirs,* 45.

15. Courtney Whitney, *MacArthur: His Rendezvous with Destiny* (New York: Alfred A. Knopf, Inc., 1956), 251.

16. Kagawa, interview.

17. William J. Sebald, *With MacArthur in Japan* (New York: W. W. Norton & Co., 1965), 257.

18. John M. Allison, *Ambassador from the Prairie, or Allison Wonderland* (Boston: Houghton Mifflin, 1973), 148.

19. Ibid.

20. Townsend Hoopes, *The Devil and John Foster Dulles* (Boston: Little, Brown & Company, 1973), 105.

21. Michael Schaller, *The American Occupation of Japan: The Origins of the Cold War in Asia* (New York and Oxford: Oxford University Press, 1985), 297.

22. Michael M. Yoshitsu, *Japan and the San Francisco Peace Settlement* (New York: Columbia University Press, 1983), 28.

23. E. J. Lewe Van Aduard, *Japan from Surrender to Peace* (New York: Frederick A. Praeger, 1954), 126–27.

24. Douglas H. Mendel, *The Japanese People and Foreign Policy* (Berkeley and Los Angeles: University of California Press, 1961), 43.

25. Frederick S. Dunn, *Peacemaking and the Settlement with Japan* (Princeton: Princeton University Press, 1966), 93.

26. George R. Packard III, *Protest in Tokyo* (Princeton: Princeton University Press, 1966), 12.

27. Robert A. Fearey, *The Occupation of Japan, Second Phase, 1948–50* (New York: The Macmillan Co., 1950), 189.

28. Hugh Borton et al., eds., *Japan Between East and West* (Westport, Conn.: Greenwood Press, 1957), 312.

29. Mendel, *The Japanese People,* 102.

30. Allen B. Cole and Naomichi Nakanishi, eds., *Japanese Opinion Polls with Socio-Political Significance, 1947–57* (Ann Arbor: Microfilm, 1960), 612.

31. Mendel, *The Japanese People,* 85.

32. Ibid., 61.

33. Borton, *Japan Between East and West,* 310.

34. Mendel, *The Japanese People,* 234.

35. Cited in Dower, *Empire and Aftermath,* 391.

36. Matsui, interview.

37. *The Nation* 168: 20, May 14, 1949.

38. Kagawa, interview.

39. Ibid.

40. Allison, *Ambassador,* 157.

41. Cole and Nakanishi, *Japanese Opinion Polls,* 64.

42. Kiichi Miyazawa, *Tokyo-Washington No Mitsudan*, (Secret Talks in Tokyo and Washington) (Tokyo: Jitsu-Gyo No Nipponshi, 1956), 44–46, 52–56.

43. *Asahi Shimbun* staff, *Pacific Rivals: A Japanese View of Japanese-American Relations* (New York and Tokyo: Weatherhill/Asahi, 1972), 205.

44. Dower, *Empire and Aftermath*, 408.

45. Cole and Nakanishi, *Japanese Opinion Polls*, 128.

46. Ibid., 191.

47. Dower, *Empire and Aftermath*, 370–71.

48. *Asahi Shimbun* staff, *Pacific Rivals*, 119.

49. Mikanagi, interview.

50. Ibid.

51. Matsui, interview.

Chapter Five

1. Richard E. Caves and Masu Uekusa, "Industrial Organization" in Hugh Patrick and Henry Rosovsky, eds. *Asia's New Giant: How the Japanese Economy Works* (Washington: The Brookings Institution, 1976), 465.

2. Peter F. Drucker, "What We Can Learn from Japanese Management," *Harvard Business Review* March-April 1971, 110–22.

3. James G. Abegglen, *The Japanese Factory* (Glencoe, Ill.: The Free Press, 1958), 134.

4. Bela Balassa and Marcus Noland, *Japan in the World Economy* (Washington: Institute for International Economics, 1988), 81.

5. Nathan Glazer, "Social and Cultural Factors in Japanese Economic Growth," in Patrick and Rosovsky, *Asia's New Giant*, 858.

6. Naohiro Amaya, in a speech at a seminar of the Multinational Insurance Arrangement, Tokyo, December 3, 1987.

7. Cited in Yonosuke Nagai, "The Roots of Cold War Doctrine" in Nagai and Akira Iriye, eds. *The Origins of the Cold War in Asia* (Tokyo: University of Tokyo Press, 1977), 28.

8. George F. Kennan, *Memoirs 1925–1950* (Boston: Little, Brown & Co., 1967), 388.

9. Chalmers Johnson, *MITI and the Japanese Miracle: The Growth of Industrial Policy, 1925–1975* (Stanford: Stanford University Press, 1982). I have relied much on Professor Johnson's excellent study of MITI for details in this section.

10. Yasuyuki Maeda, interview.

11. Ibid.

12. Ibid.

13. Ibid.

14. Ibid.

15. Yoshihisa Ojima, vice-minister of MITI, in speech to the Industrial

Committee of the Organisation for Economic Cooperation and Development, in Tokyo, June 24, 1970.

16. Maeda, interview.

17. Ibid.

18. Kozo Yamamura, *Economic Policy in Post-war Japan* (Berkeley and Los Angeles: University of California Press, 1967), 77.

19. Saburo Okita, *The Developing Economies and Japan* (Tokyo: University of Tokyo Press, 1980), 97.

20. William W. Lockwood, "Japan's 'New Capitalism,' " in Lockwood, ed., *The State and Economic Enterprise in Japan* (Princeton: Princeton University Press, 1965), 503.

21. Ibid., 510.

22. Maeda, interview.

23. Ministry of Foreign Affairs, "Labor Relations in Japan," 1977.

24. Robert S. Ozaki, "The Humanistic Enterprise System in Japan," *Asian Survey* 27:8 (August 1988), 831.

25. Konosuke Matsushita, *Quest for Prosperity: The Life of a Japanese Industrialist* (Tokyo: PHP Institute Inc., 1988), 61.

26. Takeshi Inagami, "Japanese Workplace Industrial Relations," Japanese Institute of Labor, 1988, 5.

27. Yasumitsu Nihei, interview.

28. Kazuo Okochi, *The Japan Labor Union Story*, Vol. 1 (Tokyo: Chikuma Shobo, 1974), 398.

29. Cohen, *Remaking Japan*, 449.

30. Ochiai, interview.

31. Yamamura, *Economic Policy*, 48.

32. Seigo Kojima, interview.

33. Okochi, *The Japan Labor Union Story*, 2, 314.

34. Miyata, interview.

Chapter Six

1. Yutaka Kosai, *The Era of High-Speed Growth: Notes on the Post-War Japanese Economy* (Tokyo: University of Tokyo Press, 1986), 130.

2. Matsushita, *Quest for Prosperity*, 288.

3. Lockwood, "Japan's 'New Capitalism,' " Lockwood; *The State and Economic Enterprise*, 474.

4. Patrick and Rosovsky, "Japan's Economic Performance: An Overview" in *Asia's New Giant*, 18.

5. Johnson, *MITI and the Japanese Miracle*, 251–52.

6. Kazuo Okochi, et al., eds. *Workers and Employers in Japan* (Princeton: Princeton University Press, 1974), 178.

7. Anonymous, interview.

8. Lockwood, "Japan's 'New Capitalism' " in Lockwood, *The State and Economic Enterprise*, 450.

9. Yasumitsu Nihei, interview.

10. Rodney Clark, *The Japanese Company* (New Haven: Yale University Press, 1979). Clark is one of three foreign authorities on whose investigations I rely for part of what follows. Their work, I believe, provides the best glimpses into what was actually happening in Japanese plants during the sixties and seventies. Clark studied a medium-sized box factory for fourteen months. Robert E. Cole, an American, lived in a factory neighborhood for a year and worked as a blue-collar employee in both a Tokyo die-cast plant and in a rural automobile factory. Ronald P. Dore, like Clark a British scholar, examined two Hitachi factories at close range and compared them with comparable British plants.

11. Clark, *The Japanese Company*, especially 158.

12. Quoted in Abegglen, *The Japanese Factory*, 133.

13. Ronald P. Dore, *British Factory—Japanese Factory* (Berkeley and Los Angeles: University of California Press, 1973), 203.

14. Ibid., 214.

15. Ronald P. Dore, "Mobility, Equality and Individuation in Modern Japan" in Dore, ed. *Aspects of Social Change in Modern Japan* (Princeton: Princeton University Press, 1967), 141.

16. Matsushita, *Quest for Prosperity*, 302.

17. Kichinosuke Yamazaki, interview.

18. Dore, *British Factory—Japanese Factory*, 52.

19. Cited in Robert E. Cole, *Japanese Blue Collar* (Berkeley: University of California Press, 1971), 117.

20. Ibid., 64–65.

21. Clark, *The Japanese Company*, 205.

22. Cited in Ministry of Foreign Affairs, "Labor Relations in Japan," 1977.

23. Robert M. Marsh and Hiroshi Mannari, *Modernization and the Japanese Factory* (Princeton: Princeton University Press, 1976), 101.

24. Dore, *British Factory—Japanese Factory*, 216.

25. Takeshi Ishida, *Japanese Political Culture* (New Brunswick, N.J.: Transaction Books, 1983), 44.

26. Iwao Nakatani, *The Japanese Firm in Transition* (Tokyo: Asian Productivity Organization, 1988), 13.

27. A. M. Whitehill, Jr., and Shinichi Takezawa, *The Other Worker: A Comparative Study of Industrial Relations in the United States and Japan* (Honolulu: East-West Center Press, 1968), 110.

28. Dore, *British Factory—Japanese Factory*, 215.

29. Keita Genji, *The Lucky One and Other Humorous Stories*, trans. Hugh Cortazzi (Tokyo: The Japan Times Limited, 1980). This story and those subsequently mentioned are from this volume.

Chapter Seven

1. Masayoshi Takamura, address to Foreign Correspondents Club of Japan, April 21, 1989.

2. Bradley M. Richardson and Scott C. Flanagan, *Politics in Japan* (Boston: Little, Brown & Co., 1984), 176.

3. Shunsuke Tsurumi, *A Cultural History of Post-war Japan* (London and New York: KPI Limited, 1987), 111, 120.

4. Kenzo Uchida, address to Foreign Correspondents Club of Japan, April 21, 1989.

5. *Asahi Evening News*, May 11, 1989.

6. Takeshi Ishida, interview.

7. Matsushita, *Quest for Prosperity*, 286.

8. Cited in the *Washington Post*, November 26, 1978.

9. Richardson and Flanagan, *Politics in Japan*, 174–95.

10. *Hoso Kenkyu To Chosa Ripoto* (Broadcast Research and Investigation Report), March 1989.

11. The *Washington Post*, April 10, 1988.

12. Kan Ori, interview.

13. Seiichi Tagawa, interview.

14. Dan Kurzman, *Kishi and Japan: The Search for the Sun* (New York: Ivan Obolensky Inc., 1960), 274.

15. Chitoshi Yanaga, *Big Business in Japanese Politics* (New Haven: Yale University Press, 1968), 135.

16. Ibid., 80, 141.

17. Nihachiro Hanamura's recollections were provided in an interview with the author in 1989 when he was semiretired but still serving as a *Keidanaren* advisor. His account of Tanaka's plea for funds was contained in an interview with the newspaper *Mainichi*, April 10, 1988.

18. Hirotatsu Fujiwara, *Tanaka Kakuei: Godfather of Japan* (Tokyo: Nihon Shoko Shinkokai, 1985). Fujiwara accepted the deal in principle, but somehow negotiations faltered and the book was freely distributed.

19. Michio Watanabe, address to Foreign Correspondents Club of Japan, December 16, 1988.

20. *Asahi Evening News*, January 3, 1989.

Chapter Eight

1. Aron Viner, *The Emerging Power of Japanese Money* (Homewood, Ill.: Dow Jones–Irwin, 1988), 2.

2. Kuniko Inoguchi, "Prosperity Without the Amenities," in Kenneth B. Pyle, ed., *The Trade Crisis: How Will Japan Respond?* (Seattle: Society for Japanese Studies, 1987), 62.

3. Ibid.

4. *OECD Handbook 1988*, 22, 16.

5. The *Washington Post*, September 30, 1979.

6. Martin Bronfenbrenner and Yasukichi Yasuba, "Economic Welfare," in Yasuba and Kozo Yamamura, eds., *The Political Economy of Japan: Vol. 1—The Domestic Transformation* (Stanford: Stanford University Press, 1987), 107.

7. Reports of the Ministry of Construction and "Living Conditions in OECD Countries," (Paris: OECD, 1986).

8. Economic Planning Agency, "Annual Report on National Life, 1987," 135.

9. These statistics are reported in "Practical Handbook of Productivity and Labor Statistics, 1987–88," published by the Japan Productivity Center, 129, 12, 109.

10. *The Economist*, May 19, 1990, 26.

11. Economic Planning Agency, "Annual Report on the National Life for Fiscal 1988."

12. Economic Planning Agency, "New Social Indicators, 1989."

13. From survey by Rengo, The Japanese Private Sector Trade Union Confederation, November, 1989.

14. Economic Planning Agency, "1989 Price Report."

15. OECD, "Statistics on the Member Countries," 1988 edition.

16. From accounts in *Asahi* and *Nihon Keizai* newspapers, October and September, respectively, 1989.

17. *Nihon Keizai*, November 14, 1989.

18. *Asahi*, October 26–November 5, 1989.

19. Economic Planning Agency, "Annual Report on the National Life for Fiscal 1988," 99.

20. Ibid., "Poll on Preferences in the National Life," 1988, 101.

Chapter Nine

1. Hirobumi Kato, interview.

2. Takamitsu Sawa, "What Happened to Ethics?" The *Japan Times*, January 30, 1989.

3. Toshiaki Izeki, interview.

4. *Asahi Evening News*, January 8, 1988.

5. Hikoharu Kure, interview.

6. *The Economist*, April 15, 1989, 29.

7. *Journal of Social and Political Ideas in Japan* 1:2 (August 1963), 76.

8. Jinnosuke Miyai, interview.

9. Peter Tasker, *Inside Japan: Wealth, Work and Power in the New Japanese Empire* (London: Sidgwick and Jackson, 1987), 256.

10. Malcolm Sawyer, "Income Distribution in OECD Countries," OECD, July 1976.

11. Noboru Takeshita, *The Furusato Concept: Toward a Humanistic and Prosperous Japan* (1987, unbound).

12. Economic Planning Agency, "Economic Survey" 1987–88.

13. Nobuaki Takahashi, "Tai Koku Nihon No Uchinaru Mazushisa" (*Poverty in Superpower Japan*), *Chuo Koron*, February 1989.

14. *The Economist*, March 18, 1989, 15.

15. "Public Opinion Survey on the Life of the Nation," The Prime Minister's Office, October 1987.

16. *Asaki Evening News*, January 8, 1988.

Chapter Ten

1. Rokuro Hidaka, *The Price of Affluence: Dilemmas of Contemporary Japan* (Tokyo: Kodansha International, 1984) 71–73.

2. Naohiro Amaya and Kanji Nishio, "Education Reform: How Far, How Fast," in *Japan Echo* 12:2 (1985), 53.

3. Takeshita, *The Furusato Concept*, 58.

4. Public-opinion surveys conducted by the prime minister's office, November 1986 and October 1987.

5. Economic Planning Agency, Annual Report, 1987.

6. Yasuo Tanaka, *Nanto-naku Kuristaru* (Somewhat Crystal), (Tokyo: Kawade Shoten, 1981).

7. Christine Chapman, *International Herald Tribune*, March 27, 1981.

8. The *Japan Times*, March 13, 1988.

9. Nihon Recruit Center survey, cited in *Japan Echo* 12:2 (1985), 71.

10. Dai Ichi Kangyo Ginko Bank survey of new recruits, 1987.

11. Economic Planning Agency, "Annual Report on the National Life for Fiscal 1987," 125.

12. Economic Planning Agency, "Annual Report on the National Life for Fiscal 1988," 1982.

13. Cited in Iwao Nakatani, *The Japanese Firm in Transition*, 55.

14. Survey by Fukoku Mutual Life Insurance Co., cited in *The Daily Yomiuri*, November 22, 1988.

15. Economic Planning Agency, "Annual Report on the National Life for Fiscal 1988," 61–62.

16. Toshiaki Izeki, "The New Rich," *Next* magazine, August 1988.

17. Vincent Canby, the *New York Times*, June 28, 1989.

18. Christine Chapman, *International Herald Tribune*, May 6, 1985.

19. Juzo Itami, quoted in the *Daily Yomiuri*, January 23, 1988.

20. Takahashi, "Tai Koku Nihon," 87.

Chapter Eleven

1. Kai Oi, "Toward the Formation of a New Japanese Nationalism," *The Journal of Social and Political Ideas in Japan* 2:2, (August 1964), 16–18. Excerpted from *Chuo Koron*, July 1963.

2. Hidaka, *The Price of Affluence*, 37.

3. Michiko Hasegawa, "A Post-war View of the Greater East Asia War," *Japan Echo* 11 Special Issue (1984), 29.

4. Saburo Shiroyama, *Rakujitsu Moyu* (The Sunset Aglow), trans. by John Bester as *War Criminal: The Life and Death of Hirota Koki* (Tokyo: Kodansha International, 1977).

5. Fusao Hayashi, *Dai Toa Senso Kotei Ron* (In Affirmation of the Greater East Asian War) (Tokyo: Bancho Shobo, 1964).

6. John Nathan, *Mishima: A Biography* (London: Hamish Hamilton, 1974), 174.

7. Yukio Mishima, "An Ideology for an Age of Languid Peace," *Journal of Social and Political Ideas in Japan* 2:2 (August 1964). Excerpted from *Ronso*, September 1963.

8. *Mishima, On Hagakure: The Samurai Ethic and Modern Japan*, trans. Kathryn Sparling (New York: Basic Books, 1977), 17.

9. Ibid., 24.

10. Mishima, "Patriotism," from *Death in Midsummer and Other Stories* (New York: New Directions Publishing Co., 1966), 100.

11. Nathan, *Mishima*, 229, 246.

12. *Bungei Shunju*, August 1985.

13. Peter N. Dale, *The Myth of Japanese Uniqueness* (London: Croom Helm and Nissan Institute for Japanese Studies, Oxford, 1986), 15.

14. Shozaburo Kimura, *Journal of Japanese Trade and Industry* 1 (1987), 55.

15. Tadanobu Tsunoda, Foreword to *The Japanese Brain*, trans. Yoshinori Oiwa (Tokyo: Taishukan Publishing Co., 1985), vi.

16. Takeo Kuwabara, *Japan and Western Civilization*, trans. Tsutomu Kano and Patricia Murray (Tokyo: University of Tokyo Press, 1983), 83–84.

. 17. Haruhiko Kindaichi, *The Japanese Language*, trans. Umeyo Hirano (Rutland, Vt., and Tokyo: Charles F. Tuttle Co., 1978), 30.

18. Winston Davis, "The Hollow Onion: The Secularization of Japanese Civil Religion," in Hiroshi Mannari and Harumi Befu, eds., *The Challenge of Japan's Internationalization: Organization and Culture* (Tokyo: Kodansha International Ltd., 1983), 228.

19. The *Japan Times*, December 27, 1986. The comment had first appeared in *Jomo Shimbun*, a newspaper published in Gunma Prefecture.

20. From "Public Opinion Survey on Society and State," an annual poll conducted by the prime minister's office, and a survey conducted by the Management and Coordination Agency, released January 1989.

21. Surveys of the *Hoso Kenkyu Chosa*, published February 1989, as *Seiron Chosa Ripoto*.

Chapter Twelve

1. Keigo Okonogi, "The Age of the Moratorium People," *Japan Echo*, 5:7 (1978).

2. Jun-ichi Kyogaku, *The Political Dynamics of Japan*, trans. Nobutaka Ike (Tokyo: University of Tokyo Press, 1983), 18.

3. Lockwood, "Japan's 'New Capitalism' " *The State and Economic Enterprise*, 479.

4. Dower, *Empire and Aftermath*, 388–89.

5. Masataka Kosaka, "Japan: A Nation Without a Foreign Policy," *Journal of Social and Political Ideas in Japan* 2:3 (1964), 56.

6. Cited in Akio Watanabe, "Japanese Public Opinion and Foreign Affairs, 1964–73," in Robert A. Scalapino, ed., *The Foreign Policy of Modern Japan* (Berkeley: University of California Press, 1977), 114.

7. Donald C. Hellman, "Japanese Security and Post-war Japanese Foreign Policy," in Scalapino, ed., *The Foreign Policy of Modern Japan*, 325.

8. Takashi Hosomi, interview.

9. *The Economist*, July 1, 1989, 21.

10. Sunao Sonoda, in statement dated August 6, 1979. Cited in Manabu Shimizu, "Japan's Middle East Policy," *Japan Quarterly* 35:4 (October–December 1988), 385.

11. Shigeru Yoshida, *Japan's Decisive Century, 1867–1967* (New York: Frederick A. Praeger, 1967), 85.

12. Yoshida, cited in Makoto Momoi, "Basic Trends in Japanese Security Policies," in Scalapino, ed., *The Foreign Policy of Modern Japan*, 342–43.

13. *Asahi Shimbun* staff, *The Pacific Rivals*, 362.

14. William H. Jorden, "Japan's Diplomacy Between East and West," in Borton et al., eds., *Japan Between East and West*, 279.

15. Packard, *Protest in Tokyo*, 334.

16. Cited in C. Martin Wilbur, "Some Findings of Japanese Opinion Polls," in Borton et al., eds., *Japan Between East and West*, 312.

17. Cited in Akio Watanabe, "Japanese Public Opinion and Foreign Affairs," in Scalapino, ed., *The Foreign Policy of Modern Japan*, 116.

18. Mendel, *The Japanese People*, 112.

19. "Public Opinion Survey on Japan's Peace and Security," The prime minister's office, August 1989.

20. Masamichi Inoki, interview.

Chapter Thirteen

1. Seizaburo Sato, "The Foundations of Modern Japanese Foreign Policy," in Scalapino, ed., *The Foreign Policy of Modern Japan*, 381.

2. John Dower, *War Without Mercy: Race and Power in the Pacific War* (New York: Pantheon Books, 1986).

3. Hajime Tamura, quoted in *Japan Economic Journal*, October 17, 1987.

4. *Asahi Shimbun* staff, *The Pacific Rivals*, 26.

5. Ibid., 233.

6. *Newsweek*, October 9, 1989, 12.

7. Department of Defense, "A Strategic Framework for the Asian Pacific Rim: Looking Toward the 21st Century" (1990).

8. The *Washington Post*, March 17, 1990.

9. *Asahi Shimbun*, "Let Go of American Apron Strings," April 28, 1988.

10. Ken Otani, interview.

11. Susumu Ohara, untitled article in *Speaking of Japan*, March 1987.

12. Hajime Karatsu, interview and article in the *Japan Times*, September 10, 1990.

13. Takakazu Kuriyama, *Gaiko Forum*, May 1990.

14. Ichiro Naito, *Shukan Post*, October 9, 1987.

15. *Japan Economic Journal*, October 17, 1987.

16. Takeshi Igarashi, interview.

17. Jun Eto, *Nichibei Senso wa Owatteinai: Shukumei no Taiketsu*, (The Japan-U.S. War Is Not Over: Fatal Conflict), (Tokyo: Bungei Shunju, 1987).

18. *Business Week*, December 18, 1989, 27.

19. The New York Times News Service, in *Asahi Evening News*, June 5, 1987.

20. James Fallows, "Containing Japan," *The Atlantic Monthly*, May 1989, 40–54.

21. Kenichi Ohmae, "America, Japan Has Economic Deterrent Power," *Chuo Koron*, August 1989.

22. Shintaro Ishihara, "Frustration of FSX—The Post-war Structure Has Still Not Come to an End," *Chuo Koron*, July 1989.

Chapter Fourteen

1. Kiichi Miyazawa, *Japan Economic Journal*, November 3, 1990.

2. Ministry of International Trade and Industry, "International Trade and Industrial Policy in the 1990s: Toward Creating Human Values in the Global Age" (July, 1990).

Index

●